U.S. STAMP YEARBOOK 1996

A comprehensive record of technical data, design development and stories behind all of the stamps, stamped envelopes, postal cards and souvenir cards issued by the United States Postal Service in 1996.

By
George Amick

Published by *Linn's Stamp News*, the largest and most informative stamp newspaper in the world. *Linn's* is owned by Amos Press, 911 Vandemark Road, Sidney, Ohio 45365. Amos Press also publishes *Scott Stamp Monthly* and the Scott line of catalogs.

ISSN 0748-996X

Acknowledgments

Again I must thank scores of persons whose help made another *Linn's U.S. Stamp Yearbook* possible.

At the Postal Service and the Citizens' Stamp Advisory Committee, they are Azeezaly Jaffer, James Tolbert, Terrence McCaffrey, Joe Brockert, Elizabeth Altobell, Vance Harris, Frank Thomas, Catherine Caggiano, Robert Williams, Robin Wright, Andrew Gunn Wilinski, Kathryn Miller and members of CSAC.

Also, these art directors, artists and photographers who create the stamp designs: Howard Paine, Richard Sheaff, Derry Noyes, Carl Herrman, Phil Jordan, John Boyd, Tom Mann, Howard Koslow, David LaFleur, Michael Deas, Wilhelm Goebel, Margaret Bauer, Bill Nelson, Davis Meltzer, James Balog, McRay Magleby, Fred Otnes, Michael Bartalos, Richard Waldrep, Keith Birdsong, Dean Ellis, M. Gregory Rudd, Dennis Lyall and Harry Devlin.

And these officials of the establishments that print U.S. stamps: Leonard Buckley and Cecilia Hatfield Wertheimer of the Bureau of Engraving and Printing; Richard Sennett, Sandra Lane and Don Woo of Stamp Venturers; and Barry Switzer and Joe Sheeran of Ashton-Potter.

My thanks go also to Louis Plummer, Sidney Brown and Jana Belsky of PhotoAssist; Janet Tennyson and Anita Noguera of the Federal Duck Stamp Office; Dr. Cynthia Field of the Smithsonian Institution; Lloyd Shaw, Utah Centennial Commission; Don Nichols and Michael White, United States Mint; Dorothy L. Bedford and Mary Caffrey, Princeton University; Barbara Goyette, St. John's College; Diane Sackett Nannery, advocate of the Breast Cancer Awareness stamp; Hoyt Purvis of the Fulbright Institute; Scottie B. Hicks of the National Rural Letter Carriers Association; and the staffs of the New Jersey State Library, the College of New Jersey Library and the Mercer County, New Jersey, Library.

Thanks as well to my philatelic colleagues, Michael Schreiber, Michael Baadke, Rob Haeseler, Ken Lawrence, Kim Johnson, Michael Perry, Robert Kitson and Richard Schulman, and to stamp dealers Bob Dumaine, Jacques Schiff Jr., William R. Weiss Jr. and Richard E. Drews.

Finally, my personal appreciation, as always, goes to my incomparable editor at *Linn's Stamp News*, Donna Houseman, and to my wife, Donna Amick, whose contributions to the successful completion of this work each year are many and huge.

Contents

Legend for Linn's Yearbook Specification Charts

The following is an explanation of the terminology used in the charts that appear at the beginning of each chapter in this *Yearbook:*

Date of Issue: The official first-day-sale date designated by the Postal Service.

Catalog Number: The number or numbers assigned to the stamp or other postal item by the Scott *Specialized Catalogue of U.S. Stamps.*

Colors: The color or colors in which the stamp is printed. A number in parentheses preceded by the letters PMS refers to the color's designation under the Pantone Matching System.

First-Day Cancel: The post office location that is identified in the official first-day cancellations.

FDCs Canceled: This figure represents the total number of first-day covers hand-canceled and machine-canceled for collectors and dealers by the Philatelic Fulfillment Service Center in Kansas City, Missouri. It does not include covers canceled at the first-day site on the day of issue.

Format: The number and arrangement of stamps in the panes and printing plates.

Perf: The number of teeth or holes per 2 centimeters, as measured with a perforation gauge, and the type of perforator used.

Selvage Inscriptions: Informational or promotional material printed in the selvage of certain sheet stamps.

Selvage Markings: Standard markings, other than plate numbers, of the kind found on most sheet stamps.

Cover Markings: Material printed on inside and outside of booklet covers.

Designer: The artist commissioned by USPS to prepare the artwork for the stamp.

Project Manager: The USPS staff member who oversees and coordinates the planning, research, design and manufacture of the stamp.

Art Director: The USPS staff member or private-sector graphic arts specialist assigned to work with the designer.

Typographer: The specialist who selects and arranges the kind and size of type for the letters and numbers in the stamp design.

Engraver: The person who engraves the die for a stamp with an intaglio component.

Modeler: The specialist who takes the artwork and typography and makes any adaptions that are necessary to meet the requirements of the printing process. After completing this work, the modeler makes a stamp-size, full-color model of the design, which must be approved by USPS before production begins.

Stamp Manufacturing: The agency or company that manufactured the stamp, and the process by which it was made.

Quantity Ordered and Distributed: The number of stamps or other postal items ordered by USPS, and the number actually distributed for sale to the public.

Plate/Sleeve/Cylinder Number Detail: The number and location of plate, sleeve and/or cylinder numbers on the selvage of sheet stamps, on the tabs of booklet panes, and on coil stamps at constant intervals along the strip.

Plate/Sleeve/Cylinder Numbers Reported: The numbers or combinations of numbers of plates or cylinders used to print the stamp as reported and compiled by members of the Bureau Issues Association.

Tagging: The method used to add phosphor to the stamp in order to activate automated mail-handling equipment in post offices.

Introduction

By recent Postal Service standards, 1996 was a year of relative restraint. With no rate change to require new denominations, USPS issued "only" 166 new varieties of stamps and postal stationery during the 12 months. It was the lowest total since 1993 and a substantial drop from the all-time high of 214 varieties that appeared in 1995.

Seventy of the varieties were accounted for by only two issues: a Classic Collections pane of 20 designs for the Atlanta Centennial Olympic Games and a 15-design pane depicting endangered species of animal wildlife, each with a matching set of picture postal cards.

Self-adhesive stamps, hugely popular with the public, continued to represent a fast-growing share of total stamp production. The Postal Service expected to sell 32.8 billion self-adhesives in 1996 — 60 percent of all stamps sold — compared to a mere 8.8 billion in 1995. There were 28 distinct varieties of self-adhesive stamps issued in 1996, compared to 12 the year before.

Photography was increasingly used as the source of stamp designs, thanks to fine-screen offset printing and the ability of technicians to refine images on the computer. No fewer than 25 stamp designs and one stamped envelope were based on photographs rather than on drawings or paintings.

On the other hand, lovers of fine intaglio craftsmanship were disappointed in 1996. Only two stamps — Olympic Games Centennial and Cal Farley — had engraved vignettes, and both were printed by private contractors. For the first time in at least 20 years, the Bureau of Engraving and Printing's premier engraver, Tom Hipschen, had no postage stamp to his credit.

In this, the 14th annual edition of *Linn's U.S. Stamp Yearbook*, we have tried to present as complete a verbal and pictorial record as possible of the Postal Service's stamps and stamp-related activities in 1996. As always, we hope you enjoy reading the book as much as we at *Linn's Stamp News* have enjoyed creating it.

COMMEMORATIVES

As usual, commemorative stamps comprised the largest single category of the year, with 89 varieties. The Atlanta Centennial Olympic Games Classic Collection pane (20 designs) and the Endangered Species pane (15 designs) accounted for 35 of these. Several other commemoratives were issued in four-stamp and five-stamp multiples.

The major development in this category was the appearance of the first self-adhesive commemoratives. As if testing the waters (no pun intended), USPS first issued the Tennessee and Iowa Statehood stamps in both lick-and-stick and self-stick versions, then followed these with a set of five Riverboats stamps as self-adhesives only.

Continuing commemorative series that received new entries in 1996 ranged in longevity from Black Heritage, which got its 19th annual stamp, to Legends of Hollywood, which got its second. The fourth and final installment of the seasonal Garden Flowers series appeared, featuring winter blossoms; this set may have represented the last hurrah as well for a long and honored postal artifact, the booklet of conventional lick-and-stick stamps. The Lunar New Year, Literary Arts and Legends of American Music series also were represented in 1996. A block of four Prehistoric Animals stamps, which had been scheduled for 1995 and then postponed, finally made its appearance.

More commemoratives than ever before were issued in panes with extra-wide pictorial selvage, a feature that USPS hopes will entice buyers to save the entire pane. This group included the Endangered Species set of 15 and the Indian Dances set of five, as well as single stamps for Georgia O'Keeffe, James Dean and the Olympic Games centennial, and a pair of 50¢ stamps celebrating competitive cycling.

One commemorative issue that was announced in the *Postal Bulletin* and confirmed by USPS spokespersons never materialized. It was a special self-adhesive stamp or stamps to mark the 25th anniversary of the Postal Service, which occurred July 1. After a vigorous internal debate at USPS the project was dropped. (See The Year in Review.)

Date of Issue: January 4, 1996

Catalog Number: Scott 3024

Colors: black, purple (PMS 272), blue (PMS 306), orange (PMS 1585), yellow-orange (PMS 136)

First-Day Cancel: Salt Lake City, Utah

First-Day Cancellations: 207,089

Format: Panes of 50, vertical, 10 across, 5 down. Offset printing plates of 200 subjects (20 across, 10 around).

Overall Stamp Size: .99 by 1.56 inches; 25.1mm by 39.6mm

Perforations: 11.1 (Wista and Bickell stroke perforator)

Selvage Markings: "© USPS/1995." ".32/x50/$16.00." "PLATE/POSITION" and diagram.

Designer and Typographer: McRay Magleby of Provo, Utah

Modeler: Joseph Sheeran of Ashton-Potter (USA) Ltd.

Art Director: Richard Sheaff

Project Manager: Terrence McCaffrey, USPS

Stamp Manufacturing: Stamps printed for Ashton-Potter (USA) Ltd. of Williamsville, New York, by Sterling Sommer, Tonawanda, New York, on Akiyama 628 offset press. Stamps perforated and processed at Ashton-Potter.

Quantity Ordered and Distributed: 102,000,000

Plate Number Detail: 1 set of 5 offset plate numbers preceded by the letter P in selvage above or below each corner stamp

Plate Number Combinations Reported: P11111, P22222

Paper Supplier: Westvaco/Ivex

Tagging: block tagging

The Stamp

For six years prior to 1996, the state of Utah had a unique status as far as stamp collectors were concerned. It was the only one of the 50 states that never had been honored with a statehood commemorative stamp. That deficiency was remedied January 4, 1996, when the 100th anniversary of Utah's entry into the union was postally recognized.

Statehood anniversary stamps originated in 1935 with a commemorative for Michigan's centennial. One by one thereafter, the other states were honored; the 49th was Rhode Island, in 1990. In recent years, several states even received second-time-around stamps, including the two latecomers, Alaska and Hawaii, which had their actual entries into the Union celebrated with stamps in 1959 — and then, in 1984, got 25th anniversary commemoratives, as well.

In neglecting Utah in the past, postal officials had missed both the state's 50th anniversary, in 1946, and 75th anniversary, in 1971. Why no stamp was issued in 1946, after several other Western states had been honored on their 50th anniversaries, is unclear. It may be that Utahns were looking ahead to 1947, when they planned to celebrate the 100th anniversary of the arrival of Brigham Young and the first Mormon settlers in the valley of the Great Salt Lake. The Post Office Department did mark that anniversary with a stamp (Scott 950), and officials may have felt — in those days of greater postal restraint — that two commemoratives in two years for one state would have been excessive.

In 1993 and early 1994, representatives of the Utah Statehood Centennial Commission began corresponding with the Postal Service about a stamp for the forthcoming anniversary. They had some specific things in mind. They had a design of their own to offer (see below, under "The Design"). They wanted the stamp to be a self-adhesive, and, if possible, die-cut in the shape of the state — a rectangle with the upper-right corner cut out. And they asked that Utah printing firms be permitted to bid on the contract to produce the stamp.

This 3¢ purple stamp of 1947 (Scott 950), designed by Charles R. Chickering, commemorated the centennial of the arrival of Brigham Young and the Mormon pioneers in the Valley of Great Salt Lake.

USPS officials replied that it was Postal Service policy to create its own stamp designs rather than use designs submitted from the outside. They turned down the request for a self-adhesive on grounds that their program of developing such stamps wasn't advanced enough to produce commemoratives. (However, a few months after the Utah stamp was issued in conventional lick-and-stick form, the Postal Service did issue self-adhesive versions of commemorative stamps for two other states, Tennessee and Iowa — a fact that did not go unnoticed in Utah.)

Finally, USPS explained that its list of approved security printers under contract was a limited one, and that it would have to stay with one of its regular companies. The Utah stamp was assigned to Ashton-Potter (USA) Ltd., which printed it by offset lithography.

Although most stamps now are made on paper with a phosphor component, Ashton-Potter used nonphosphored paper and applied tagging to the stamp on press. The reason, explained Barry Switzer, the company's general manager, was that the design of the stamp called for "full ink coverage with some heavy pigments in the ink," which "tends to kill a phosphor signal that comes through from the paper."

Two different tagging types were identified by collectors, including one in which a fluorescent agent was added to the tagging compound, causing the variety to glow a slight orangish color when viewed under longwave ultraviolet light. The variation first was spotted by Victor Bove, a specialist and dealer in modern U.S. varieties, and reported in *Stamp Collector*.

Utah was named from a Ute Indian word "Eutaw," meaning "in the tops of the mountains." The area first was extensively explored in 1776 by two Franciscan missionaries, Silvestre Velez de Escalante and Francisco Atanasis Dominguez. Part of the course they followed became the Old Spanish Trail.

The Mormons who settled Utah were fleeing from persecution in the East. In 1847, when Brigham Young's pioneers arrived, Utah belonged to Mexico. It became part of the United States at the conclusion of the Mexican War.

Young and his followers established the State of Deseret, a name from the Book of Mormon meaning "honeybee" and signifying industriousness. Utah today is known as the Beehive State, and the beehive appears on the state seal and state flag.

Congress denied initial requests by the Mormons for admission of Deseret to the Union as a state. However, it created the Utah Territory in 1850, with Young appointed the first territorial governor. Four decades later, in 1890, the Mormons formally abandoned the practice of polygamy, a step that finally opened the way for Utah's statehood in 1896.

Today about two-thirds of the state's people are Mormons, or members of the Church of Jesus Christ of Latter-Day Saints. The church still is the most important social and political force in Utah. It owns much property and manages many cooperative enterprises.

Besides the 1947 commemorative stamp that honored the Brigham Young expedition, several other stamps have had Utah connections.

Two 50-stamp panes, the State Flags of 1976 and the State Birds and Flowers of 1982, each contained Utah stamps. Zion National Park's Great White Throne is shown on a stamp in the National Parks series of 1934. A 1944 stamp marked the 75th anniversary of the driving of the Golden Spike near Promontory Point, Utah, linking the two halves of the first transcontinental railroad. James Bridger, the first white man to see Great Salt Lake, and Utah-born Philo T. Farnsworth, television pioneer, have been pictured on commemoratives.

The Design

In 1993 the Utah Statehood Centennial Commission asked for stamp design suggestions from its members, stamp collectors and the public, and chose one winner and two runners-up from among the submissions. These were sent to the Postal Service, with a supporting letter from Governor Michael O. Leavitt, asking that the winning design be used for the statehood stamp. The work of Mike Sullivan, a past president of the Utah Philatelic Society, this design showed the Utah state capitol in Salt Lake City as seen through Eagle Gate, a structure that was built in 1859 to mark the entrance to Brigham Young's farm. The vignette was enclosed in a Utah-shaped frame.

Sullivan's design wasn't universally admired, even in Utah. The *Salt Lake City Tribune*, in an editorial headed "Return to Sender," pronounced it unimaginative and urged the centennial commission to "start over again." In any event, there was little chance the Postal Service would accept unsolicited artwork from an outsider. Stamp Services officials and the Citizens' Stamp Advisory Committee prefer to closely control the design process, and they already had commissioned an artist — a Utah resident, McRay Magleby, of Provo — to create the Utah stamp.

It was the first Postal Service assignment for Magleby, who is creative director for Brigham Young University and a professor of graphic design

This is Utah stamp collector Mike Sullivan's color sketch of the Utah state capitol framed by Eagle Gate that the Utah Statehood Centennial Commission submitted to USPS as its preferred design for the stamp.

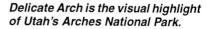
Delicate Arch is the visual highlight of Utah's Arches National Park.

at the University of Utah. In 1986 he was named "designer of the decade" by the Council for Advancement and Support of Education. *HOW Magazine* recently named him one of the "12 most influential designers today."

Magleby, working with Art Director Richard Sheaff, decided to create on his computer a stylized representation of Delicate Arch in eastern Utah's Arches National Park, a landmark so closely identified with Utah that it is pictured on the state's centennial license plate. Desert winds and wind-blown sand carved this spectacular formation out of red sandstone.

For reference, Magleby consulted a selection of picture postcards and color photographs. In his finished design, the arch, in vivid red-orange, is shown against a blue sky and a deep blue and purple landscape. "There's a kind of lavender or purple edge around the arch," Mableby noted. "I put that in at the last minute. It just needed some complementary color to make the orange pop out." A yellow orb hangs in the sky — "It's the moon or the sun, take your pick," Mableby said — and its color is duplicated in a broad band of sand in the foreground.

Mableby confessed that he had second thoughts afterward about the placement of the moon/sun. "I wasn't sure if the arch was actually oriented to where the moon or the sun could be in that place in the sky," he said. "I was a little worried about getting caught on that. But then I found a picture of the arch that had the moon in it. It wasn't in the same place that I had put it, but I could see that its arc would go in that direction. So I felt relieved."

The artist first created an image by cutting papers of different colors to the desired shapes with an Exacto knife and pasting them down. He then made a color photocopy of his cut-paper artwork and sent it to the Postal Service. After CSAC had approved the concept, Magleby took a blank sheet, drew pencil lines to indicate the edges of each color and scanned the drawing into his computer. Using the Adobe Illustrator program, he filled in the outlines with vivid hues, then output it on a color printer.

The words "Utah 1896," in a typeface called New Century School-

13

In this semijumbo version of McRay Magleby's Utah stamp design, the Utah-like shape of the frame enclosing the picture of Delicate Arch is accompanied by a dropped shadow and is more obvious than it is on the stamp as issued.

book, are in dropout white on a black band at the bottom, and "32 USA" is dropped out of a black square in the upper right corner. The shape and placement of the black areas leave an image area with a shape that suggests the outline of Utah — a subtle design touch that the Postal Service didn't mention in its publicity for the stamp. (In one of his preliminary concept sketches, Magleby had placed the Delicate Arch in a frame that was more obviously Utah-shaped.)

Postmaster General Marvin T. Runyon approved the finished design August 29, 1995, and the design was unveiled in Salt Lake City in November. Not all the reaction in Utah was enthusiastic, according to one member of the statehood centennial commission. However, Magleby reported that Governor Leavitt extended his personal compliments to him at the January 4 first-day ceremony.

Some collectors professed to see more in the design than a stylized arch. One reader wrote to *Linn's Stamp News* that the image "resembles a fireman's hat with a hole blown through the center." Another *Linn's* reader found in the pattern of light and shade on the right side of the arch "a

This version of Magleby's stamp design, made from cut colored paper and photocopied, doesn't have the black areas that the artist added to the final version to create a Utah-shaped frame around the image. It also lacks some of the shading subtleties that appear on the finished stamp.

Lafayette, Louisiana, was one of two cities where Utah stamps were postmarked on December 28, 1995, one week before the first-day ceremony.

stylized outline of a woman complete with head, arm, breast, bottom, leg and foot." A third reader then wrote to the newspaper to suggest that the writer of the previous letter had been "away at sea too long."

First-Day Facts

The stamp was dedicated by Stephen L. Johnson, USPS district manager for customer service and sales, in a ceremony at the Utah State Fairgrounds in Salt Lake City, held in conjunction with the Utah Philatelic Society's Centennial Philatelic Exhibition. The speakers were Governor Leavitt and Catherine Wilcox Smith, chairperson of the Centennial Stamp Citizens' Task Force.

The earliest-reported prerelease use of the Utah stamp was on covers machine canceled at Lafayette, Louisiana, and Atlanta, Georgia, December 28, 1995, one week before the dedication date.

32¢ GARDEN FLOWERS BOOKLET STAMPS (5 DESIGNS)

Date of Issue: January 19, 1996

Catalog Numbers: Scott 3025-3029, single stamps; 3029a, pane of 5

Colors: yellow, magenta, cyan, black (offset); black (intaglio)

First-Day Cancel: Kennett Square, Pennsylvania

First-Day Cancellations: 876,176

Format: 4 panes of 5 vertical stamps, arranged horizontally. Offset printing plates of 360 subjects (20 across, 18 down). Intaglio printing sleeves of 720 subjects (20 across, 36 around).

Overall Stamp Size: 0.96 by 1.74 inches; 24.384mm by 14.196mm

Perforations: 10.9

Selvage Markings: Sleeve numbers printed on each pane binding stub; narrow or wide cross-register lines and other markings on some binding stubs

Cover Markings: "© United States Postal Service 1995" and promotion for 1995 Commemorative Collection on inside of front cover. Universal Product Code (UPC) and promotion for Commemorative Collection on outside of back cover. Coupon for Commemorative Collection on inside of back cover.

Designer: Ned Seidler of Hampton Bay, New York

Typographer: John Boyd, Anagraphics Inc., New York, New York

16

Modeler: Clarence Holbert, Bureau of Engraving and Printing

Engraver: photoengraved by BEP

Art Director: Derry Noyes

Project Manager: Elizabeth A. Altobell, USPS

Stamp Manufacturing: Stamps printed by BEP on the 4-color offset, 3-color Giori intaglio webfed F press (801). Covers printed and booklets formed on a Goebel booklet-forming machine.

Quantity Ordered and Distributed: 800,000,000

Sleeve Number Detail: 1 intaglio sleeve number printed on each pane binding stub

Sleeve Number Reported: 1

Paper Supplier: Westvaco/Ivex

Tagging: phosphored paper

The Stamps

On January 19, the Postal Service issued a booklet of 20 stamps in four identical panes of five varieties each. Each stamp featured a garden flower that blooms somewhere in the United States during the winter months.

The booklet was the fourth and last in an annual series of booklets containing garden flower stamps. The first, issued in 1993, was devoted to spring flowers; the second, in 1994, to summer flowers; and the third comprised flowers that characteristically bloom in the fall. The fall flowers booklet was issued September 19, 1995, and therefore saw only four months' exclusive service before the final booklet in the series appeared.

The seasonal categories actually are somewhat fluid, according to postal officials. "The idea with the series was to show a grouping of flowers that would be together somewhere in a garden at the same time," said Elizabeth A. Altobell, the USPS project manager for the Garden Flowers stamps. "It's not scientific. It's meant to be more for mass-market appeal, as opposed to botanical."

For each year's set, USPS prepared a list of potential subjects, with input from the Citizens' Stamp Advisory Committee and flower experts consulted by PhotoAssist, the Postal Service's research firm. The list then was given to Ned Seidler, the designer of all the stamps in the series, who made the final selection of five varieties based on which ones would look best together on a booklet pane.

The flowers in the 1996 booklet were the crocus, winter aconyte, pansy, snowdrop and anemone. The choices for this last booklet were more limited than for the first three because of the relatively small number of flowers that could be considered winter bloomers.

"We try to get a good variety of color on a pane," explained Derry Noyes, the series art director. "Some people might think other flowers belonged in this booklet, but we wanted to avoid having a whole bunch of white blossoms. So we had to think of the visual aspect as well as what made sense content-wise."

As with its three predecessors, the stamps in this set were printed by a combination of offset (images) and intaglio (the black Galliard type) and assembled into booklets at the Bureau of Engraving and Printing.

Early blooming crocuses, mostly developed in Holland and called "Dutch crocuses," are among the best-known garden plants. Many American gardens exhibit the crocus alongside tulips, daffodils and hyacinths. Crocuses bear grasslike leaves and cup-shaped white, yellow, pink, lilac or deep purple flowers held close to the ground. The stigmas in the centers of the blooms often are showy. In some species, the leaves appear after the flowers; in others, with the flowers. All arise from corms and generally are three to six inches in height. A member of the iris family Iridaceae, the crocus is found in the wild from the Mediterranean region to Afghanistan.

Winter aconites (Eranthis) are members of the buttercup family that arise from tuberous roots. Planted in large clusters, the hardy aconite forms a yellow carpet of blooms in late winter. The foliage is deeply divided and found at the base of the plant, with the exception of one dissected leaf that is carried just below the flower. Flowers are borne one per stem and consist of showy sepals surrounding small, nectar-producing petals. Winter aconites make fine additions to woodland and rock gardens. The hybrid variety found in most gardens is Eranthis tubergenii, raised in Holland and named in 1924.

Pansies are among the most commonly grown and widely known of all cultivated flowers. The pansy's distinctive blossom consists of five overlapping petals and comes in a range of pale and rich colors including white, cream, yellow, purple, blue, dark red and maroon, combined in almost endless variations of stripes and blotches. In the early 19th century, British and French horticulturists developed the modern varieties of pansy from hundreds of hybrids cultivated over a span of 10 to 15 years. The "johnny-jump-up" was the starting point of this breeding program, resulting in the modern hybrid species Viola tricolor hortensis. These pansies, with blooms from two to four inches wide, are quite different from their miniature ancestors, except for their distinctive facelike markings.

Snowdrops are members of the amaryllis family that bloom in late winter or very early spring. Grown from bulbs, they are small plants with two or three grasslike leaves and nodding, waxy white flowers borne one per stem. Each bloom consists of six petal-like segments; there are three large outer segments that are white and three inner ones that are marked with green and appear tubular. Snowdrops are grown in rock gardens and naturalized under deciduous trees and shrubs. Galanthus nivalis, the common snowdrop, bears four-inch leaves that are ¼ inch wide and has one-inch-long flowers.

The anemone is a large genus, belonging to the buttercup family, that contains many popular perennials, some of which grow from tubers. Fern-like leaves are divided or composed of two or more leaflets. Flowers may be daisylike or poppylike and double or single, but have petal-like sepals, not true petals. Clustered stamens at the center of the flowers also are often showy. Blossoms are usually borne singly on stems that rise above the foliage. The leaves are deeply lobed or fernlike. The flowers close at night and during cloudy weather. Anemones are fine for beds and borders as well as rock gardens.

The Designs

Artist Ned Seidler retired from *National Geographic* magazine in 1985 after 18 years. His specialty is nature paintings, and his USPS stamp-design credits, in addition to the Garden Flowers series, include the 1993 African Violet booklet stamp and the 1995 Peach and Pear booklet and self-adhesive stamps.

Seidler used the same approach to the 1996 Garden Flowers that he had used for the previous three sets. He painted the pane of five as a single piece of art, with the flowers arranged as a bouquet, seemingly growing from a central source somewhere below the bottom edge of the pane, and the foliage crossing the perforations. Thus, the design of each stamp, when it is separated from the pane, has a jagged edge along at least one of its vertical sides.

The 1996 booklet pane differs from the other three in one respect, how-ever. Because each of the flowers selected for the five stamps blooms low to the ground, Seidler painted a curving brown horizon, suggesting the nearness of the garden surface, behind the five confluent stamp designs.

Seidler does his paintings in a combination of watercolor and gouache (opaque watercolor). For visual reference for the Garden Flowers series he used color photographs from reference books and flower catalogs as well as pictures he had taken in his own garden.

Seidler's crocus stamp displayed two different species, one with pointed petals of a delicate lilac color and the other with rounded yellowish pet-als. His pansy stamp also showed two species, and his anemone stamp displayed flowers of red, pink, white and blue.

Typographer John Boyd reproduced Seidler's crocus painting in full color on the cover of the booklet.

First-Day Facts

Jon Steele, vice president of the Postal Service's Allegheny Area, dedi-cated the stamps at a noon ceremony at the Longwood Gardens in Kennett Square, Pennsylvania. Featured speakers included Mary Ann Owens, a CSAC member; Fred Roberts, director of Longwood Gardens; and Gary McCurdy, manager of the USPS Lancaster District.

Longwood Gardens, one of the world's best-known horticultural dis-plays, is located on property purchased from William Penn in 1700. Pierre du Pont bought Longwood in 1906 to protect the gardens from impending destruction and went on to assemble most of what is there today: 40 indoor/outdoor gardens, 11,000 different types of plants, spectacular fountains, an open-air theater and a 10,010-pipe organ. The facility annually is host to 700 educational and performing arts events, trains many of the country's professional gardeners and attracts more than 800,000 visitors from all over the world.

Robert Rabinowitz, writing in *Linn's Stamp News*, reported that USPS officials went out of their way to make sure that never-folded Winter Garden Flowers panes with all possible combinations of tab markings were available for collectors and dealers at Kennett Square January 19. These were rationed, one set of panes to a customer, to make them as broadly available as possible. Thereafter, sets were offered for sale by mail; in all, more than $8,000 worth of unfolded panes were sold by the Kennett Square post office. Rabinowitz gave specific credit to Scott DiNolfi, the local postmaster; Linda Peffer, USPS customer service support manager from Lancaster, Pennsylvania; and Kay Herr, Lancaster's philatelic clerk.

The earliest-known prerelease use of a 1996 Garden Flowers stamp was on a cover bearing a crocus stamp and postmarked Minneapolis, Minnesota, January 11, eight days before the stamps were dedicated.

32¢ ERNEST E. JUST
BLACK HERITAGE SERIES

Date of Issue: February 1, 1996

Catalog Number: Scott 3058

Colors: yellow, magenta, black, cyan

First-Day Cancel: Washington, D.C.

First-Day Cancellations: 191,360

Format: Panes of 20, vertical, 5 across, 4 down. Offset printing plates of 160 subjects (8 across, 20 around).

Overall Stamp Size: .99 by 1.56 inches; 25.146mm by 39.624mm

Perforations: 11.1 (Wista stroke perforator)

Selvage Markings: "©/USPS/1995." ".32/x20/$6.40." "PANE POSITION" and diagram.

Designer, Art Director and Typographer: Richard Sheaff of Norwood, Massachusetts

Project Manager: Vance Harris, USPS

Stamp Manufacturing: Stamps printed by Banknote Corporation of America, Browns Summit, North Carolina, on a Goebel 670 webfed offset press.

Quantity Ordered and Distributed: 92,100,000

Plate Number Detail: 1 set of 4 offset plate numbers preceded by the letter B in selvage above or below each corner stamp

Plate Number Combinations Reported: B1111

Paper Supplier: Ivex

Tagging: phosphored paper

21

The Stamp

The 19th person to be honored in the Postal Service's series of annual Black Heritage stamps was Ernest E. Just, a marine biologist and Howard University faculty member who died in 1941. The stamp bearing Just's portrait was issued in Washington, D.C., on February 1, the first day of Black History Month.

Just was one of the first academically trained African American scientists. In 1915 he became the first recipient of the Spingarn Medal, which the National Association for the Advancement of Colored People awards annually to an American of African descent who "shall have made the highest achievement during the preceding year or years in an honorable field of human endeavor." Even so, his name was unfamiliar to most Americans until his stamp brought the name and his face to the attention of millions of postal customers.

The stamp was the result of an intensive lobbying campaign begun in 1990 by Don Lyons, vice president of Lane One Inc., a management consulting firm in East Brunswick, New Jersey. Although Lyons is a history buff with a fondness for African-American trivia, he had never heard of Just before 1984, when he read a then-new book titled *Black Apollo of Science: The Life of Ernest Everett Just.* The biography, by Massachusetts Institute of Technology historian Kenneth R. Manning, made a strong impression on Lyons.

"How can it be that nobody knows about this man of such achievement?" Lyons said to a *Philadelphia Inquirer* reporter. "His work on abnormal cell life has a direct relationship to leukemia and sickle-cell anemia and cancer. He was a forerunner in the field.

"It just didn't register why I didn't know, and other people didn't know, about Dr. Just. I figured it just shouldn't be allowed to be. What can I do to rectify this oversight? It occurred to me, why not an American stamp?"

Lyons embarked on a campaign of telephoning and letter-writing to convince the Citizens' Stamp Advisory Committee of the merits of Ernest Just. "He was constantly on the phone," Lyons' wife Lanetta told the newspaper. "Our bills were astronomical. Stamp, stamp, stamp. It was bizarre. But it was something he had to do, so I supported him the best I could."

Among those who enlisted in the campaign were scholars and scientists at MIT, Harvard, the American Society of Cell Biology and the American Medical Association. Many letters came from members of the influential Omega Psi Phi Fraternity Inc., which Just had helped found. When Lyons contacted the fraternity, it called on each of its 100,000 members to have 10 friends send letters of support to the Postal Service. John S. Epps, executive director of Omega Psi Phi, told *The Inquirer* he personally received 2,000 letters of support at his office.

These efforts were rewarded with success when the CSAC approved Just for a Black Heritage stamp and placed it in the 1996 commemorative program. It was printed by Banknote Corporation of America by offset lithography and issued in panes of 20.

Ernest E. Just was born August 14, 1883, in Charleston, South Carolina. As a youth he applied for admission to the Kimbell Union Academy in New Hampshire and entered in 1900, after working his way north on a ship. He completed the four-year course in three years and won a scholarship to Dartmouth College, where he specialized in zoology, was elected to Phi Beta Kappa and graduated magna cum laude in 1907. He then became an instructor at Howard, where he would remain a faculty member for the rest of his life and head the departments of zoology and physiology.

At the Marine Biological Laboratory at Woods Hole, Massachusetts, Just studied the fertilization and early development of the eggs of sea urchins and marine worms, and published his first paper in 1912. He was awarded the Spingarn Medal on the basis of his record in research and his effective efforts to improve the quality of medical training at Howard. He received his Ph.D. from the University of Chicago in 1916.

A resourceful experimentalist whose command of French and German gave him full access to the literature, Just had an unusually full understanding of the embryology of marine organisms. As a black man, however, he never was invited to a post at an American university or research institute where he would have had a permanent laboratory and facilities commensurate with his abilities. In Europe, however, he was not only recognized as a scientist but warmly received as a person, and throughout the 1930s, he conducted research in institutes and marine laboratories in Berlin, Paris and Naples. From 1912 to 1937 he published 50 papers based on his research, and in 1939 published two books, *Basic Methods for Experiments on Eggs of Marine Animals* and *The Biology of the Cell Surface*.

Just returned to the United States, where he died of cancer October 27, 1941. He is buried in Washington's Lincoln Cemetery.

The Design

The Ernest E. Just stamp marks the second change in the design style of Black Heritage stamps since the series began in 1978.

The first 16 stamps were multicolored, were printed by gravure (or, in one case, offset/intaglio), and showed a large portrait of the subject along with a small vignette representative of his or her area of achievement. The next two — in 1994 and 1995 — were engraved, had no small vignette, and depicted the honored individual against a patterned background suggestive of African art.

On each of those 16 stamps, the portrait was based on a painting or drawing commissioned by the Postal Service. The Just stamp, however, is different. Its design source was a black and white photograph. There is no extraneous pictorial material in the stamp design; there is, instead, the word "Biologist," marking the first time the subject's career field has been stated in the design. Although the stamp is printed in the standard four process colors, it has a duotone look to it, suggestive of an old sepia photograph. About the only link between the Just stamp and previous stamps in the series, in fact, is the inclusion of the inscription "BLACK HERITAGE."

"The original style, we thought, was too much format — and kind of an old, boring format at that — and so we made the first change (in 1994) in the hope of having a fresher appearance, and making the person's face more prominent," said Richard Sheaff, the designer of the Just stamp. "We got rid of the secondary vignette, and made the stamp look more African-American in typography and background.

"Then, when Ernest Just came along, two factors were involved. One was that the new people on the design subcommittee (of CSAC) were interested in doing some photography-based stamps once in a while. I was all for that; I'd been wanting to do it for a long time. So they became sort of a lobby for trying to find opportunities to use photographs.

"And, with the Black Heritage series, I had the feeling that even the new format (used in 1994 and 1995) was too much format and not enough of the person that was being honored. As it turned out, there were some good photos available of Ernest Just. I particularly liked the one we used, and it's really the only one I dummied up for a design ...

"So the Just stamp gave us, first, a chance to use a photograph, and second, suggested to us that we should do away with formats for the series, and just put in the background the words 'Black Heritage' — or maybe not even that — and have the person front and center."

The plan now is to continue to use photographs, as long as satisfactory ones can be found, Sheaff said. "If we come to somebody for whom we can't find a good photograph, we'll paint the portrait, but with the same idea: that there isn't a format. The stamps aren't going to look exactly

Shown are unused combinations of portrait and type for the Ernest E. Just stamp. The one in which the words "Black Heritage" are above the frameline is similar to the format used for the two previous stamps in the series, in 1994 and 1995.

The earliest-known use of a Just stamp was on this cover machine-canceled January 27 in Atlanta, Georgia.

alike. The type will be handled a little differently in each case. In each case the important thing will be to show the person — to show something of the individual's personality."

The source photograph for the Just stamp was made in 1912 by Robert Scurlock, a Washington, D.C., photographer. Later, Scurlock's photographs of black intellectuals, artists, musicians and politicians would appear in black newspapers, and in magazines like *Ebony*, *Life* and *Time*.

The typefaces chosen by Sheaff for the stamp are Lithos ("Black Heritage"), New Astor Semi-Bold, New Astor Bold and Futura Bold.

First-Day Facts

LeGree Daniels, a USPS governor and former assistant secretary for civil rights in the Department of Education, dedicated the stamp February 1 at a ceremony in the Tower auditorium of Howard University Hospital's Ambulatory Care Building. Speakers included Dr. Dorsey C. Miller, grand basileus of the Omega Psi Phi Fraternity; Just's biographer, Kenneth R. Manning; and Dr. Lee Virn Leak, research professor in Howard's anatomy department. Also attending the ceremony was Just's daughter, Maribel Just Butler, and Mrs. Robert Scurlock, widow of the photographer whose picure of Just was used on the stamp.

The earliest-reported prerelease use of an Ernest Just stamp was on a cover machine-canceled in Atlanta, Georgia, January 27, five days before the dedication date.

32¢ SMITHSONIAN INSTITUTION SESQUICENTENNIAL

Date of Issue: February 7, 1996

Catalog Number: Scott 3059

Colors: black, cyan, magenta, yellow

First-Day Cancel: Washington, D.C.

First-Day Cancellations: 221,399

Format: Panes of 20, horizontal, 4 across, 5 down. Offset printing plates of 160 subjects (20 across, 8 around).

Overall Stamp Size: 1.56 by .99 inches; 39.6mm by 25.1mm

Perforations: 11.1 (Wista and Bickell stroke perforator)

Selvage Markings: "© USPS/1995." ".32/x20/$6.40." "PLATE/POSITION" and diagram.

Designer: Tom Engeman of Carbondale, Colorado

Typographer and Art Director: Phil Jordan

Modeler: Joseph Sheeran of Ashton-Potter (USA) Ltd.

Project Manager: Terrence McCaffrey, USPS

Stamp Manufacturing: Stamps printed for Ashton-Potter, Williamsville, New York, by Sterling Sommer, Tonawanda, New York, on an Akiyama 628 offset press. Stamps perforated and processed by Ashton-Potter.

Quantity Ordered and Distributed: 115,600,000

Plate Number Detail: 1 set of 4 offset plate numbers preceded by the letter P in selvage above or below each corner stamp

Plate Number Combinations Reported: P1111, P2222

Paper Supplier: Westvaco/Ivex

Tagging: phosphored paper

The Stamp

On February 7, the Postal Service issued a stamp commemorating the 150th anniversary of the establishment of the Smithsonian Institution, the national museum in Washington, D.C., that has been affectionately called

"America's attic."

The stamp depicts the north front of the original building on the Mall that is universally known as the Castle. The Castle had been shown twice before on U.S. stamps: in 1946, on a 3¢ commemorative for the institution's centennial (Scott 943), and in 1980, on a 15¢ stamp that was part of the American Architecture series and honored the building's designer, James Renwick Jr. (Scott 1838).

In addition, the opening of the National Postal Museum, a branch of the Smithsonian, was commemorated in 1993 with a block of four se-tenant stamps.

Officials of the institution, in planning the 150th birthday, had asked USPS for a multiple-stamp issue, with a separate stamp for each of the Smithsonian's numerous component museums and galleries. They subsequently scaled down their request to a block of four, but the Postal Service was determined to issue only a single stamp.

"We told them that a block would resemble the look of the National Postal Museum block," recalled Terrence McCaffrey, the stamp's project manager. "We pointed out that the stamps in it would have to feature artifacts from only a few of the museums and that the people at the other museums would be offended. In the end, they agreed that they could live with a single stamp that pictured the Castle."

The stamp was printed by Ashton-Potter (USA) Ltd. by offset lithography. Its design includes a microtype element consisting of the letters "USPS," in black, in the lower-right corner.

The United States Mint also commemorated the Smithsonian's anni-

These earlier commemorative stamps, like the new one, pictured the north front of the old Smithsonian Institution building on the Mall in Washington. The 3¢ maroon-colored stamp of 1946 (Scott 943), designed by William K. Schrage, marked the Smithsonian's centennial. The 15¢ red and black stamp of 1980 (Scott 1838), designed by Walter D. Richards, was part of the American Architecture series and honored the building's designer, James Renwick Jr. The 1946 stamp differs from the two later ones in that it shows the smaller of the two central towers without the peaked roof that it has today. The roof was part of the original building but was destroyed by the fire of 1865. It wasn't restored until 1970, 105 years later.

The letters "USPS," in microprinting, can be found in the lower-right corner of the design.

versary, with two coins. A $5 gold, with a mintage of 100,000, bore a bust of James Smithson, the institution's benefactor, on the obverse and the Smithsonian's sunburst logo on the reverse. A silver dollar (mintage 650,000) showed the Castle on the obverse and an allegorical figure atop the world, carrying the torch of knowledge and a scroll inscribed "art, history and science" on the reverse.

The Smithsonian Institution had its beginnings in an unusual bequest. In 1829, Smithson, a British chemist and mineralogist, died and left $508,318 to the United States "to found at Washington, under the name of the Smithsonian Institution, an establishment for the increase & diffusion of knowledge among men." (The Smithsonian, in its press releases relating to the anniversary, gave that quote a politically correct spin by omitting the last two words. Congress did the same when it specified the wording to appear on the two commemorative coins.)

The sum bequeathed by Smithson amounted to one and one-half times the federal budget of the day. Former President John Quincy Adams, by then a member of the House of Representatives, led the effort to persuade Congress to accept the bequest and meet the terms of Smithson's will. On July 1, 1836, President Andrew Jackson signed into law a bill to authorize the United States to pursue its claim to the legacy. Ten years later, on August 10, 1846, with the money in hand, President James K. Polk signed the measure officially creating the Smithsonian Institution. It was to include a library, art gallery, museum, and lecture and scientific research facilities.

The board of regents held a competition to design the building. Thirteen architects sent in plans, and the winner was 28-year-old James Renwick Jr. of New York City. Renwick later would design New York's St. Patrick's Cathedral, but his best-known work at that time was another New York church, Grace Episcopal, which was known as "Renwick's Toothpick" for its elegant wooden steeple.

Renwick's plan called for a "Norman" building of red sandstone, with nine towers of varying heights, to be built on the Mall between 12th and 14th Streets in Washington. Eight years went into its construction. A recent history of the Smithsonian described the building as "a solid if somewhat whimsical structure, its towers and extensive crennelation constituting what might be considered excessive ornament." It was "an amalgam — like the Smithsonian itself — of history and intellectual fashion," the writer concluded.

In January 1865, a fire broke out, consuming most of the collected papers and effects of James Smithson, as well as books, art and scientific equipment. The flames destroyed part of the building's roof, the upper story and the interior of three of the towers. Reconstruction and repair required an additional 12 years and $125,000.

The institution's first secretary was Joseph Henry, a professor of natural philosophy at Princeton University. Under his leadership and that of his successors, the Smithsonian became a major patron of scientific research around the globe, as well as an important tourist attraction and cultural center. (One of those successors, aviation pioneer Samuel P. Langley, was pictured on a U.S. airmail stamp in 1988). James Smithson, who made it all possible, never visited the United States in life, but in

These are the obverse and reverse sides of the $1 silver and $5 gold coins issued by the U.S. Mint to commemorate the 150th anniversary of the Smithsonian Institution. When James Smithson bequeathed his estate to the United States, it was conveyed in gold sovereigns, which made coins a particularly appropriate medium for commemorating the event. The surcharge portion of the coins' sale price went to the Smithsonian to support the National Numismatic Collection and for other purposes.

1904 his body was removed from Italy, his original resting place, and re-interred in a crypt in the Smithsonian's Castle.

Today the Smithsonian complex includes 16 museums and galleries housing more than 140 million artifacts and specimens. Its divisions include the Air and Space Museum, the National Zoological Park and the National Postal Museum, home of the national stamp collection.

The 1946 stamp that commemorated the Smithsonian's centennial was largely the work of Harlan F. Stone, chief justice of the United States and chancellor of the Smithsonian's board of regents, who personally lobbied for it with President Harry S. Truman. At Stone's suggestion, the stamp's design included the defining words from Smithson's will, in their entirety: "For the increase and diffusion of knowledge among men." Unfortunately, when the stamp was issued on the anniversary date, August 10, 1946, the chief justice wasn't present to see it. He had died the previous April.

On the 1946 stamp, the smaller of the two towers that flank the main entrance on the north side is shown without a roof. The tower originally had been crowned by a peaked roof, but the roof was destroyed in the 1865 fire, and it wasn't replaced until 1970, more than a century later. The restored roof can be seen on the 1980 and 1996 stamps.

The Design

"We started out asking ourselves, what can you do with the Smithsonian?" recalled Phil Jordan, the stamp's art director. "We had already done two views of the Castle over the years, and I had wanted to explore other avenues; and the Smithsonian would have preferred that we try to speak to different aspects of the organization.

"But we concluded that, because there are so many entities in the Smithsonian, if we had tried to extract anything, the next thing we knew we would have had to have 16 or so symbols and that doesn't necessarily translate into a coherent stamp image. So we sort of gravitated toward the Castle itself as being the keystone of the whole organization. In the minds of the public, I felt, the Mall is where it's all going on."

The finished design that emerged from the process is horizontally arranged. Instead of the head-on view of the Smithsonian's north front that was shown on the two earlier commemorative stamps, the 1996 stamp depicts the structure from a vantage point on the Mall somewhat to the east (closer to the Capitol), so that the east sides of the towers and roofs are visible. The time is early morning. The sky behind the building is golden, those eastern surfaces are bathed in light, and streaks of light penetrate the complex and illuminate the green lawn in the foreground.

The artist was Tom Engeman, a former Washington, D.C., resident whose previous work for the Postal Service had featured similar masses of light and shade: the Holocaust Museum picture postal card of 1993, the Statue of Liberty self-adhesive of 1994, and the Butte and Mountain Scene nondenominated nonprofit-mail coil stamps of 1995 and 1996.

"That's his trademark, the real strong contrast between the lights and

These are two design concepts by Phil Jordan using a 19th-century line drawing of the Castle that appears monthly with the secretary of the institution's column in Smithsonian *magazine. The type is New Baskerville, which is a font created especially for the publication by the late Bradbury Thompson, who designed many U.S. stamps. The sun symbol was part of the Smithsonian's 150th anniversary logo.*

the darks, and the unique color combinations," said project manager McCaffrey. "That's why we like Tom's work so much. It's very distinctive."

In developing his acrylic painting, Engeman worked from a selection of photographs provided by PhotoAssist, the Postal Service's research firm. He made three concept sketches for the Citizens' Stamp Advisory Committee's consideration. Two were verticals that were dominated by the two central towers at the building's main entrance. The third, the horizontal view that CSAC chose, included much more of the Castle complex.

After trying several other typefaces, Phil Jordan chose a Garamond font for the stamp's wording and numerals.

Early in the design planning, before commissioning Engeman to paint the building, Jordan had tried adapting some 19th-century views of the Castle for use on the stamp. One of these was a line drawing that *Smithsonian* magazine uses with a monthly column written by the secre-

Phil Jordan tried adapting this early view of the Castle, complete with horse and buggy in front, for the stamp design.

tary. Jordan, a graphic designer, was a design consultant to the magazine for many years.

First-Day Facts

Michael Coughlin, deputy postmaster general, dedicated the Smithsonian stamp in a public ceremony in the Baird Auditorium of the National Museum of Natural History, located across the Mall from the Castle. He was introduced by Marc Pachter, chair of the Smithsonian's 150th Anniversary Coordinating Committee. David Clark, postmaster of Washington, D.C., presided. Honored guests were Lillian Scheffries Turner, founder of the Smithsonian Society; Spencer Crew, director of the National Museum of American History; and Jim Bruns, director of the National Postal Museum.

The earliest-reported prerelease use of the Smithsonian Institution stamp was on an envelope postmarked in Erie, Pennsylvania, February 3, four days early.

32¢ LUNAR NEW YEAR (YEAR OF THE RAT)

Date of Issue: February 8, 1996

Catalog Number: Scott 3060

Colors: yellow, magenta, cyan, purple

First-Day Cancel: San Francisco, California

First-Day Cancellations: 237,451

Format: Panes of 20, horizontal, 4 across, 5 down. Gravure printing cylinders of 180 subjects (15 across, 12 around) manufactured by Armotek Industries, Palmyra, New Jersey.

Overall Stamp Size: 1.56 by .99 inches; 39.624mm by 25.146mm

Perforations: 11.1 (APS rotary perforator)

Selvage Markings: "© USPS/1995." ".32/X20/$6.40." "PLATE/POSITION" and diagram.

Designer and Typographer: Clarence Lee of Honolulu, Hawaii

Modeler: Richard C. Sennett, Sennett Industries

Art Director and Project Manager: Terrence McCaffrey, USPS

Stamp Manufacturing: Stamps printed for Stamp Venturers by J.W. Fergusson and Sons, Richmond, Virginia, on Champlain webfed gravure press 1. Stamps perforated and processed by Stamp Venturers, Fredericksburg, Virginia.

Quantity Ordered and Distributed: 93,150,000

Cylinder Number Detail: 1 set of 4 gravure cylinder numbers preceded by the letter S in selvage above or below each corner stamp

Cylinder Number Combinations Reported: S1111

Paper Supplier: Coated Paper Unlimited, Bollington, England

Tagging: phosphored paper

The Stamp

February 19, 1996, was the first day of the year 4694 on the modified lunar (lunisolar) calendar that is used in China and other parts of the Orient. Eleven days before the new year began, the Postal Service issued a commemorative stamp to mark the occasion. The first-day city was San Francisco, California, home to a large Asian-American population.

Each Chinese lunisolar year is designated by one of 12 animal symbols. The year 4694 was a Year of the Rat, which is the first year of the 12-year cycle, and the stamp that was issued February 8 bore a rat image — the first U.S. stamp to depict this particular kind of rodent.

The stamp was the fourth in a series. The series began on an experimental note late in 1992 with a stamp to mark the impending Year of the Rooster. The Year of the Rooster stamp proved popular with Asian-Americans and overseas buyers, and it was followed by similar stamps for the Year of the Dog and the Year of the Boar. USPS plans to continue the series with annual stamps through the entire 12-year cycle.

Each stamp bears the appropriate Chinese New Year inscription in Kanji characters and the words "HAPPY NEW YEAR!" in English. Despite the inclusion of the latter phrase in the design, the Postal Service makes no attempt to time the release of the stamps to accommodate non-Asians who might want to convey Happy New Year greetings on their mail during December. None of the four stamps has been available in time for that purpose.

The Year of the Rat stamp was gravure-printed by Stamp Venturers and issued in panes of 20.

The traditional Chinese calendar, unlike the Islamic calendar, isn't lunar — based solely on the moon — but lunisolar, based on both the moon and the sun, to keep it closer to seasonal changes. The New Year occurs during the first new moon in the Far East after the sun enters Aquarius.

On that day the Chinese begin their four-day celebration, Hsin Nien. On the same day the Vietnamese begin a three-day event called Tet, and the Koreans commence their three-to-four-day event, Suhl. A lunisolar year sometimes has 12 months and sometimes 13, but in either case, the first day of the Chinese lunisolar New Year never comes before solar January 21 or after solar February 22.

The Chinese lunisolar calendar was used officially in China until 1912 and in Japan until 1873, being supplanted by the Gregorian solar calendar in use elsewhere in the world. In the Chinese calendar, the months of the year and the hours of the day share the same 12 animal designations that are appended to the years: rat, ox, tiger, hare, dragon, snake, horse, sheep, monkey, rooster, dog and boar.

Asians celebrate the arrival of a new year with fireworks, food and family reunions. Beforehand, many housekeepers clean house thoroughly to sweep away any lingering bad spirits from the previous year, and some people cut out artistic floral patterns from red paper to decorate the walls at home or work.

The Design

Clarence Lee of Honolulu, Hawaii, a Chinese-American graphic designer, was commissioned by USPS to design all 12 stamps in the Chinese New Year series. At the time the Year of the Rat stamp was issued, Lee had completed the next five designs: ox, tiger, hare, dragon and snake.

Each stamp in the series shows the featured animal in a way that suggests Chinese cut-paper art. Lee cuts the figure from paper with an Exacto knife, then photographs the cutout and overlays the negative on an airbrushed background so the background color shows through the transparent parts of the figure.

The artist subcontracts the Kanji characters to Lau Bun, a professional calligrapher in Honolulu. Lau Bun is an elderly man, an emigrant from China, who comes from a long line of calligraphers. On the Year of the Rat stamp, the character at the lower left signifies "year" and the character at the upper left stands for "rat."

Lee originally submitted four alternative design concepts for the Year of the Rat to the Postal Service. "Evidently there are no rats in Hawaii," said Terrence McCaffrey, the project manager and art director for the stamp, "because none of the designs looked like rats. The one that probably resembled a rat more than any of the others was a little too ferocious, with a very pointed nose. The others just looked too round and cute and too much like a chipmunk with a long tail.

"So I told Clarence to go back and start over, using some reference photos of rats. He then came up with a version that was usable, with a couple of changes."

Clarence Lee submitted these four concept sketches for the Year of the Rat stamp, but they were unsatisfactory to CSAC. None looked ratlike enough, and the creature with the pointed nose, whatever it was, was too fierce looking. The artist was told to get some reference photographs of rats and try again.

This image of a rat proved to be acceptable, but a few minor modifications were needed. "Extend and round out tail to show curve behind type," Lee was instructed in a note. "Revise, slightly, the interior markings. It's felt that the 'star' pattern on the back leg resembles an Amish hex symbol design." Lee replaced the "hex symbol" with a pinwheel pattern similar to one he had used on some of the earlier sketches.

The rat on the stamp, like the previous animals in the series, is yellow with subtle tones of red, orange and green, and is silhouetted against a blue-violet background. The first three Chinese New Year stamps had backgrounds of brilliant Chinese red, terra-cotta red and maroon, respectively. McCaffrey and Lee originally had planned to use a different background color for each of the 12 stamps, proceeding through the full spectrum. However, they realized that when they reached the lighter colors, particularly the yellows, they would have to make the animal figures dark, which would mean reversing the light-figure-dark-background pattern they had started out with. So they decided to use different background colors only for the first six stamps and then begin the sequence anew.

First-Day Facts

Deputy Postmaster General Michael Coughlin dedicated the Year of the Rat stamp February 8 in a ceremony at the Chinese Cultural Center in San Francisco. George S. Kikuchi, San Francisco's postmaster, presided, and participants included Martin Yan, host of "Yan Can Cook"; Stephen McLin, a member of the Citizens' Stamp Advisory Committee; and Clarence Lee, the stamp designer.

The earliest-known prerelease use of a Year of the Rat stamp was on an envelope machine-postmarked in Oakland, California, February 5, three days before its official first day of sale.

32¢ PIONEERS OF COMMUNICATION (4 DESIGNS)

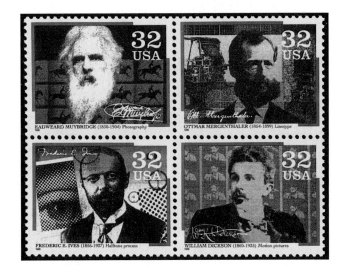

Date of Issue: February 22, 1996

Catalog Number: Scott 3061-3064, individual stamps; 3064a, block of 4

Colors: black, cyan, magenta, yellow, brick red (PMS 1807)

First-Day Cancel: New York, New York

First-Day Cancellations: 567,205

Format: Panes of 20, horizontal, 4 across, 5 down. Offset printing plates of 120 subjects (8 across, 15 around).

Overall Stamp Size: 1.56 by 1.225 inches; 39.59mm by 31.09mm

Perforations: 11.1 by 10.9 (Wista and Gammeller stroke perforator)

Selvage Markings: "© USPS/1995." ".32/X20/$6.40." "PLATE/POSITION" and diagram.

Designer: Fred Otnes of West Redding, Connecticut

Tyopgrapher: Tom Mann, Mann & Mann Graphics, Warrenton, Virginia

Modeler: Joseph Sheeran, Ashton-Potter (USA) Ltd.

Art Director: Howard Paine

Project Manager: Terrence McCaffrey, USPS

Stamp Manufacturing: Stamps printed by Ashton-Potter, Williamsville, New York, by offset on Stevens Varisize Security press. Stamps perforated and processed by Ashton-Potter.

Quantity Ordered: 96,000,000

Quantity Distributed: 93,170,000

Plate Number Detail: 1 set of 5 offset plate numbers preceded by the letter P in selvage above or below each corner stamp

Plate Number Combinations Reported: P11111, P22222

Paper Supplier: Westvaco/Ivex

Tagging: phosphored paper

The Stamps

On February 22, the Postal Service issued a block of four stamps honoring "Pioneers of Communication." The first-day ceremony was held on the opening day of the Postage Stamp Mega-Event at New York City's Jacob K. Javits Convention Center.

The four men depicted on the stamps were Americans whose inventions and discoveries in the late 19th century helped usher in the era of mass public communications. They were: Eadweard Muybridge, whose zoopraxiscope converted still photos into moving images; Ottmar Mergenthaler, inventor of the Linotype; Frederic Ives, who helped develop the halftone printing process; and William Dickson, who, building on Muybridge's work, helped invent the kinetoscope, a forerunner of the motion picture film projector. Of the four, only Ives was born in the United States.

The stamps were printed by Ashton-Potter (USA) Ltd. by offset lithography and issued in panes of 20, four across by five deep. They are laid out on the pane so that any block of four, or any horizontal strip of four, will contain one of each variety. Each vertical strip of five comprises two alternating varieties.

Two of the inventors shown on the block, Mergenthaler and Muybridge, had been on the Citizens' Stamp Advisory Committee's lengthy "hold list," which contains stamp proposals that CSAC has considered and neither rejected nor scheduled for specific issues. This list was reviewed by Phil Meggs, a Richmond, Virginia, graphic designer and typographer who teaches design history at Virginia Commonwealth University, shortly after he was appointed to CSAC in May 1993. Meggs was pleased to find Mergenthaler's name on it.

Years earlier, as a member of the American Printing History Association, Meggs had written a letter to CSAC supporting the association's campaign for a stamp to honor Mergenthaler on the 100th anniversary of the Linotype in 1986. That campaign was unsuccessful, but now, as a CSAC member himself, Meggs made a motion that a Mergenthaler stamp be issued. He reminded his colleagues of the key role the Linotype had played in the great growth of the publishing industry in the 20th century.

In the discussion of Meggs's motion, another CSAC member, David Lewis Eynon, pointed out that Eadweard Muybridge also was on the hold list, and suggested that Meggs look for two more people who had played roles in developing mass-communications technology comparable to those of Mergenthaler and Muybridge, so that a block of four could be issued. Meggs agreed to research the subject and report back.

At the next CSAC meeting, Meggs made his presentation. After considering Thomas A. Edison, who usually is credited with the invention of the kinetoscope, for one of the two additional stamps, he settled instead on the virtually unknown William Dickson, who, unlike Edison, never had been postally honored. For the remaining stamp, he chose Frederic Ives. The quartet was well-balanced, Meggs told the committee; two had made their contributions in the field of print and the other two in the kinetic media, photography and cinematography. CSAC then approved the project.

Eadweard Muybridge was born in England April 9, 1830. He became interested in photography and was employed by the U.S. Coast and Geodetic Survey to photograph the Pacific Coast. He gained recognition for his early photos of Yosemite and Alaska.

In 1872 former Governor Leland Stanford of California hired him to prove that at one point in its gallop a horse has all four feet off the ground. Muybridge's first efforts were unsuccessful because his camera lacked a fast shutter. The project then was interrupted while Muybridge was tried for the murder of his wife's lover. Although he was acquitted, he found it expedient to travel for a number of years in Mexico and Central America, making publicity photographs for Stanford's Union Pacific Railroad.

In 1877 he returned to California and resumed his experiments in motion photography. He set up a series of 12 cameras with trip wires attached to the shutters. As one of Stanford's horses passed through the prearranged course, it triggered the cameras, creating a dozen photographs of the running horse in various stages. One dim silhouette from a wet plate showed that Stanford was correct; all four feet were off the ground.

Refining his technique, Muybridge conducted motion studies of horses and other animals, and developed the zoopraxiscope, forerunner of modern motion-picture projectors, to project sequences of his pictures. An 11-volume work, *Animal Locomotion* (1887), contained 100,000 of his photographic plates. He returned to England, where he died May 8, 1904.

Ottmar Mergenthaler was born in Germany May 11, 1854. As a youngster, he apprenticed as a watchmaker in Wurttemberg. After emigrating to the United States in 1872, he worked in a scientific instrument shop in Washington, D.C. He became a naturalized citizen in 1878.

Responding to the need for a machine to replace the laborious hand-typesetting process, Mergenthaler invented the Linotype, a keyboard-operated machine that used an assembly of metal matrices into which hot lead was poured, producing a "line of type" as a single unit. The first 12 Linotype machines were installed in *The New York Tribune* in 1886. This model was called "the blower machine" because a blast of air carried each matrix to its place in the assembling line of matrices after a touch of the proper key had released it from the magazine.

In the next few years, Mergenthaler continued to refine and improve the Linotype. Although he lived only until October 18, 1899, he saw the use of his invention flourish, revolutionizing the publishing industry. Savings from the reduction in production costs meant lower prices and vastly increased circulation for newspapers, magazines and books.

William Kennedy Laurie Dickson was born in France in 1860 and moved to the United States at age 19. He began working at the Edison Machine Works in New York and later became a photographer at Thomas Edison's West Orange, New Jersey, laboratory.

It was to provide a visual accompaniment to his phonograph that Edison commissioned Dickson to invent a motion-picture camera in 1888. Five years later Dickson patented a device, the kinetograph, to ensure the intermittent but regular motion of a celluloid film strip through a camera. He perforated the strip in such a way as to ensure precise synchronization between strip and shutter. The resulting images, shown in rapid succession, would produce the visual effect of continuous action. The moving image wasn't projected, but was viewed through a kind of peep-show device that Dickson and Edison called the kinetoscope. In 1944, 50 years after the kinetoscope's invention, the U.S. Post Office Department issued a 3¢ stamp commemorating a half century of motion pictures (Scott 926).

Dickson later designed and constructed what would be the world's first movie studio, the "Black Maria," at the West Orange location. In 1892 he and his wife Antonia published *The Life and Inventions of Thomas Alva Edison*. Dickson died in 1935.

Frederick Eugene Ives was born February 17, 1856, in Litchfield, Connecticut, where at age 11 he began a three-year apprenticeship at the local newspaper to learn the art of making printing blocks by wood engraving. After mastering wet-plate photography while working with a cousin, Ives headed up the photographic laboratory at Cornell University when he was 18 years old.

In 1878 Ives formulated the halftone printing process using a swelled gelatin relief, which translated an image such as a photograph into a pattern of dots that varied in size to re-create the appropriate tones of the image. A printing plate made using this process would reproduce the tonal range of the original image for publication in a newspaper or magazine. Ives refined the halftone process in 1885 with the use of screening.

Along with his patent for halftone photogravure, Ives also patented the photochromoscope camera and the modern short-tube, single-objective binocular microscope. In the late 1920s he developed a two-color photographic process known as polychrome. He died May 27, 1937, in Philadelphia, Pennsylvania.

The Pioneers of Communication block was reminiscent of an earlier block of four commemorative stamps that honored American inventors who pioneered in the development of electrical devices. Issued in 1983, those stamps depicted Charles Steinmetz, Edwin Armstrong, Nikola Tesla and Philo T. Farnsworth.

The Designs

Phil Meggs, the CSAC member and graphic designer who had set the Communications Pioneers project in motion, suggested that instead of showing "typical severed heads," as he put it, the stamps should feature a more complex design approach, such as a montage combining portrait and appropriate artifacts.

To create the designs, Meggs nominated Fred Otnes, who had created the collage-like covers for the five books produced by the Postal Service from 1991 to 1995 to accompany its annual sets of World War II commemorative stamps. (Otnes' only previous stamp design, the D.W. Griffith commemorative of 1975, had been of a more conventional nature.) Howard Paine, a CSAC art director, volunteered to sign up Otnes, an old friend, and to oversee the design process.

At the outset, PhotoAssist, the Postal Service's research firm in Washington, D.C., assembled for Otnes an assortment of visual reference material, consisting of photographs of the men to be honored and of artifacts representative of their inventions or discoveries, as well as samples of their signatures.

Otnes converted this visual material into composite stamp designs, using a complicated transfer technique of his own devising. For each design he made high-contrast photographs of the portrait and the selected artifact or artifacts, then combined them on a textured linen background that had been prepared with white acrylic paint. He then overlaid the subject's

Art director Howard Paine made this concept sketch of a Mergenthaler stamp at the beginning of the process of planning the Pioneers of Communication block of four to show researchers and others what design elements he had in mind.

autograph, enlarged and reproduced in white on acetate, onto the montage. A bit of touching up with an airbrush completed the job.

What he and Otnes sought and achieved, said Paine, was the impression of grainy, old-time photographs. The stamps' colors are muted, with black, gray and sepia predominating; two of the stamps, Dickson and Ives, have a yellowish cast that heightens the effect of an aging photographic print.

"We couldn't make all our stamps look like this," Paine said. "But these are sober and important and appropriate to their 19th-century subjects." The designs made a nice complement, he added, to the "colorful things ... cartoons and Florida alligators ... Elvis and Marilyn Monroe."

To Terrence McCaffrey, head of stamp design for USPS, the Pioneers of Communication were "some of the most European-looking stamps we've ever done." "That's a compliment," McCaffrey said, "because there are a lot of really nice European portrait-type stamps, and to me they represent real class."

In a strip of small Cochin type across the bottom of each stamp are the name of the pioneer, his years of birth and death, and a descriptive word or two ("Linotype," "Halftone process," "Motion pictures," "Photography"). Although Stamp Services had stopped including birth and death years on stamps in the Legends of Music series because of the difficulty of determining the right year of birth for some of the subjects, "we all felt that in this case we really needed the years," McCaffrey explained. "It put the individuals in the context of the period of history in which they worked." The "32 USA" is in a Clarendon typeface.

To provide a touch of color, Paine added to Otnes' original designs an interrupted frame line that bracketed the upper-left and lower-right corners of each stamp. Postal officials tested several bright hues for the brackets before settling on a more subdued brick red.

For the Muybridge stamp, Otnes used a photograph showing the subject with flowing white hair and beard. He used the subject's head only; the other three stamps feature head-and-shoulders portraits. Muybridge's picture is reversed from the source photo so that he looks to the left rather than to the right, and is superimposed on three horizontal film strips showing sequential views of a running horse.

Both the Muybridge portrait and signature were found in the Library of Congress. The film strips, titled " 'Bouquet' galloping," are from Muybridge's book *Animal Locomotion*.

The Mergenthaler stamp shows, to the left of the portrait, a picture of an 1890 Linotype machine. On the right side, barely visible against a dark background, is a line drawing of the inventor's 1886 "blower" machine. The portrait was made by Bachrach and Brothers of Baltimore, Maryland, in 1894, and was found in the Library of Congress, as was the inventor's signature. The 1890 Linotype, described as "improved Model 1," is from an illustration in Carl Schlesinger's 1989 book *The Biography of Ottmar Mergenthaler*. The drawing of the blower, from the original patent, is reproduced from a booklet published by the National Inventors Hall of Fame.

The Ives stamp depicts two enlargements of the dot patterns of halftone photo reproductions, one of them recognizable as a human eye, along with two circular registration marks used by printers. The inventor's portrait and signature were reproduced from his 1928 book *The Autobiography of an Amateur Inventor*.

On the Dickson stamp, the inventor's portrait is superimposed over a series of vertical film strips made by a kinetograph. The portrait, circa

 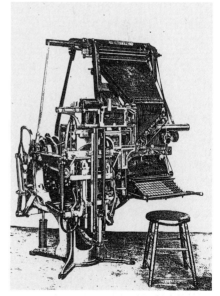

Ottmar Mergenthaler's 1894 portrait, by Bachrach and Brothers of Baltimore, and his signature were obtained from the Library of Congress. The drawing of his 1890 Linotype machine, described as "Improved Model 1," is from Carl Schlesinger's book, The Biography of Ottmar Mergenthaler.

The portrait of Frederic Ives used on the stamp was found in the inventor's 1928 book, **The Autobiography of an Amateur Inventor.**

1898, and signature were supplied by the Edison National Historical Site. The picture frames are from *Edison Kinetoscopic Record of a Sneeze.* The latter, according to Douglas G. Tarr, archivist at the historical site, is a "short film made for publicity purposes during the first week of January 1894. Copyrighted on January 9, 1894, it is the oldest surviving copyrighted film. (One prior film is known to have been copyrighted but has not survived.) Fred Ott, a long-time Edison associate and employee, is the gentleman sneezing. Dickson was the cameraman."

In advance pictures of the block of four released by the Postal Service, the designs were arranged with Muybridge and Ives on top and Mergenthaler and Dickson beneath. However, when the block was issued, collectors found that the Ives and Mergenthaler stamps had exchanged places. The preliminary layout, before the diagonal switch of designs was made, was the one reproduced by the American Stamp Dealers Association on the souvenir card that was prepared for and sold at the New York Postage Stamp Mega-Event, where the block was issued February 22.

First-Day Facts

The Postage Stamp Mega-Event, scene of the stamps' first-day sale, was a joint presentation of the American Stamp Dealers Association, the American Philatelic Society and USPS. One of its exhibits was an operating linotype, an appropriate tie-in to the Mergenthaler stamp. The linotype was borrowed from the True Type Printing Company of New York City.

Azeezaly S. Jaffer, manager of stamp services for USPS, dedicated the stamps at the opening-day ceremony. Other speakers included ASDA president Philip Bansner and APS president Randy Neil. Sylvester Black, post-

This photograph of an elegantly dressed William K.L. Dickson was supplied by the Edison National Historical Site, along with frames from a short film strip made by Dickson in 1894 called **Edison Kinetoscopic Record of a Sneeze.**

master of New York City, presided.

Stephen Brand, executive director of the National Inventors Hall of Fame, told the audience that the four men shown on the stamps "changed many things about the way we line up our lives." "We need people to look up to, not just sports stars and musicians," Brand said.

Among the honored guests were CSAC member Mary Ann Owens; Dani Herzka, a vice president of the Linotype-Hell Company; and Carl Schlesinger, author of the Mergenthaler biography mentioned above and a retired printer for *The New York Times*, who had been a long-time advocate of a stamp for the Linotype inventor.

32¢ FULBRIGHT SCHOLARSHIPS

Date of Issue: February 28, 1996

Catalog Number: Scott 3065

Colors: magenta, yellow, cyan, black (offset); black (intaglio)

First-Day Cancel: Washington, D.C.

First-Day Cancellations: 227,330

Format: Panes of 50, vertical, 10 across, 5 down. Offset printing plates of 200 subjects (20 across, 10 around). Intaglio printing sleeves of 400 subjects (20 across, 20 around).

Overall Stamp Size: .99 by 1.56 inches; 25.146mm by 39.624mm

Perforations: 11.1 (Eureka stroke perforator)

Selvage Markings: "© USPS 1996." "50 x .32=$16.00." "PLATE/POSITION" and diagram.

Designer, Typographer and Art Director: Richard Sheaff of Norwood, Massachusetts

Modeler: Peter Cocci, Bureau of Engraving and Printing

Engraver: BEP (chemical etching)

Project Manager: Elizabeth A. Altobell, USPS

Stamp Manufacturing: Stamps printed by BEP on Giori offset-intaglio F press (801).

Quantity Ordered: 129,900,000

Quantity Distributed: 111,000,000

Plate Number Detail: 1 set of 4 offset plate numbers and 1 black intaglio sleeve number in selvage above 2 upper corner stamps or below 2 lower corner stamps.

Plate Number Combinations Reported: 1111-1

Paper Supplier: Westvaco/Ivex

Tagging: phosphored paper

The Stamp

On February 28, the Postal Service issued a stamp commemorating the 50th anniversary of the Fulbright Scholarships. The stamp was issued in Fayetteville, Arkansas, home state of the late U.S. Senator J. William Fulbright, whose legislation initiated the international educational exchange program and for whom it is named.

Over the years, proposals for a stamp honoring the Fulbright program had been made by former Fulbright scholars and other interested individuals. Late in 1993, members of the presidentially appointed J. William Fulbright Foreign Scholarship Board, which administers the program, discussed plans for observing the 50th anniversary and decided it would be an appropriate time to make an all-out push for the stamp. Also enlisting in the campaign were the Fulbright Institute of International Relations at the University of Arkansas — whose director, Hoyt Purvis, now is chairman of the Fulbright Scholarship Board — and the Fulbright Association of Washington, D.C., which is the program's alumni organization.

"The three organizations, independently and collectively, set out to do whatever we could to get support for the stamp," Purvis said. "Letters were written to the postal authorities, and we had members of Congress, and others who were willing to do so, express their support for the idea."

As luck would have it, the group had a sympathetic friend at the Postal Service. Ron Robinson, chairman and chief executive officer of Cranford Johnson Robinson Woods, a public relations company in Little Rock, Arkansas, and an admirer of Senator Fulbright, had been appointed to the Citizens' Stamp Advisory Committee in 1993. "It didn't hurt our prospects that we had Ron's support as well," Purvis said.

The stamp was printed by the Bureau of Engraving and Printing by a combination of offset and intaglio.

The Fulbright Scholarship program of annual awards, authorized by the Fulbright Act of 1946, allows U.S. citizens to study or work in other lands and permits persons of other countries to study or work in the United States. Money for the awards came at first from the sale of surplus World War II equipment abroad. The U.S. government and participating nations and universities now fund the scholarships, which are administered by the U.S. Information Agency with cooperation from 130 countries.

Some 250,000 students have participated in the program during its half-century of existence. Each year, nearly 5,000 individuals receive the opportunity to broaden their professional or academic knowledge by, among other things, studying or lecturing at renowned international universities, or conducting collaborative research with foreign nations.

Fulbright alumni include U.S. Senator Daniel Patrick Moynihan of New York, Actor Stacy Keach and former United Nations Secretary General Boutros Boutros-Ghali.

Senator Fulbright, who founded the program and gave it his name, died February 9, 1995. He had served in the Senate from 1945 to 1974, and for the last 16 years of that period was chairman of the Foreign Relations Committee.

The Design

The unusual design of the stamp was the work of Postal Service art director Richard Sheaff, and features a human face seen through an overlay of marbled bookbinding paper. A compass rose is superimposed on one eye, and the top of the head is a globe with an old map of Eurasia and North Africa on it.

"The design emphasizes the fact that the scholarships of the Fulbright program facilitate the international exchange of students and artists," Sheaff explained. "It suggests the power of the mind applied to all points of the compass. The bookbinding paper background is meant to subtly symbolize both academics (books) and the arts (decorative printmaking)."

The words "Fulbright Scholarships," in an unusual typeface called Walbaum Bold, are reversed out of the design, as is the "USA 32," which is in New Astor Bold and Semi-Bold type.

Sheaff put together the design on his computer, using the Adobe. PhotoShop program, a program that lends itself to the kind of layering and juxtaposition of design elements that comprise the stamp. The face, of indeterminate sex, is a generic one, based on an old sketch but basi-

Stamp designer Richard Sheaff experimented with a background of interlocking colored flags of several nations before deciding on a different approach, an overlay of marbled bookbinding paper.

cally computer-developed by Sheaff himself. The map is based on Mappe-Monde (map of the world), by Pierre van der aa Layden, circa 1713, a copy of which is in the Harvard University map collection. The compass was adapted from 1920s-vintage clip art in Sheaff's collection.

The designer experimented with various backgrounds, including one that featured flags of many nations in an interlocking pattern, before deciding to use a marbled-paper overlay. Sheaff had written his graduate thesis in college on the marbling of paper, and the pattern he used — called a French swirl, and taken from a book published in 1875 — came from his own extensive collection of samples.

The individuals who had led the campaign for the Fulbright Scholarships stamp were "generally enthusiastic about it," said board chairman Hoyt Purvis.

"It's suitably symbolic of the Fulbright program," Purvis said. "The only reservation I heard expressed is that it was a shame the stamp wasn't bigger, because the graphic artwork shows up much better in a larger format. At the first-day ceremony we had a blowup of the stamp that showed the detail and the color much more vividly. But it's a very attractive and distinctive stamp."

The engraved element of the stamp is the compass rose, which is printed in black. Its recessed lines were etched into a die by a photochemical process at the Bureau. The lines as printed are delicate, and specimens of the stamps have been seen on which portions of the directional lettering ("North, NE, East, SE, South, SW, West, NW") are broken off.

First-Day Facts

Gerald J. McKiernan, USPS vice president for legislative affairs, dedicated the stamp at the Walton Arts Center on the edge of the University of Arkansas campus in Fayetteville as part of a four-day Fulbright symposium at the university. Speakers included Joseph Duffey, director of the U.S. Information Agency; Harriet Mayor Fulbright, widow of Senator Fulbright; George W. Haley, a member of the Postal Rate Commission; Daniel E. Ferritor, chancellor, University of Arkansas; and the Fulbright Institute's Hoyt Purvis. CSAC's Ron Robinson and stamp designer Richard Sheaff were honored guests.

32¢ MARATHON

Date of Issue: April 11, 1996

Catalog Number: Scott 3067

Colors: yellow, magenta, cyan, black

First-Day Cancel: Boston, Massachusetts

First-Day Cancellations: 177,050

Format: Panes of 20, vertical, 5 across, 4 down. Offset printing plates of 160 subjects (8 across, 20 around).

Overall Stamp Size: .99 by 1.56 inches; 25.146mm by 39.624mm

Perforations: 11.1 (Wista stroke perforator)

Selvage Markings: "©/USPS/1995." ".32/x20/$6.40." "PANE POSITION" and diagram.

Designer and Typographer: Michael Bartalos of San Francisco, California

Art Director: Richard Sheaff

Project Manager: Vance Harris, USPS

Stamp Manufacturing: Stamps printed by Banknote Corporation of America, Browns Summit, North Carolina, on a Goebel 670 offset press.

Quantity Ordered and Distributed: 209,450,000

Plate Number Detail: 1 set of 4 offset plate numbers preceded by the letter B in selvage above or below each corner stamp

Plate Number Combination Reported: B1111

Paper Supplier: Ivex

Tagging: phosphored paper

The Stamp

On April 15, 1996, in Boston, Massachusetts, there took place the 100th running of the Boston Marathon, an event that has become as much a part of the city's heritage as beans, cod and Cabots. The Boston Marathon is a footrace over 26.2 miles of rural road, suburban boulevard and city street (and a hill with the evocative name of "Heartbreak"). It first was run in 1897, and, with the exception of the wartime year of 1918, when it was replaced by a military relay race, it has been held each spring since then.

As the 1996 renewal drew near, its sponsors and fans sought a commemorative stamp to mark this milestone. After due consideration, the Citizens' Stamp Advisory Committee decided to honor Boston's 100th running indirectly by issuing a stamp in conjunction with it, but one that celebrated all marathons. The first-day ceremony was held in Boston's Copley Square, near the finish line of the race, on April 11.

Numerous U.S. stamps have depicted athletes on the run, but this one was the first to mark the marathon, which is not a generic term but describes a specific kind of race at a specific distance. The stamp was printed by Banknote Corporation of America by offset lithography and issued in panes of 20.

Marathons once were considered to be for superior athletes only, demanding endurance beyond the capability of ordinary mortals. But with the running boom that began in the 1960s came the revelation that to complete a marathon — and in a respectable time — was, with a reasonable amount of training, an achievement accessible to vast numbers of people: young, old, male, female.

Never was that more clear than in the Boston Marathon on April 15, 1996. The sponsoring Boston Athletic Association normally limits the race field by imposing qualifying times, graded according to age and sex, but for this occasion it admitted additional thousands through a lottery and other procedures. As a result, an unprecedented horde of 37,500 runners set out from the starting line in Hopkinton toward the finish line in downtown Boston, to be cheered on by a million or more spectators along the way.

The marathon has a classic heritage. The first one, in 490 B.C., wasn't a race in the usual sense. It was the legendary run of Pheidippides, the swiftest messenger of the ancient Greeks, who carried word to Athens of the victory of its armies over the Persians under Darius the Great on the Plains of Marathon some 23 miles away. Communicating the news was essential so that Athens would not be lured into surrendering to the Persian army retreating from the battlefield by sea.

Pheidippides reached the city, gasped, "Rejoice, we conquer!" and fell dead — a thought for modern-day Boston contestants to ponder as they struggle through the final weary miles on Commonwealth Avenue. The messenger did have a valid excuse, though, for "hitting the wall" in this ultimate fashion; he had just finished a run to Sparta, some 140 miles away, and back in a quest for reinforcements before setting out on his

Athens mission.

Now fast-forward 2,386 years, to 1896, when Greece hosted the first modern Olympic Games. The organizers deemed it appropriate to include a "marathon" run of 25 miles, a shade over the original distance. Even more appropriate was the result: It was won by a Greek, the shepherd Spyridon Loues, to the delight of his countrymen.

This first Olympic marathon inspired officials of the Boston Athletic Association to hold their own marathon back home on New England soil. For the date, they picked Patriot's Day, when Massachusetts celebrates Paul Revere's ride; and ever since, the nation's premier footrace has been held on the holiday that marks a horse's gallop.

At 12:15 p.m., April 19, 1897, the starter scraped the toe of his boot across the narrow dirt road in front of Metcalf's Mill in Ashland, announced: "That's the starting line, gents," and called the roll. Fifteen men answered, some wearing toreador pants, all with heavy shoes or boots on their feet. The course they followed would take them to a Boston finish line 24.5 miles distant, with a handful of curious spectators watching along the way. The winner that day was the favorite, J.J. McDermott of New York — although he caused some consternation by running through the middle of a funeral procession, causing two of the newfangled electric automobiles to stall.

The Boston Marathon was launched, and has been held each year since then — with the single wartime exception — in rain and sunshine, raw cold and near-100 degree heat. The course and distance were altered occasionally, and it was not until 1927 that it settled at the "official" marathon distance of 26 miles, 385 yards. This curious measurement dates to the 1908 Olympics in London, when the course was stretched so the race could begin in front of the royal family at Windsor Castle.

The Design

The whimsical design of the Marathon stamp was the work of Michael Bartalos of San Francisco, California. Bartalos is an editorial and advertising illustrator, printmaker and designer of neoprene jewelry, display mannikins and department store windows for such stores as Barneys in New York and Tokyo.

Composed of simple, angular blocks of color, the stamp design depicts a male marathoner in shorts and tank-top in the foreground, with the silhouette of a female runner in the distance. A generic urban skyline and a tree provide the backdrop. The single word "MARATHON," the "USA" and the "32" are in capital letters and numbers of Bartalos' own devising.

The male runner has wings on his feet, evocative of the Greek messenger-god Hermes. "I'm pleased that they allowed me to include the winged feet," Bartalos said. "I kind of liked it, because it was a reference to the Greek origins of the sport. I think stamps can afford to have a sense of humor."

The design was one of three alternative designs, with similar graphic elements, that Bartalos had offered to CSAC. Their purpose was "to suggest the joy of running," said Richard Sheaff, the art director. "Not just for marathon runners, but for people who go out and jog every day, through city streets, as suggested by the buildings, and on country lanes, as suggested by the tree."

The male runner, an odd-looking angular fellow with spiky hair, is a variation of a character who shows up frequently in Bartalos designs. "That style came about because I used to do cut paper a lot. That was my original medium," the artist said. "When the Macintosh computer came along, I found I could achieve the same style much faster and much more conveniently, both for myself and my clients, by using the computer. Also, I can e-mail my drawings to my clients."

To create each of his alternative Marathon stamp designs, Bartalos first made a pencil sketch, then scanned it into the Macintosh, where he re-

These are unused variations on Michael Bartalos' design for the Marathon stamp. One shows four silhouettes, in green, blue and black, against a white background. The female figure running off the stamp at the left connects with the figure running onto the stamp at the right, so that a horizontal strip of stamps would make a long row of runners, as shown here. The other design, in a semijumbo format, shows a lone male runner against a sky of maroon and brown. Note that the word on each design is "Marathons." For the finished version, the form was changed to the singular.

Another artist made these concept sketches for the Marathon stamp, one of which was turned into a finished design, also shown here.

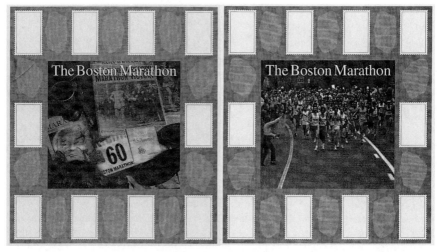

At one point, USPS contemplated issuing the Marathon stamp in a miniature pane of 10 stamps framing a central photographic image of the best-known distance race of all, the Boston Marathon, and Richard Sheaff made these mockups on his computer. The free-form shapes between the stamps were included to show where images of various marathon artifacts could appear, such as medals, laurel crowns and runners' numbers.

The earliest-reported prerelease use of the Marathon stamp is on a cover bearing an April 5 San Diego, California, machine postmark and a Carlsbad, California, handstamp with the same date.

fined and completed the artwork using Adobe Illustrator software.

Bartalos was one of two artists who submitted concept sketches for the Marathon stamp. The other artist's sketches were also stylized, but were somewhat more realistic than the one that was chosen.

At one point officials considered issuing the Marathon stamp in a miniature pane of 10 stamps framing a photograph or photo montage of the Boston Marathon, and Sheaff made some mockups of such a pane.

First-Day Facts

Deputy Postmaster General Michael Coughlin dedicated the Marathon stamp at a noon ceremony April 11. A 20-degree wind chill in Copley Square made conditions uncomfortable for participants and spectators alike. Bill Rodgers, a four-time men's winner at Boston, and Joan Benoit Samuelson, an Olympic gold medalist who won the women's division at Boston twice, were the main speakers. Guy L. Morse III, director of the Boston Athletic Association, gave the welcome. An honored guest was a local hero, John A. Kelly, who won the Boston Marathon 61 years earlier in 1935, and again in 1945.

The earliest-reported prerelease use of the Marathon stamp was on a cover bearing an April 5 San Diego, California, machine postmark and a Carlsbad, California, handstamp with the same date.

32¢ CENTENNIAL OLYMPIC GAMES (20 DESIGNS) CLASSIC COLLECTIONS SERIES

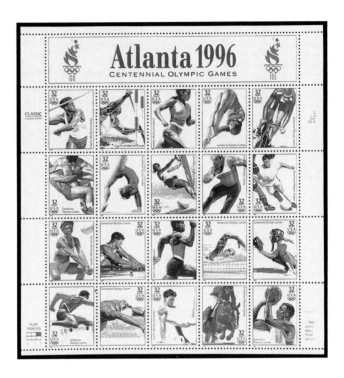

Date of Issue: May 2, 1996

Catalog Numbers: Scott 3068a-t, individual stamps; 3068, pane of 20

Colors: tan, yellow, magenta, cyan, black

First-Day Cancel: Washington, D.C.

First-Day Cancellations: 1,807,316 (includes Centennial Olympic Games picture postal cards and Atlanta Paralympic Games envelope)

Format: Panes of 20, vertical, 5 across, 4 down. Gravure printing cylinders of 120 subjects (8 across, 15 around). Also sold in uncut sheets of 6 panes, 3 across, 2 down.

Overall Stamp Size: 1.24 by 1.56 inches; 31.5mm by 39.6mm

Perforations: 10.2 by 10.1 (APS rotary perforator)

Selvage Inscription: "Atlanta 1996/CENTENNIAL OLYMPIC GAMES" and Olympic logo.

Selvage Markings: "CLASSIC/COLLECTIONS." "© 1996/United/States/Postal/Service." "36 USC 380." "32/x20/$6.40." "PLATE/POSITION" and diagram.

Back Markings: On header: " 'What is important in the Olympic Games is not winning, but taking part./What is important in life is not the triumph, but the struggle.' " " 'Atlanta 1996' and the Centennial Torch Logo, ™, © 1992 ACOG."

On individual stamps:

"Men's/Cycling/Sprint cycling was one/of the original events/in the 1896 Games./ It combines speed and/strategy on a banked/track. A women's event/was added in 1988."

"Women's/Diving/Platform diving is performed/from a board 10 meters/above the water. The most/difficult dive is the back 1½/somersault with 4½ twists./ The U.S. has won over half/the medals awarded in both/men's and women's events."

"Women's/Running/There are 8 women's/running events, from/100 meters to/ the marathon/(26 miles, 385 yards)./Until 1964,/the longest race/was only 200 meters."

"Men's/Canoeing/Whitewater, or slalom,/events were added/temporarily in 1972 and/permanently in 1988./Flatwater canoeing/has been part of/the Games since 1936."

"Decathlon/The decathlon consists of 10/events. On the first day,/athletes compete in the/100-meter dash, long jump,/shot put, high jump, and/400-meter run. On the second/day, they perform the/110-meter hurdles, discus/throw, pole vault, javelin/throw, and 1500-meter run."

"Women's/Soccer/Although men's soccer/has been a part of the/Games since 1900,/a women's tournament/will be held for the first/time in 1996. Eight/ teams will take part."

"Men's/Shot Put/The shot put has been/included in all/Games since 1896./A shot is a 16-pound/ball of iron or brass./The United States/has won 15/of 22 gold medals."

"Women's/Sailboarding/The first sailboarding/contest was included/in the 1984/ Los Angeles Games./A separate/women's event/was added in 1992."

"Women's/Gymnastics/Women gymnasts compete/in an all-around event,/a team event, floor/exercises, balance beam,/uneven bars, and vault./Contestants must be at/least 15 years old by/the end of 1996."

"Freestyle/Wrestling/Wrestling has 10 weight/divisions. It is the only sport/with a maximum weight/limit: wrestlers must be/less than 286 pounds./The United States has/earned more medals than/any other nation."

"Women's/Softball/Softball will make/its first appearance/in the 1996 Games./ The United States team/is the world champion/and one of the teams/favored to win a medal."

"Women's/Swimming/The women's 400-meter/freestyle event was/first held in 1920;/the 800-meter event was/added in 1968./American women have/won 15 of 24 gold medals/in these events."

"Men's/Sprinting Events/The 100 meters and 400/meters were part of the/first games in 1896./In the 100, 200, and 400/meters and the two sprint/relays, the United States/has won two-thirds/of the gold medals."

"Men's/Rowing/There will be 14 rowing/events contested at the/1996 Games: 8 for men/and 6 for women. For the/first time, lightweight/events will be included for/men under 160 lbs. and/for women under 130 lbs."

"Beach/Volleyball/Beach volleyball, played/with two-person teams,/will be added to the/Games program for the/first time in 1996./There will be both men's/ and women's events."

"Men's/Basketball/Since basketball first made/its appearance in 1936,/the United States has won/92 games and lost only 2./Professionals from the/NBA were allowed to/compete for the first/time in 1992."

"Equestrian/Equestrian is one of only/two sports in which women/compete against men./The jumping event was/first included in the 1900/Games. The sport was/opened to women/in 1952."

"Men's/Gymnastics/Male gymnasts compete/in 6 events: horizontal/bar, parallel bars, vault,/pommel horse, rings,/and floor exercises./There are also an/ all-around event and/a team event."

"Men's/Swimming/The backstroke event was/first included in the Games/of 1900. There are now/two events: the 100 meters,/which is two lengths/of the pool,/ and the 200 meters,/which is four lengths."

"Men's/Hurdles/The 110-meter hurdles/event has been included/in all Games since/1896. The United States/has earned 48 medals./No other nation has/ won more than 5."

Designer: Richard Waldrep of Sparks, Maryland

Typographer: John Boyd, Anagraphics Inc., New York, New York

Modeler: Richard C. Sennett

Art Director: Carl Herrman

Project Manager: Terrence McCaffrey, USPS

Stamp Manufacturing: Stamps printed for Stamp Venturers at J.W. Fergusson and Sons, Richmond, Virginia, on Champlain webfed gravure press 1. Polyvinyl acetate (PVA) gum applied at Ivex Company, Troy, Ohio. Stamps perforated, processed and shipped at Stamp Venturers, Fredericksburg, Virginia.

Quantity Ordered and Distributed: 324,150,000

Cylinder Number Detail: 1 set of 5 gravure cylinder numbers preceded by the letter S in selvage beside lower-left (Men's Hurdles) stamp

Cylinder Number Combination Reported: S11111

Paper Supplier: Westvaco/Ivex

Tagging: block tagged

The Stamps

On May 2, USPS issued a pane of 20 stamps to commemorate the Centennial Olympic Games that would open some 2½ months later in Atlanta, Georgia. Each stamp bore a different design featuring one of the sports of the summer Olympics.

The pane was the fourth in the Postal Service's "Classic Collections" series that was launched in 1994 with Legends of the West and continued in 1995 with Civil War and Comic Strip Classics. The first three panes in the series bore the wording "Classic Collection" (singular) in the selvage. On this one, however, the wording was plural.

Classic Collections panes are characterized by 20 designs, a decorative selvage at the top called a header and descriptive text printed on the back of each stamp beneath the gum. They are gravure-printed by Stamp Venturers. Each set of stamps is accompanied by a matching set of picture postal cards reproducing the stamp designs on the picture side as well as in the indicium stamp. (See separate chapter.)

The issuance of the Olympic Games pane was attended by a temporary but bitter dispute between the Postal Service and organizers of the Games in which the Postal Service was accused of "ambush marketing" and threatened with legal action. One consequence was that USPS abruptly moved the first-day ceremony from Atlanta to Washington, D.C., announcing its

This is the reverse side of the Centennial Olympic Games pane, showing the descriptive information printed beneath the gum on each stamp and on the header.

change of plans only six days before the issue date. At the same ceremony, USPS dedicated the 32¢ Paralympics stamped envelope it had planned to issue in Atlanta May 9. No Olympics officials attended the relocated event.

This falling-out was in sharp contrast to the amicable relations between the parties in 1992, when USPS was an official sponsor of the Olympic Games in Barcelona. However, when Marvin T. Runyon Jr. became postmaster general in July of that year, one of his first acts was to announce that the sponsorship wouldn't be renewed. Subsequently, United Parcel Service, one of the Postal Service's strongest competitors, became the "official overnight carrier" of the 1996 Games.

Even so, there was no hint of trouble February 1, 1996, when USPS and Olympic Games officials joined in Atlanta to unveil the designs of the 20 stamps for the 1996 Games. Taking part in the event at the Sport Summit '96, a major sports trade show, were Loren E. Smith, Postal Service senior vice president and chief marketing officer; John Krimsky Jr., deputy secretary general of the U.S. Olympic Committee (USOC), and Craig Tartasky, vice president and executive director of the sports division of

E.J. Krause and Associates Inc. "With the Centennial Games right around the corner and back on U.S. soil, I think it is especially fitting for us to be here in Atlanta to unveil our stamp designs," Smith said.

The atmosphere cooled, however, when USOC and the Atlanta Committee for the Olympic Games learned of the Postal Service's intention to sell T-shirts bearing reproductions of its Olympic stamps.

USPS had modified the stamp designs on the shirts to comply with the letter, if not the spirit, of its November 20, 1995, philatelic licensing agreement with the USOC that governed the stamps commemorating the Olympics. The stamps, as shown on the shirts, were minus the text "Centennial Olympic Games," the five interlocking Olympic rings and the denomination "32," leaving basically the central stamp image. The word "ATLANTA" appeared above the design in large letters, and "USA 96" was displayed prominently.

These alterations didn't mollify USOC. On April 27, *The Washington Post* carried a story by Bill McAllister and Thomas Heath reporting that increasing friction between the Postal Service and USOC officials had come to a head two days earlier when USOC's John Krimsky "accused

the federal agency of infringing on the upcoming Atlanta Games by selling Olympic T-shirts without paying licensing fees to his group." The story quoted Krimsky as saying: "I told them to move their (stamp) ceremonies out of Atlanta and into Washington."

On April 26, the day before the *Post* story appeared, the Postal Service tersely announced its change in first-day plans, but gave no reason for it. A half-page media advisory provided only bare details about the ceremony that now would be held in Washington. The only emphasis in the advisory was to note that the new stamps and envelope would be available only in Washington May 2, with the word "only" underlined.

Linn's Stamp News called Mark Weinberg, a Postal Service spokesman, and was told that the ceremony was moved to Washington following a request by Olympic officials that USPS hold the event at a postal facility in Atlanta rather than at Atlanta's CNN center, the original planned ceremony site.

Weinberg told *Linn's* that USPS agreed to the request in an attempt "to be a good neighbor" of the Games organizers. However, he said, none of the post office locations in Atlanta proved to be appropriate for such a

ceremony. Asked if the Olympic officials' request may have stemmed from the conflict reported in *The Post*, Weinberg replied: "You'd have to ask the Olympic officials."

On May 1, the day before the stamps were dedicated in Washington, the Postal Service announced more details, including the fact that two former Olympic gold medalists would be featured speakers. Conspicuous by its absence was any mention of participation by any officials of the 1996 Games. The news release did reveal, however, that the stamps would be sold in Atlanta post offices as well as in Washington May 2, although the Paralympics envelope would be available only in Washington that day.

The day after the stamps were issued, the dispute was reviewed in detail by Atlanta reporter Brian Cabell in a televised report that appeared on CNN's Headline News. According to Cabell, the Postal Service's T-shirts "upset (the) Hanes (Company), which spent millions to be the official apparel sponsor, and UPS (the United Parcel Service), which paid millions to be the official postal sponsor" of the 1996 Summer Games.

In its broadcast, CNN displayed a portion of a May 1 letter from King & Spaulding, the Atlanta-based attorneys for the Olympic organizers, to

Postmaster General Runyon, outlining their objections. The letter, which the lawyers sent by fax and UPS — but not by mail — said the planned sale of the T-shirts was "unlawful in several respects" and called on the Postal Service to "cease and desist."

The Olympic Committee's Krimsky elaborated to the media. "It's mean-spirited and it hurts the athletes and it hurts the organizing committee," he said of USPS' merchandising plans. "We've sold those rights, and this is very confusing.

"Clearly, it is an Olympic-wannabe T-shirt ... If these steps continue, I would hope and expect to pursue further legal action."

An Associated Press story on the dispute said Olympic organizers accused USPS of "ambush marketing," contending "that the post office wanted to appear associated with the Games without paying for sponsorship." In Cabell's report, UPS spokeswoman Susan Rosenburg characterized the relationship of USPS to the Olympics as that of a parasite.

But USPS' Loren Smith told the AP: "We do not suggest we are a Games sponsor. We are only selling Olympic stamps on a T-shirt."

The dispute took on an added dimension when Olympic officials sought

64

to limit the Postal Service's official role at the Games to delivering mail and selling stamps. Loren Smith rejected the demand, according to the AP. If there was a post office at the Olympic Village, Smith said, it would offer full service; this would include overnight mail, in competition with the Olympic sponsor, UPS. Games organizers then announced that they would handle mail deliveries in the Olympic Village themselves.

The tempest over T-shirts ended May 14, a few days before the Games opened, when the two sides reached an agreement under which, Loren Smith said, "we both win."

The Postal Service agreed to allow a marketing firm created by the USOC and the Atlanta Committee for the Olympic Games to share in revenues USPS was to receive from the T-shirts. USPS withdrew from sale some 5,000 of its shirts, which had been created by a suburban Atlanta firm. These would be offered for sale to postal workers after the Games ended. For their part, the Olympic committees agreed to market new shirts carrying both the stamp images and the five-ring Olympic logo.

The agreement allowed the Atlanta committees to expand the number of products carrying images of the stamps. Both sides predicted that the wider sales of both the T-shirts and other merchandise would mean additional revenues for both the organizers and USPS. Bill McCahan, chief marketing officer of the Atlanta Centennial Olympic Properties, described the agreement as strictly a business deal in licensing, with no other nuances to it.

The dispute was unprecedented in the history of U.S. postal commemoration of the Olympic Games, which spanned 64 years.

In the early years, the U.S. Post Office Department issued stamps only when the Games were in the United States: namely, for the 1932 Winter Games at Lake Placid, New York, the 1932 Summer Games in Los Angeles, California, and the 1960 Winter Games at Squaw Valley, California. But beginning in 1972, with the Winter Games of Sapporo, Japan, and the Summer Games of Munich, Germany, the Postal Service produced stamps and, in some cases, postal stationery to salute every quadrennial Olympic gathering, winter and summer, regardless of where it was held. The total from 1932 through 1994 was 82 face-different varieties, plus some perforation varieties that turned up in the 1980 and 1984 sets.

The 1996 pane for the Centennial Olympic Games included in its selvage the inscription "36 USC 380," a reference to the Amateur Sports Act of 1987, which gave the United States Olympic Committee authority to control the use of Olympic-related marks, images and terminology in this country.

Like the three previous Classic Collections, the new one was offered for sale to collectors in uncut press sheets of 120 stamps (six panes) that could be kept intact or broken into gutter pairs or cross-gutter blocks. The uncut sheets were available at face value, $38.40.

Fifteen thousand uncut sheets were signed by the artist who designed the stamps, Richard Waldrep, and sold for $125. Waldrep also signed

20,000 individual panes that the Post Office priced at $29.95. (Asked by an interviewer from the Graphics Philately Association whether he got hand cramps in the process, Waldrep replied: "My signature will never be the same. I kid you not! It's very graphic now. You used to be able to see letters in the signature, but it's graphic now.")

The text on the backs of the stamps was written by David Wallechinsky of Santa Monica, California, an author and authority on the Olympic Games. It produced one minor controversy.

When the Postal Service announced details of the stamps February 1, including the backside wording, it reported that the text for the women's diving stamp would begin with the sentence: "Platform diving is performed from a board 10 meters above the water." Bruce Bradley, a member of the 1968 and 1972 U.S. Olympic water polo teams, then wrote to *Linn's Stamp News* pointing out that there is no diving board on the 10-meter platform, and *Linn's* published an article based on Bradley's observation.

After the article appeared, postal officials conferred among themselves and consulted their experts. It's true that there literally is no board on a diving platform, they were told, but some divers use the term "board" when referring to a platform. Although a revision of the type was made for the stamp in anticipation of a change, Stamp Services management in the end decided to leave the wording as it was.

The decision wasn't communicated to two places in the Postal Service, however. One was the Corporate Relations Department, which prepares the press releases on new stamps. A release dated May 1 — the day before the stamps were issued — again included the full text description from the back of each stamp. This time, however, the wording provided for the women's diving stamp had been changed to read: "Platform diving is performed from 10 meters above the water." The reference to a board had been eliminated.

The other section was the stamp and product marketing section of Stamp Services, which had taken over responsibility for preparing the Classic Collections picture postal cards. These cards normally carry the same wording as is found on the backs of the stamps whose designs they reproduce. However, the women's diving postal card, which was issued on the same day as the women's diving stamp, carried the revised version of the text: "Platform diving is performed from 10 meters above the water."

(A similar alteration had been made in 1995 with the Comic Strip Classics set. The text on the back of the Little Orphan Annie stamp included the word "indispensible," a spelling that purists would call incorrect, although it is listed as a variant in *Webster's Third International Dictionary*. On the Little Orphan Annie postal card, however, the spelling was the more standard "indispensable.")

Normally, an event of the magnitude of the Olympics would inspire many organizations to prepare commemorative postmarks. However, so stringent were the rules and limitations imposed on these postmarks by USPS at the behest of USOC that few were made by organizations other than the Postal Service itself.

The rules, as published in the *Postal Bulletin*, forbade any use in a pictorial cancellation of the Olympic rings, the Olympic torch, the word Olympics in any form, the 1996 Olympic mascot (a character named "Izzy"), or any reference to Atlanta in an Olympic context. Applications for Olympic-related cancellations had to be made on a special form provided by USPS. The form then was sent to Atlanta, where no fewer than four Olympic and USPS functionaries had to sign it, indicating their approval, before going to USPS headquarters for a final determination. The *Bulletin* candidly warned that it would be "unlikely" that any cancellation containing any of the listed marks or words would be approved.

The rules applied even to the official Olympic-venue handstamps prepared by the Postal Service. These comprised 25 different pictorial designs representing 25 athletic events, most with datestamps covering a range of dates rather than single days. The designs all showed the outlines of athletes in action at various events. But none of them bore the words "Olympic" or "venue," the Olympic rings or the Atlanta 1996 torch logo. The datestamps all read "ATLANTA GA 30303."

Coin collectors, as well as stamp collectors, were targeted for Olympic-related marketing. The U.S. Mint issued the largest commemorative coin series in its history in connection with the Atlanta Centennial games. It created a total of 14 coins — seven in 1995 and seven in 1996 — for the Olympic Games and an additional two coins for the Paralympics, the international games for disabled athletes, which also took place in Atlanta in 1996. There were four $5 gold, eight $1 silver and four 50¢ cupro-nickel clad coins (see illustration). Proceeds helped fund the training of U.S. Olympic athletes and the staging of the Atlanta Olympics.

The Centennial Olympic Games, held from July 19 to August 4, were memorable for their record-breaking attendance and their many outstanding athletic performances, but they also will be remembered for tragedy. A pipe bomb that exploded in Atlanta's Centennial Olympic Park early on the morning of July 27 caused the death of two people and wounded 111 others.

The Games went on after that with heightened security, and escaped further criminal incident. For the first time in recent history, no nation boycotted the Games, and all 197 eligible countries were represented. In the end, the United States won the most medals, with 87, followed by Russia (53), Germany (52), and China (49). The host country also won the most golds (36), with Russia second with 23 and China third with 16.

More than 25 world records were broken during the Games, 15 of them by weightlifters. American Michael Johnson became the first Olympian ever to win both the men's 200- and 400-meter runs in the same Games; he set a world record of 19.32 seconds in the 200. On the women's side, France's Marie-Jose Perec won those same two races as well. Canada's Donovan Bailey set a world record of 9.84 seconds in winning the 100 meter dash, and also anchored his country's 4- by 100-meter relay team to an upset victory over the Americans.

American Carl Lewis, at age 35, won his ninth gold medal over a span of four Olympiads by taking the long jump, and his countryman, Dan O'Brien, who in 1992 had failed to make the U.S. team in the decathlon, came back to win the event at Atlanta. Aleksei Nemov of Russia took home six medals in men's gymnastics: two gold, one silver and three bronze. Amy Van Dyken of the United States won four gold medals and Michelle Smith of Ireland won three, both in women's swimming. Fu Mingxia of China became the first woman in 36 years to win two golds in diving. Team sports winners included the United States in men's and women's basketball, women's softball and women's soccer, and Cuba in baseball.

The Designs

Having issued 82 Olympic Games stamps over the years, the Postal Service was hard-pressed to come up with a novel look for the 20 new ones scheduled for 1996. Members of the Citizens' Stamp Advisory

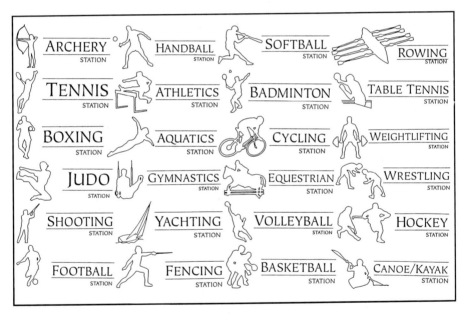

Pictorial portions taken from 24 so-called Olympic-venue postmarks and a complete Baseball Station handstamp.

Committee's design subcommittee suggested that photographs of athletes rather than the customary paintings be used, but Stamp Services staffers pointed out that it would be impossible to find and adapt 20 photos that wouldn't be recognizable as specific living people.

However, artist Richard Waldrep, who was chosen to paint the images for the stamps, did need photographs for reference. PhotoAssist, the Postal Service's research firm, assembled a large quantity of photos of world-class athletes for his use. Waldrep was instructed by art director Carl Herrman to alter the faces and other features in his paintings as necessary to make the athletes on the stamps anonymous, but, as we will see, that turned out to be not as easy as it might have appeared.

Shown here are the designs of some of the 14 U.S. coins issued in 1995 and 1996 to commemorate the Centennial Olympic Games. Altogether, the U.S. Mint produced four $5 gold, eight $1 silver and four 50¢ cupronickel clad coins depicting Olympic athletes and symbols. The obverse sides bear the words "In God We Trust"; the reverse sides, which were common to more than one coin, are inscribed "E Pluribus Unum."

Waldrep previously had designed the five se-tenant Summer Olympics stamps of 1992 and the four Country and Western Music stamps of 1993. A free-lance illustrator for 20 years, he has a wide range of credits, from Parker Brothers and Milton Bradley board games to the cover of the 1996 National Football League *Pro Bowl* magazine.

The artist used gouache and airbrush to create his Olympic stamp paintings. Like his 1992 Summer Olympic designs, the 20 new designs incorporated cropped images of bodies in action typical of their sports. The cropping was less severe, however, than in the 1992 designs, which postal officials came to describe as "the severed-head approach."

"The stamps were to be vertical," Herrman said. "But some sports, like swimming, aren't vertical. Instead of trying to fit whole figures into the vertical boxes, Richard zoomed in on them, and cropped off part of their bodies in some cases. This really added to the impact.

"What we tried to achieve was to hit a moment of peak action and drama for each of the sports: the wrestler about to escape, or the other one at the bottom about to drop his opponent to the mat ... the moment when the kayaker is just clearing the gates by inches ... the thrower about to release the javelin."

Waldrep emphasized the athletes' musculature, using highlights and reflections to bring out the texture of skin and fabric. "The figures are beyond real," the artist himself told an interviewer. "They're very graphic." Carl Herrman's word for the style was "heroic."

The 20 designs featured 20 different Olympic activities: (men's) decathlon, men's canoeing, women's running, women's diving, men's cycling, (men's) freestyle wrestling, women's gymnastics, women's sailboarding, men's shot put, women's soccer, (women's) beach volleyball, men's rowing, men's sprinting events, women's swimming, women's softball, men's hurdles, men's swimming, men's gymnastics, equestrian (a sport in which women compete against men) and men's basketball.

In choosing the 20 sports, Herrman considered several things. He gave his highest priority to events in which U.S. athletes were expected to excel. He also wanted to focus on sports that would get the most exposure on American television; for this purpose, PhotoAssist made a careful tally, down to the minute, of how much TV time had been devoted to each sport in 1992. Another factor was the Postal Service's desire to show men and women athletes in approximately equal numbers. Finally, Herrman wanted to include one or two sports that were unfamiliar and new to stamps — which is how sailboarding, for example, was selected.

"Richard (Waldrep) was a participant in this," Herrman said. "I wanted him to be comfortable that he could do a good stamp, based on the photographic reference material that was provided to him. So that was another part of the decision-making process."

At one point Herrman had planned to include men's boxing, and Waldrep made a finished painting showing two fighters confronting each other in the ring. However, CSAC members and USPS officials were cool to the idea of again featuring this violent event — it had been depicted on three previous U.S. Olympic stamps — and it was decided to replace boxing with women's softball, a first-time Olympic medal sport.

Another substitution was beach volleyball, also a first-time Olympic activity, for the men's long jump, but this was done mostly for compositional reasons. Waldrep's sketch of a long jumper "just didn't fit into our format," Herrman said. "It would have been great as a horizontal, but we couldn't get enough of the body into the vertical frame without cropping, and if you start cropping the long jumper, it's hard for the viewer to know what the figure is doing. If we had reduced him down to avoid cropping, his body would have been half the size of the other bodies on the pane, and it just wouldn't have looked right."

These changes gave the stamps an even 10-10 male-female division. One more major change was made, however, and it unbalanced the genders.

The first stamp on the pane was intended to represent the women's heptathlon. For this stamp, Waldrep painted an African-American woman preparing to hurl the javelin. He based his painting on a photo of U.S. heptathlete Jackie Joyner-Kersee, and, despite the alterations he made in her features, the sports experts and Olympic officials who reviewed each painting for accuracy said the resemblance to Joyner-Kersee was too strong. Waldrep went back to work, changed her hairdo and revised the features even more extensively, but the experts still weren't satisfied.

Finally, USPS officials gave up and told the artist to make the javelin thrower a male. He did so — and the event represented by the stamp became the men's decathlon.

Not only did the athletes have to be generic, but so did uniforms and equipment. In most cases, even after a painting was finished, Waldrep made additional small changes to ensure that no uniform resembled too closely that of a prominent university or athletic club. Shoes and other gear with stripes or other decorations suggestive of commercial insignia also had to be revised.

Often, in stamp design, such minor changes are made electronically by computer graphics specialists during the production process. In this case, however, postal officials had Waldrep do most of the alterations with his paintbrush. The reason, said Terrence McCaffrey, head of stamp design for USPS, was that postal officials hoped to exhibit the original finished art, just as it appeared on the stamps, at the Games. Because of the falling-out between USPS and Olympic officials, however, this plan had to be abandoned.

Following is a listing of the 20 designs, along with some of the revisions Waldrep made after submitting his paintings. PhotoAssist furnished the names of the athletes in most of the source photographs.

Men's Decathlon: Unidentified.

Men's Canoeing: Thierry Saidi of France.

Women's Running: Meredith Rainey. At the suggestion of the experts,

Waldrep removed the runner's headband and an earring and changed her hairstyle.

Women's Diving: Mary Hammer. Waldrep repainted the athlete's hair to lighten the color.

Men's Cycling: David Brinton.

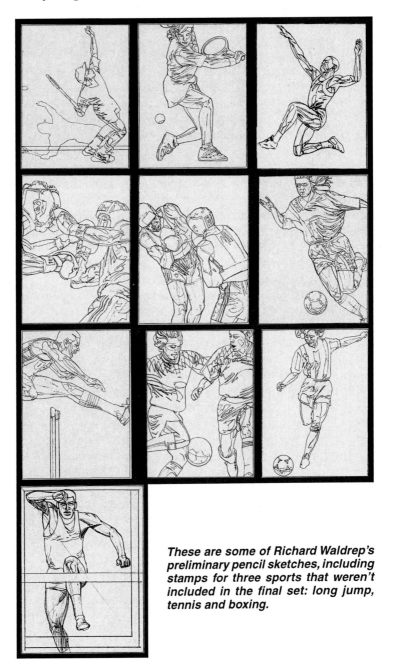

These are some of Richard Waldrep's preliminary pencil sketches, including stamps for three sports that weren't included in the final set: long jump, tennis and boxing.

Richard Waldrep painted this picture for a boxing stamp, but the subject was dropped in favor of a stamp for women's softball.

Freestyle Wrestling: Ghani Yulouz and Julien Jasko of France. Waldrep repainted the stripes on the shoe of the wrestler in red to reduce its resemblance to Adidas. He also removed a bandage from the wrestler's knee.

Women's Gymnastics: Kelly Garrison-Steves. The artist de-emphasized the gymnast's headband. He also added a shadow beneath the figure to make it clear that the gymnast was on the floor and not in mid-air.

Women's Sailboarding: Unidentified. Waldrep lengthened the sailboarder's hair, gave her sunglasses and modified the harness holding her to the mast.

Shot Put: Art McDermott. The athlete's hair was lightened and re-

These are two versions of the javelin thrower, who was intended to appear on a stamp honoring the women's heptathlon. Richard Waldrep painted her with and without a pony tail, and altered and re-altered her features. However, the experts consulted by USPS continued to insist she looked too much like Jackie Joyner-Kersee, whose photograph the artist had used for visual reference. Finally the design was scrapped and a male javelin thrower, representing the men's decathlon, was substituted.

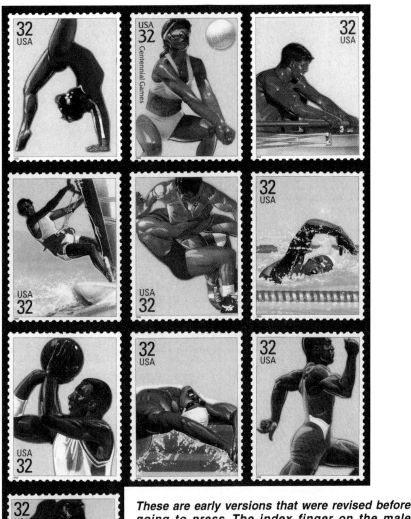

These are early versions that were revised before going to press. The index finger on the male sprinter's left hand, shown here extended, was folded back with his other fingers. The shoe on one of the wrestlers looked too much like an Adidas product and had to be changed. The windsurfer was given long hair and sunglasses, and her harness was modified. On the equestrian stamp, the distinctive blaze on the horse's nose was reshaped. The male rower, shown here barechested, was provided with a shirt. The beach volleyball player, despite her visor and sunglasses, was deemed too recognizable and was shorn of her ponytail and given a changed jawline and lips. The woman gymnast's headband was made less prominent, the stripes on her sleeves were removed and a shadow added to the floor. The two swimmers were raised higher in their stamp frames and more water inserted beneath them. The male basketball player's face, as shown here, was altered on the recommendation of critics who thought he looked too much like the photographic model, Scottie Pippen.

shaped to reduce his resemblance to McDermott.

Women's Soccer: Mia Hamm. Waldrep's original painting had shown the player in a light blue jersey with a blue stripe on her white shorts. But the uniform too closely resembled the uniform of the University of North Carolina, where Hamm had been a collegiate soccer star, so Waldrep lightened the shirt and changed the stripe to red.

Beach Volleyball: Janice Harrer. Although the figure in Waldrep's original painting wore sunglasses and a visor, the experts thought she resembled Harrer too closely, so the artist eliminated her ponytail, altered her lips and rounded her jawline.

Men's Rowing: Unidentified. Originally, Waldrep painted the rower bare-chested, but after the experts informed him that Olympic rowers were required to wear tops, he provided one.

Men's Sprinting Events: Dennis Mitchell. Waldrep's early sketches for this stamp showed the runner coming straight at the viewer, but he and Herrman agreed that a profile view would be better. The painting that Waldrep submitted showed the runner with his index finger extended in an unusual manner, the way it looked in the source photograph. But the Postal Service's consultants suggested that the extended finger might be an identifiable characteristic, so the artist repainted the hand.

Women's Swimming: Mary Wayte. This painting, and the men's swimming painting, were the only ones on which significant changes were made electronically. Using Adobe PhotoShop, a computer graphics specialist raised the figures higher in their designs and electronically "cloned" additional blue water.

Women's Softball: Suzy Brazney. The painted figure wore a catcher's mask, and Waldrep changed her hair beneath her cap. Even so, Brazney telephoned the Postal Service's Terrence McCaffrey after the designs were made public to announce with pleasure that she recognized herself on the stamp.

Men's Hurdles: Greg Foster.

Men's Swimming: Martin Lopez-Subard of Spain.

Men's Gymnastics: Valery Lyukin of Russia.

Equestrian: Katie Monahan Prudent, aboard her horse "The Empress." Waldrep made the blaze on the nose of the horse narrower to prevent The Empress and, by extension, the rider from being identified on the stamp. On the advice of the experts, Waldrep made sure the horse's mane was braided and that it had the kind of bridle and ankle gear required in Olympic competition.

Men's Basketball: Scottie Pippen. Waldrep revised his painting extensively to satisfy experts who insisted that the player's profile and way of holding the ball bore too close a resemblance to the Chicago Bulls star.

CSAC and USPS staff suggested that the stamps be given backgrounds of different colors, but in the end Carl Herrman opted for a single color, a pale yellow, that would complement the flesh tones and uniforms of the athletes and, when extended to the header, would unify the pane.

In painting the backgrounds Waldrep included what he called "nice little variations throughout that I thought were interesting." However, Herrman wanted the backgrounds to have a uniform flatness, and the variations were eliminated electronically during the prepress work.

Waldrep outlined each figure and item of equipment in orange. "It's a technique that goes back to the early days of illustration," Herrman explained. "It gives the art a little sense of motion, as if the edges were blurred. Also, on some of them, like the male gymnast with the white uniform, you really needed the outline to hold the edge.

"If Richard had given the figures a black outline it would have been

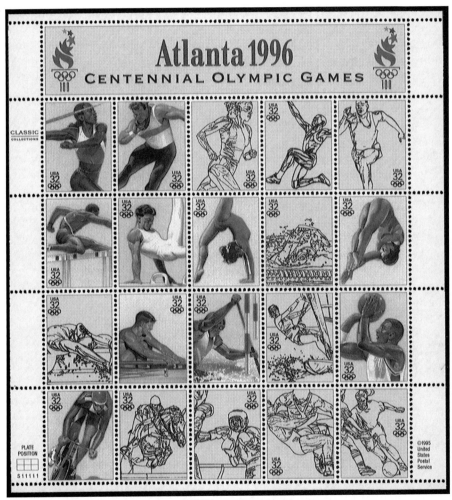

This is an early layout of the pane in which Waldrep's finished paintings were combined with designs that still were in the pencil-sketch stage. The stamps were arranged generally in the order in which their sports were introduced at the Olympic Games, with the first five stamps featuring track and field events; that scheme soon was dropped.

76

ghastly — like a cartoon — but for some reason the orange works."

During much of the design process, USPS was uncertain whether it would be allowed to use the interlocking Olympic rings and the words "Centennial Olympic Games" in the stamp designs. Accordingly, Herrman had to position the art in the frames and crop it in a way that would leave room for the wording and rings, but also look attractive with a simple "USA 32."

In the end, when the use of the rings and wording was allowed under the November 1995 philatelic licensing agreement, Herrman was able to find enough free area on most of the designs in which to tuck the typography without impinging on the images. The exceptions were the shot put, men's sprinting events, sailboarding and canoeing stamps, on which the words "Centennial Olympic Games" overlap the design. On the men's hurdles stamp, the "32" is printed over one of the hurdle crossbars; a dark square that Waldrep had painted on the bar was removed to make the denomination more visible.

The type chosen by typographer John Boyd is called Friz Quadrata, a modern font with lines of varying thickness.

Normally the Postal Service presents the denomination and "USA" as a unified logo on its stamps. However, the U.S. Olympic Committee specified that the "USA" and the rings be next to each other and that they be separated from the denomination by a thin horizontal bar.

The uncertainty over what logos and wording could be used also complicated the designing of the header. Several different designs were tried out, some of which featured a color photograph of the Atlanta skyline. (Postmaster General Runyon warned the designers to make sure the city didn't add a new skyscraper or two while the stamps were being printed.) In the end, the skyline wasn't used, and for the final header design, USPS was allowed to use the official torch-and-rings logo of the Centennial Games.

Herrman laid out the stamps in a way that seemed to him to be attractive and logical. The four blue-water stamps, for example, are on four different rows; the basketball player is in the bottom-right corner, where he is aiming the ball up into the pane. CSAC's first suggestion was that he place the stamps in the order in which the sports became part of the Olympics, but that idea proved unsatisfactory.

Varieties

Several panes of the Centennial Olympic Games stamps were found imperforate or with partial perforations.

The first such find was an imperforate pane that was bought May 22 in a Skokie, Illinois, post office by stamp collector Howard Jancy. Jancy told *Linn's Stamp News* that he had gone to the post office to buy stamps for postage. He recognized the pane as an error and asked for two additional panes, but these were normally perforated.

Later, stamp dealer Bob Rosenbaum of Prescott, Arizona, told *Linn's*

These are three proposed header treatments, each featuring a color photograph of the Atlanta skyline. Postmaster General Runyon warned the designers that the skyline might change between the time the stamps went to press and the time they were issued.

that a caller had told him May 14 that 10 error panes were bought in Prescott. Nine of the panes were imperforate and one had perforations at the upper left corner only, affecting the first two stamps of the left-hand column (positions 1 and 6). The dealer purchased the partially imperforate pane and one fully imperforate pane and sold them to a customer, Rosenbaum said.

The dealer told *Linn's* he had learned that three more imperforate panes were found in the post office in Prescott Valley, eight miles from Prescott. All 13 panes in the Arizona find were from the upper-right position of the press sheet, according to the plate position diagram in the selvage.

James Kabatek, a Colorado Springs, Colorado, collector, purchased a pane of the Centennial Olympic Games stamps on which the printing on the reverse is shifted exactly one stamp width to the left across the entire back of the pane. The result is that a vertical strip of four stamps has the printing omitted, and the remaining 16 stamps on the pane have the wrong descriptive text on the back. The front of the pane is normal.

Kabatek told *Linn's* he went to a post office early in September and, while waiting in line, overheard a woman patron requesting "a sheet of those Olympic stamps." As the woman left, Kabatek noticed that the back of the pane she was carrying looked odd. When he reached the front of the line, Kabatek asked to look through the clerk's stock of Olympic Games stamps. From the 20 panes remaining, he found the single error pane illustrated here. He also was allowed to examine additional stock at the same location, but no other errors were found.

The four stamps on the pane that have no printing on the back are Decathlon, Freestyle Wrestling, Beach Volleyball and Men's Hurdles. As an example of the mismatch between front and back printing on the remaining stamps, the stamp in the upper-right corner of the pane depicting men's cycling is backed by a description of the women's diving event. The description for the men's cycling stamp, like the descriptions of all the stamps in the far-right column on the pane, is split between the left and right vertical selvage.

The shift affects all aspects of the reverse printing, including the quote from modern Olympic Games founder Pierre de Coubertin that appears on the back of the header at the top of the pane.

First-Day Facts

Robert F. Harris, USPS vice president for diversity development, dedicated the Olympics stamps in a noon ceremony at Washington's L'Enfant Plaza in front of Postal Service headquarters. Harris had excelled in track and field at Florida A&M and qualified for the 1964 Tokyo Olympics before being injured in a parachute jump.

"What is important in the Olympic Games is not winning, but taking part. What is important in life is not the triumph, but the struggle."

...the Centennial ...ch Logo, TM © 1992 ACOG   Atlanta 1996

	Women's Diving	Women's Running	Men's Canoeing	Decathlon	
n's ing ng was one nal events 6 Games. speed and a banked men's event d in 1988.	Platform diving is performed from a board 10 meters above the water. The most difficult dive is the back 1½ somersault with 4½ twists. The U.S. has won over half the medals awarded in both men's and women's events.	There are 8 women's running events, from 100 meters to the marathon (26 miles, 385 yards). Until 1964, the longest race was only 200 meters.	Whitewater, or slalom, events were added temporarily in 1972 and permanently in 1988. Flatwater canoeing has been part of the Games since 1936.	The decathlon consists of 10 events. On the first day, athletes compete in the 100-meter dash, long jump, shot put, high jump, and 400-meter run. On the second day, they perform the 110-meter hurdles, discus throw, pole vault, javelin throw, and 1500-meter run.	M Cy Sprint cyc of the ori in the 19 it combine strategy o track. A w was adde
	Men's Shot Put	Women's Sailboarding	Women's Gymnastics	Freestyle Wrestling	
en's cer n's soccer part of the ce 1900. tournament for the first 96. Eight take part.	The shot put has been included in all Games since 1896. A shot is a 16-pound ball of iron or brass. The United States has won 15 of 22 gold medals.	The first sailboarding contest was included in the 1984 Los Angeles Games. A separate women's event was added in 1992.	Women gymnasts compete in an all-around event, a team event, floor exercises, balance beam, uneven bars, and vault. Contestants must be at least 15 years old by the end of 1996.	Wrestling has 10 weight divisions. It is the only sport with a maximum weight limit; wrestlers must be less than 286 pounds. The United States has earned more medals than any other nation.	Wo So Although m has been has been Games s a women's will be hel teams wil
	Women's Swimming	Men's Sprinting Events	Men's Rowing	Beach Volleyball	
en's ball ill make pearance 6 Games. States team a champion the teams win a medal.	The women's 400-meter freestyle event was first held in 1920. The 800-meter event was added in 1968. American women have won 15 of 24 gold medals in these events.	The 100 meters and 400 meters were part of the first Games in 1896. In the 100, 200, and 400 meters and the two sprint relays, the United States has won two-thirds of the gold medals.	There will be 14 rowing events contested at the 1996 Games: 8 for men and 6 for women. For the first time, lightweight events will be included for men under 160 lbs. and for women under 130 lbs.	Beach volleyball, played with two-person teams, will be added to the Games program for the first time in 1996. There will be both men's and women's events.	Wo Sof Softball in all Games its first a in the 199 The United is the wor and one o favored to
	Equestrian	Men's Gymnastics	Men's Swimming	Men's Hurdles	
n's tball ball first made nce in 1936. ates has won d lost only 2. s from the allowed to r the first 1992.	Equestrian is one of only two sports in which women compete against men. The jumping event was first included in the 1900 Games. The sport was opened to women in 1952.	Male gymnasts compete in 6 events: horizontal bar, parallel bars, vault, pommel horse, rings, and floor exercises. There are also an all-around event and a team event.	The backstroke event was first included in the Games of 1900. There are now two events: the 100 meters, which is two lengths of the pool, and the 200 meters, which is four lengths.	The 110-meter hurdles event has been included in all Games since 1896. The United States has earned 48 medals. No other nation has won more than 5.	M Bask Since basket its appeara the United 92 games a Professiona NBA were compete in time in

A shift in the printing on the reverse of this Centennial Olympic Games pane resulted in four stamps that have the back printing omitted. Each of the remaining 16 stamps has the wrong event description printed on the back.

Featured speakers included two Olympic gold medalists: Evelyn Ashford, who won three golds in the women's 4- by 100-meter relay (1984, 1988 and 1992) and a gold in the 100 meters in 1984, and Mitch Gaylord, who won his gold as a member of the U.S. men's gymnastics team in 1984 and also won a silver and two bronze medals during individual competition that year. Also speaking was C. Thomas McMillen, co-chair of the President's Council on Physical Fitness and Sports. Azeezaly S. Jaffer, Stamp Services manager, gave welcoming and closing remarks. Honored guests included CSAC vice chairman C. Douglas Lewis; Sandra Perlmutter, executive director of the President's Council on Physical Fitness and Sports; and stamp designer Richard Waldrep.

The earliest-known prerelease use of one of the 20 Olympics stamps was a men's cycling stamp on a cover machine-postmarked in Huntsville, Alabama, April 30, two days before the first-day ceremony.

Date of Issue: May 23, 1996

Catalog Number: Scott 3069

Colors: yellow, magenta, cyan, black (2)

First-Day Cancel: Santa Fe, New Mexico

First-Day Cancellations: 200,522

Format: Panes of 15, horizontal, 3 across, 5 down. Gravure printing cylinders of 90 subjects (6 across, 15 around) made by Armotek Industries of Palmyra, New Jersey

Overall Stamp Size: 1.56 by 1.24 inches; 39.624mm by 31.496mm

Perforations: 11.6 by 11.5 (APS rotary perforator)

Selvage Inscription: "Nobody sees a flower,/really — it is so small — we haven't/ time, and to see takes time,/like to have a friend takes time./GEORGIA O'KEEFFE." "Red Poppy, 1927." "Reproduced by permission of the owner and the Georgia O'Keeffe Foundation."

Selvage Markings: ©/USPS/1995." "15 x .32 = $4.80." "PLATE/POSITION" and diagram.

Designer and Typographer: Margaret Bauer of Washington, D.C.

Modeler: Richard C. Sennett

Art Director: Derry Noyes

Project Manager: Terrence McCaffrey, USPS

Stamp Manufacturing: Stamps printed for Stamp Venturers, Chantilly, Virginia, at J.W. Fergusson and Sons, Richmond, Virginia, on a Champlain webfed gravure press. Stamps perforated, processed and shipped at Stamp Venturers, Fredericksburg, Virginia.

Quantity Ordered and Distributed: 156,300,000

Cylinder Number Detail: 1 set of 5 gravure cylinder numbers preceded by the letter S in selvage next to upper-left and lower-left stamps

Cylinder Number Combination Reported: S11111

Tagging: block tagging over stamps

The Stamp

On May 23, 1996, USPS issued a commemorative stamp honoring artist Georgia O'Keeffe. The first-day city was Santa Fe, New Mexico, where O'Keeffe died in 1986.

The stamp was the latest of many issued over the years to depict the work of American artists and sculptors. Several of these, in the 1960s and 1970s, were included in an informal series called "American artists." The more recent ones, however, such as the 1994 stamp honoring Norman Rockwell, have had no series designation.

O'Keeffe got her stamp shortly after becoming eligible for postal honors under the Citizens' Stamp Advisory Committee's 10-year (after death) rule. Her distinguished reputation as an artist, plus the fact that CSAC makes extra effort to find women to honor on stamps, made for quick approval, with strong support from the committee's chairperson, Virginia Noelke; its vice chair, C. Douglas Lewis; and Phil Meggs, a member of CSAC's literary and visual arts subcommittee.

The stamp's design was a photographic reproduction of O'Keeffe's painting *Red Poppy, 1927*. It was issued in a mini-pane of 15 stamps with wide decorative selvage that featured a photograph of the artist, along with a brief excerpt from one of her writings.

This mini-pane format was devised by Carl Burcham, former head of stamp and product marketing for USPS, as a way to entice collectors to buy entire panes rather than single stamps. It first was used in 1994 for the 29¢ Moon Landing commemorative and was used again the following year for the 32¢ Marilyn Monroe stamp. Postal officials speculate that if this format had been available for the Elvis Presley stamp of 1993 — the stamp that spectacularly demonstrated the profit potential in pop-culture figures — USPS would have netted even more than the $36 million it says it made from Elvis.

"We would have had Elvis gyrating in the selvage," laughed Terrence McCaffrey, head of stamp design. "But we hadn't really gotten to that point in our thinking yet."

The contractor for the O'Keeffe stamp was Stamp Venturers, which did the printing job by gravure. The block of 15 stamps was enclosed in a single row of perforations, with the six horizontal rows extending to the edge of the pane on the left to facilitate sale of individual stamps by postal clerks.

Red Poppy, 1927 was one of more than 200 flower paintings created by O'Keeffe in her lifetime. Done in oil on canvas, 9 inches wide by 7½ inches deep, it is owned by an anonymous private collector in Geneva, Switzerland.

Most of the flower paintings were done between 1918 and 1932. In O'Keeffe's oversized views of natural objects — blossoms, leaves, rocks, shells, feathers, animal bones — she frequently integrated abstract and objective imagery. Many of these paintings were influenced by photographic techniques, especially close-ups and cropping. She tended to ex-

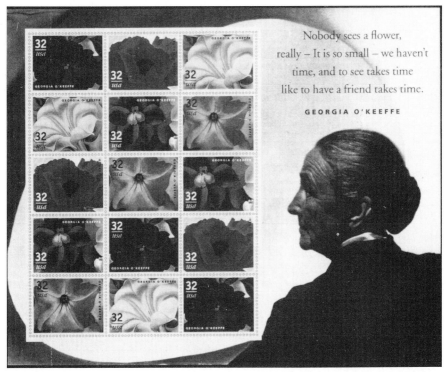

Designer Margaret Bauer prepared this mockup of a pane of se-tenant stamps incorporating five of Georgia O'Keeffe's paintings. The paintings are, starting at the top left: Petunias, 1925; Red Poppy, 1927 *(the painting ultimately used for the O'Keeffe stamp);* White Trumpet Flower, *1932 (used twice in succession);* White Rose with Larkspur No. 1, 1927 *(detail);* Petunia No. 2, 1924 *(detail).*

aggerate sizes, simplify forms, eliminate middle distances and employ surrealistic techniques, such as a floating animal skull against a distant mountain range.

Photographer Alfred Stieglitz first exhibited her charcoal drawings and watercolors at his avant-garde gallery on New York City's Fifth Avenue in 1916-17. Stieglitz was a strong advocate of the first generation of American modern artists, and he brought O'Keeffe into this circle, convinced that she expressed a female sensibility in a new, original and bold manner. He and O'Keeffe were married in 1924.

The artist was born November 15, 1887, near Sun Prairie, Wisconsin. She studied at the Art Institute of Chicago, the Art Students League of New York, the University of Virginia and Columbia University.

She first experienced the American Southwest when she taught art at West Texas State Normal School (now West Texas State University) in the small town of Canyon, near Amarillo, Texas, in 1914-16. Her love of the region grew stronger over decades of summer visits, and it eventually led her to settle in the small village of Abiquiu, 50 miles from Santa Fe. After Stieglitz died in 1946, O'Keeffe lived full time in New Mexico.

She was elected to the National Institute of Arts and Letters in 1949 and the American Academy of Arts and Letters in 1962. In 1976 her autobiography was published. She died March 6, 1986, at the age of 98.

Among the ancillary products produced by USPS for the O'Keeffe stamp were what USPS called a "first-day souvenir," containing a pane of stamps bearing the first-day postmark and a biographical overview, which sold for $14.95; a stamp pane matted and ready for framing, for $19.95; and the customary American Commemoratives panel with a mint block of four and vintage engravings, for $7.95.

The Design

To convert an O'Keeffe painting into a stamp, the project's art director, Derry Noyes, chose Margaret Bauer of Washington, D.C. Bauer is a staff designer for the National Gallery of Art who prepares exhibition catalogs and other National Gallery publications. Her familiarity with fine art, as well as her design skills, were assets in the project.

Bauer and Noyes considered making the O'Keeffe stamp a se-tenant block of multiple varieties, using different flower paintings either as details or in full. Among the paintings they considered, besides *Red Poppy, 1927*, were *White Rose with Larkspur No. 1, 1927*; *Petunia No. 2, 1924*; *Petunias, 1925*; and *White Trumpet Flower, 1932*. In the end, however, CSAC and the Postal Service staff decided they would be unable to justify to collectors the creation of several stamp varieties for a single subject.

"If it had looked as if we were saying more about Georgia O'Keeffe by using multiple designs — if it gave more information about her, and made a stronger sheet — I think we would have stuck with that idea," said Derry Noyes. "But the red poppy was such a strong image ... It was far more striking than the others. It made a stronger sheet by itself than it would have if it were combined with the other paintings."

Red Poppy, 1927 had several pluses as a design subject. It "reads well as a flower," Noyes said, meaning that it isn't as abstract as many of O'Keeffe's flower images. Unlike the other flower paintings that were considered, *Red Poppy*'s dimensions were perfectly suited for a horizontal semijumbo stamp without cropping. And it is the artist's "most famous small still life," according to writer Jan Garden Castro. In *The Art and Life of Georgia O'Keeffe*, Castro goes on to say:

"The sensuous, China-red petals delicately curve inward toward the mauve and black central mound of seeds. The green neck of the flower head and the gray-white ground at the petal edges lead the eye toward the vibrant flower. The compositional features — a central, dark oval; surrounding triangles of bright color enclosed in knife-sharp edges of color; and pale ground — again show O'Keeffe's original use of the basic symmetry of circle and triangle."

The problem with *Red Poppy*, however, was that it is privately owned. CSAC normally resists the use of privately owned paintings because of a theory held by some of its members that showing a painting on a stamp automatically enhances its value in the art market. As an alternative to *Red Poppy*, CSAC vice chairman C. Douglas Lewis, who is curator of sculpture at the National Gallery of Art, proposed the use of another O'Keeffe painting, *Oriental Poppies, 1927*, which is in the University Art Museum at the University of Minnesota. However, after examining a trial design using *Oriental Poppies*, CSAC decided that *Red Poppy* made a much stronger stamp.

USPS lawyers located the anonymous owner through an intermediary. The owner initially refused permission to use the painting on grounds that it had been overexposed, but ultimately relented. Noyes believes the owner was won over by the fact that the stamp and pane were tastefully designed, with a "sensitive" use of typography, which, although superimposed on the flower, didn't detract from its pictorial effectiveness.

The typefaces chosen by Margaret Bauer for the stamp are Frutiger, for the name "Georgia O'Keeffe" in black capitals down the right side; Officiana, for the "32" in dropout white in the lower left; and Garamond italic, for the lowercase "USA," also in dropout white, below the denomination. "It's rare that you can combine typefaces like that and make them work," said Noyes.

For the photograph of O'Keeffe in the selvage, Bauer and Noyes narrowed the choices to two: a 1918 photo of the artist at work in Lake George, New York, taken by her future husband, Alfred Stieglitz, and a color photo of the artist as an older woman, made around 1960 by Tony Vaccaro.

CSAC thought that O'Keeffe as she looked in the Vaccaro photo would be more recognizable to the general public. The committee also liked the way her image could be positioned on the selvage to suggest that the artist was looking at the Red Poppy stamps. In the original photograph, the artist is holding up one of her large canvases titled *Pelvis, Red with Yellow*,

Designer Margaret Bauer and art director Derry Noyes originally considered using this photograph of O'Keeffe in the selvage of the pane. It was made by Alfred Stieglitz at Lake George, New York, in 1918, when the artist was 30.

and is profiled against it. It is part of her so-called "pelvis series" of paintings, which feature closeups of a cow's pelvic girdle with blue sky appearing inside the bone's ovoid hollow.

"It would have been nice to use a Stieglitz photograph because there was such a famous bond between those two people," Noyes said. "But you can't let yourself get stuck on an idea. You should go with what looks best."

The selvage photo and typography are printed in tones of black, an attractive contrast to the bright red of the stamp images. Stamp Venturers originally made one gravure cylinder for all the black portions of the pane, selvage as well as stamps. The result, however, was that the black used on the stamps to help give the flower definition was printing too dark.

Richard Sennett, founder of Stamp Venturers, was called in for consultation and quickly diagnosed the problem. "He said the black in the selvage was so strong that it was killing the red in the stamp," project manager Terrence McCaffrey recalled. "He said they needed two separate color stations on the press. They stopped production and made a separate cylinder for the black process color they were using for the stamp. It made a world of difference."

The quotation above the artist's portrait is from O'Keeffe's *About Myself*, a text published in the catalog that accompanied her 1939 exhibition at An American Place, New York. The context of the quotation is as follows:

"A flower is relatively small. Everyone has many associations with a flower — the idea of flowers. You put out your hand to touch the flower

— lean forward to smell it — maybe touch it with your lips almost without thinking — or give it to someone to please them. Still — in a way — nobody sees a flower — really — it is so small — we haven't time — and to see takes time like to have a friend takes time. If I could paint the flower exactly as I see it no one would see what I see because I would paint it small like the flower is small.

"So I said to myself — I'll paint what I see — what the flower is to me but I'll paint it big and they will be surprised into taking time to look at it."

Varieties

Ten imperforate panes of the Georgia O'Keeffe stamp were found in the Boston, Massachusetts, area. All were from the right-center position on the printing sheet, as indicated by the plate position diagram in the selvage. The error was reported to *Linn's Stamp News* in July by dealer Jacques C. Schiff Jr. of Ridgefield Park, New Jersey. At that time Schiff had sold a majority of the panes, he told *Linn's*.

This is the original photograph, made in color around 1960 by Michael Vaccaro, that was adapted for use on the pane selvage. It shows Georgia O'Keeffe holding up her painting, Pelvis, Red and Yellow.

First-Day Facts

Loren Smith, chief marketing officer and senior vice president of USPS, dedicated the O'Keeffe stamp in a noon ceremony on The Plaza in Santa Fe. Actress Marsha Mason was the host.

The participants were: Raymond R. Krueger of the board of directors of the Georgia O'Keeffe Foundation and a grand-nephew of the artist; John L. Marion of the board of directors of the Georgia O'Keeffe Museum; Thomas A. Livesay, director, Museum of New Mexico; and Charles M. Davis, district manager, USPS.

Also present were Maria Chabot, O'Keeffe's long-time friend; Elizabeth Glassman, president of the O'Keeffe Foundation; Anne W. Marion, president of the O'Keeffe Museum board of directors; Jean Firstenberg, a director of the American Film Institute; and stamp designer Margaret Bauer.

Later that day, the participants were taken to Abiquiu for what was in effect a second first-day ceremony. Ceremony programs were prepared for both locations. In the Santa Fe programs, the O'Keeffe stamps were tied by the standard "first day of issue" postmark. In the Abiquiu programs, a special pictorial cancellation was used, showing the outline of a mesa and the words "The Georgia O'Keeffe Foundation Station." Both groups of programs were canceled by Minnesota Diversified, a company that produces many USPS items. In addition, the pictorial cancellation was available in Abiquiu as a handstamp. Eleanor Caponigro, its designer, was an honored guest at the Abiquiu ceremony.

As part of the May 23 celebration, the Museum of Fine Arts on the Santa Fe Plaza opened a special exhibit of *Red Poppy, 1927*, the painting featured on the stamp, on loan from its anonymous Swiss owner. Eleven O'Keeffes from the museum's permanent collection, plus paintings loaned by the O'Keeffe Foundation and the O'Keeffe Museum, were on view. Admission was free for the day, courtesy of USPS.

In addition to issuing the stamp, USPS also underwrote the broadcast of a Public Broadcasting System "American Masters" documentary on Georgia O'Keeffe made before her death.

The earliest-reported prerelease use of a Georgia O'Keeffe stamp was on a cover machine-postmarked Queens, New York, May 14, nine days before the official dedication date. The stamp also was sold one day early at the main post office in Las Cruces, New Mexico, a mistake that was publicized in a front-page story in the Las Cruces *Sun-News*.

32¢ TENNESSEE STATEHOOD BICENTENNIAL

Date of Issue: May 31, 1996

Catalog Number: Scott 3070

Colors: light blue (PMS 291), yellow, magenta, cyan, black

First-Day Cancel: Nashville, Tennessee. First-day ceremonies also held in Memphis and Knoxville, Tennessee.

First-Day Cancellations: 217,281 (includes self-adhesive version)

Format: Panes of 50, vertical, 10 across, 5 down. Gravure printing cylinders of 200 (10 across, 20 around) manufactured by Armotek Industries, Palmyra, New Jersey.

Overall Stamp Size: .99 by 1.56 inches; 25.146mm by 39.624mm

Perforations: 11.1 (APS rotary perforator)

Selvage Markings: "© 1996 USPS." "50 x .32 = $16.00." "PLATE/POSITION" and diagram.

Designer, Art Director and Typographer: Phil Jordan of Falls Church, Virginia

Photographer: Robin Hood of Franklin, Tennessee

Project Manager: Elizabeth A. Altobell, USPS

Stamp Manufacturing: Stamps printed for Stamp Venturers by J.W. Fergusson and Sons, Richmond, Virginia, on Champlain gravure press 1. Stamps processed by Stamp Venturers, Fredericksburg, Virginia.

Quantity Ordered and Distributed: 100,000,000

Cylinder Number Detail: 1 set of 5 gravure cylinder numbers preceded by the letter S in selvage above 2 top corner stamps or below 2 bottom corner stamps

Cylinder Number Combination Reported: S11111

Paper Supplier: Paper Corporation/Brown Bridge

Tagging: One large tagging block over all 50 stamps. The block does not cover the stamps to the edges.

The Stamp

On May 31, the Postal Service issued a 32¢ stamp commemorating the 200th anniversary of Tennessee's entry into the Union as the 16th state. It was the second time the event had been postally recognized. Fifty years earlier, on June 1, 1946, a 3¢ stamp (Scott 941) had marked the 150th anniversary of Tennessee statehood.

Two versions of the new stamp were issued using the same design,

This 3¢ purple stamp issued in 1946 (Scott 941) commemorated Tennessee's statehood centennial. Designed by Victor S. McCloskey Jr., it depicted the state capitol in Nashville flanked by oval portraits of Andrew Jackson, whose home was in Tennessee, and John Sevier, the state's first governor.

which was based on a nighttime photograph of the Tennessee State Capitol in Nashville. One was a conventional "lick-and-stick" stamp with moisture-activated gum. The other was a self-adhesive, the first commemorative stamp to be produced in this popular format. The lick-and-stick variety was sold nationwide, whereas sale of the self-adhesive was limited to Tennessee post offices and philatelic centers elsewhere (see next chapter).

The stamps were officially dedicated at three of the state's major cities during the day: Knoxville, in the east; Memphis, in the west; and Nashville, the capital, near the center. At each of the three ceremonies, Postmaster General Marvin T. Runyon — a Tennessee resident — performed the dedication, Tennessee Governor Donald S. Sundquist was the principal speaker and Andrew S. Walker, USPS district manager for Tennessee, presided.

"Tennessee divides naturally into three 'grand divisions,' both geographically and politically," explained Runyon in a news release. "There's the mountainous upland of East Tennessee, Middle Tennessee with its foothills and basin, and the low plain of West Tennessee. It is only natural that we dedicate the Tennessee bicentennial stamp in all three."

Almost five months earlier, on January 11, Runyon had unveiled the design of the stamp on the grounds of the capitol in Nashville. Taking part in the ceremony were Governor Sundquist; Ned R. McWherter, a former governor of the state and now a member of the USPS Board of Governors; U.S. Senator Bill Frist, Republican of Tennessee; and Martha Ingram, chairman of the "Tennessee 200" Bicentennial Committee.

Both the conventional and self-adhesive versions of the stamp were printed by the gravure process by Stamp Venturers.

Tennessee's name comes from the Indian word "Tenassee," the early capital of the Cherokee Nation. A long, narrow strip of land, it is bordered by eight other states; Missouri is the only other state to touch as many.

Tennessee originally was part of North Carolina and was a U.S. territory from 1790 to 1796. It became the 16th state June 1, 1796, with Knoxville as its capital and John Sevier as its governor. The westernmost section of the state, west of the lower Tennessee River, was purchased from the Chickasaw Indians in 1818.

Nashville was made the permanent capital in 1843, and the present capitol building, designed by William Strickland and combining three styles of Greek Revival architecture, was completed in 1855. Strickland, who also designed George Washington's sarcophagus at Mount Vernon and the Masonic Hall and Customs House in Philadelphia, died in Nashville while overseeing the capitol's construction and is buried in the building.

The well-known nickname "Volunteer State" came from the large number of Tennesseans who volunteered for service in the War of 1812, particularly in the battle of New Orleans. In the Mexican War also, the number of Tennessee volunteers far exceeded the quota set for the state.

Tennessee was the last state to secede from the Union when the Civil War began and the first Confederate state to be readmitted after the war. During the conflict, more battles were fought in Tennessee than in any other state except Virginia. Tennessee has four national military parks: the sites of the battles of Chattanooga and Chickamauga, Fort Donelson, Shiloh, and Stone's River.

In the 1930s, Congress and President Franklin D. Roosevelt created the Tennessee Valley Authority (TVA), creating thousands of jobs as well as providing flood control and recreational areas through a series of dams on the Tennessee River. During World War II, Oak Ridge, Tennessee, was the secret site of the first plant for purifying uranium, the raw material of the first atomic bombs.

During the past half-century, the state has grown from an almost totally agrarian community to a balanced one of farming, business and industry. In 1960, for the first time, Tennessee had more urban than rural dwellers. Among its major "products" is country music, showcased in the world-famous Grand Old Opry in Nashville.

Tennessee has been well-represented on U.S. stamps.

The earlier statehood stamp, in 1946, pictured the state capitol and two major figures out of the state's early history, President Andrew Jackson and John Sevier, the first governor. Jackson wasn't born in Tennessee, but he made his home in the state, died and is buried there, and his residence, the Hermitage, has been pictured in two different stamp designs.

Two other U.S. presidents, although natives of North Carolina, achieved their political fame in their adopted Tennessee homes: James K. Polk and Andrew Johnson. Both men were governors of Tennessee, as was Sam Houston, who was born in Virginia, reared in Tennessee and later became president of the Republic of Texas. All three have been pictured on stamps. Native Tennesseeans who have been postally portrayed include Davy Crockett, Sequoyah, Sam Rayburn, Admiral David Farragut and Cordell Hull.

The Civil War battle of Shiloh has twice been commemorated on stamps. Mount Le Conte, in the Tennessee portion of the Great Smoky Mountains National Park, is shown on a stamp in the National Parks series. The Knoxville World's Fair of 1982 was marked with a se-tenant block of four. The Norris Dam, near Knoxville, has been pictured on two stamps; one honored Senator George Norris, for whom it was named, and the other marked the 50th anniversary of the Tennessee Valley Authority.

Two 50-stamp panes, the State Flags pane of 1976 and the State Birds and Flowers pane of 1982, each included a stamp honoring Tennessee.

The Design

The Postal Service's original plan for the Tennessee stamp was to follow normal procedure and commission a piece of original art. Phil Jordan, the stamp's art director, asked an illustrator in Memphis to work on the project.

After much consultation and many sketches, the artist produced a composite painting showing a steamboat, a country musician and a Tennessee volunteer in the Great Smoky Mountains, representing the three geographic divisions of the state from west to east. The musician's jacket was the orange color of the University of Tennessee. "I thought it looked real good," Jordan said, "and so did all the art directors."

But when Jordan and Elizabeth A. Altobell of the Postal Service, the stamp's project manager, took the artwork to Nashville to show it to the executive director of the Bicentennial Committee, she reacted negatively. "We came away thinking that we had better take another direction rather than continue this way and perhaps incur the displeasure of the committee and lose time in the process," Jordan recalled.

Back home, the art director cast about for another idea and remembered a calendar featuring photographs of Tennessee that a printer had

Art director Phil Jordan commissioned a Memphis illustrator to prepare this concept sketch that reflects the three major geographic divisions of Tennessee: a steamboat, for the Mississippi River basin in the west; a country musician (in an orange jacket, the color of the University of Tennessee), for the home of the Grand Old Opry in the central part of the state; and a volunteer in coonskin cap in the Great Smoky Mountains, for the east.

sent him and that he had kept on file because he found its images so appealing. The pictures were the work of a freelance commercial photographer from Franklin, Tennessee, with the evocative name of Robin Hood.

Hood was trained as a painter, and his photo work shows a painter's eye for the use of light in defining form, giving colors their identity and creating patterns. In 1977, as a member of the photo staff of *The Chattanooga News-Free Press*, Hood won the Pulitzer Prize for feature photography. From 1980 to 1984, he served as director of photography for the state of Tennessee. His photographs can be found in many magazines, books, art galleries and private collections.

In the past, photographs would not have been considered for stamp designs, but fine-screen offset printing and electronic prepress image refinement had improved to the point that the Postal Service had begun to experiment with photo-based designs. While in Nashville, Jordan had looked over the state capitol, but he didn't begin to see stamp-design possibilities until C. Douglas Lewis, vice chairman of CSAC and the curator of sculpture at the National Gallery of Art, told him that the building was highly regarded for its architecture and was considered William Strickland's finest work.

"We began to focus on the capitol," Jordan said. "I talked to Robin Hood on the telephone, and he sent some beautiful photographs that he had taken of it, and some of them were really unique. There was a photograph of it in the fog, and some really stunning photos of it in either the setting or the rising sun. They really did illustrate the jewel-like quality of the building."

Jordan mocked up some of the photographs as stamp designs. The one he liked best was a vertical arrangement of a 35-millimeter photo showing a night view of the east front. The cupola, topped by the red state flag, is bathed in light against a dark blue sky, and Clark Mills' equestrian statue of Andrew Jackson — a duplicate of one in Lafayette Park in Washington, D.C., near the White House — is silhouetted against the massive pillars of the front porch.

"Everybody said, 'Great,'" Jordan recalled. "The postmaster general recognized the photograph — he had a book of Robin Hood's photography — and he responded very well to it, and we figured at that point we were in. Evidently Governor Sundquist liked it, and from there it was an easy trip. I think it was the grace of God, if you will, that all of a sudden this photograph rose up to present itself."

The typography is dropped out of the dark background and is a light blue in color. The word "Tennessee" in Garamond Light capitals reads vertically along the left side. The single year date "1796," also vertical, is on the right side, and "USA 32" in two horizontal lines is in the upper right.

First-Day Facts

The May 31 stamp dedication odyssey began at 7:15 a.m. (EDT) in

These are unused alternative design treatments using two additional photographs of the Tennessee capitol made by Robin Hood. One shows a closeup of the statue of Andrew Jackson outside the east front, with the building's cupola looming in the background. Officials decided this picture didn't "read" as the capitol building clearly enough. The other is a view of the building with exaggerated perspective.

Knoxville, in a ceremony outside the Blount Mansion Interpretive Center. Honored guests included U.S. Representatives John J. "Jimmy" Duncan Jr., James H. Quillen, Van Hilleary and Zach Wamp; Knoxville Mayor Victor Ashe; and Tommy Schumpert, Knox County executive.

At Memphis, at the other end of the state and in another time zone, the dedication took place at 11:45 a.m. (CDT) at the Brooks Museum of Art. Here the honored guests included U.S. Representatives Harold E. Ford, Ed Bryant and John Tanner; W.W. Herenton, mayor of Memphis; and Jim Rout, mayor of Shelby County.

The final ceremony was held at 5 p.m. (CDT) in the amphitheater of Nashville's Bicentennial Capitol Mall, just north of the capitol, which would stage its grand-opening ceremony the following day. Here the honored guests were John S. Wilder, lieutenant governor of Tennessee; Ned R. McWherter of the USPS Board of Governors; Jimmy Naifeh, speaker of the House in the Tennessee Legislature; and Nashville Mayor Phil Bredesen.

Among those present at each of the three ceremonies were Martha Ingram, chairman of "Tennessee 200," and Martha Sundquist, honorary chairman.

Separate first-day ceremony programs were prepared by USPS for each of the three ceremonies.

32¢ TENNESSEE STATEHOOD BICENTENNIAL (SELF-ADHESIVE)

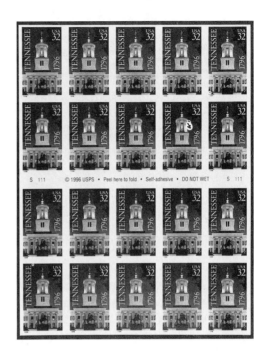

Date of Issue: May 31, 1996

Catalog Numbers: Scott 3071, single stamp; 3071a, pane of 20

Colors: light blue (PMS 291), yellow, magenta, cyan, black (stamp); blue (back)

First-Day Cancel: Nashville, Tennessee. First-day ceremonies also held in Memphis and Knoxville, Tennessee.

First-Day Cancellations: 217,281 (includes water-activated version)

Format: Panes of 20, vertical, 5 across, 4 down, with horizontal peel-off strip between second and third horizontal row. Gravure printing cylinders of 160 (8 across, 20 around) manufactured by Armotek Industries, Palmyra, New Jersey.

Overall Stamp Size: .99 by 1.56 inches; 25.146mm by 39.624mm

Perforations: die-cut simulated perforations

Selvage Markings: on peel-off strip: "© 1996 USPS • Peel here to fold • Self-adhesive • DO NOT WET"

Liner Markings: none

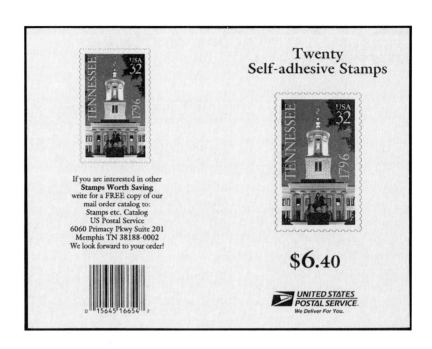

Back Markings: "Twenty/Self-adhesive Stamps/$6.40/UNITED STATES/POSTAL SERVICE./We Deliver For You." USPS logo. Universal Product Code (UPC), promotion for *Stamps etc.* catalog, all on backing paper.

Designer, Art Director and Typographer: Phil Jordan of Falls Church, Virginia

Photographer: Robin Hood of Franklin, Tennessee

Project Manager: Elizabeth A. Altobell, USPS

Stamp Manufacturing: Stamps printed for Stamp Venturers by J.W. Fergusson and Sons, Richmond, Virginia, on Champlain gravure press 1. Stamps processed by Stamp Venturers, Fredericksburg, Virginia.

Quantity Ordered and Distributed: 60,120,000

Cylinder Number Detail: 1 set of 5 gravure cylinder numbers preceded by the letter S at each end of peel-off strip

Cylinder Number Combination Reported: S11111

Paper Supplier: Nichimen/Kanzaki

Tagging: One large tagging block over each block of 10 stamps. Tagging does not extend to peel-off strip. Bottom perforations on stamps from second row and top perforations on stamps from third row have untagged tips.

The Stamp

The self-adhesive version of the Tennessee Statehood stamp was the first U.S. commemorative stamp to be issued in the popular peel-and-stick format. A total of 60,120,000 of these stamps were printed. They

Postal officials originally considered issuing the Tennessee self-adhesive stamp in the smaller size used for previous peel-and-sticks. This is how the stamp would have looked if that plan had been followed. In the end, however, the self-adhesive was issued in commemorative size, the same as the water-activated version.

Like the conventional version of the stamp, the self-adhesive was printed by Stamp Venturers by the gravure process. It was issued in panes of 20, with a narrow selvage strip across the center. After peeling off the selvage strip, a buyer could fold the pane into a kind of booklet, with the back of the stamps' backing paper serving as the cover.

The panes are die-cut with the now-familiar simulated perforations separating the stamps from each other and from the peel-off strip. The six interior stamps on a pane are "perforated" on all four sides, while each of the remaining stamps has at least one straight edge; the four corner stamps have two straight edges.

The Design

Phil Jordan's design, based on Robin Hood's nighttime photograph of the east front of the Tennessee Capitol in Nashville, was used on the self-adhesive version as well as the water-activated version of the stamp. Except for the die-cut "perforations" and straight edges on the self-adhesives, the faces of the two varieties are the same.

Officials at first considered producing the self-adhesive version in the special-stamp dimensions used for recent Christmas and Love stamps, instead of the commemorative size used for the conventional version, and Jordan mocked up Hood's photograph to fit those specifications. Later, they decided to make the self-stick stamp the same size as the conventional stamp. The only previous U.S. self-adhesive to be issued in commemorative size was the first one — the experimental Dove Weathervane Christmas stamp of 1974 (Scott 1552).

First-Day Facts

The conventional and self-adhesive versions of the Tennessee Statehood stamp were dedicated at three first-day ceremonies held in sequence in Knoxville, Memphis and Nashville. For information on the ceremonies, see the preceding chapter.

Date of Issue: June 7, 1996

Catalog Number: Scott 3072-3076, single stamps; 3076a, strip of 5

Colors: black, cyan, magenta, yellow

First-Day Cancel: Oklahoma City, Oklahoma

First-Day Cancellations: 653,057

Format: Panes of 20, vertical, 5 across, 4 down. Offset printing plates of 120 subjects (8 across, 15 around).

Overall Stamp Size: 0.99 by 1.56 inches; 25.146mm by 39.624mm

Perforations: 11.1 (Wista stroke perforator)

Selvage Inscription: "American Indian dancers perform to assure/the continuation of ancient life ways, to honor/deities and each other, and to affirm their/Indian identities." "American Indian Dances."

Selvage Markings: "United States Postal Service/© 1995." ".32 x 20 = $6.40." "PLATE/POSITION" and diagram.

Designer: Keith Birdsong of Muskogee, Oklahoma

Typographer: John Boyd, Anagraphics Inc., New York, New York

Modeler: Joseph Sheeran, Ashton-Potter (USA) Ltd.

Art Director: Carl Herrman

Project Manager: Terrence McCaffrey, USPS

Stamp Manufacturing: Stamps printed by Ashton-Potter (USA) Ltd., Williamsville, New York, on offset portion of a Stevens Varisize Security Documents webfed 6-color offset, 3-color intaglio press. Stamps perforated, processed and shipped by Ashton-Potter (USA).

Quantity Ordered and Distributed: 139,250,000

Plate Number Detail: 1 set of 4 offset plate numbers preceded by the letter P in selvage next to each corner stamp

Plate Number Combinations Reported: P1111, P2222, P3333

Paper Supplier: Westvaco/Ivex

Tagging: block tagging

The Stamps

Over the past several years, the Postal Service has periodically issued se-tenant sets of four or five stamps each, featuring a wide range of subjects popular with topical collectors, from locomotives to lighthouses, from cats to carousel animals. Most of the earlier sets were in the booklet format, but as conventional booklets have gone out of style the more recent topicals have been issued in panes.

On June 7, the Postal Service issued five such stamps featuring American Indian dances: Fancy, Butterfly, Traditional, Raven and Hoop. The five dances are contemporary interpretations of traditional tribal or regional dances and were selected by USPS to represent different regions of the United States.

Ashton-Potter (USA) Ltd. printed the stamps by the offset process and distributed them in panes of 20. Each vertical strip of stamps on the pane comprises four specimens of a single design, and each horizontal strip consists of five

different designs.

There is a wide decorative selvage, or header, at the top. The green of the grass in the header picture is carried down the sides of the pane and across the bottom, bleeding off the three edges; a narrow vertical strip of white frames the block of 20 stamps on the left and right. Four sets of plate numbers appear in this white strip, one beside each of the four corner stamps. A plate block, as defined by the Scott catalog, consists of 10 stamps, constituting either the top or bottom half of the pane.

The Postal Service offered for sale several related products: a poster bearing enlarged reproductions of the dancers on the stamps, for $12.95; a first-day souvenir, with a pane of stamps affixed ($14.95); a StampFolio that included a compact disk of Native American music by the Cedar Tree Singers and Smithsonian Folkways ($9.95); and a commemorative panel ($7.95). In addition, panes of stamps signed by the designer, Keith Birdsong, were available for $29.95.

For advice on the designs and other matters related to the stamps and to ensure accuracy, PhotoAssist, the Postal Service's research firm, enlisted the services of a large number of experts on American Indian culture. One of the first questions they addressed was how to title the stamps and pane: "American Indian Dances" or "Native American Dances"? The consensus was that it should be the former.

"American Indian Dance(s) is more appropriate," the chief consultant, Dr. William C. Sturtevant, curator at the Smithsonian Institution's Museum of Natural History, Division of Anthropology and North American Ethnology, told the Postal Service. "... Native American Dance(s) would do, but most of those sensitive to political correctness are increasingly aware that most Indians prefer 'Indians' in most contexts."

Della Warrior, a professor at the Institute of American Indian Art, agreed. In the 1970s through the 1980s "Native American" was in vogue, she explained, but today "American Indian" is used.

For centuries, dance has been part of the Indian culture. Indian dances tell stories — of battles and the hunt, of the spirit world and the kinship of humans to all living things.

The Traditional, Fancy and Hoop dances are considered pan-Indian and are performed regularly at competitions known as powwows, held every weekend throughout North America. They arise from the dances of the Plains and Pueblo Indians. The Raven Dance is performed by fish-

100

ermen of the Pacific Northwest to ensure a productive catch. It is done by two dancers representing ravens, who mock the fishing ability of a third dancer, representing a grizzly bear.

The Butterfly Dance is performed in Southwest Pueblo Indian villages and recognizes the Zuni tribe's most honored insect, one with special meaning for children, who learn industry from its work in pollinating flowers and an appreciation of the natural world from its beauty.

Many U.S. stamps have depicted American Indians and their culture since the Columbian Exposition commemorative set of 1893, which pictured Indians on four of its values. An Indian dance, described as the Dog Dance, was shown on one of the 20 Legends of the West stamps in 1994.

The Designs

The stamps are commemorative-size, vertically arranged. Each contains the image of a Native American in appropriate costume performing one of the dances, against a plain background of a brownish-yellow color. Across the bottom of each design is a band containing a colorful pattern representative of Indian art.

The dancers' images were painted by Keith Birdsong, an illustrator from Muskogee, Oklahoma, using airbrush with acrylic and colored pencil for the details. Although he is, appropriately, of Cherokee and Creek descent, postal officials were surprised to learn that the name Birdsong isn't an Indian name but is an Anglicization of the German name Vogelsang.

Birdsong's specialty is book covers — he has done hundreds of them, including the Star Trek series — and commemorative plates. He once designed a set of World Cup Soccer stamps for The Gambia, but the Indian Dances issue was his first U.S. stamp assignment. He had worked for

USPS before, however, having designed souvenir envelopes for the 1992 Olympic Games, of which the Postal Service was a sponsor, and the 1994 25th anniversary of the first manned moon landing.

Birdsong based each of his illustrations on a color photograph of an actual dancer, revising the facial features and some of the details of makeup and costume to conform to U.S. law against picturing a living person on a postage stamp. Two of these photos, for the Fancy Dance and Traditional Dance stamps, were made at a powwow by Roy Campbell, a Muskogee photographer. Two others, showing members of the

American Indian Dance Theatre performing the Hoop Dance and Butterfly Dance, were taken by Theo Westenberger and published in the February 1993 issue of *Smithsonian* magazine.

Each of the artist's paintings was reviewed at the sketch and finished stages by three experts on that particular tribe or tribal group, after which the artist made revisions based on their recommendations.

In spite of the best efforts of the Postal Service to avoid problems with the designs, the design of the Traditional Dance stamp generated not only controversy but a threatened lawsuit against USPS. It happened because of a mistake by a local expert on whom Birdsong relied to identify the individual in the source photograph. The expert identified the dancer as his son — a performer who wears a costume similar to that of the man in the photograph — and the Postal Service proceeded to obtain written authorization from the son to base the stamp design on his photo.

Only after the stamps were well into the production process did USPS learn that the man in the photo actually was Pat Moore of Pawnee, Oklahoma, a Pawnee Indian dancer who performs at powwows around the country and who danced at the Olympic Games in Atlanta. Roy Campbell's photograph shows Moore in a costume of his own design, holding in one hand a club with a simulated bald eagle's head and talons and an eagle wing in the other. Birdsong changed the dancer's face, giving it red and blue makeup, but followed the photograph fairly closely in reproducing the costume and accessories.

After Moore saw the design, he telephoned postal officials and Birdsong himself, demanding to be compensated. He was dissatisfied with what he was offered, and

This photo of Pat Moore, a Pawnee Indian from Oklahoma, in full regalia and brandishing an eagle club in his right hand, was used by Keith Birdsong as the model for the Traditional Dance stamp design. Unfortunately, the local expert on whom Birdsong relied to identify the subject of the photo made an error, leading USPS to obtain the release to use the picture from the wrong person. Birdsong's painting is different in some respects from the photograph: His dancer has red and blue facial paint, and he modified a few of the costume details. (Photo by Roy Campbell)

This photograph of an Oklahoma dancer, whom the Yearbook *was unable to identify, served as Keith Birdsong's model for the Fancy Dance stamp design. In his painting, Birdsong altered the colors of the subject's facial paint, feathers and headgear.*

commenced action through his attorney, Valerie Corzine of Oklahoma City, under the federal Tort Claims Act. This act would give Moore the right to sue the Postal Service if he was unable to reach a satisfactory settlement with the agency in a reasonable period of time.

Asked what an appropriate settlement would be, Corzine told the *Yearbook* her client was claiming "all the profits resulting from the use of his image, which we estimate is in excess of $10 million." As of this writing, no resolution had been reached.

The name of the model in the Fancy Dance source photograph wasn't available to the *Yearbook*. The Hoop Dance stamp design was based on a photograph of Eddie Swimmer, a North Carolina Cherokee, published in *Smithsonian* magazine. In both cases, Birdsong changed the color of the leg wraps, but later restored them to their original white after the consultants pointed out that they are made of angora goatskin with the hair on and are left in their natural color.

Swimmer, the hoop dancer, "is truly a lightning contortionist, manipulating up to 36 hoops into natural forms: snakes, butterflies, flowers," the *Smithsonian* caption said. "This (the routine shown on the stamp) will be an eagle. Dancing staccato, using every muscle in his body to wriggle in, out, of hoops, he will create a globe representing the Earth."

Birdsong based his Butterfly Dance illustration on a *Smithsonian* photograph of Cassie Soldierwolf of the American Indian Dance Theatre, an Arapaho. The artist changed the belt and sash, known as the "maiden shawl," from white to green and the necklace from turquoise to green, but once again restored the original colors on the advice of the consultants.

For the Raven Dance stamp, Birdsong based his first illustration on a photograph that Carl Herrman, the stamps' art director, found in a magazine advertisement produced by the Alaska Department of Tourism. The dancer shown in the photo was a member of the Nwa Kahidi Theater of the Sealaska Foundation, a Native American corporation.

But Rosita Worl, anthropologist at the University of Alaska, correctly deduced that the mask and regalia in the photo — and in Birdsong's illustration — were a theatrical costume. These items were "all wrong," she told the Postal Service. Specifically, she said, the beak was too long, the regalia patterns weren't identifiable, and there were no ears on the mask and too much fluffy material at the top.

Steve Henrikson, collections manager at the Alaska State Museum in Juneau, agreed with Worl that the stamp should depict an authentic costume. On Henrikson's recommendation, the Postal Service contacted Nathan Jackson, a Tlingit Indian master carver and performer. Jackson supplied photographs of himself in costume, as well as a watercolor card painted by a local artist, and Birdsong used these in creating the final version of the Raven Dance design.

"I liked the first raven better," said Herrman, "but we were delighted that it ended up an accurate portrayal."

For the pane header, Herrman wanted to show a historical dance that would complement the dances shown on the stamps as they are performed today. To accomplish this, Birdsong turned to an 1847 painting by the American artist George Catlin, who spent eight years in the West creating a pictorial record of Indian life. The painting depicted a group of Plains Indians performing the Bear Dance, with tepees in the background.

Birdsong followed Catlin's artwork closely in painting the header illustration, but made several modifications on the advice of the Smithsonian's Dr. Sturtevant. Most of these related to the num-

Keith Birdsong's illustration for the Hoop Dance stamp was based on this photograph of Eddie Swimmer of the American Indian DanceTheatre, who is using his hoops to simulate an eagle. For the stamp, Birdson gave the dancer red and black facial paint and made alterations in the designs of the vest, apron, belt and mocassins. To make the image fit into the vertical stamp format, the artist omitted the two extended hoops in each of the dancer's hands. (Photo by Theo Westenberger, published in Smithsonian *magazine.)*

Cassie Soldierwolf of the American Indian Dance Theatre, an Arapaho, holds a bouquet of flowers in each hand as she portrays the Zuni tribe's most honored insect in the Butterfly Dance. This photograph served as the model for Keith Birdsong's stamp painting. Birdsong changed several of the colors in Soldierwolf's costume in his painting, but on the advice of the Postal Service's expert consultants he restored the original white color of the belt and sash, known as the "maiden shawl," and the turquoise color of the necklace. (Photo by Theo Westenberger, in Smithsonian *magazine)*

ber and location of the flaps and poles at the tops of the tepees. To help him get the details right, Carl Herrman visited the Smithsonian's Museum of Natural History, sketched the tepees on display there and sent the sketches to the artist. USPS originally had planned to give Catlin a credit line on the header, but decided against it because of the revisions that had been required.

The multicolored band across the bottom of each design came from digital clip art; it was the first time such art had been used on a U.S. stamp. Herrman found the bands in the Santa Fe Collection and Plains Collection of RT Computer Graphics, a Rio Rancho, New Mexico, software company. He confirmed through the Smithsonian's Dr. Sturtevant that each of the bands he wanted to use would be appropriate for the region represented by the accompanying dancer.

Using his computer and Adobe Illustrator software, Herrman created slight variations in each of the repeated motifs, such as they would display if they had been hand-painted or woven by Indian craftsmen. Because the clip art was in black and white, Herrman had to select the colors

Birdsong's original painting for the Raven Dance was scrapped after the Postal Service's experts determined that the dancer in the source photograph, found in an Alaska Department of Tourism advertisement, was wearing a theatrical costume rather than an authentic one. The lettering and numerals shown here are in a typeface called Caricature. It later was changed, as was the decorative band at the bottom of the design.

This is Keith Birdsong's original illustration for the header of the pane, adapted from George Catlin's 1847 painting of Plains Indians performing the Bear Dance. On the advice of an expert consulted by the Postal Service, Birdsong later revised several of the tepees, adding flaps and subtracting a number of tent poles.

arbitrarily. "There are almost no rules," he said. "Today's Indians choose more or less on the basis of what looks good, and they use a lot of primary colors, so I just took my best shot at it. Again, we ran it by the experts, and they approved the coloring."

As printed, the background color on the stamps turned out more yellow than Herrman had intended. "We had wanted a light buckskin color with almost no yellow at all," he said.

The typography, chosen by John Boyd of Anagraphics Inc., was a traditional font called Tiepolo.

First-Day Facts

Bert H. Mackie, a USPS governor from Enid, Oklahoma, dedicated the stamps in the June 7 ceremony that kicked off the three-day Red Earth Native American Cultural Festival at the Myriad Convention Center and Plaza in Oklahoma City.

The festival, in its 10th year, is the largest of its kind in the world. It annually draws more than 125,000 spectators to the festivities that include juried art and dance competitions. The 1996 event was attended by more than 1,500 Native American dancers and artists representing tribes from across North America.

Speakers at the first-day ceremony were Mary Fallin, lieutenant governor of Oklahoma; Ann Simank, vice mayor of Oklahoma City; and Don Moses, USPS district manager. Virginia Noelke, CSAC chairperson, presided, and Senator Enoch Kelly Haney of the Red Earth board of directors gave the welcome. Honored guests were Phil Lujan, president of the Red Earth board of directors; Clarence Hopkins, Oklahoma City postmaster; Keith Birdsong, the stamps' designer; and Irma Zandl of CSAC.

The Indian Dances stamps were sold two days early in Middletown, New York. Seven covers are known with a June 5 postmark.

32¢ PREHISTORIC ANIMALS (4 DESIGNS)

Date of Issue: June 8, 1996

Catalog Number: Scott 3077-3080, single stamps; 3080a, block or strip of 4

Colors: black, cyan, magenta, yellow

First-Day Cancel: Toronto, Ontario, Canada

First-Day Cancellations: 485,929

Format: Panes of 20, horizontal, 4 across, 5 down. Offset printing plates of 120 subjects (8 across, 15 around).

Overall Stamp Size: 1.56 by 1.225 inches; 39.624mm by 31.115mm

Perforations: 11.1 by 10.9 (Wista stroke perforator)

Selvage Markings: "© USPS/1994." ".32/x20/$6.40." "PLATE POSITION" and diagram.

Designer: Davis Meltzer of Huntingdon Valley, Pennsylvania

Typographer: Tom Mann, Mann and Mann Graphics, Warrenton, Virginia

Modeler: Joseph Sheeran, Ashton-Potter (USA) Ltd.

Art Director: Howard Paine

Project Manager: Terrence McCaffrey, USPS

Stamp Manufacturing: Stamps printed by Ashton-Potter (USA) Ltd., Williamsville, New York, on offset portion of a Stevens Varisize Security Documents webfed 6-color offset, 3-color intaglio press. Stamps perforated, processed and shipped by Ashton-Potter.

Quantity Ordered: 150,000,000

Quantity Distributed: 111,090,000

Plate Number Detail: 1 set of 4 offset plate numbers preceded by the letter P in selvage above or below each corner stamp

Plate Number Combinations Reported: P1111, P2222, P3333

Paper Supplier: Westvaco/Ivex

Tagging: phosphored paper

The Stamps

On June 8, at the CAPEX 96 World Philatelic Exhibition in Toronto, Ontario, Canada, USPS issued a se-tenant block of four semijumbo stamps depicting prehistoric animals: eohippus, woolly mammoth, mastodon and saber-tooth cat.

The idea for such a block had been in the minds of postal officials for at least 15 years. In 1981 Howard Paine, then a newly appointed art director at USPS, was discussing the possibility of a block of Indian arrowhead stamps with Dr. Dennis Stanford, a paleontologist at the Smithsonian Institution, and Stanford suggested four stamps depicting a mastodon, woolly mammoth, saber-tooth tiger and prehistoric camel. Paine didn't pursue Stanford's proposal then, but six years later, coming across a newspaper advertisement with a painting by artist John Dawson, he cut it out and sent it to the late Jack Williams of the Stamps Division. In an accompanying letter, Paine recalled Stanford's idea for the four prehistoric animals stamps ("a fearsome foursome indeed," in Paine's words) and added that Dawson would be a good choice to design them. Dawson, working with Paine, subsequently designed the four Domestic Cats stamps of 1988.

More time went by. In 1989 the Postal Service sought to appeal to young collectors and potential collectors by issuing a block of four stamps depicting dinosaurs. A few years later, the Citizens' Stamp Advisory Committee, at the urging of USPS marketing officials, approved another block of stamps featuring prehistoric creatures, but mammals this time rather than reptiles.

The four beasts chosen for the stamps were the same ones that Dennis Stanford had listed for Howard Paine back in 1981, with one exception: the eohippus (dawn horse) replaced the primitive camel. Eohippus was, in a sense, a leftover from still another previous set. CSAC's subject subcommittee had suggested that eohippus be shown on one of four topical stamps depicting horses to be issued in 1993, but the committee decided that to juxtapose three present-day breeds of horse with their ancient ancestor would make no sense, and the block as issued showed four modern sports horses.

The 1996 Prehistoric Animals stamps originally were scheduled to make their debut in 1995, at the American Philatelic Society's annual convention and Stampshow in St. Louis, Missouri. However, on August 1, 1995, 23 days before the planned day of issue, the Postal Service announced that the issuance had been "deferred to a future date due to technical problems in the printing process."

"The Prehistoric Animals stamps were put on hold," the USPS news release said, "when the contract printer, Ashton-Potter (USA), encountered technical difficulties in the offset-intaglio production of the stamps and could not provide the Postal Service with sufficient quantities of product to meet its quality standards by the scheduled release date."

Terrence McCaffrey, head of stamp design for USPS, provided further details for the *Yearbook*. Ashton-Potter had made preparations to print the stamps by a combination of offset and intaglio on its new Stevens Varisize Security Documents press. The company had booked the same press and the same combination process to print the 32¢ stamp commemorating the 75th anniversary of Woman Suffrage, which also was scheduled for an August 1995 release.

But in breaking in its new press, Ashton-Potter encountered problems, particularly in ensuring proper registration between the offset and intaglio portions of the stamps (see illustration). Production schedules were thrown off, and sufficient quantities of the two issues couldn't be ensured in time for the first-day ceremonies. Ultimately, USPS had to decide to sacrifice one of the issues.

Because the Woman Suffrage stamp was linked to an anniversary that fell in 1995 — and also because it had strong political support in Congress — the choice was an easy one. (As it turned out, registration problems plagued the Woman Suffrage stamp as well, and numerous poorly registered specimens reached the public.)

The 11th-hour cancellation of the Prehistoric Animals had widespread ramifications. Many plans were thrown into disarray, particularly those of dealers specializing in first-day covers.

For example, eight days before the Postal Service announcement, Unicover Corporation, which creates the Fleetwood first-day-cover line, mailed 100,000 special full-color promotional flyers related to the Prehistoric Animals stamps. The company had the production of cacheted envelopes under way, with artwork complete and ready for the press. Now it faced the prospect of receiving many orders for covers, collectors' albums and specially designed private-issue souvenir pages that it would be unable to fill.

Yale University's Peabody Museum of Natural History had promoted plans for a second-day cancellation and reception, including a specially designed limited-edition cachet and a postcard depicting prehistoric animals. A Yale University pictorial postmark was designed and prepared for the scheduled August 25, 1995, reception. Flyer notices were sent to 1,100 museum members, and a second mailing was necessary to tell members the plans had been changed.

USPS gave the American Philatelic Society an alternative first-day item, the 50¢ Soaring Eagle postal card, to replace the Prehistoric Animals at its Stampshow. Nevertheless, APS had distributed a large amount of advance information based on the original plan, and it was too late to correct it. In addition, show organizers had arranged to obtain a 38-foot dinosaur exhibit from the St. Louis Science Center and had invited the president of the center and representatives of the Mastodon State Park Friends Group to the first-day ceremony.

"These groups represent only a minute percentage of the shows, local festivals, museums and parks planning activities around the release of the Prehistoric Animals stamps," wrote Michael Baadke in *Linn's Stamp News.* "If the announcement of the delay had come a lot earlier, a great deal of wasted time, wasted money and headaches nationwide could have been avoided."

USPS faced problems of its own as a result of the change of plans. Terrence McCaffrey, who also oversees the illustrated books that accompany the Postal Service's annual commemorative mint sets, was forced to "pull out the middle spread" of the 1995 book, he said, "redo all the pages, redo the table of contents, redo the cover page, redo the cover. We had commemorative stamp panels for the Prehistoric Animals, we had all this promotional stuff, we had T-shirts that were going to be handed out to kids at the Stampshow ... It was a domino effect."

But to McCaffrey and others involved in designing the stamp, there also was a positive side to the delay. When Ashton-Potter finally printed the stamps, it printed them entirely by offset, with no intaglio. That was the method the Postal Service's design section had wanted all along.

There are three ways to combine offset and intaglio in printing stamps. One is to use offset for the image and intaglio for the typography. Another is to print the image in intaglio and use offset colors for tinting, which is how most of the Christmas Madonna and Child stamps of recent years have been produced. Both these methods are favored by the Postal Service's stamp design section.

The third method, which the design experts deplore, is to print the image by offset and add intaglio to it in spots, on a more or less random basis. "If you just go in there and put hairs or wrinkles here and there by intaglio, it looks like hell," is how one veteran stamp designer put it. "It looks as if a truck had driven over the stamp."

Officials of the stamp design section hadn't known in 1995 that their associates in the stamp acquisition section had authorized Ashton-Potter to print the Prehistoric Animals stamps by the spot-intaglio method. When the team responsible for the stamps' designs first saw the proofs, they were startled to discover that the animals' fur and the foliage or rocks around them had been "enhanced" with patches of engraved lines.

"It was killing the illustrations. It was heavying it up too much," recalled McCaffrey. "We thought the illustrations stood on their own, without the intaglio...

"So, when they went back to press this year, we (in the design section) said we didn't want the intaglio because it didn't enhance the design at all, and it was dropped."

When the set first was planned, USPS contemplated issuing it in the form of a booklet containing five panes, each of which would consist of

This enlargement of a section of a plate proof of the original 1995 inta-glio-offset version of the Prehistoric Animals stamps shows how the printer applied patches of engraved lines on a spot basis to the offset-printed illustrations, and how badly out of register they were. The intaglio plate in this example is registered downward, so that bits of the intaglio printing extend below the bottom of the designs. On the saber-tooth cat stamp, the engraved lines that were meant to be printed on one of the mountain peaks are printed over the cat's hind foot instead. On the woolly mammoth stamp, engraved lines that are supposed to represent hairs on the animal's coat are superimposed on its tusk. On the eohippus stamp, the engraved lines that were meant to reinforce the shadow of the foliage on the creature's back are similarly displaced. Later, the Postal Service instructed the printer to abandon the intaglio, and when the stamps fi-nally were printed in 1996, the job was done by offset only.

111

four of the semijumbo stamps stacked vertically. But the decision later was made to issue the stamps in a pane of 20. The pane is so arranged that all four varieties can be obtained in either a block or a horizontal strip of four.

Eohippus lived in the early Cenozoic era (the age of mammals), about 55 million years ago, in what is now North America and Europe. Standing only 10 to 20 inches high, it had an arched back and a snoutlike nose and looked more like a racing dog, such as a greyhound or whippet, than like the straight-backed, long-faced modern horse. It had four toes on its front feet and three toes on its hind feet. Each toe ended in a separate small hoof. Eohippus' scientific name — which some authorities thought should have been used on the stamp — is Hyracotherium.

In the middle of the Cenozoic era, about 40 million years ago, carnivores began to develop into doglike and catlike animals. Some catlike animals were called saber-tooth cats or saber-tooth tigers because they had a pair of upper canine teeth, up to eight inches long, that were shaped like sabers. They became extinct about 12,000 years ago. Their fossils have been found in Africa, Europe and North and South America. The cats probably were as heavy as today's tigers and preyed on thick-skinned animals, including elephants, mastodons and ground sloths.

Later in the Cenozoic era, the climate became drier and colder. Mammoths — huge, lumbering beasts closely related to present-day elephants — roamed the plains of North America, Europe and Siberia, and were hunted for food by prehistoric people. Perfectly preserved mammoth bodies have been found in the Siberian ice by modern-day explorers. Some mammoths measured more than 14 feet high at the shoulders and had curving tusks 15 feet long. The woolly mammoth, one of two varieties that lived in what is now the U.S. Midwest, had long hair on its body, which helped protect it from the severe cold of the Ice Age. Mammoths died out about 10,000 years ago.

Another elephant-like beast was the mastodon. Mastodons first lived in North Africa about 40 million years ago. They spread to Asia, Europe and the rest of Africa. They reached America about 15 million years ago and lived there until at least 8,000 years ago. They were stockier than elephants and not as tall. Early mastodons had tusks in both jaws; some of the later species lost the lower tusks.

A portion of a mastodon previously had been depicted on the 3¢ Pennsylvania Academy of the Fine Arts commemorative stamp of 1955 (Scott 1064). That stamp reproduced an 1822 self-portrait of artist Charles Willson Peale in his own Peale's Museum in Philadelphia. Peale is holding up a curtain to reveal the museum's Long Room and a portion of its most celebrated exhibit, a reconstructed mastodon skeleton.

The Designs

Perhaps the leading artist in the field of prehistoric animals and prehistoric man was the late Charles R. Knight, who wrote and illustrated books

These early versions of Davis Meltzer's designs were laid out as a booklet pane at a time when officials were considering issuing the Prehistoric Animals stamps as a booklet. Changes later were made in two of the designs. The mastodon, as shown here, failed to fill the stamp frame adequately, so the artist depicted the animal from a different angle. The eohippus design was revised to remove some of the heavy foliage and lower the bottom frameline. The Postal Service's researchers determined that the mammoth in Meltzer's painting was a woolly mammoth and not the imperial mammoth named in the inscription, and the wording was changed.

on the subject and also created many of the paintings at the Museum of Natural History in New York. One expert whom the Postal Service consulted for the Prehistoric Animals stamps, Dr. John J. Flynn of the Field Museum in Chicago, asked why USPS didn't use Knight's existing artwork for the stamps rather than commissioning new paintings.

The answer, art director Howard Paine said, was that it would have been difficult if not impossible to find Knight paintings of the four specified animals that would have been colorful and would have fit neatly onto individual stamps that in turn would fit together in a coherent block of four. However, artist Davis Meltzer, in creating his four acrylic paintings for the stamps, did refer to Knight's work, along with other visual reference materials.

The Postal Service's efforts to ensure accuracy were extensive. For example, the questionnaire accompanying Meltzer's eohippus painting that was sent to Dr. Flynn read as follows: "Is the name correct? If not, exactly what name would be correct? We believe this mammal is representative of the Eocene period. If not, what period does it represent? ... Are the following physical traits depicted accurately: shape of the head, the tail, the length of the tuft at the end of it, the shape of the feet, toes, location and shape of the ears, overall coloring and markings? Are the flora and background appropriate to the period?"

Dr. Flynn's response read, in part: "Shape of the head: reasonable. Tail length and tuft at end: Length seems reasonable, impossible to know the size, shape or occurrence of tuft based on available evidence. Shape of the feet and toes: Hind feet OK, front feet need modification, see attached drawing of toes from McFadden book, has toe numbers correct but shape should be asymmetrical, more toes on the outside of the foot and main weight-bearing toe second from inside should be the biggest.

"Location and shape of the ears: Probably reasonable, ears may have been slightly lower on head, shape impossible to know from fossil material but seems reasonable to scale them down in size from comparison to modern horses. Overall coloring: Impossible to know. Flora and background forestation: Appropriate; plant types seem fine."

Similar queries were made and replies received for the other animals, and Meltzer revised his artwork in accordance with this information.

The artist's original painting of a mastodon showed a side view of an animal on the run, but the resulting figure was too long and low to adequately fill the semijumbo stamp dimensions, so Meltzer repainted the creature in more of a head-on view and added a baby mastodon to the composition.

Because the eohippus was a much smaller animal than the other three, and couldn't be shown on the same scale as the others, officials asked Meltzer to surround it with foliage to put its size in the proper perspective. "Then we found the leaves were overpowering everything, so we had him take out some of them so the picture would 'read' better," said Terrence McCaffrey. "We think it now 'reads' as a small horse — but I'm sure that someone just glancing at the stamp might not make that connection."

Meltzer rounded the two bottom corners of each painting. The corners and edges didn't come out uniformly on the four pieces, however, so Paine told him to paint each one out to the full corners and let the curves be provided when the art was made ready for the press. The two upper corners were defined by typography: "32 USA" at the right and the name of the animal at the left. The typeface chosen by typographer Tom Mann for the animals' names and the "USA" was Caligraphic 429BT, a computer font made by Bitstream. The "32" was Adobe Garamond.

First-Day Facts

Capex 96, where the stamps were dedicated on the show's first day, was held at the Metro Toronto Convention Center, near downtown Toronto's famous CN Tower. The ceremony was held in the convention center's Bassett Theater.

Azeezaly S. Jaffer, manager of stamp services for USPS, did the dedication honors. Virginia Noelke, chair of CSAC, presided, and Kenneth Rowe, chair of Capex 96, welcomed the audience. Speakers were E.A. Scott, marketing manager of Canada Post Corporation, and Kevin Seymour, assistant curator of the Royal Ontario Museum.

The Buffalo, New York, post office handled sales of the new stamps and cancellations at Capex 96, and also processed all mail orders for first-day covers. However, the cancellations bore a Toronto postmark.

On June 9, the Peabody Museum at Yale belatedly made good on its plan to celebrate the issuance of the stamps with a second-day-of-issue reception, complete with pictorial cancel. The event originally had been scheduled for August 25, 1995.

32¢ BREAST CANCER AWARENESS

Date of Issue: June 15, 1996

Catalog Number: Scott 3081

Colors: black, cyan, magenta, yellow, rust (PMS 491c)

First-Day Cancel: Washington, D.C. (Stamp was placed on sale nationwide.)

First-Day Cancellations: 183,896

Format: Panes of 20, vertical, 5 across, 4 down. Offset printing plates of 120 subjects (8 across, 15 down).

Overall Stamp Size: .99 by 1.56 inches; 25.146mm by 39.624mm

Perforations: 11.1 (Wista and Gammeler stroke perforator)

Selvage Inscription: "HELP/CONQUER/BREAST/CANCER." "To learn more, call/The Cancer Infor-/mation Service:/1-800-4-CANCER." "CIS — the public's/link to information/from the National/Cancer Institute." "Hearing im-paired/callers with TTY/TDD/equipment, dial/1-800-332-8615." "With this stamp/USPS continues a/long tradition of/public service."

Selvage Markings: "© USPS/1995." ".32/X 20/$6.40." "PLATE/POSITION" and diagram.

Designer and Typographer: Tom Mann, Mann & Mann Graphics, Warrenton, Virginia

Modeler: Joseph Sheeran, Ashton-Potter (USA) Ltd.

Art Director: Howard Paine

Project Manager: Elizabeth A. Altobell, USPS

Stamp Manufacturing: Stamps printed by Ashton-Potter, Williamsville, New York, on offset portion of a Stevens Varisize Security Documents webfed 6-color offset, 3-color intaglio press. Stamps perforated, processed and shipped by Ashton-Potter.

Quantity Ordered and Distributed: 95,600,000

Plate Number Detail: 1 set of 5 offset plate numbers preceded by the letter P in selvage next to each corner stamp

Plate Number Combinations Reported: P11111, P22222

Paper Supplier: Westvaco/Ivex

Tagging: phosphored paper

The Stamp

On June 15, the Postal Service issued a stamp to increase public awareness of breast cancer and the need for research, education, screening and treatment related to the disease. Its official dedication ceremony was held in Washington, D.C., but it went on sale nationwide on the first day.

The stamp was similar in purpose to the AIDS Awareness stamp that was issued in sheet and booklet form in 1993. Like the AIDS stamp, the new commemorative featured in its design a picture of the colored ribbon that is worn to call attention to the affliction. And, like the AIDS stamp, its issuance was the result of the determined advocacy of one woman.

The AIDS commemorative came about because of a seven-year campaign led by Jean Anne Hlavacek, a Madison, Wisconsin, nurse-clinician. The person responsible for the Breast Cancer Awareness stamp was Diane Sackett Nannery, a supervisor at the Long Island, New York, District Office of USPS and a survivor of breast cancer herself.

"It was Diane's courageous fight to overcome this disease and her personal crusade to empower others that helped convince me that it was time to issue a Breast Cancer Awareness stamp," said Postmaster General Marvin T. Runyon when he announced details of the first-day ceremony.

Nannery, of Manorville, New York, was diagnosed with breast cancer October 1, 1993, at the age of 41. She'll never forget the feeling, she said. "It was like the sides of my throat were closing in and choking me," she said. "I couldn't eat, sleep or think."

It was after undergoing a biopsy and the start of chemotherapy that Nannery first got the idea of a stamp to publicize breast cancer. "I wanted a stamp for the 184,000 women that are diagnosed each year, and for all of those who died — I wanted them remembered," she said.

She was convinced at first that such a stamp never would be approved, however, especially after she learned that the National Cancer Institute and others had tried unsuccessfully for years to obtain a stamp publicizing all forms of cancer. But she changed her mind one day in February 1994 when her husband showed her an AIDS stamp.

116

For Diane Sackett Nannery, the Postal Service "opened the door" to a Breast Cancer Awareness stamp when it issued this AIDS Awareness commemorative in 1993.

"That was the day I wrote my first letter," Nannery said, "because I thought, 'Now you (the Postal Service) have opened the door.'" The letter went to the Citizens' Stamp Advisory Committee; another went to President Clinton. As a postal employee, she sent a courtesy copy of these letters to Postmaster General Runyon, as she did with each of the hundreds of letters she sent out thereafter.

CSAC sent her a standard form letter of rejection. Undeterred, she went after public support.

She wrote to 100 newspapers — one major daily and one weekly in each state — urging people to write to CSAC on behalf of the stamp. While waiting in line at the supermarket, she would thumb through women's magazines for the names of the editors, and send letters to them as well.

Her letters began appearing in print; some of the magazines ran brief commentaries about her crusade and published her telephone number. She gave talks and interviews at every opportunity. Calls of support came in. A woman in Seattle promised to take petitions to an international health fair. A Philadelphia couple drove the length of Pennsylvania, collecting 10,000 signatures. A fax from Anchorage contained 700 more names.

"I had friends that died of this disease," Nannery said with emotion. "We became friends through our breast cancer experience. And these women wrote letters when I asked for support. I can tell you as a survivor how sick you are when you are going through that, how frightened you are. They took the time, while they were dying, to write a letter, because it meant that much to them.

"The Postal Service received letters and petition signatures from men and children too. I heard from one little girl whose mother died of this disease. She was so little that her grandmother dialed the phone. She told me how her mother 'went away.' She was going to write to the post office to get a stamp, and her grandmother was going to help her."

As a visual prop for her speeches and media photo opportunities,

Nannery used a large picture of what a breast cancer awareness stamp might look like; it resembled the AIDS stamp, with a looped pink ribbon instead of a red one filling the frame. She considered it essential that the stamp show the pink ribbon, the national symbol of the fight against breast cancer. The ribbon represents both "awareness and remembrance," she said, "and those were the two things that for me the stamp would represent."

In spite of all her efforts, the campaign was getting nowhere until the spring of 1995, when three New York members of Congress volunteered to help. One was her congressman, Representative Michael Forbes, Republican of Quogue, New York. Another was Representative Peter King, Republican of Seaford, who obtained 102 signatures of House members on a letter to the Postal Service on behalf of the stamp. On the Senate side of the Capitol, New York's Republican senator, Alfonse D'Amato, did even better percentagewise; after delivering a pro-stamp speech on the Senate floor that C-SPAN televised, D'Amato persuaded all 99 of his fellow senators to join him in signing their own letter to USPS.

Early in July 1995, Nannery was invited to Washington to present her case in person to representatives of CSAC and Postal Service staffers. The meeting was held in Representative Forbes' office. A few days later, she got a fax from Senator D'Amato, who had good news from Postmaster General Runyon. "Well, Dee, you did it," D'Amato wrote. "It's official. We've got a stamp." The next day, Nannery said, her house was besieged by television cameramen and reporters and radio and newspaper interviewers.

Representative King invited her to return to Capitol Hill. Here she met

Diane Sackett Nannery holds up a copy of her proposed design for the Breast Cancer Awareness stamp, featuring the pink "awareness" ribbon, as she speaks to an audience on behalf of the stamp prior to its approval by the Postal Service.

Runyon, who told her: "Congratulations, Diane. You did a wonderful job. You should be very proud of yourself."

On December 18, the postmaster general unveiled the design in New York City during the taping of a two-hour Lifetime Network television special, "Lifetime Applauds: The Fight Against Breast Cancer," to be aired two days later. Nannery was there, along with Representative Forbes and some of the performers in the TV show.

On March 7, 1996, at the National Postal Museum, Runyon announced that the stamp would be dedicated June 15 in conjunction with the 1996 Race for the Cure in Washington, the largest 5-kilometer footrace in America. The Race for the Cure, held in 65 American cities in 1996, raises money to fund all aspects of the fight against breast cancer. It was founded by the Susan G. Komen Breast Cancer Foundation, which was established in 1982 by Nancy Brinker in memory of her sister Susan Komen, who died of breast cancer at the age of 36.

Nannery was on hand at this ceremony as well, as were Representatives Forbes and King; Mary E. McAuliffe, 1996 chair of the National Race for the Cure; and officials of organizations involved in the fight against breast cancer. Also present was Senator Wendell Ford, Republican of Kentucky. Ford was honorary co-chair of the Federal Teams Committee for the 1996 race, which was dedicated to his long-time Capitol Hill aide, Martha Moloney, who succumbed to breast cancer in November 1995.

The issuance of the stamp June 15 launched a four-month public service campaign in which USPS joined with the YWCA of the U.S.A.'s ENCORE plus program, the American Cancer Society, Lifetime television, the American Association of Retired Persons regional and state offices, and several breast cancer groups in providing health information forums and mammography screenings at post offices and other community locations. USPS developed a breast cancer awareness brochure for distribution at post offices during the campaign, along with other informational brochures about the disease.

In addition to the symbolic message of the stamp itself, the selvage on the stamp panes contained an explicit one. This message, longer and in larger type than is customary for selvage text, gave two toll-free 800 numbers for the Cancer Information Service, the regular number and one for hearing-impaired callers. It was written by Elizabeth A. Altobell, the stamp's project manager, and Howard Paine, the art director.

Ashton-Potter (USA) Ltd. printed the stamp by offset in panes of 20. The printer placed the word "AWARENESS," in microtype, in the lower-right corner of the design, parallel to the woman's arm.

As it had done with the AIDS Awareness stamp, USPS waived its usual fee to use the stamp design for nonprofit organizations. These organizations were free to reproduce the design on T-shirts, mugs, key rings and other sales items for fund-raising purposes. The necessary color artwork was made available to them through Hamilton Projects Inc. of New York,

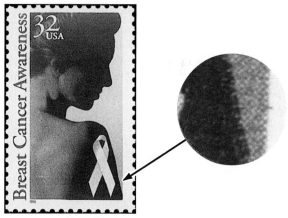

Ashton-Potter (USA) Ltd. printed the word "AWARE-NESS" in microtype in the lower-right corner of the stamp as a security device.

the Postal Services' licensing agency.

Diane Sackett Nannery is proud of the stamp. "When it came out and I knew that information on breast cancer was going to be available at every post office, and that women were going to see the stamp every day and be reminded to do their mammograms and their breast examinations, there have been moments when I have been completely overcome by the magnitude of it," she said.

"And there have been times where I've thought: I didn't just pass through here. I made a difference."

She continues to be a breast-cancer activist. She successfully lobbied the New York State Senate to approve a checkoff box on the state income tax form to earmark funds for breast-cancer research. She is leading a national campaign for the "pink wristband" that 140 hospitals have adopted to identify cancer survivors who have undergone removal or radiation of the lymph nodes. This treatment leaves them at risk for a condition called lymphodema, a blockage of the lymph flow, and the wristband alerts medical personnel to their situation.

Nannery believes the Postal Service should issue many more stamps to help raise awareness of health and social issues.

"I don't ever want to see the day come when we don't have stamps about American musicians and flowers and prehistoric animals, because stamps should be used as a learning tool," she said. "They should be a mirror image of what our country is, what it was and what it will be. But there's a negative side to life, and there also should be stamps calling attention to such things as child abuse — to domestic violence — to homelessness. It's a wonderful vehicle for that purpose."

The Design

The same design team that created the AIDS Awareness stamp, art di-

120

rector Howard Paine and designer Tom Mann, was assigned to the Breast Cancer Awareness project. The stamp they produced is vertically arranged and shows a pensive-appearing woman in profile, her face in shadow. The pink ribbon that Diane Sackett Nannery considered essential is superimposed on the woman's bare shoulder. The stamp's graduated pink background echoes the color of the ribbon, and the words "Breast Cancer Awareness" in brown Adobe Garamond type read up the left side.

Focus groups consulted by the Postal Service found the design "strong and poignant," according to project manager Elizabeth Altobell. To *Linn's Stamp News*, the woman's pose suggested that she was performing the monthly breast self-examination that is recommended for early breast-cancer detection.

Before arriving at the finished design, however, Paine and Mann experimented with a variety of visual concepts.

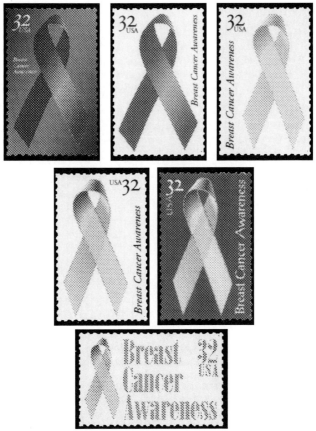

Tom Mann developed several vertical concept sketches using the looped pink ribbon alone, with a blue or white background. He also prepared a horizontal sketch with the words "Breast Cancer Awareness" in large type.

These are some of the dozens of design treatments developed by Tom Mann and art director Howard Paine, using the anonymous woman's profile that was chosen to be the central subject of the stamp. Some of their treatments showed the figure in close-up; others farther back. Some included the pink ribbon in one location or another; others omitted it. Design elements that were tried included a mammography machine and a windowlike background. Different type styles and placements were tested. The woman's hair was altered in different ways and her skin darkened.

At the outset, Paine studied dozens of color photographs of women undergoing mammography, as well as actual mammograms, and concluded that such literal images wouldn't work. Turning to symbolism, he asked Mann to work up some designs in which the pink ribbon was the central focus. These included verticals that showed the ribbon alone, similar to Nannery's own original sketch, virtually replicating the 1993 AIDS Awareness commemorative. A horizontal concept sketch consisted of the ribbon alongside the words "Breast Cancer Awareness."

The designers decided that a human figure was necessary, and they found the one they wanted in a stock photograph of a Caucasian woman from the files of Allstock Inc./Tony Stone Images. In the photo, the woman's left hand is holding her right upper arm, and her hair is tied in a bun with loose strands hanging beside her face. Mann used his computer graphics program to remove the hand, alter her hairdo and darken her skin in an attempt to make her race more ambiguous.

In some of the designs Mann incorporated a picture of a mammography machine, but the visual effect was unsatisfactory. "It looked like a big white refrigerator with a drill press hanging off the front end," said Paine.

The "32 USA" is dropped out of a dark portion of the design. It is unusual in that Mann used old-style digits, with a portion of the "3" descending below the baseline. "USA" is tucked under the normal-size "2."

One of Tom Mann's earliest concept sketches showed a woman's figure silhouetted against a window, with the pink ribbon visible pinned to her dress.

This is a preliminary draft of the selvage text. The wording was extensively revised, and an 800 telephone number for hearing-impaired callers included in the final version.

First-Day Facts

Postmaster General Runyon dedicated the stamps in a ceremony at the National Race for the Cure in Washington June 15. The ceremony was held at the post-race rally site near the Washington Monument. Speakers included Vice President Al Gore and his wife Tipper, honorary co-chairs of the race; Kentucky's Senator Wendell Ford; and Dr. Richard Klausner, director of the National Cancer Institute. Barbara Harrison, anchor of WRC Channel 4, presided, and the welcome was given by the race's chairperson, Mary McAuliffe.

Honored guests included Dr. Susan Blumenthal, director, Women's Health, U.S. Department of Health and Human Resources; Susan Alvarado and Robert Rider, Postal Service governors; M. Richard Porras, vice president and controller of USPS; Nancy Brinker of the Susan G. Komen Breast Cancer Foundation; Chris Thomsen, chief of the Cancer Information Service for the National Cancer Institute; and David Clark, postmaster of Washington, D.C.

First-day ceremonies were held elsewhere as well. The most significant of these was at Stony Brook, on New York's Long Island, an area that has the highest incidence of breast cancer in the United States. The speakers at this ceremony were Diane Sackett Nannery; Senator D'Amato; Representatives King and Forbes; and Anita Redrick McFarlane, an official at Memorial Sloan Kettering Cancer Center. The stamp was dedicated by Thomas F. Rosati, Long Island district manager for USPS. Dr. Shirley Strum Kenny, president of the University at Stony Brook, welcomed the guests.

The earliest-known use of a Breast Cancer Awareness stamp was on a cover machine-postmarked in The Bronx, New York, June 10, five days before the first-day ceremony.

32¢ JAMES DEAN
LEGENDS OF HOLLYWOOD SERIES

Date of Issue: June 24, 1996

Catalog Number: Scott 3082

Colors: yellow, magenta, cyan, black (2), taupe (PMS 453), warm red

First-Day Cancel: Burbank, California

First-Day Cancellations: 263,593

Format: Panes of 20, vertical, 5 across, 4 down. Gravure printing cylinders of 6 panes containing 120 stamp subjects (10 stamps across, 12 stamps around) manufactured by Armotek Industries, Palmyra, New Jersey.

Overall Stamp Size: 0.99 by 1.56 inches; 25.1mm by 39.6mm

Pane Size: 8.75 by 7.25 inches

Perforations: 11.1. Star-shaped perforations at corner of each stamp. (APS rotary perforator).

Selvage Inscription: "LEGENDS OF HOLLYWOOD." "In a brief but brilliant career, the actor/James Dean (1931-1955) spoke for/millions of American teenagers as the/misunderstood youth in East of Eden/and Rebel Without a Cause./His stature grew mythic after he/died in a car crash, shortly/before his final film, Giant,/was completed." "James Dean TM James Dean Foundation Trust/c/o CMG Worldwide, Indianapolis, IN."

Selvage Markings: "© USPS 1996." "20 X .32 = $6.40." "PLATE/POSITION" and diagram.

Designer: Michael Deas of New Orleans, Louisiana

Typographer: John Boyd, Anagraphics Inc. New York, New York

Modeler: Richard C. Sennett

Art Director: Carl Herrman

Project Manager: Terrence McCaffrey, USPS

Stamp Manufacturing: Stamps printed for Stamp Venturers by J.W. Fergusson and Sons, Richmond, Virginia, on Champlain webfed gravure press 1. Stamps perforated, processed and shipped at Stamp Venturers, Fredericksburg, Virginia.

Quantity Ordered: 300,000,000

Quantity Distributed: 150,000,000

Cylinder Number Detail: 1 set of 7 gravure cylinder numbers preceded by the letter S in selvage next to each corner stamp

Cylinder Number Combination Reported: S1111111

Paper Supplier: Paper Corporation U.S./Brown Bridge

Tagging: Large tagging block over all 20 stamps. The block does not cover the stamps to the edges.

The Stamp

On June 24, the Postal Service issued the second stamp in the "Legends of Hollywood" series that it had launched in 1995 with a stamp picturing Marilyn Monroe. The new stamp honored James Dean, whose rebel image — which he created in a career of only three films — and accidental death at age 24 turned him into an enduring cult figure.

The first-day ceremony was held at the Warner Bros. Studios lot in Burbank, California, where Dean's movies were made, but the stamp also

was available June 24 at all Warner Bros. Studio Stores nationwide, as well as the Burbank post office.

Postmaster General Marvin T. Runyon officially unveiled the stamp design January 3 at a ceremony at New York's Planet Hollywood theme restaurant, where he had unveiled the Marilyn Monroe design one year earlier. With him for the event was Dean's first cousin, Marcus Winslow.

"In 1995, Marilyn Monroe brought a new sizzle to the world of stamps," Runyon said. "This year, James Dean will deliver a special brand of cool that is just as hot. Even today, his very name stirs up powerful memories of leather jackets, diners and drive-ins, and living on the edge."

The day before, Runyon had provided what was termed "a sneak peek" at the Dean stamp design during the "Picture of the Week" segment of the NBC television program *Dateline*.

According to USPS, the Legends of Hollywood series "showcases individuals who made a major impact on the development of American films." The series epitomizes the Postal Service's ongoing efforts to broaden the appeal of its stamps and maximize "retention revenue" from stamps that are saved rather than used on mail.

The Dean stamp, like the Monroe, was issued in panes of 20, five across by four down. The pictorial selvage was intended to make the pane so attractive that collectors and Dean fans would save it intact. Also like its predecessor, it was printed by the gravure process by Stamp Venturers and given star-shaped perforations at the four corners of each stamp. A double row of perforations around the outer edges of the block of 20 stamps creates a narrow inner selvage, which is blank except for a set of plate numbers in each corner.

The tagging also is identical to that on the Monroe pane. It consists of a large block of taggant applied over the 20 stamps so that it covers only the design areas, leaving the outer margins of the 14 "border" stamps untagged. Thus, when one of those 14 stamps is examined under ultraviolet (UV) light, at least one of its outer margins doesn't glow because the taggant doesn't extend that far. Each of the four corner stamps has two adjacent margins that are "dead."

USPS offered uncut sheets of six panes for sale to collectors, as it had done with the Monroe stamp and with the stamps in its so-called Classic Collections series. Artist Michael Deas signed 15,000 of the sheets, which sold for $125. Unsigned sheets went for their $38.40 face value. Deas also signed individual panes of 20 stamps that sold for $29.95.

Other Dean items marketed by USPS were a StampFolio containing a block of four stamps ($4.95), a poster featuring an enlargement of the stamp design, also with four stamps affixed ($12.95), and a first-day program with a pane of 20 stamps and the first-day cancellation ($14.95).

To promote all these products, the Postal Service distributed a colorful brochure at post offices featuring Deas' stamp portrait of Dean on the cover and urging its readers to "be first in line for one-of-a-kind James Dean commemoratives — as lasting as the movies he starred in over 40 years ago."

The rights to Dean's name and image are owned by the James Dean Foundation Trust, whose beneficiaries are the actor's cousins and their descendants. CMG Worldwide of Indianapolis, Indiana, formerly the Curtis Management Group, markets and protects those rights for the trust.

As a condition of granting permission to the Postal Service to issue the Dean stamp, CMG specified that each pane must include the name of the trust and CMG; these appear in a line of small lettering along the lower edge of the pane. In addition, USPS was required to incorporate the trademark symbol, "™," beneath the actor's name on each stamp.

The same demand had been made in connection with the Marilyn Monroe stamp by the Roger Richman Agency, the licensing agency for Monroe's name and image. USPS design officials resented this requirement — no previous U.S. stamp had borne a trademark designation — and they resolved to fulfill it in the least obtrusive way possible. They printed the "™" in tiny black letters on the Monroe stamp's dark blue background, making it virtually impossible to see with the naked eye. On the Dean stamp, with its dark gray background, the "™" is, if anything, even harder to detect.

Once again, first-day cover cachetmakers had to decide whether to pay a licensing fee for the right to use the subject's name and picture or create a generic cachet that would have much less sales appeal. Most of the major ones opted to use the Dean name and features, for which CMG charged them 5 percent of the face value of the covers or 50¢ per cachet sold, whichever was higher.

For the second consecutive year, the Republic of the Marshall Islands seized the opportunity to piggyback a stamp of its own on a USPS "Legends of Hollywood" stamp. It issued a James Dean commemorative on June 1, beating the Postal Service by three weeks and using the USPS format of 20-stamp panes with decorative selvage. In 1995, the Marshalls had issued a Marilyn Monroe stamp on the same day that the U.S. Marilyn Monroe stamp was released. The Marshall Islands' agent in the United States is Unicover World Trade Corporation of Cheyenne, Wyoming, and its stamps are printed by Unicover.

James Byron Dean was born February 8, 1931, in Marion, Indiana, the only child of Winton R. and Mildred M. Wilson Dean. The family moved to California in 1935, but four years later Mildred Dean died of cancer and Winton Dean, considering himself incapable of raising his son, sent the boy back to the farm of his sister and her husband near Fairmount, Indiana. In spite of the affection and parental concern he received from

The Republic of the Marshall Islands issued this James Dean stamp, designed by Tom McNeely, on June 1, 23 days before the U.S. Postal Service's Dean stamp was issued. It bore a reproduction of Dean's signature. USPS was denied the right to use the signature on the U.S. stamp.

his Quaker aunt and uncle, Dean would acknowledge later the deep pain and rejection he felt at being orphaned at such a young age.

At Fairmount High School he took part in school plays, and after graduation he returned to California, where he studied drama at Santa Monica City College. He launched his professional career by appearing in a Coca-Cola television commercial and landing a small part in a TV drama. In 1951 he moved to New York City, where he honed his acting skills through personal discipline and study at the Actors' Studio. His strongest asset was his face, described by writer Alfred F. McLean as "delicate and somewhat androgynous" and "particularly expressive of intense states of personal conflict."

Dean landed roles in Broadway plays and caught the attention of motion-picture director Elia Kazan, who cast him as the volatile and bitter son, Cal Trask, in Warner Bros. 1955 adaptation of John Steinbeck's novel *East of Eden*. "Dean became prime material for Hollywood publicity agents," McLean writes. "Floods of fan mail, fan clubs, gossip items and Dean's own enigmatic personality established a cultism among young people that persisted for two decades after his death."

His next role, which fixed his image as the dissatisfied hero-victim, was that of the brooding teenager Jim Stark in *Rebel Without a Cause* (1955). Next, George Stevens cast him in the role of Jett Rink, the ranchhand who becomes an oil tycoon in *Giant*, based on Edna Ferber's novel. After completing the film, Dean was killed on September 30, 1955, while driving from Los Angeles to a sports-car race in Salinas, California. His Porsche crashed at high speed into another car that was making a left turn across his lane on California Route 49 near Paso Robles, California. *Rebel Without a Cause* opened four days later and *Giant* was released the following year.

Coincidentally, the other two lead actors in *Rebel Without a Cause* — also youth idols of the 1950s — would also die under tragic circumstances. Dean's death on the highway was followed two decades later by the stabbing homicide of Sal Mineo. In 1981 Natalie Wood drowned after slipping off a yacht.

The Design

The portrait used on the Marilyn Monroe stamp of 1995 was picked from among sketches submitted by nine artists who had been invited to compete for the design job. The James Dean stamp required no such process. Art director Carl Herrman and the Postal Service staff knew they wanted the same designer whose Monroe portrait had been the consensus choice: Michael Deas of New York City.

To prepare, Deas viewed videotapes of the three Dean movies. "I had never seen any of them in their entirety and had never been a particular fan of Dean, but suddenly I understood what all the fuss was about," Deas said. "He really was quite spectacular. He's so natural in his films he makes everybody else's performance look like acting."

This brooding photo of Dean with a stubble beard, one of the "torn sweater series" that Roy Schatt shot December 29, 1954, was the model for Michael Deas' stamp design.

The artist found the photograph on which he based the Dean design in the picture collection of the New York Public Library. It was taken by Roy Schatt, who made many photographs of Dean in New York in 1954 and also taught the actor photography, and is one of a group of photos known as the "torn sweater series." The pictures are published in Schatt's book *James Dean: A Portrait.*

"Dean was just becoming known when I began photographing him," Schatt writes in the book. "... *Life* was the important magazine to appear in at the time and, naturally, Jimmy wanted to be in it. He asked me to show them my shots. Frank D. Campion, the man to see, liked the photos, but said he wanted a serious, more manly sitting. What *Life* wanted we were more than happy to provide.

"The day I shot the photos (December 29, 1954) the session went extraordinarily well. After a certain amount of horsing around, Jimmy behaved and became serious when I got the lighting set just right. He clicked, I clicked, and the photos clicked. He now had quite a bit of photographic experience himself, and after a while I allowed him to direct some of the shots. It was all pretty heady. At one point he commented, 'Don't you think I look like Michelangelo's David?'

"The pictures from that sitting became the 'torn sweater' series. *Life* magazine, as it turned out, had an exclusive contract with a big agency and couldn't use the pictures I had taken. But to this day, the 'torn sweater' series are the best known and most popular shots of Dean in the world, even though *Life* never published them."

The photograph on which Deas based his stamp portrait "is a little bit on the moody side for a stamp," the artist said. "But then again, that's what James Dean is all about."

This is Michael Deas' original pencil sketch of what would become the design for the James Dean stamp. One of several poses that Deas sketched, it was "far and away the best" in the artist's opinion.

Deas offered the Postal Service and Citizens' Stamp Advisory Committee an alternative sketch based on a different photo, but he was gratified when the officials in Washington agreed with his first choice.

His oil painting of Dean showed the actor out of doors under a lowering sky, with a flat country landscape behind him. "In all three of his films, he played someone who is a bit at odds with himself, and I wanted to capture that sense of inner turbulence," Deas explained. "I thought the stormy skies were a good way of representing that.

"The open plain behind him has multiple meaning. He was from the farmlands of Indiana, with wide open, flat fields. Then he moved to California and his first film was *East of Eden*, which is set in California's Salinas Valley — and that, coincidentally, is where he died. *Giant* was set on the plains of Texas. I wanted to be deliberately ambiguous about the background.

"He's an American film icon, so I wanted to give the sense of an American landscape."

Deas considered this alternative image of Dean, which he presented in a pencil sketch, his "second-best" portrait for the stamp. "Don't worry about the hunchback effect," he wrote to art director Carl Herrman. "I'll fix it in the finish. Also, Dean can be reclining against a brick wall OR we can have him against an all-white background — very graphic — as we see here."

131

The original Schatt photograph was dark, with one side of Dean's face completely in shadow. "I had to invent that side of his face," Deas said. "I had to refer to other photographs of him to make sure I was getting the features right." Deas also gave his subject "a little cleanup," removing the stubble beard that showed in Schatt's photo.

Deas' preliminary color sketches are as detailed as many illustrators' finished art. When he submitted his sketch of Dean to the Postal Service, he configured it so that the commemorative-size stamp could be arranged either vertically, with Dean's face centered and filling most of the design, or horizontally, with the portrait on the right side. To make the stamp consistent with the first one in the new series, USPS chose the vertical arrangement.

For the selvage design, Deas made a pencil drawing of Dean walking down the middle of a residential street in Manhattan, hands in pockets, sports jacket open, hair blowing in the breeze. He based the drawing on another Schatt photograph. In the photo, a cigarette dangles from Dean's lips, but in conformance with Postal Service policy of not depicting smok-

Michael Deas sent CSAC this color sketch, done in oil, of the approved Dean image with an extended sky and horizon on the left so the design could be used as either a horizontal or a vertical stamp.

ing on stamps, the artist deleted the cigarette.

Dean's figure itself is shown on the wide portion of selvage to the right of the block of 20 stamps, but the drawing extends behind the stamps and bleeds off all four edges of the pane. The parts of buildings shown along the left and top edges don't exist in the original photograph, and Deas had to invent them.

Postal officials intended to use a replica of Dean's autograph as a name identification line on the stamp, as they had done with Marilyn Monroe. But CMG Worldwide vetoed the idea. The management firm has its own "corporate identity program" for Dean, with a specified typeface (Bernhard Modern) and color (PMS 453, a brownish gray called taupe) for the display of Dean's name, and it wanted USPS to follow those guidelines on the stamp.

"Here's the ultimate rebel of the 1950s," Terrence McCaffrey, head of stamp design for USPS, said with a laugh, "and he's now branded with a 'corporate identity program.'"

Fortunately, Bernhard Modern is a handsome typeface for lettering and worked well with the stamp design. USPS was allowed to use a bold weight for the letters in "JAMES DEAN," rather than standard weight, after McCaffrey demonstrated to the company's representatives that standard-weight lettering would be too fragile to be visually effective when it was reversed out of the stamp's background color and printed in the specified PMS color.

This Roy Schatt photograph of James Dean sauntering along a New York City street, cigarette between his lips, was the model for Michael Deas' pencil drawing for the selvage of the Dean stamp pane. In his finished version of the drawing, Deas removed the cigarette in conformance with USPS' policy against depicting smoking.

These two essays utilized two versions of Dean's signature as the name line, one in gold and the other in a metallic silver that was repeated in a border around the design. However, CMG Worldwide, which licenses the use of the Dean name and image, specified that the name should be printed in the "corporate identity" typeface, Bernhard Modern.

Postal officials didn't like the numerals in the Bernhard Modern font, however. Typographer John Boyd tried several compatible typefaces for the "32," including Copperplate 29BC, Simoncini Garamond, Adobe Garamond, Garamond Export, Caslon 540 and Sabon, finally settling on a typeface called Trajan. At Deas' suggestion, the denomination and "USA" were printed in red.

"Michael's thought was that in red, it wouldn't 'chop a hole' in Dean's shoulder," said Carl Herrman. "If we had done it in white, it would have been the brightest thing on the stamp and would have been very distract-

Michael Deas made this alternative concept sketch for the selvage of the stamp pane, based on a different Roy Schatt photo in which the actor is wearing a topcoat over a buttoned jacket.

ing. Now it's not distracting at all. The red is sort of absorbed by the dark background and it doesn't look as if Dean has some big monogram on his sweater."

Stamp Venturers used two black gravure cylinders in the printing operation, one for the selvage, the other for the black process portion of the stamps. It had done the same thing with the Georgia O'Keeffe stamp, and for the same reason: to be able to get the proper intensity of ink for each of the two different uses of the color.

In March 1996, before the stamp was issued, its design was awarded a gold medal by the Society of Illustrators. The society said it selected the design from more than 7,000 entries. Deas' design for the 32¢ Tennessee Williams commemorative was honored by the society in 1995.

Varieties

Panes of James Dean stamps were found completely and partly imperforate.

In August, Jacques C. Schiff Jr. of Ridgefield Park, New Jersey, a dealer in stamp errors, reported to *Linn's Stamp News* that four fully imperforate panes had been bought in southern Illinois by a collector. The collector retained one pane and sold the others through Schiff.

Another pane was found containing three fully imperforate vertical pairs as well as some partial perforations and a slight doubling of perfs called the "snowman effect." Dealer Richard E. Drews offered the pane at his February 21, 1997, auction, but it failed to reach the $1,500 reserve price set by the consignor.

Wayne Youngblood, writing in *Stamp Collector*, explained how this error pane illustrated several characteristics of a new type of perforator used by Unique Binders of Fredericksburg, Virginia, the finishing firm of the Stamp Venturers partnership.

Standard perforators puncture or remove paper through the use of male and female perforating pins in dies that move either in a rotary or stroke direction. The resulting scrap, tiny dots of paper, is called chad.

The new units, called APS grinding perforators, produce dust and don't puncture the paper. A perforation die, with the appropriate pattern for a stamp issue, pushes the stamp paper from the front, while sharp steel rotary blades that resemble large pencil-sharpener blades scrape it from the back. This produces perforation holes for the stamps. The so-called pins never puncture the paper. The distance between the perforation die and the blade is only 4½ one-thousandths of an inch.

Youngblood explained the creation of the error pane this way:

"As the web of stamp paper travels through the perforator, it passes by one cutting head on the lead end, then under a take-up roll to preserve tension, and finally passes by two other cutting heads on the tail end.

"The cutting heads are positioned so that the first one cuts through the center portion of the web. The remaining two heads cut the outer portions. The cutting heads have an overlap distance of between two and three

This is the partly imperforate error pane offered but not sold by Richard E. Drews. It shows several characteristics of Unique Binders' perforators, including partially ground, partial-hole and "snowman-effect" perforations.

perforation holes. If all goes well, the overlap is precise and is not noticed, but any web chatter or movement causes a misalignment that results in doubled perforation holes known as the 'snowman effect.'

"... The abrupt half-perforation holes that appear on this and other partially perforated panes are caused by the side edge of the cutting blade. There simply is nothing to cut, and if the adjacent cutting blade is disengaged it will show an immediate and abrupt end of perforations.

"The partially ground-out perforations are caused by the slow disengagement of the cutters, with full perforations slowly changing to imperfs.

"By looking at the plate position of the (Dean error) pane (upper right), we can reconstruct exactly what happened. The stamps, two panes wide by three down, were traveling through the perforator foot-to-head (bottom to top), when a problem developed. Some slight malfunction caused web chatter and the resulting snowman effect on the bottom two rows of stamps just left of center (where the blades were supposed to meet).

"As a result, the center cutter (the first one on the lead end) disengaged, causing the fade-out perfs and six fully imperforate stamps to occur. Because of the delicate nature of this high-precision equipment, the slightest problem will shut down the cutting heads, resulting in partially perforated and imperf errors that are later removed and destroyed.

"Assuming that both of the outer tail-end cutting blades were still operating properly, the top-left position pane should be a more or less mirror image of this pane, with imperf stamps at right, changing to normal stamps at left, depending on the original width of the trimmed-out center gutter."

136

This is the Rebel Without a Cause station cancellation that was used at Warner Brothers Studio Stores around the country on the Dean stamp's first day of issue.

First-Day Facts

Postmaster General Runyon dedicated the James Dean stamp at the first-day ceremony, held on Warner Bros.' Midwestern Street, the section of the lot where Dean filmed his first two movies.

Remembrances of the actor were given by his cousin, Marcus Winslow; Frank Mazzola, Dean's co-star in *Rebel Without a Cause*; Carroll Baker, co-star of *Giant*; and other friends and colleagues of Dean. Jean Picker Firstenberg, director and chief executive officer of the American Film Institute, and Tirso del Junco, chairman of the USPS Board of Governors, also spoke. The welcome was extended by Robert A. Daly, chairman and co-CEO of Warner Bros. and the Warner Music Group, and excerpts from Dean's three films were shown.

Guests included Loren E. Smith, chief marketing officer and senior vice president of USPS; Richard Ordonez, USPS district manager for customer service; CSAC members Karl Malden and Michael Brock; stamp designer Michael Deas; and three actors billed as *Rebel Without a Cause* gang members, Jack Grinnage, Beverly Long and Steffi Sydney.

A special cancellation was available June 24 at 118 Warner Bros. Studio Stores around the country, where the stamps and related products were sold. The stamps could be purchased at post offices the following day.

Fairmount, Indiana, where Dean grew up and went to high school and where he is buried, had wanted to be allowed to share the first-day ceremony with Burbank. In March, Senator Dan Coats, Indiana Republican, wrote a letter to Postmaster General Runyon on the town's behalf. The Postal Service declined to change its first-day plans, but did agree to hold a second-day ceremony in Fairmount June 25.

The earliest-known prerelease use of a James Dean stamp was on a cover machine-canceled in Lancaster, Pennsylvania, June 21, three days before the first-day ceremony.

32¢ FOLK HEROES (4 DESIGNS)

Date of Issue: July 11, 1996

Catalog Numbers: Scott 3083-3086

Colors: black, cyan, magenta, yellow

First-Day Cancel: Anaheim, California

First-Day Cancellations: 739,706

Format: Panes of 20, vertical, 5 across, 4 down. Offset printing plates of 120 subjects (8 across, 15 down).

Overall Stamp Size: 1.105 by 1.44 inches; 28.067mm by 36.576mm

Perforations: 11.1 (Wista and Gammeller stroke perforator)

Selvage Markings: "© USPS/1995." ".32/x20/$6.40." "PLATE/POSITION" and diagram.

Designer: David LaFleur of Derby, Kansas

Typographer and Art Director: Richard Sheaff

Modeler: Joseph Sheeran, Ashton-Potter (USA) Ltd.

Project Manager: Elizabeth A. Altobell, USPS

Stamp Manufacturing: Stamps printed by Ashton-Potter (USA) Ltd., Williamsville, New York, on offset portion of a Stevens Varisize Security Documents webfed 6-color offset, 3-color intaglio press. Stamps perforated, processed and shipped by Ashton Potter.

Quantity Ordered: 112,780,000

Quantity Distributed: 94,725,000

Plate Number Detail: 1 set of 4 offset plate numbers preceded by the letter P in selvage above or below each corner stamp

Plate Number Combinations Reported: P1111, P2222

Paper Supplier: Westvaco/Ivex

Tagging: phosphored paper

The Stamps

On July 11, USPS issued a block of four se-tenant stamps depicting well-known characters from American folklore: Mighty Casey, Pecos Bill, John Henry and Paul Bunyan. The stamps were issued at Anaheim, California, on the first day of the American Stamp Dealers Association's Postage Stamp Mega-Event.

The idea for such a set went back at least to 1962. On January 7 of that year, the old *Los Angeles Examiner* published an article by its stamp writer, Phil Glickman, proposing a series of stamps to celebrate "the folklore of America." The stamps, depicting characters like Paul Bunyan, Pecos Bill, Johnny Appleseed, John Henry and Rip Van Winkle, would be an asset in "the international propaganda war," Glickman wrote, by showing that "this nation's heritage is reflected more in the deeds and legends of our people than in the economic levels we have attained."

Whether the article was read in Washington isn't known, but in 1966 the U.S. Post Office Department did issue the first of six commemorative stamps that would appear over the next eight years under the loose heading of "American Folklore." These stamps honored characters both real (Johnny Appleseed, Davy Crockett, Daniel Boone, Grandma Moses) and fictional (Tom Sawyer, Ichabod Crane and the Headless Horseman).

Early in the 1990s, the Citizens' Stamp Advisory Committee and the Postal Service's marketing specialists decided that the theme was worth revisiting. Art director Richard Sheaff, intrigued by the idea of a set of

These three images were created by Charles Schneeman, staff artist for the Los Angeles Examiner, *to illustrate an article by* Examiner *stamp editor Phil Glickman that was published January 7, 1962. The stamps Glickman proposed in the article for Pecos Bill, John Henry and Paul Bunyan became a reality more than 34 years later.*

stamps depicting legendary Americans, set to work on the project.

Sheaff began by developing three lists on which he jotted down every possible candidate for the set he could think of. The lists were as follows:

"American Myths and Heroes": Johnny Appleseed, Bowleg Bill, Virginia Dare, John Henry, Jonathan the Yankee, Stackalee, Pecos Bill, Bigfoot (Sasquatch), Casey Jones, Casey at the Bat, Joe Magarac, Rip Van Winkle, Mose the Bowery B'hoy, Superman, Paul Bunyan, the Lone Ranger, Uncle Sam, Raven (Northwest Coast Indians), Pele (Hawaiian goddess of volcanoes), Jubilation T. Cornpone, Tom Sawyer, Huckleberry Finn, Zozobra (Old Man Gloom), the Headless Horseman, Natty Bumppo (Leatherstocking), Captain Ahab, Davy Crockett, Daniel Boone, Uncle Remus.

"Legendary Real People, Larger Than Life": Davy Crockett, Daniel Boone, Kit Carson, Sam Bass, Judge Roy Bean, Butch Cassidy, the Sundance Kid, Bonnie and Clyde, Billy the Kid, Captain Lightfoot (Michael Martin), Jim Bridger, John Brown, Buffalo Bill, Annie Oakley, Calamity Jane, Wild Bill Hickok, Jesse James, Sam Patch, Sequoya, Phineas T. Barnum, Nellie Bly, Jim Bowie, Diamond Jim Brady, Wyatt Earp, Hiawatha, Betsy Ross, Pocahontas, Belle Starr, Squanto.

"American Archetypes": the Maine Guide, the Indian Tracker, the Mountain Man, the Lawman/Marshal, the Cowboy, the Lobsterman, the Minuteman, the Pioneer, the Pilgrim, the Girl Next Door, the Kentucky Rifleman, the Country Gentleman, the Pony Express Rider, the Sodbuster.

Sheaff's first two lists overlapped to some extent. "American Myths and Heroes" contained the names of several real persons along with legendary, fictional and even comic-strip characters. Both lists included individuals who had made previous appearances on U.S. stamps, plus six from the second list who would be pictured in 1994 on the Legends of the West pane of 20 varieties.

Sheaff commissioned Dave LaFleur, an illustrator from Derby, Kansas, to prepare some sketches. LaFleur made pencil drawings of six of the people from Sheaff's lists: the four who eventually ended up on the stamps, plus Rip Van Winkle — author Washington Irving's fictional character who slept for 20 years — and Johnny Appleseed. "As soon as he did the sketches, everybody (on CSAC) loved them," Sheaff said. "When he did the final art, everybody loved them even more."

The stamps were offset-printed by Ashton-Potter (USA) Ltd. and issued in panes of 20. They were so arranged that any block of four or vertical strip of four would include one of each of the four varieties.

Mighty Casey was the brainchild of Ernest L. Thayer, whose *Casey at the Bat*, first published in *The San Francisco Examiner* June 3, 1888, is the most famous poem ever written about the game of baseball. Subtitled by Thayer *A Ballad of the Republic*, the poem focuses on a critical moment for the team from Mudville. Down 6-4 with two outs in the ninth inning, Mudville's outlook is bleak. But then two light-hitting batters manage to get on base, bringing up the team's slugger, Mighty Casey, to the anticipatory roar of the crowd.

Casey disdainfully watches two called strikes go by, then gets serious. As he digs in, a heroic ending seems imminent. But fate rules otherwise, as the familiar concluding stanza relates:

"Oh somewhere in this favored land the sun is shining bright.

"The band is playing somewhere, and somewhere hearts are light,

"And somewhere men are laughing, and somewhere children shout,

"But there is no joy in Mudville — Mighty Casey has struck out!"

Cowboy hero Pecos Bill originated in a magazine article by journalist Edward O'Reilly in 1923. But as the story passed among real cowboys sitting around their campfires, Bill took on a number of fantastic attributes.

Born in Texas with 16 brothers and sisters, Bill, as the story went, used a bowie knife as a teething ring and played with bears and other wild animals. While still a baby, he fell off the end of a wagon when his family moved west, and he was raised by coyotes.

He became the strongest, toughest cowboy ever. He rode a mountain lion using a rattlesnake for a quirt, roped a railroad train and rode an Oklahoma cyclone without a saddle. The cyclone couldn't throw him and finally "rained out" from under him in Arizona. The rain fell so heavily that it created the Grand Canyon. Bill crashed in California and the force of his fall created Death Valley. Astride his horse, Widow-Maker, Pecos Bill waged war on robbers and outlaws throughout the West.

The saga of the giant lumberman Paul Bunyan got its start in the logging camps of Minnesota. The real Paul Bunyon (spelled with an o) was a French-Canadian lumber-camp operator in the mid-1800s whose crews told marvelous stories of his strength and bravery. These anecdotes were picked up by American lumberjacks, who seized on Paul as a hero to personify their exciting life. They had him cross the border into the United States, anglicize his name to Bunyan, invent logging and then begin his career of unmatched exploits.

Paul towered above the treetops, covered 24 townships in a stride when he was in a hurry, combed his beard with a young pine and could bellow loud enough to cause a landslide on Pike's Peak. When his ax got too hot from felling trees two at a time, he cooled it in a spring that to this day is known as the boiling spring. He made the Great Lakes as drinking-water reservoirs for his great blue ox, Babe; the Alleghenies and Rockies piled up when he dug a channel for the Mississippi; and Kansas is flat because Paul hitched Babe to it and turned it over to make good corn land.

The story of John Henry, celebrated in a steel drivers' ballad, has its roots more firmly planted in reality than the other three folk-hero stories, although what parts of the story are true and what are myth remains uncertain.

Researchers say there really was a John Henry working on the mile-long Big Bend railroad tunnel in West Virginia in the early 1870s. Many laborers perished as they dug and blasted through the hard red shale of Big Bend Mountain. According to the story, John Henry, a black man of prodigious strength, was the finest steel driver of them all. When the steam drill came to Big Bend, John Henry bet that he could drive spikes into the rock as fast as the new machine could do it. "Before I'd let your steam drill beat me down," the song has him telling the boss, "I would die with my hammer in my hand." John Henry won the race and the wager — but he perished from his mighty effort.

A 1969 *Washington Post* article by Hank Burchard concludes: "That John Henry lived seems beyond doubt. That he drove steel in Big Bend tunnel ... seems certain. That he drove steel against a steam drill and beat it seems likely. That he died from overexertion in the contest seems somewhat less likely, if wonderfully poetic.

"But there is no doubt that John Henry is high among America's towering authentic folk heroes, symbol of the proud working man who would not yield his human strength and skill to the coming of the machine."

The Designs

Many of the pictures in Dave LaFleur's portfolio of commercial illustrations are of square-jawed people, with features that are heavy with planes and angles. Even his animals have this strong, stylized appearance. The style, which LaFleur's admirers call "heroic" or "archetypal," has its roots in early Soviet propaganda art and, in the United States, in the WPA-sponsored murals and posters of the New Deal era. Both glorified the working man as a burly icon with thick neck and strong arms.

"The heroic look was a very big trend about 15 years ago," LaFleur said. "You didn't see it in the 1960s and 1970s, but then a couple of well-known illustrators began using it, and it made its way into advertising.

"It's on the wane now. In fact, I do a lot fewer heroic type figures now than I did five or six years ago. Illustration is very trendy that way. Today, everything has kind of a computer look to it."

It was the heroic effect in LaFleur's art, however, that convinced Richard Sheaff that he would be the ideal person to design the Folk Heroes stamps. "Dave has a way of kind of making things look more monumental than they are, which seemed to be right for this set," Sheaff said. "His work is whimsical but it has a strength to it as well."

For the stamp assignment, LaFleur said, he "definitely set out to make the folk heroes look very cool, very macho. Square jaws? Heck, even the beard on Paul Bunyan is square.

"The only regret I have about the stamps is that the figures were more outlined — a little more cartoony looking — than I would have made them if I had been doing them for a print and they weren't going to have to be reduced to stamp size."

Sheaff told LaFleur to focus on the characters' faces, rather than show them full length, and to give each one a background or bit of costume that would tell something about him. On the stamps, a mustachioed Casey, in turn-of-the-century baseball uniform, brandishes his bat against a background of stadium and blue sky. Pecos Bill flaunts a similar handlebar mustache, along with a white 10-gallon hat and a live rattlesnake for a neckpiece; a Western landscape is outlined against a red sky in the distance. John Henry, in an undershirt, holds up his mallet as a locomotive rumbles by on a trestle overhead. A bearded Paul Bunyan, with his axhead next to his chest, towers over the treetops in the foreground. His blue ox, Babe, stands behind him.

LaFleur devoured all the written material he could find on the four legendary characters, but he deliberately avoided looking at other artists'

Dave LaFleur made these pencil sketches for two Folk Heroes stamps that weren't included in the "final four." One shows Rip Van Winkle, leaves clinging to his long flowing beard, awakening from his 20-year sleep in the woods; the other depicts Johnny Appleseed, wearing his saucepan hat, a bag of apples over his shoulder, with stylized apple trees in the background.

These are Dave LaFleur's preliminary pencil sketches for the four Folk Heroes stamps.

representations of them — particularly the Walt Disney Studios' versions — for fear of being subconsciously influenced. "The faces (on the stamps) came completely out of my head," he said.

The artist made his finished paintings in oil, rather than the acrylic or gouache that many stamp designers prefer because of their faster drying times. He was surprised to see that the printed stamps were considerably darker than his original artwork, he said.

For the stamps' typography, Richard Sheaff selected fonts called Lubalin Graph, Serifa Roman and Serifa Bold.

Postal officials were so pleased with LaFleur's designs for the Folk Heroes stamps that Sheaff subsequently assigned the job of creating the Flag Over Porch definitive stamp to the Kansas illustrator. As it turned

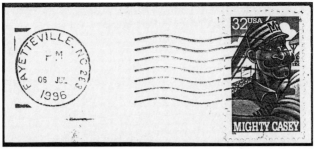

The earliest-known prerelease use of a Folk Heroes stamp is this cover bearing a Mighty Casey stamp postmarked in Fayetteville, North Carolina, July 6, five days before the stamps officially went on sale.

out, however, the first stamp to bear the Flag Over Porch design was issued in April 1995, some 15 months before the Folk Heroes quartet finally made it to the post offices.

First-Day Facts

Michael S. Coughlin, deputy postmaster general, dedicated the stamps at a ceremony at the Anaheim Convention Center that featured the appearance of four actors portraying the depicted folk heroes. Phil Bansner, president of the American Stamp Dealers Association, gave the welcome, and Robert C. Gillis, USPS district manager for customer service and sales, presided. Stamp designer Dave LaFleur was a special guest.

The earliest-known prerelease use of a Folk Heroes stamp was a cover bearing a Mighty Casey stamp postmarked in Fayetteville, North Carolina, July 6, five days before the stamps officially went on sale.

32¢ CENTENNIAL OLYMPIC GAMES (DISCUS THROWER)

Date of Issue: July 19, 1996

Catalog Number: Scott 3087

Colors: black, magenta, yellow, beige (PMS 155), brown (PMS 469) (offset, selvage); brown (PMS 469) (intaglio, stamp). A varnish coating also was applied over the selvage area.

First-Day Cancel: Atlanta, Georgia

First-Day Cancellations: 269,056

Format: Panes of 20 stamps, vertical, 5 across, 4 down. Intaglio printing plates of 80 stamps, 8 across, 10 around. Offset printing plates of 4 panes, 2 across, 2 down.

Overall Stamp Size: 0.99 by 1.56 inches; 25.1mm by 39.6mm

Perforations: 11.1

Selvage Inscription: "Centennial Olympic Games/The ancient Greek Olympic Games were held every four/years from at least 776 BC until 393 AD. Inpsired by the/original Olympics, Baron Pierre de Coubertin of France/proposed a modern version in 1892. The first Games were/staged in Athens in 1896. The 1996 Centennial/Games will be hosted by Atlanta." "1896/Athens,/Greece/ 1996/Atlanta,/Georgia." "USA" and Olympic rings. "Discus Thrower/Roman marble copy after a/bronze original of c. 450 BC/by Myron, Museo Nazionale/Romano delle Terme, Rome, Italy."

146

Selvage Markings: © 1995 USPS." ".32 x 20 = $6.40." "PLATE/POSITION" and diagram.

Designer and Art Director: Carl Herrman of Ponte Vedra Beach, Florida

Typographer: John Boyd, Anagraphics Inc., New York, New York

Modeler: Joseph Sheeran, Ashton-Potter (USA) Ltd.

Engraver: Armandina Lozano

Project Manager: Terrence McCaffrey, USPS

Stamp Manufacturing: Stamps printed by Ashton-Potter (USA) Ltd., Williamsville, New York, on a Stevens Varisize Security Documents webfed 6-color offset, 3-color intaglio press. Stamps perforated, processed and shipped by Ashton-Potter (USA).

Quantity Ordered and Distributed: 133,613,000

Plate Number Detail: 1 intaglio plate number preceded by the letter P in selvage above or below each corner stamp

Plate Number Reported: P1

Tagging: phosphored paper

The Stamp

On July 19, the opening day of the Centennial Olympic Games in Atlanta, Georgia, the Postal Service issued a 32¢ commemorative stamp to mark the 100th anniversary of the first modern Olympics. The place was the Merchandise Mart in downtown Atlanta, where Olymphilex 96, an international Olympic and sports stamp show, had opened the day before.

The event brought to 21 the number of U.S. stamps issued in 1996 to salute the Games of Atlanta. It was the first, however, to be dedicated in the host city. The 20-variety Centennial Olympic Games pane, which USPS originally had intended to issue in Atlanta May 2, was issued on that date in Washington, D.C., instead, after a falling-out between USPS and the U.S. Olympic Committee over the Postal Service's plans to market T-shirts bearing modified replicas of the stamps. That dispute later was resolved amicably (see separate chapter).

For the July 19 event, the Postal Service, in the words of its news release, issued "a classic stamp evoking visions of the Olympics' origins in ancient Greece." The stamp bore the image of *Discobolus*, a statue of a nude athlete throwing the discus, by the Greek sculptor Myron of Eleutherae. Printed in single-color intaglio by Ashton-Potter (USA) Ltd., it was the first all-intaglio stamp to be produced for USPS by the

147

Williamsville, New York, printer.

The stamp was issued in panes of 20 with a wide selvage on the left bearing an enlarged photographic reproduction of the statue and a descriptive text. The picture and wording on the selvage were printed by offset, making this the first U.S. stamp issue in which the stamp and the selvage were printed by different processes. The perforations extended to the edges of the pane at top and bottom and on the right to make it easier for postal clerks to break the pane into smaller units.

Because the panes were printed on phosphored paper, Ashton-Potter added a varnish coating to the selvage area in order to forestall any possible use of the selvage, or a portion of it, as a "stamp." Without a coating to kill the phosphor signal from the paper, the selvage would activate the automated facer-canceler equipment in post offices in the same way the stamps themselves do.

Discobolus was no stranger to U.S. stamps. The statue's first postal appearance was on a 5¢ stamp issued in 1932 to mark the Summer Olympics in Los Angeles. It next appeared as part of the emblem of the American Turners Society on a 3¢ stamp of 1948 commemorating the Turners' 100th anniversary. It was featured again in 1965 on a 5¢ Physical Fitness stamp marking the centennial of the American Sokol Organization, a chapter of the international Sokol gymnastic society founded in Prague in 1862.

Although Myron's original bronze sculpture of *Discobolus* (circa 450 B.C.) no longer exists, several copies sculpted in marble during Roman times survive today. The image on the 1996 stamp was based on the marble copy housed in the Museo Nazionale Romano delle Terme in Rome. The statue captures the athlete at the maximum point in his backswing before

From left to right, these three stamps were issued in 1932, 1948 and 1965. Their designs are based on different copies of Myron's classic statue Discobolus. *The first commemorated the 1932 Olympic Games in Los Angeles, while the other two honored organizations that promote physical fitness.*

Art director Carl Herrman commissioned McRay Magleby to prepare these concept sketches for an international-rate stamp, to be issued jointly with Australia, commemorating the passing of the Olympic torch from Atlanta, site of the 1996 summer Olympic Games, to Sydney, site of the games of 2000. CSAC gave its approval to the semijumbo vertical design showing a stylized torch with portions of the two countries' flags comprising the flame. The joint issue never got beyond the early planning stages, however. On the alternative design, the runner in the Northern Hemisphere is red, the figure in the Southern Hemisphere is green and the globe is blue.

launching the discus. His torso is twisted into a crouching position, his head is nearly parallel to the ground and looking to the right, and his left hand rests on his right knee.

This image differs from the one engraved on the 1932 Olympic commemorative, which was modeled after a somewhat different marble copy of *Discobolus*, on display at the British Museum in London. In that sculpture, the athlete is more erect and is looking down instead of to the side. It also differs from the image on the 1965 Sokol commemorative, which was based on a bronze reproduction cast in Florence, Italy, and given by Italy to the people of the United States in 1956. The statue stands in Edward J. Kelley Park in Washington, D.C.

The first appearance of *Discobolus* on any postage stamp was on two Greek stamps of 1896 issued to celebrate the first Olympic Games of the modern era, held that year in Athens. Since then, the statue has been shown numerous times on stamps of the world.

In addition to the 20 Classic Collection stamps and the Discobolus stamp, the Postal Service might have issued yet another commemorative in 1996 in connection with the Centennial Olympic Games. Australia, where the summer Olympics of 2000 will be held, had proposed to USPS in mid-1995 that the two countries issue matching stamps with a design featuring the "passing of the torch" from Atlanta to Sydney, the next host city. Carl

Carl Herrman himself created this whimsical design for the proposed U.S.-Australia joint issue, showing an Australian kangaroo carrying the American torch-bearer in its pouch.

Herrman, the art director for the Classic Collections and Discobolus stamps, commissioned McRay Magleby (designer of the Utah Statehood Centennial stamp of 1996) to develop some design concepts, and one of his images — a stylized torch with portions of the U.S. and Australia flags comprising the flame — actually was approved by the Citizens' Stamp Advisory Committee.

But the project never came off. There wasn't adequate time in which to work out all the details, according to a USPS official. In addition, the official said, "Australia really wanted to do a hologram stamp, and not only did we not have time to develop one, we didn't have the OK from the Environmental Protection Agency to do holograms as stamps because of the environmental issues involved. We now have that OK.

Carl Herrman proposed these four triangular stamps to commemorate the centennial of the modern Olympic Games. Each one bears a photographic reproduction of the gold medals of one of the summer Games held in the United States: St. Louis, 1904; Los Angeles, 1932 and 1984; and Atlanta, 1996. The decorative frame and "USA 32" were designed on scratchboard by John Thompson of Hellman Associates, who had designed the James K. Polk commemorative stamp of 1995.

"Also, by then the opening salvo of the hassle with the U.S. Olympic Committee had taken place, and we said, 'Enough is enough.' "

If the joint issue had materialized, it would have been the second between the United States and Australia. In 1988 the two countries each had issued a single stamp with a common design commemorating Australia's bicentennial.

The Design

Discobolus wasn't Carl Herrman's first choice of design subject. His original idea for the 100th anniversary of the Olympics was of something quite different.

What Herrman proposed was a set of four triangular stamps — a first for the United States. Each stamp would have featured one of the four summer Olympic Games held in the United States: 1904, St. Louis; 1932 and 1984, Los Angeles; and 1996, Atlanta.

The centerpiece of each triangle-shaped design would have been a pho-

Herrman's plan called for the triangle-shaped stamps to be arranged on a souvenir-type pane in this manner, 16 stamps to a pane. The idea was turned down because officials weren't confident that the stamps' printer could master the problems this novel format would present in time to meet the production schedule. However, the format later was used for a pair of commemoratives in 1997.

tographic reproduction of the gold medal made for that city's Olympic Games. The stamps would have been laid out on the pane in se-tenant groups of four, with the points of each quartet of stamps meeting in the center.

CSAC and the USPS staff were intrigued by the concept. However, the production staff was unable to assure them that the printer could successfully overcome the problems of printing and perforating stamps in this unfamiliar format and get them out on time. So Herrman was sent back to the drawing board. (The format and frame design were kept in mind, however, and used in 1997 for a pair of 32¢ stamps issued to promote Pacific 97, the world philatelic exhibition in San Francisco, California.)

Seeking ideas in a local library, Herrman found a book about the Olym-

After the triangular stamps were turned down, Carl Herrman produced this design concept for five stamps depicting the Discobolus *reproduction in the British Museum. The stamps would differ only in background color (each color matching one of the Olympic rings) and inscription (calling attention to the first modern Olympics in Athens in 1896, and each of the four summer Olympic Games held in the United States). The colors were: Athens, black; St. Louis, blue; Los Angeles 1932, yellow; Los Angeles 1984, red; Atlanta, green.*

After USPS officials decided that five varieties of a stamp with the same basic design were four too many, Herrman produced this single all-purpose Discobolus design. For the stamp that ultimately was issued, however, he abandoned the anatomically revealing British Museum version of the statue in favor of the more modest version in Rome's Museo delle Terme.

pics containing a picture of the *Discobolus* statue at the British Museum. Working with this illustration, he designed a set of five conventionally shaped stamps, each with a background in the color of one of the five Olympic rings: black, red, yellow, blue and green. Again, the stamps celebrated the four U.S. summer Olympic Games, with the fifth stamp commemorating the first modern Olympics in Athens in 1896.

This design concept met a more favorable reception at USPS headquarters. In the end, however, officials decided that to issue multiple stamps that differed only in background color and inscription would be to invite justified criticism that they were manufacturing unnecessary additional varieties. Herrman was told to design a single stamp and drop the idea of recalling the U.S. Olympic Games of the past.

In his finished design, Herrman showed the Rome version of *Discobolus* instead of the one in the British Museum. The Rome statue's pose was superior aesthetically, he thought. Also, by using it he could avoid a debate within the Postal Service over propriety. The nude athlete's genitals were visible on the picture of the British Museum statue, but were discreetly out of sight in the photograph that he obtained from the national museum in Rome.

Herrman placed the statue against a white background inside a single-line frame. The athlete's right hand, holding the discus, covers and extends beyond the frameline in the upper-left corner. "Centennial Olympic Games" and "1896 1996" are in Friz Quadrata type, the same font used on the 20-variety pane that was issued May 2 for the Atlanta Olympics. In the lower-right corner is the denomination, "USA" and the Olympic rings in the same style and relationship in which they appear on the 20 earlier stamps — a style and relationship that were dictated by the U.S. Olympic Committee.

The color of the intaglio stamp itself is brown. The offset colors used in the selvage are black, magenta, yellow and beige. Some postal officials expressed disappointment in the quality of the engraving on the stamp, which was done by Armandina Lozano for Ashton-Potter. "It was very weak," said one. "The light and shadow and the beauty of the statue weren't interpreted well."

First-Day Facts

Loren E. Smith, USPS senior vice president and chief marketing officer, dedicated the stamp at Olymphilex 96. Speakers included John Krimsky Jr., deputy secretary general of the U.S. Olympic Committee; Manfred Bergman of the philatelic department of the International Olympic Committee; and Ralph Boston, who won medals in the long jump for the United States in three successive Olympic Games (gold, 1960; silver, 1964; and bronze, 1968).

Azeezaly S. Jaffer, manager of stamp services for USPS, presided. Honored guests included Nancy B. Zielinski Clark, chairman of Olymphilex 96, and Joan Benoit Samuelson, 1984 Olympic gold medalist in the marathon.

Olymphilex, the World Olympic and Sports Stamp Exhibition, was cre-

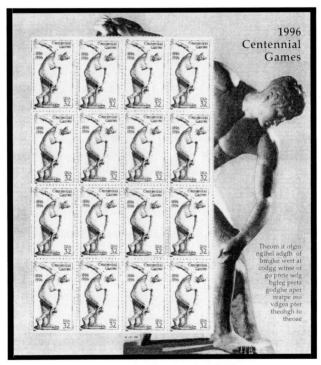

This is an early mockup of a pane of Discobolus stamps, with dummy text in the selvage. It contains only 16 stamps instead of the 20 that were on the pane as issued. Notice that this mockup uses both versions of the statue that had been considered for the stamp design: the Rome version on the stamps and the British Museum version — anatomy discreetly covered — for the selvage.

ated in 1985 by H.E. Juan Antonio Samaranch, president of the IOC. Previous exhibitions were held in Lausanne, Switzerland; Rome, Italy; Seoul, South Korea; Warna, Bulgaria; and Barcelona, Spain.

In addition to Olympic and sports stamps, Olymphilex 96 showcased coins and Olympic memorabilia. The stamps section contained more than 17,000 pages of exhibits, including rare covers, early Olympic postmarks and errors on Olympic stamps and souvenir sheets. Besides the United States, four other stamp-issuing entities held first-day ceremonies for Olympic stamps at Olymphilex: the United Nations, Nauru, Australia and Papua New Guinea.

Olymphilex was the only place in Atlanta where collectors could obtain official cancellations from all Olympic venues.

The earliest-known prerelease use of a Discobolus stamp was on covers machine-canceled in Providence, Rhode Island, and San Francisco, California, on July 13, six days before its official first-day sale.

Date of Issue: August 1, 1996

Catalog Number: Scott 3088

Colors: black, cyan, magenta, yellow

First-Day Cancel: Dubuque, Iowa

First-Day Cancellations: 215,181 (includes self-adhesive version)

Format: Panes of 50, vertical, 10 across, 5 down. Offset printing plates of 200 subjects (10 across, 20 around).

Overall Stamp Size: .99 by 1.56 inches; 25.1mm by 39.6mm

Perforations: 11.1 (Wista and Gammeler stroke perforator)

Selvage Markings: "© USPS/1995." ".32/x50/$16.00." "PLATE/POSITION" and diagram.

Designer and Art Director: Carl Herrman of Ponte Vedra Beach, Florida

Typographer: John Boyd, Anagraphics Inc., New York, New York

Modeler: Joseph Sheeran of Ashton-Potter (USA) Ltd.

Project Manager: Vance Harris, USPS

Stamp Manufacturing: Stamps printed by Ashton-Potter (USA) Ltd. of Williamsville, New York, on offset portion of a Stevens Varisize Security Documents webfed 6-color offset, 3-color intaglio press. Stamps perforated, processed and shipped by Ashton-Potter.

Quantity Ordered and Distributed: 103,400,000

Plate Number Detail: 1 set of 4 offset plate numbers preceded by the letter P in selvage above or below each corner stamp

Plate Number Combinations Reported: P1111, P2222

Paper Supplier: Paper Corporation of the United States/Brown Bridge

Tagging: phosphored paper

The Stamp

On August 1, USPS issued a stamp to commemorate the 150th anniversary of the statehood of Iowa. The first-day city was Dubuque, Iowa's first incorporated community.

Like the Tennessee Bicentennial stamp issued two months earlier, the Iowa stamp was produced by two different printers in two versions: conventional lick-and-stick and self-adhesive. The conventional version was available nationwide August 2. The self-adhesive version was sold only at post offices in Iowa and at philatelic centers around the country (see next chapter).

The Iowa stamp had one other thing in common with the Tennessee commemorative, and with the Smithsonian Institution stamp issued earlier in the year as well. Each of the three 1996 stamps marked the anniversary of an event that had been postally commemorated on a previous anniversary 50 years before, in 1946. The earlier Iowa stamp (Scott 942), for the state's centennial, bore a 3¢ denomination and depicted the state flag on an outline map of Iowa flanked by cornstalks, representing Iowa's best-known agricultural product.

Ashton-Potter (USA) Ltd. printed the 1996 Iowa lick-and-stick variety in panes of 50. As the company often does with its single-design offset-printed stamps, it incorporated microprinting in the design for added security against counterfeiting. The word "IOWA" in black capitals can be found running vertically between the first and second full rows of corn from the right in the lower-right portion of the stamp.

In addition to the earlier statehood stamp, two previous U.S. postal issues had commemorated Iowa's attainment of territorial status, preceding statehood. The territorial centennial was marked with a 3¢ stamp in 1938 (Scott 838) picturing the Old Capitol in Iowa City, and its sesqui-

This 3¢ blue stamp of 1946 (Scott 942) commemorated Iowa's centennial of statehood. Designed by Victor S. McCloskey Jr., it depicts an Iowa flag on an outline map of the state flanked by cornstalks.

157

On the lick-and-stick version of the stamp (but not the self-adhesive), the word IOWA in microtype can be found between the vertical rows of corn on the right side.

centennial inspired a postal card in 1988 (Scott UX123).

Like the other 49 states, Iowa was represented with a stamp on each of two 50-stamp panes: the State Flags of 1976 (Scott 1661) and the State Birds and Flowers of 1982 (Scott 1967). Iowa native Herbert Hoover, 31st president of the United States, has been pictured on two stamps, and another Iowan, Lee De Forest, the "Father of Radio," was postally recognized when his audion tube, an invention that made possible radio broadcasting, was shown on a Progress in Electronics airmail stamp (Scott C86).

The United States obtained Iowa from France in the Louisiana Purchase of 1803. Until the early 1830s, Iowa remained Indian land, officially closed to permanent settlement. But as a result of the Black Hawk War of 1832, the Sauk and Fox Indians ceded a 50-mile-wide strip along the Mississippi River for $640,000 and settlers quickly staked their claims in this so-called "Black Hawk Purchase."

Two years later Iowa was attached to the Michigan Territory for governmental purposes. Later it was transferred to the newly created Wisconsin Territory, and Burlington, in the territory's Iowa District, served as a temporary capital of Wisconsin. Finally, on June 12, 1838, President Martin Van Buren signed the bill creating the Territory of Iowa and including in its borders much of Minnesota and the Dakotas. Iowa City was made the territorial capital.

Iowans resisted statehood at first for a very practical reason: As long as the region was a territory, they didn't have to pay the salaries of local officials. Even after Congress had passed a bill admitting Iowa to the Union, residents rejected the honor out of dissatisfaction with the proposed boundaries.

Eventually, however, the voters and Congress agreed on a compromise, and on December 28, 1846, President James K. Polk signed the act making Iowa the 29th state. Iowa adopted its present state constitution in 1857, and under that document the capital was moved from Iowa City to its present location, Des Moines.

The Design

The Iowa stamp is commemorative size, vertically arranged, and reproduces a detail from *Young Corn*, Iowa artist Grant Wood's 1931 painting of an idealized farm landscape.

Art director-designer Carl Herrman made the necessary adaptation after experimenting with a semijumbo stamp that showed the entire painting. The decision to use the smaller commemorative size, which necessitated using only a portion of the picture, was made to avoid any accusations of favoritism by other states. The detail Herrman selected was from the right side of Wood's artwork, containing the farmhouse and the more heavily wooded area.

The staff of Hellman Associates of Waterloo, Iowa, prepared this assortment of concept sketches as possible designs for the Iowa Statehood stamp. The illustrators found most of their subjects in Iowa's farms, people and livestock; one suggested a design based on bicycle racing, a sport that has become very popular in Iowa. Some added rainbows or shooting stars in the skies overhead.

More concept sketches for the Iowa Statehood stamp, by the staff of Hellman Associates.

Herrman had worked up an alternative design, also in semijumbo size, based on another 1931 Grant Wood painting, *Fall Plowing*. The composition of this one didn't lend itself to cropping, and it was put aside in favor of *Young Corn*.

Although a work by Grant Wood might seem a natural choice for an Iowa statehood stamp, Herrman and USPS officials arrived at this solution only after a long and involved design-selection process that saw their first-choice design summarily rejected by Iowa's governor, Terry Branstad, and the Iowa Sesquicentennial Commission.

Herrman had begun the process by asking Bob Hellman of Hellman Associates of Waterloo, Iowa, a design company, to put his large staff of illustrators to work turning out design concepts for the Iowa stamp. The firm had given Herrman similar help in developing a design for the POW-MIA commemorative stamp of 1995, and a Hellman artist, John Thompson, had designed the James K. Polk commemorative, also issued in 1995.

The staff responded to the assignment with nearly two dozen sketches, most of them in colored pencil, pastel or felt-tip marker. The artists focused mostly on Iowa's rural areas, people and livestock, although some showed cities on the horizon. Rainbows or shooting stars added a romantic touch to a few of the sketches.

The design that Herrman and CSAC liked best showed a plump, smiling, grandmotherly looking woman with her arms full of home-canned vegetables and preserves. They told the illustrator to make some alterations ("slim face but keep robust look," a note of instruction said) and the committee approved it for the finished stamp, subject to the approval of the appropriate officials in Iowa.

That approval wasn't forthcoming. In a letter to Frank Thomas, a Postal Service marketing specialist, dated July 19, Governor Branstad and Robert D. Ray, chairman of the Sesquicentennial Commission, called the design "unacceptable."

"It reinforces a stereotypical image of Iowa which does not appropriately represent our state," the officials wrote. "We strongly encourage the committee to develop and review alternative designs which would depict

Carl Herrman developed this design in the semijumbo size from a color photograph he found in a brochure distributed by the Iowa Division of Tourism. The farm and its red barn are in a hilly area of northeast Iowa known as "Little Switzerland."

the scenic beauty and progressive nature of Iowa.

"Consideration should be given to an attractive symbol of Iowa which represents our strong track record on human rights. Iowa's motto, 'Our Liberties We Prize and Our Rights We will Maintain,' should be a guiding influence in stamp development."

Pondering this abundance of specifications, Herrman went back to the drawing board. He had Hellman prepare a design containing the state bird, the state flower and a portion of the state flag containing the motto that Governor Branstad had quoted. That would be the design he would recommend if all else failed, Herrman said. In the meantime, he sought other ideas.

He found one idea in a brochure distributed by the Iowa Division of Tourism: a picture-book color photograph of a farm, complete with red barn, located in a hilly area of northeast Iowa known as "Little Switzerland." He developed a semijumbo stamp design using a portion of that photograph.

But Herrman drew more solid inspiration from a book from the Sesquicentennial Commission depicting merchandise related to the anniversary. "Grant Wood was a common thread throughout this book," Herrman recalled. "So I started tracking down Grant Wood paintings ...

"Even though a Grant Wood painting wasn't what the governor had

This collection of state symbols — state bird (Eastern goldfinch), flower (wild rose) and flag — would have been the Postal Service's next offering to Governor Branstad and the Sesquicentennial Commission if they hadn't approved the Grant Wood design.

162

Young Corn, *the 1931 Grant Wood painting from which a detail was extracted for use on the Iowa Statehood stamp.*

asked for, I said to myself: How could any state with such a famous artist, who paints the landscapes of his state so beautifully, not find one of those acceptable? So I took a gamble. We worked up a couple of the images. The best one was *Young Corn*, which became the stamp, and it went out there (to Iowa) and was approved."

Young Corn is in oil on masonite panel and is 30 inches wide by 24 inches deep. It is part of the Cedar Rapids, Iowa, Community School District Collection in the Cedar Rapids Museum of Art. The collection furnished a color transparency of the painting to the Postal Service for use in preparing the stamp.

Herrman placed the word "Iowa," in Clarendon capitals, in the lower-left corner of the design, using the colors of the University of Iowa: gold for the letters, black for the dropped shadow. In a preliminary version of the design, he included a line

Grant Wood, in a 1932 self-portrait.

163

Grant Wood's Young Corn *was depicted virtually in its entirety on this semijumbo-size design. However, the Postal Service decided it would be best not to give Iowa a larger stamp than other states had received for their anniversaries, and so the painting had to be cropped to fit into a vertical commemorative-size design. USPS also turned down the idea of identifying the painter and painting on the stamp, as is done here in small type beneath the bottom frameline.*

of small type beneath the bottom frameline identifying the painting and painter, but officials rejected that idea as contrary to Postal Service policy.

Grant Wood's farm landscapes were analyzed by Wanda M. Corn in *Grant Wood: The Regionalist Vision*, a catalog of a 1983-84 traveling exhibit of the artist's works. She called these landscapes "without a doubt, the most sensuous and passionate works he painted."

"Mingling eroticism with ecstacy, Wood made the relationship between the farmer and mother earth into a Wagnerian love duet," Corn continued. "While mother earth is always the principal protagonist, overwhelming the farmer in scale and vitality, she is always loving and benevolent. In Wood's idyllic farmscapes, man lives in complete harmony with nature; he is the earth's caretaker, coaxing her into abundance, bringing coherence and beauty to her surfaces.

"Wood's way of describing the earth's goodness and fertility is an obvious one; he turned the landscape into a gigantic, reclining goddess, anthropomorphizing the contours of fields and hills so that they look like rounded thighs, bulging breasts, and pregnant bellies, all of them swelling and breathing with sexual fullness. Within nature's fecund forms, Wood tucks a tiny farmhouse, the home of those who tend and order this gigantic living force. Like artists or seamstresses, the farmers make abstract art out of their fields ...

"In *Young Corn*, the farmer and his children tend herringbone rows of new plants; and in *Fall Plowing*, the farmers have lovingly arranged tidy rows of corn shocks and plowed fields into perfectly parallel furrows."

Another 1931 Grant Wood painting, Fall Plowing, *also was considered for use on the stamp. It is shown here in the semijumbo format. However, unlike* Young Corn, *its composition made it difficult to adapt to the smaller commemorative size the Postal Service chose to use.*

Wood (1891-1942), who was born near Cedar Rapids and lived most of his life in that city and Iowa City, was one of a group of Midwestern contemporaries who specialized in painting the people and landscapes of their native region. By far his best-known work is his painting of a solemn farm father and equally solemn unmarried daughter, *American Gothic*.

Another of those Midwestern regional artists, Wood's friend Thomas Hart Benton, had one of his works adapted for use on an earlier statehood commemorative: the Missouri Sesquicentennial stamp of 1971 (Scott 1426). At that time the Postal Service had no objection to reproducing artists' names on stamps, and Benton — who was still living at the time — got full credit in the stamp design.

First-Day Facts

Deputy Postmaster General Michael Coughlin, a former Iowan, dedicated the Iowa stamps at a first-day ceremony at the Dubuque Five Flags Center. Also participating were Governor Branstad; Robert Ray, the Sesquicentennial Commission chairman; Thomas C. Johnson, USPS district manager for customer service and sales; and Terry Duggan, mayor of Dubuque.

It was Governor Branstad's second first-day ceremony that focused on an Iowa anniversary. As governor, he also had taken part in the dedication of the Iowa Territory postal card in Burlington, Iowa, July 2, 1988.

32¢ IOWA STATEHOOD SESQUICENTENNIAL (SELF-ADHESIVE)

Date of Issue: August 1, 1996

Catalog Number: Scott 3089, single stamp; 3089a, pane of 20

Colors: yellow, magenta, cyan, black (stamp); blue (back)

First-Day Cancel: Dubuque, Iowa

First-Day Cancellations: 215,181 (includes water-activated version)

Format: Panes of 20, vertical, 5 across, 4 down, with horizontal peel-off strip between second and third horizontal rows. Offset printing plates of 240 subjects (20 across, 12 around).

Overall Stamp Size: .99 by 1.56 inches; 25.14mm by 39.62mm

Perforations: Die-cut simulated perforations

Selvage Markings: on peel-off strip: "© USPS 1995 * Peel here to fold * Self-adhesive * DO NOT WET"

Liner Markings: none

Back Markings: "Twenty/Self-adhesive Stamps/$6.40/UNITED STATES/POSTAL SERVICE ™/We Deliver For You." USPS logo. Universal Product Code (UPC), promotion for *Stamps etc.* catalog, all on backing paper.

Designer and Art Director: Carl Herrman of Ponte Vedra Beach, Florida

Typographer: John Boyd, Anagraphics Inc., New York, New York

Project Manager: Vance Harris, USPS

Stamp Manufacturing: Stamps manufactured by Banknote Corporation of America (BCA), Browns Summit, North Carolina, on a Goebel offset press. Stamps processed and finished at BCA.

Quantity Ordered and Distributed: 60,000,000

Plate Number Detail: 1 set of 4 offset plate numbers preceded by the letter B at each end of peel-off strip

Plate Number Combination Reported: B1111

Paper Supplier: Paper Corporation of the United States/Brown Bridge

Tagging: phosphored paper

The Stamp

The Iowa Statehood self-adhesive stamp was printed by Banknote Corporation of America and sold in panes of 20. Removal of a narrow peel-off strip across the center of the pane enabled the user to fold the pane into a kind of booklet.

The Iowa stamp was the second U.S. commemorative to be issued in self-adhesive form. The first was the Tennessee Statehood stamp that was issued May 31, 1996. Like the Iowa stamp, the Tennessee stamp also was issued in a conventional water-activated version.

The Iowa self-adhesive panes contained serpentine die-cutting between the stamps, forming simulated perforations. The six interior stamps of each pane were "perforated" on all four sides. Each of the remaining 14 stamps had at least one straight edge.

Like the water-activated version of the Iowa stamp, which was made by Ashton-Potter (USA) Ltd., the self-adhesive was printed by the offset method. But whereas Ashton-Potter included only one piece of security microprinting in the design of its stamp, Banknote Corporation of America provided three. In fact, the microprinting on the Iowa self-adhesive stamp is more varied and at the same time more difficult to see than on any previous U.S. stamp.

Each of the three tiny "USPS" inscriptions is printed in one of the process colors used for the stamp: black, cyan and yellow. All three require a good magnifying glass to discern, and, in addition, the yellow "USPS," because of its lightness and location, can only be seen through a blue film. The microprinting can be found in these locations:

Black — Along the left edge of the design, just above the lowest tree-

This enlargement shows where a microprinted "USPS" can be found in three locations on the Iowa self-adhesive stamp. The black "USPS," the clearest of the three, is on the left edge of the design, just above the lowest treetop. The cyan microprinting is in the cornfield in the extreme lower-right corner of the design, between the second and third rows of corn from the right. The yellow "USPS," which can only be seen through a blue film, is on the right edge of the design, on the light-blue sky, just above the distant horizon.

top. This is the clearest of the three pieces of microprinting.

Cyan — In the cornfield in the extreme lower-right corner of the design, between the second and third rows of corn from the right.

Yellow — Along the right edge of the design, on the light-blue sky, just above the distant horizon.

BNA originally intended to print a fourth "USPS" — in magenta, the remaining process color — in the upper-left portion of the stamp over a light-green part of the distant meadow. However, on the proofs this microprinting could be seen with the naked eye, and officials decided it would have detracted from the design, so the printer removed it.

The Iowa self-adhesives were intended for sale only at Iowa post offices, but collectors could obtain them at philatelic centers nationwide, as well as by mail from the Philatelic Fulfillment Service Center.

The Design

Because the water-activated and self-adhesive versions of the Iowa Statehood stamp were produced by two different printers, there are subtle differences in the appearance of the two stamps. These are in addition to the differences in the microprinting (see above).

The self-adhesive design is about ½ millimeter taller than the design of the conventional stamp. The year date "1996" in the lower-left corner, outside the design frame, is smaller on the self-adhesive. The two designs are cropped slightly differently, so that on the water-activated version, the back porch on the farmhouse in Grant Wood's painting can be seen. On the self-adhesive, it is missing. The "USA 32" is closer to the treetops on the self-adhesive.

First-Day Facts

For details on the first-day ceremony in Dubuque August 1, see previous chapter.

32¢ RURAL FREE DELIVERY CENTENNIAL

Date of Issue: August 7, 1996

Catalog Number: Scott 3090

Colors: magenta, yellow, cyan, black (offset); red (PMS 200C), blue (PMS 301C) (intaglio)

First-Day Cancel: Charleston, West Virginia

First-Day Cancellations: 192,070

Format: Panes of 20, horizontal, 4 across, 5 down. Offset printing plates of 120 subjects (10 across, 12 around). Intaglio printing sleeves of 120 subjects (10 across, 12 around).

Overall Stamp Size: .99 by 1.56 inches; 25.1mm by 39.6mm

Perforations: 11.1 (Eureka perforator)

Selvage Markings: "© USPS 1995." "20 x .32 = $6.40." "PLATE/POSITION" and diagram.

Designer, Typographer and Art Director: Richard Sheaff of Norwood, Massachusetts

Modeler: Peter Cocci, Bureau of Engraving and Printing

Engraver: BEP (chemical etching)

Project Manager: Vance Harris, USPS

Stamp Manufacturing: Stamps printed by BEP on the 4-color offset, 3-color intaglio webfed F press (801).

Quantity Ordered and Distributed: 134,000,000

Plate/Cylinder Number Detail: 1 set of 4 offset plate numbers and 1 red intaglio cylinder number in selvage above or below each corner stamp

Plate/Cylinder Number Combinations Reported: 1111-1, 1112-1, 1122-1, 1123-1, 2223-1, 2224-1, 2235-1, 3235-1, 3236-1

Paper Supplier: Westvaco/Ivex

Tagging: phosphored paper

The Stamp

On August 7, the Postal Service issued a stamp to commemorate the 100th anniversary of Rural Free Delivery (RFD), the service that brought mail directly to the homes of farmers and other residents of the nation's countryside.

The stamp was the result of a long lobbying campaign by the National Rural Letter Carriers' Association (NRLCA). As far back as 1984, officers of NRLCA wrote to the postmaster general asking for an RFD centennial stamp when the time came. Thereafter, said Scottie B. Hicks, the association's president, the officers would put in a word on behalf of the stamp whenever they met with Postal Service officials.

"Tony Frank (Anthony M. Frank, the immediate past postmaster general) had said that he couldn't envision anything being an impairment to getting it done," Hicks said. "But, of course, postmaster generals come and go. So it was a matter of having a constant awareness of the commitment ... and following up to make sure it didn't fall through the cracks."

Frank's successor, Postmaster General Marvin T. Runyon, was happy to honor his predecessors' commitment to a group whose good will is of such great importance to the Postal Service. On August 11, 1995, almost a year before the stamp's issuance, Runyon joined with Hicks to unveil its design at the organization's 91st national convention in Washington, D.C. And the stamp itself was dedicated at NRLCA's 92nd convention in Charleston, West Virginia.

Unfortunately, the selection of Charleston as the first-day city came at the expense of another West Virginia municipality, Charles Town, 325 miles to the east, where RFD actually had its beginning October 1, 1896. Among those in Charles Town who were offended at the slight was Tom Owens, the community's former postmaster. "There is nothing to connect Charleston to this event at all," Owens told Bill McAllister of *Linn's Stamp News*. "This is the one time for this community to get its name in the limelight."

Owens appealed to the Postal Service and to members of the West Virginia congressional delegation for dual first-day ceremonies, one in Charleston, the other in Charles Town. But although there was ample precedent for such events — the Tennessee Statehood stamp issued a little more than two months earlier had had three official first-day cities — the idea was turned down.

However, Charles Town wasn't forgotten. On October 1, the actual centennial of the service, the community was the site of a special ceremony attended by the entire governing board of NRLCA, high officials of the Postal Service and other dignitaries. A rider on horseback re-enacted the first mail deliveries, and USPS contributed a commemorative postmark for the occasion.

Coincidentally, 50 years earlier Charles Town had gotten another cancellation, in lieu of a stamp, to commemorate an RFD anniversary. In 1946, the Post Office Department had been urged to issue commemora-

The urban predecessor of Rural Free Delivery was City Mail Delivery, the centennial of which was commemorated by this Norman Rockwell-designed stamp in 1963 (Scott 1238).

tive stamps marking 50 years of Rural Free Delivery and of the automobile industry as well. However, postal officials had decided to focus on centennials and sesquicentennials and to resist pleas for additional 50th anniversary stamps, of which several recently had been issued. So Charles Town had to settle for a two-line machine-cancel slogan, in use between August 12 and October 15, 1946, to call attention to RFD's 50th birthday.

The 1996 RFD stamp was printed by the Bureau of Engraving and Printing by a combination of offset and intaglio and issued in panes of 20.

RFD had its origins in the late 19th century when farmers and farm groups, principally the National Grange, began to press for mail delivery service comparable to that provided to residents of large cities since 1863. (The 100th anniversary of free city delivery was commemorated in 1963 with a 5¢ stamp, Scott 1238, designed by popular illustrator Norman Rockwell.)

"It's hard to imagine the isolation in rural America back in the 1800s," as Postmaster General Runyon said in announcing the RFD stamp. "There was not much in the way of communications — no telephones, radios or television. People stayed in touch by mail, period. The problem was, they had to go to the post office to do it. For many people, it was weeks between trips to town, and many, many miles to stay in touch and informed."

The prime congressional advocate of Rural Free Delivery was Representative Thomas Watson of Georgia. Watson, a fervent defender of the small farmer, later would abandon the Democratic Party for the newly formed Populist Party and be its candidate for vice president in 1896 and president in 1904. He had an ally in the Republican postmaster general,

A horse-drawn rural mail vehicle almost identical to the one shown on the 1996 commemorative was depicted on the 4¢ stamp of the parcel post series in 1912 (Scott Q4). C.A. Huston's design reportedly was based on a photograph of a wagon used on a rural route around Schuyler, Nebraska.

John Wanamaker, who in 1891 conducted a test of free delivery in 40-odd small towns and villages as a forerunner of a possible rural delivery service.

However, Wanamaker had left office in 1893 when Congress finally enacted Watson's bill for an experimental Rural Free Delivery service and appropriated a modest $10,000 to cover the cost. The new postmaster general was Wilson S. Bissell, an appointee of Democratic President Grover Cleveland, and Bissell refused to spend the money, contending that RFD would bankrupt the nation. Bissell's successor, William L. Wilson of West Virginia, was more open-minded; his objection to the congressional mandate was that $10,000 was too small an amount to launch such a bold new initiative.

In 1896 Congress obliged by putting up $40,000, and Wilson chose to test Rural Free Delivery in his own hometown of Charles Town and two nearby villages, Halltown and Uvilla. Here RFD began October 1 with five routes covered by carriers on horseback with mail in their saddlebags. By the end of the year, Wilson's test had been extended to 41 additional routes in 28 states.

In his October 1897 annual report, Postmaster General James A. Gary said:

"It would be difficult to point to any like expenditure of public money which has been more generously appreciated by the people, or which has conferred greater benefits in proportion to the amount expended ...

"Another noticeable fact is the loyal service of the carriers employed in the rural districts. Though receiving a maximum pay of but $300 a year and furnishing their own means of conveyance, many of those men ride 20 or 30 miles a day in all kinds of weather, over every description of road, and often across farms where there are no roads at all, with cheerful alacrity."

To apply for a rural-delivery route at the turn of the century, at least 100 families along the proposed route had to sign a petition, which then went to the local congressman or senator for a recommendation. Such a recommendation rarely was denied, and the number of RFD routes grew rapidly. RFD transformed rural life, enabling farmers to stay in touch with the outside world — and each other — on a daily basis. For the first time, for example, they could receive daily newspapers by mail. The authorization of the parcel post system in 1912 gave them a convenient way to shop. The combination of the Rural Free Delivery and parcel post systems made it possible for enterprising merchants to develop the great catalog mail-order firms.

Today, rural carriers deliver the mail daily on 54,442 rural routes over 2.7 million miles to 24.7 million delivery points. The National Rural Letter Carriers' Association, the union that represents these workers, has a membership of more than 93,000 regular, substitute, auxiliary and retired rural carriers.

The Design

When the RFD centennial stamp first was approved, art director Richard Sheaff commissioned Jim Lamb, the illustrator who designed the four Children's Classic Books stamps of 1993, to prepare some concept sketches. In the end, however, Sheaff and members of the Citizens' Stamp Advisory Committee's design subcommittee decided to base the design on photographs.

For this purpose, Sheaff combined two different photos. A sepia-toned picture of an early RFD carrier standing beside his horse and wagon is superimposed on a full-color image of a rural landscape, with trees and rolling hills in the distance. A red horizontal line defines the bottom edge of the inset photo. A large emblem with the initials "RFD" is in the lower-left corner. All these elements are offset-printed. The words "RURAL

Jim Lamb made these preliminary concept sketches for the Rural Free Delivery stamp. Later, it was decided to use photographs rather than a painting as the basis for the stamp design.

This is the photograph from Postal Service files of the rural mail carrier with his horse and wagon that was used on the Rural Free Delivery stamp. The identity of the carrier and the location are unknown. Based on the style of cap worn by the carrier, USPS estimates that the picture was made between 1912 and 1915.

Designer Richard Sheaff tried a variety of background and type arrangements to accompany the image of the rural mail carrier, including two different U.S. maps.

FREE DELIVERY," in blue Clarendon type, and "USA 32," in red, are intaglio.

The identity of the carrier in the photograph, and the location, are unknown. According to Jerry Mansfield of the U.S. Postal Service library, which provided the picture, it was taken sometime between 1912 and 1915, a period when carriers wore caps with a metal plate above the visor, like the one shown in the photo.

The location of the country scene in the background also is unknown. This photograph was a late replacement for another background photo showing a field of tall corn; the design with the corn actually had been approved by CSAC before Sheaff substituted the landscape photo, which he liked better. Earlier, Sheaff had tried two different maps of the United States as background, to represent the nationwide expansion of Rural Free Delivery after its modest beginning, but he was dissatisfied with the effect.

Sheaff's thought in designing the emblem in the corner with the initials "RFD" was to evoke the early rural mail service. "It suggests a postmark of the period, or a uniform badge or marking or epaulet of the period, but it's not meant to be specifically any of those things," he said.

First-Day Facts

Postmaster General Runyon dedicated the stamp in a ceremony at the Charleston Civic Center. Featured speakers included NRLCA president Scottie Hicks; Rick Morrison, a rural carrier from Charles Town, West Virginia; and Rick Esslinger, postmaster of Charleston. Diarmuid Dunne, USPS district manager, presided.

The earliest-reported prerelease use of the Rural Free Delivery stamp was on a cover machine-canceled in Madison, Wisconsin, July 27, 11 days before the dedication.

32¢ RIVERBOATS (SELF-ADHESIVE, 5 DESIGNS)

Date of Issue: August 22, 1996

Catalog Numbers: Scott 3091-3095 (single stamps); 3095a (vertical strip of 5)

Colors: yellow, magenta, cyan, black, red

First-Day Cancel: Orlando, Florida

First-Day Cancellations: 770,384

Format: Panes of 20, horizontal, 4 across, 5 down, on backing paper. Gravure printing cylinders of 200 (10 across, 20 around).

Overall Stamp Size: .99 by 1.56 inches; 25.146mm by 39.624mm

Perforations: Die-cut simulated perforations that penetrate backing paper. Backing paper on each stamp has vertical curved die-cut to facilitate its removal. Comco rotary die cutter used.

Selvage Markings: "© 1995 United States/Postal Service." ".32 x 20 = $6.40." "PLATE/POSITION" and diagram.

Designer: Dean Ellis of Amagansett, New York

Typographer: Tom Mann, Mann and Mann Graphics, Warrenton, Virginia

Art Director: Howard Paine

Project Manager: Elizabeth A. Altobell, USPS

177

Stamp Manufacturing: Stamps printed by Avery Dennison Security Printing Division, Clinton, South Carolina, on an 8-color Dai Nippon Kikko webfed gravure press. Stamps processed by Avery Dennison.

Quantity Ordered and Distributed: 160,000,000

Cylinder Number Detail: 1 set of 5 gravure cylinder numbers preceded by the letter V in selvage above upper-right and lower-left stamps on panes from right side of printing sheet and above upper-left and lower-right stamps on panes from left side of printing sheet.

Cylinder Number Combination Reported: V11111

Paper Supplier: Westvaco/Consolidated/Fasson

Tagging: phosphored paper

The Stamps

On August 22, the Postal Service issued a pane of 20 self-adhesive stamps featuring five historic steamboats that once carried passengers on inland river systems in the United States. The stamps had their first-day sale in Orlando, Florida, at Stampshow 96, the annual convention of the American Philatelic Society.

They were the first U.S. commemoratives to be issued only in the self-adhesive format. The two previous self-adhesive commemoratives, Tennessee and Iowa Statehood, had been produced as conventional lick-and-stick stamps as well.

The Riverboats stamps are laid out on the panes so that each vertical strip of five contains one specimen of each variety. Any block of six, whether two by three or three by two, will contain one of each variety plus one duplicate.

The stamps were printed by the gravure process by Avery-Dennison. They incorporated some innovative features that illustrated how swiftly the Postal Service was moving to improve the convenience and appeal of self-adhesive postage.

The die-cut simulated perforations penetrated the backing paper as well as the stamps, enabling postal clerks to divide the sheets and sell individual stamps or multiples. This feature also allowed collectors to easily remove and save mint singles, blocks or strips with the backing paper attached. Because of the novelty of it, USPS cautioned clerks in the internal *Postal Bulletin* to "first crease the section of stamps being sold vertically, then horizontally before tearing."

The peelable backing paper had a broad wavy-line die cut running down the center of each vertical row of stamps from the top edge of the pane to the bottom. Instead of having to peel a stamp off its backing paper, as they did in the past, users could separate the backing paper from a stamp at the die cut and remove it to expose the adhesive, as they would remove the backing from a standard adhesive bandage strip.

This **Linn's Stamp News** *mockup shows how a broad wavy die-cut runs down the center of the peelable backing paper on each Riverboats stamp, allowing the user to easily remove the paper from the stamp to expose the adhesive.*

Also, for the first time, USPS created a modification of the simulated-perf die cutting on selected panes to facilitate the removal of a full vertical strip of five varieties from the backing paper. This was done for the convenience of workers who make Postal Service products to be sold through the Philatelic Fulfillment Service Center, such as a Riverboats poster with the five different stamps affixed to it. The modification consisted of a partly incomplete die-cut between each of the five stamps in the strip.

Early in 1997, Philatelic Fulfillment made available to collectors strips with the die-cut variety. Sales were limited to two strips per customer.

Unlike previous self-adhesive stamp panes, the Riverboats panes had selvage on all four sides, like conventional water-activated stamps. Thus all 20 stamps on a pane had simulated perforations all around, with no straight edges.

The Riverboats stamps were a sequel to five stamps that were issued in booklet form in 1989. Those stamps, designed by Richard Schlecht, depicted vessels from the earliest period of American steamboating, the late 18th and early 19th centuries. At the time of their issuance, the Citizens' Stamp Advisory Committee and its subject subcommittee, headed by Mary Ann Owens, let it be known that they intended to issue additional stamps later, showing boats from a later era. When the time came to do it, officials at first envisioned the new set as another booklet of five varieties, but as the trend to self-stick stamps gathered momentum, they decided to change formats.

The boats on the 1989 set had been concentrated in the Eastern United States. For the second set, CSAC wanted geographic balance, with all major regions of the country represented. The committee also wanted vessels that were visually interesting as well as historically significant, with both major types of propulsion — sidewheelers and sternwheelers — represented.

In compiling a list of potential subjects, art director Howard Paine and designer Dean Ellis had access to a list of boats left over from CSAC's earlier research. But their principal resource person was Kevin Foster, a maritime historian for the U.S. National Park Service, who was enlisted for the project by PhotoAssist, the Postal Service's research consulting

179

firm. Foster helped them settle on five boats that met their specifications. He also helped PhotoAssist find accurate pictures and also verify the active service period of each vessel so year dates could be included on each stamp.

The boats chosen were: *Robert E. Lee*, which plied the Mississippi and Ohio Rivers; *Sylvan Dell*, East River/Delaware River; *Far West*, Missouri River; *Rebecca Everingham*, Apalachicola-Chattahoochee River; *Bailey Gatzert*, Columbia River/Puget Sound.

Near the turn of the century, riverboats were the fastest and most efficient way to transport goods between major inland ports in the United States. Their elegance also attracted many passengers looking to avoid the discomforts, and sometimes the hazards, of overland travel. The romance of American steamboats has been conveyed in many works of literature, most prominently *Life on the Mississippi* by Mark Twain, a reminiscence of his days as a steamboat pilot, and *Show Boat* by Edna Ferber, a novel that was made into a classic musical by Oscar Hammerstein II and Jerome Kern.

Robert E. Lee. This sidewheeler has been called "the most famous steamboat of all time," having gained its renown by winning an epic race up the Mississippi. The *Lee*, equipped with eight boilers, was launched on the Ohio River in New Albany, Indiana, in 1866, and operated between New Orleans and Vicksburg, Mississippi, before being dismantled 10 years later.

In 1870, the vessel's captain, John W. Cannon, angry over a contractual dispute, was involved in a brawl with Captain Thomas P. Leathers of the rival *Belle Lee*, which also covered the New Orleans-to-Vicksburg route. The dispute became legend later in the year after Leathers took command of the newly constructed *Natchez* and made a run from New Orleans to St. Louis in record time. A Cincinnati newspaper's published account of the feat alluded to the *Robert E. Lee* as being so slow that it would appear she was propelled by mules on a treadmill instead of by steam engines.

On June 30, 1870, both the *Robert E. Lee* and the *Natchez* were advertised as departing New Orleans at 5 p.m. on runs to Louisville and St. Louis, respectively. Both captains denied publicly that a race was in the works. Even so, the contest was widely publicized. As far away as London and Paris, bets were placed on the outcome. The levees were jammed with onlookers at the starting point, and guests were packed on six other steamboats that followed the boats upriver.

Cannon had stripped the *Lee* of all nonessential equipment. His boat started three minutes ahead of the *Natchez* and never relinquished its lead, refueling from barges en route and averaging 13 miles per hour. The *Lee* reached St. Louis in 3 days, 18 hours and 14 minutes, the all-time record for a commercial steamboat, and far ahead of the *Natchez*.

One of the tasks of PhotoAssist researcher Cameron Ruble was to determine how the *Robert E. Lee*'s name should be presented on the stamp. She consulted Jack E. Custer, publisher of *The Egregious Steamboat Journal* and a student of steamboat history for nearly 40 years. Custer wrote:

"Despite the fact that she was registered as *Robert E. Lee* and she was admeasured as the *R.E. Lee*, Captain Cannon had a sign-painter letter her as *Robt. E. Lee.* in New Albany, Indiana, in 1866. This is clearly visible in all the extant photos of the *Lee* ... It appears that *Robt. E. Lee.* was chosen to be used as a signpainter's solution for the name's symmetrical placement on the boat's sidewheel boxes.

"In our research on Cannon we have found that he was a most consistent person throughout his life and he consistently used *Robt. E. Lee.* Since Captain Cannon, a genuine luminary of steamboating, wanted the name of his boat spelled that way, it should appear as the title on the proposed stamp as well."

The Postal Service followed Custer's advice in labeling the stamp, except for one detail: It omitted the period after "Lee" that appeared on the vessel itself.

Sylvan Dell. This sidewheeler was built for the Harlem & New York Navigation Company in 1872, and was reputed to be faster than any other boat of comparable size in New York waters. It first operated on the East River between the lower end of Manhattan and its landing in Harlem, and it remained there until 1889, when it went to the Delaware River. The boat was used for the commuting trade between Philadelphia and Salem, New Jersey, until July 16, 1919, when, running on the Salem Creek without passengers, it hit a submerged obstruction and sank in mid-channel. The crew escaped on lifeboats.

Far West. The sternwheeler *Far West* was built in 1870 in Pittsburgh, Pennsylvania, for shallow-water service on the upper Missouri River. So slight was its draft that, in the words of one humorist, "when the river is low and the sand bars come out for air, the first mate can tap a keg of beer and run four miles on the suds." That wasn't all that much of an exaggeration; unloaded, *Far West* could proceed safely with as little as 20 inches of river under its flat bottom.

The boat was chartered by the Army in 1876 and served with the ill-fated expedition led by General George A. Custer. Carrying wounded survivors of the massacre of Custer's troops at the Little Big Horn, the *Far West* raced 700 miles in 54 hours down the Big Horn, Yellowstone and Missouri rivers to the Army outpost at Bis-

marck, North Dakota.

Buffalo Bill Cody once used the *Far West* on a scouting expedition before the boat's famous race with the *Nellie Peck*, a round-trip run from Sioux City, Iowa, to Fort Benton. The *Far West* won by a narrow three-hour margin after racing 17 days, 20 hours. The boat was lost on October 30, 1883, when it hit a snag and sank seven miles below St. Charles, Missouri.

Rebecca Everingham. The hull of this sternwheeler was launched August 27, 1880, and the boat was put into service on November 15 with two new steam boilers and the engines of the *William S. Holt*. The *Rebecca Everingham* was 140 feet long and could carry 120 passengers and a cargo of 1,000 bales of cotton on its normal run between Columbus, Georgia, and Chattahoochee, Florida.

On April 3, 1884, the *Rebecca Evering-ham* was steaming upriver some 40 miles below Columbus when the cotton cargo caught fire. Strong winds spread the flames quickly, and the crew set out to wake the passengers while the captain steered the doomed riverboat toward the Georgia shore. Four passengers and eight crew members died in the disaster, and the *Rebecca Everingham* was a total loss, burning to the water line.

Bailey Gatzert. A sternwheeler, *Bailey Gatzert* was launched in 1890 for service on Puget Sound between Seattle and Tacoma, Washington. It also served on the Columbia River. It was given carte blanche by its owner to "race with anything that came its way." Only days after arriving in Puget Sound, its captain, George Hill, challenged the reputed fastest boat

on the water, the *Greyhound*, and proceeded to win the race, after which he lashed the traditional victory broom to the mast. This didn't sit well with Captain Jim Troup, brother of *Greyhound* Captain Claude Troup. Jim brought his *T.J. Potter* to Tacoma for a much-anticipated faceoff with the *Bailey Gatzert* in a head-to-head race to Seattle.

It was a classic steamboat race, with the two sternwheelers neck and neck at the halfway point. Suddenly, an explosion shook the *Bailey Gatzert*. Passengers feared a boiler had blown up, but actually the pressure had blown a nozzle out of the smokestack and into Puget Sound. The *Bailey Gatzert*, crippled by the accident, pressed on, but it was no longer a match for the *T.J. Potter*.

The Designs

To adequately show the elaborate detail in the riverboats' construction, stamp designer artist Dean Ellis got permission from USPS to make his paintings larger than usual. The gouache (opaque watercolor) pieces he turned out were nine inches across rather than the seven inches that would have been normal for commemorative-size stamps such as these. The artist placed the five vessels in settings characteristic of the regions in which they operated.

In his painting of the *Robert E. Lee*, the vessel is steaming along the broad Mississippi River, with a distant wooded shore and a bank of cumulus clouds in the background. The white water coiling back from the prow indicates that the *Lee* is plowing along at top speed. This design feature was a holdover from an earlier version by Ellis, which depicted the famous 1870 race and showed the *Natchez* trailing astern. However, after consultant Kevin Foster informed him that the two boats never were in sight of each other after they left New Orleans (in spite of a Currier and Ives lithograph and other well-known illustrations of the race that show the vessels straining upriver virtually side by side), Ellis painted out the second boat. To balance the revised image, and center the *Lee*, the artist had to add more landscape on the left side.

The *Bailey Gatzert*, by contrast with the *Lee*, is shown moving at a leisurely pace over a tranquil Puget Sound. Behind the boat is the waterway's eastern shore, lined with steep, evergreen-covered hills. In the distance is seen a snow-capped Mount Rainier, making its third appearance on a U.S. stamp; it previously had been depicted on a 1934 National Parks commemorative and on the Washington Statehood Centennial stamp of 1989.

The background against which the *Far West* is steaming is a wall of green and white chalk cliffs on the upper Missouri River. Ellis relied on a set of aerial photographs of this stretch of the river for authenticity. Because the cliffs in Ellis' first version tended to blend into the boat, Howard Paine asked the artist to repaint the background to create more contrast.

Dean Ellis' original painting of the **Robert E. Lee** *depicted the famous race with the* **Natchez,** *which he showed just astern. After being told by the project consultant that the two vessels never were in sight of each other after leaving New Orleans, he painted out the* **Natchez** *and added more water and background to the left side of the painting to balance it.*

This is an early version of Dean Ellis' Far West *design. Because the green and white limestone cliffs offered too little background contrast with the steamboat, Ellis revised his painting to reduce the amount of white area.*

For his *Sylvan Dell* painting, Ellis had intended to show the boat on the Hudson River, with the New Jersey Palisades in the background. In the end, however, he painted it moving down the East River at sunset, with the sky and water a deep red-orange and the skyline of 19th-century Manhattan in the background. The steeple of Wall Street's Trinity Episcopal Church is readily recognizable on the left side of the picture; the same steeple previously was shown on the New York Statehood Bicentennial commemorative of 1988. Ellis based the skyline on a published panoramic photograph that was made in 1876 from the top of the Brooklyn tower of the then-unfinished Brooklyn Bridge.

The Southern river scene that is featured on the *Rebecca Everingham* stamp is framed by trees heavy with Spanish moss and came "from my imagination," Ellis said. The sky and water are the soft gold of late afternoon or, possibly, early morning.

In painting the *Rebecca Everingham*, Ellis relied primarily on a photograph in Edward Mueller's book *Perilous Journey: A History of Steamboating on the Chattahoochee, Apalachicola and Flint Rivers, 1828-1928*. The author acquired the photo from Herman Huhn III, who reportedly got it from an old plantation home owned by Colonel William Wadley. Mueller believes the photo is at least 110 years old.

The *Sylvan Dell* painting was based on a photograph from the Pusey & Jones Company collection of the Hagley Museum and Library. The photograph was made from the original 8- by 10-inch glass-plate negative. The label on the negative reads: "Sylvan Dell — not built by Pusey & Jones." It is undated, but the museum curator believes it would be circa 1900, judging from the other negatives with dates. The museum bought the negatives, some 7,000 in number, at auction in the 1970s after Pusey & Jones went out of business. The company built ships and manufactured papermaking machinery.

Ellis' reference photograph of *Bailey Gatzert* was found in the 1958 book *Pacific Steamboats From Sidewheeler to Motor Ferry* by Gordon Newell. His *Far West* painting was based on a photograph of a model constructed by Maynard Stephens that was obtained from the Steamship Historical Society of America. The society also provided the visual reference for the *Robert E. Lee* design: a copy of a painting of the vessel from the collection of L. Baus.

Because these reference images were black and white, the design team had to turn to Kevin Foster for information on the vessels' colors. "We couldn't just say to Dean Ellis, 'make it pretty,' " Paine explained. "We had to be accurate."

For the sake of accuracy, Ellis also made small revisions to his paintings on its expert's recommendations. These details on the finished stamps were late additions: on the *Bailey Gatzert*, the whistle in front of the stack and the faint line running from the bow to the flagstaff; on the *Rebecca Everingham*, the white puff of smoke over the small stack just astern of the pilot house; and on the *Robert E. Lee*, the two short crosspieces at the bottom of the jackstaff at the bow.

A steamboat characteristically displayed its name on some part of the vessel, and CSAC insisted that Ellis include this identifying feature in each of his paintings. He did this by painting the names separately, at a larger scale than the paintings themselves, after which computer graphics specialist Tom Mann electronically dropped the names into the pictures at the correct scale.

However, the realities of gravure printing, with its relatively coarse screens, defeated the committee's purpose. The only two printed stamps on which the tiny names can be read — using a magnifying glass — are on the wheelboxes of the two sidewheelers, *Sylvan Dell* and *Robert E. Lee*. On the other three, the names are no more than tiny fragments of color: *Rebecca Everingham* (on the boat's side near the stern), *Far West* (on the pilothouse) and *Bailey Gatzert* (on a pennant).

The one place that the names of the vessels are prominent is in the stamps' captions, which are stretched across the bottom of the stamps in red capital letters on a white background. The typeface is called Black Oak.

Paine and Ellis experimented with different ways to incorporate additional information in the designs. They tried putting each boat's year dates on a signlike panel over the bottom portion of the picture. Then they eliminated the panel and laid a line of small type containing the year dates plus the boat's service region ("Mississippi River," "Columbia River — Puget Sound," and so on) beneath the vignette. In the end, they included the year dates inside the pictures themselves, in the lower-right corner, in black or dropped-out white type.

First-Day Facts

Deputy Postmaster General Michael S. Coughlin dedicated the stamps at the Orlando Convention Center, site of Stampshow 96. Featured speakers at the ceremony included Randy Neil, president of the American Philatelic Society; Phil Bansner, president of the American Stamp Dealers Association; and Viki M. Brennan, USPS district manager.

The earliest-known prerelease use of a Riverboats stamp was a Bailey Gatzert stamp canceled in Bakersfield, California, August 16, six days before the dedication date.

32¢ BIG BAND LEADERS (4 DESIGNS)
LEGENDS OF AMERICAN MUSIC SERIES

Date of Issue: September 11, 1996

Catalog Numbers: Scott 3096-3099, single stamps; 3099a, block or strip of 4

Colors: black, cyan, magenta, yellow, blue (PMS 287), red (PMS 1935)

First-Day Cancel: New York, New York

First-Day Cancellations: 1,235,166 (includes Songwriters stamps)

Format: Panes of 20, horizontal, 4 across, 5 down. Offset printing plates of 120 subjects (12 across, 10 down).

Overall Stamp Size: 1.56 by 1.225 inches; 39.6mm by 31.1mm

Perforations: 11.1 by 11.0

Selvage Inscription: "LEGENDS OF AMERICAN MUSIC SERIES/Big Band Leaders."

Selvage Markings: "© USPS/1995." ".32/x20/$6.40." "PLATE POSITION" and diagram. "The American Music/Stamp Festival" logo.

Designer: Bill Nelson of Richmond, Virginia

Typographer: Tom Mann, Mann and Mann Graphics, Warrenton, Virginia

Selvage Typographer: Julian Waters of Gaithersburg, Maryland

Modeler: Joseph Sheeran, Ashton-Potter (USA) Ltd.

Art Director: Howard Paine

Project Manager: Terrence McCaffrey, USPS

Stamp Manufacturing: Stamps printed by Ashton-Potter (USA) Ltd., Williamsville, New York, on offset portion of a Stevens Varisize Security Documents webfed 6-color offset, 3-color intaglio press. Stamps perforated, processed and shipped by Ashton-Potter.

Quantity Ordered and Distributed: 92,100,000

Plate Number Detail: 1 set of 6 offset plate numbers preceded by the letter P in selvage next to each corner stamp

Plate Number Combinations Reported: P111111, P222222

Paper Supplier:

Tagging: phosphored paper

The Stamps

On September 11, the Postal Service issued two sets of four stamps each in its long-running Legends of American Music series. The sets honored big band leaders and songwriters, and the dedication ceremony was held at New York City's Shubert Alley.

The two sets were the seventh and eighth to appear since the Legends series was launched in 1993. The previous sets had featured rock 'n' roll/ rhythm and blues performers, including Elvis Presley, whose stamp, issued as a single, was the prototype of the series; country and western

A block of four of the Big Band Leaders stamps taken from the pane of 20.

performers; popular music singers; jazz and blues singers; and jazz instrumentalists. There also was a set honoring great Broadway musicals.

The issuance of the Big Band Leaders and Songwriters sets brought the total number of varieties in the Legends series to date to 62. This includes some earlier stamps that were issued in both pane and sheet formats. It also includes four stamps that were issued as singles as well as parts of sets, and a perforation variety on the single stamp that honored Hank Williams.

The new set for Big Band leaders depicted Count Basie, the brothers Tommy and Jimmy Dorsey, Glenn Miller and Benny Goodman. The Dorseys' stamp was the second in the series to depict more than one individual. In 1993, one of the stamps in the Country and Western set had shown the three members of the Carter Family.

The Big Band Leaders set originally was planned for release in 1995, with Fletcher Henderson as a member of the foursome instead of Benny Goodman. Goodman, who died in 1986, wouldn't have been eligible for a stamp in 1995 under the Postal Service's 10-year rule, which specifies that no postal item honoring an individual shall be issued sooner than 10 years after the individual's death.

Terrence McCaffrey, head of stamp design and project manager for the Legends series, explained the change. "I convinced the (Citizens' Stamp Advisory) Committee that we should hold off until 1996," he said, "because a Big Band group wouldn't be complete without Benny Goodman."

Other bandleaders who had been considered for the set, and had gotten as far as the preliminary design process, were Harry James, Jimmy Lunceford and Paul Whiteman.

The stamps were offset-printed by Ashton-Potter (USA) Ltd. and arranged in blocks of four on panes of 20, which has been the most commonly used format for Legends of American Music. The pane, like all previous panes in the series, has a wide selvage at the top called a header, which carries the name of the set ("Legends of American Music/Big Band Leaders") in fancy lettering created by calligrapher Julian Waters.

Plate numbers are found in the selvage next to the four corner stamps. The Scott U.S. specialized catalog lists a plate block of four from either lower corner of the pane as well as a horizontal plate block of eight, with header, from the top.

Jazz pianist and band leader Count Basie (1904-1984) was the most enduring of all the Big Band Leaders. His great legacy was to transform swing music as a solo performance to a band performance with star sidemen and vocalists.

Born William Basie in Red Bank, New Jersey, he learned piano from his mother and spent much of his youth in nearby New York City listening to such keyboard masters as James P. Johnson, Willie "The Lion" Smith and, especially, Fats Waller. Under Waller's sponsorship Basie joined a musical troupe that toured black venues throughout America (the so-called "chitlin' circuit"). Stranded in Kansas City, Missouri, when the tour collapsed, Basie found the city hospitable to a young jazz musician and stayed on for several years, forming his own band in 1935.

Jazz impresario John Hammond arranged for Basie to play in New York, where the band recorded for Decca and had a successful six-month residency at the Famous Door club on West 52nd Street. Through the 1940s, Basie's bands provided dancers with enticing rhythms and jazz fans with remarkable solos by the likes of Lester Young, Buck Clayton, Earl Warren, Hershel Evans, Illinois Jacquet and J.J. Johnson. Economic necessity pared down the Basie band to seven members at the start of the 1950s, but he maintained an ensemble until his death in 1984. His band toured Europe and Japan, became the first black band to play at New York's Waldorf-Astoria Hotel, and adapted with the times — for example, recording big band treatments of popular rock tunes in the 1960s. Basie's hits over the years included *One O'Clock Jump* (the Basie theme), *Swingin' the Blues*, *Jumpin' at the Woodside*, *Tickle Toes* and *Taxi War Dance*.

Jimmy Dorsey (James Francis Dorsey, 1904-1957) and Tommy Dorsey (Thomas Francis Dorsey Jr., 1905-1956) were born in Shenandoah, Pennsylvania. Their father was a coal miner turned music teacher.

Jimmy Dorsey, known as the "King of the Jukebox," was a clarinetist and alto saxophonist. Tommy was a trombonist. Both were known as outstanding technicians. As young men the two played together in bands, including Paul Whiteman's band, and in 1934 they formed the Dorsey Brothers Orchestra. A bitter dispute the following year led to a walkout by Tommy, leaving Jimmy to run the band on his own. Tommy took over the excellent dance band led by Joe Haymes, which he turned into the finest dance orchestra of its time. The brothers didn't reunite until 1953, after Jimmy's band had folded. In that year Jimmy joined Tommy's still-successful band, to which Tommy quickly restored the old Dorsey Brothers Orchestra name, and the group became popular through television.

Jimmy's band was considered one of the most accomplished white bands of the swing era. It retained a strong jazz element but also catered to popular demands. Its hit recordings included *Yours*, *Green Eyes* and *Tangerine*, featuring singers Bob Eberly and Helen O'Connell. Tommy, whose theme was *I'm Getting Sentimental Over You*, became known as the "sentimental gentleman of swing." He employed some of the finest singers ever to work with the big bands, including Jo Stafford, Dick Haymes and Frank Sinatra, whose stint with Dorsey made him an international star.

Trombonist, arranger and bandleader Glenn Miller (1904-1944) was born in Clarinda, Iowa, and attended the University of Colorado. He played in various bands from Los Angeles to New York City, including those of the Dorsey brothers, before forming his own in 1937.

Miller's smooth band became famous for a sweet orchestral sound, featuring a distinctive blend of four saxophones and a clarinet. Signed to a recording contract with RCA in 1939, Miller proved a sound investment with immediate consecutive best-sellers in *Little Brown Jug*, *In the Mood* and *Sunrise Serenade*. The latter was coupled with *Moonlight Serenade*,

Artist Bill Nelson made these pencil sketches of stamps for (left to right) bandleaders Paul Whiteman, Jimmy Lunceford and Harry James, but in the end none was included in the set.

an effective extrapolation of a trombone exercise that became Miller's signature tune. Other memorable Miller hits were *String of Pearls*, *Pennsylvania 6-5000*, *Tuxedo Junction*, *Jersey Bounce*, *American Patrol*, *Kalamazoo* and the first million-selling record, *Chattanooga Choo-Choo*, with a chorus by Tex Beneke, Marion Hutton and the Modernaires prominently featured.

In World War II Miller volunteered for service in the Army Air Force, where he created the Army Air Force Band that played, broadcast and recorded for the armed forces. In 1944, on a flight from England to Paris in a small plane, Major Glenn Miller perished when the aircraft disappeared in bad weather over the English Channel.

The popularity of Miller's music has never diminished. It was given a boost in the 1950s with the release of dozens of his numbers on long-playing records and Universal Picture's production of his filmed biography, *The Glenn Miller Story*, with Jimmy Stewart in the title role. His original arrangements have been preserved and duplicated by other bands in the years since his death.

Benny Goodman (1909-1986) was born into poverty in Chicago and learned to play the clarinet at Jane Addams' Hull House. A prodigy, he was playing in bands around the country in his mid-teens. By 1929 he was a much-in-demand session musician in New York City, making hundreds of record and radio dates. An ambitious perfectionist, Goodman continued to develop his craft until he was one of the most skilled clarinetists in America.

In 1934 he formed his own band, which he took on a nationwide tour.

On August 21, 1935, the band played at Los Angeles' Palomar Ballroom, a dance date so successful that it is generally considered the birth of the show-business phenomenon that became known as the "swing era." Goodman was blessed during this period and thereafter with such arrangers as Fletcher Henderson, instrumentalists like Bunny Berigan, Gene Krupa and Harry James, and vocalists like Helen Ward, Martha Tilton and Peggy Lee.

During an extended run in Chicago, Goodman integrated his band with black pianist Teddy Wilson, and, later Lionel Hampton, becoming the first major bandleader to do so. On January 16, 1938, the band played a concert at New York's Carnegie Hall, sealing its success and Goodman's reputation as the "King of Swing." His hits included *King Porter Stomp*; *Sing, Sing, Sing*; *Seven Come Eleven*; *Don't Be That Way*; *Flyin' Home*; and *Moonglow*. *Let's Dance* was his orchestra's theme, and *Goodbye* its closing number.

Goodman continued to lead dance bands through the 1940s and 1950s and took a band to the Soviet Union in 1962. A feature film, *The Benny Goodman Story*, with Steve Allen in the title role and Goodman dubbing Allen's playing, was released in 1955. He continued to record and play concert dates into the early 1980s, and cultivated a long-time affinity for classical music, performing concertos by such composers as Mozart, Bartok and Copland.

Fletcher Henderson originally was set to be one of the four Big Band leaders pictured in the stamp set, and Bill Nelson made these pencil sketches for the Henderson stamp. When the issue date for the set was pushed back to 1996, Benny Goodman became eligible for inclusion. He replaced Henderson.

The Designs

To create the stamp designs, the Postal Service picked Bill Nelson of Richmond, Virginia, an artist who works in colored pencil on recycled charcoal paper. Nelson was a logical choice, having previously designed a series of album covers for big band recordings by Time-Life Records that included portraits of Miller, the Dorseys, Harry James, Duke Ellington and Gene Krupa. After completing the Big Band Leaders stamp assignment, Nelson designed other stamps for USPS, two of which — the nondenominated Auto Tail Fin and Jukebox bulk-rate stamps — were issued in 1995.

For the Dorsey brothers stamp, Nelson drew head-and-shoulders portraits of the two brothers standing side by side, Jimmy playing his saxophone, Tommy his trombone. The portraits were based on separate photographs. Jimmy's was provided by Culver Pictures and was taken in the early 1940s, USPS consultants estimated. Tommy's photo dated from the same period and was published in a 1972 book titled *Tommy and Jimmy: The Dorsey Years* by Herb Sanford.

Nelson's preliminary pencil layout was approved, and he then produced finished art. When the Citizens' Stamp Advisory Committee and USPS staff members saw it, however, they wanted changes.

The Dorseys' heads were on the same level and close together in the picture, and they were wearing black tuxedo jackets with no detail to them that blended as though into one. This led

This early layout shows how the Big Band Leaders stamps would have looked if original plans had been followed to issue the set as a booklet pane and include Fletcher Henderson instead of Benny Goodman.

The photograph of Benny Good-man on which the stamp design was based was made by Hugh Bell and was published in Jazz Giants, A Visual Retrospective *(Abe, K, Billboard Publications Inc., 1986). USPS consultants believe it was made in the mid-1950s.*

committee members to object that the performers looked like "Siamese twins joined at the thorax," as Nelson put it, or, even more unnerving, one individual with two heads. Nelson then produced a new picture, moving the heads farther apart, setting Jimmy slightly below Tommy and giving the brothers white dinner jackets that were clearly identifiable as two separate garments.

Another problem developed when someone in the Dorsey family complained that the fingers of Tommy's left hand, which held the mouthpiece portion of the trombone, looked peculiar, even though Nelson had faithfully copied these details from the photograph. Art director Howard Paine then went to a music store and made Polaroid pictures of the left hand of

The Count Basie photograph that was the source of Bill Nelson's stamp design was provided by Archives Photos. The Postal Service had no information on when or by whom it was taken.

193

Tommy Dorsey's stamp portrait was based on this photograph, circa 1938-early 1940s, published in Tommy and Jimmy, The Dorsey Years, *by Herb Sanford (Arlington House 1972). Jimmy's portrait, also circa early 1940s, was furnished by Culver Pictures.*

The photograph of Glenn Miller that served as a model for Bill Nelson's stamp portrait is from the Frank Driggs Archives. Driggs believes it was a publicity photograph. In his painting, Nelson raised the trombone higher than Miller is holding it here to get more of the instrument into the stamp design.

an employee holding a trombone in the same position. Using these photos, Nelson redrew Dorsey's hand, showing the fingers parallel to the performer's face rather than pointed toward the face as in the first version. The family was satisfied.

Nelson's drawing of Benny Goodman showed a frontal view of the bandleader, cheeks inflated, playing his clarinet. His fingers rest lightly on the keys, with the little finger of his left hand elevated in his characteristic style. The artwork was based on a photograph by Hugh Bell, probably from the mid-1950s, that was published in a 1986 book titled *Jazz Giants, A Visual Retrospective.*

Again there were complaints about minor details from a member of the subject's family, who thought Goodman's cheeks were too fat. Karl Malden, a member of CSAC who had known Goodman, had a similar objection. The artist modified his drawing slightly to oblige them.

Glenn Miller's family also had a problem with their famous relative's stamp portrait; they thought his nose, as Nelson had drawn it, was overly prominent. Once again, a small alteration was made, and the relatives were satisfied. "Photos don't lie," said Nelson philosophically, "but families see it a different way, and you bow to that. Because they loved him, and I never knew him."

The Miller portrait, which Nelson thinks is the best of the four, shows the bandleader leaning slightly forward, the slide of his trombone in front of him in a parallel relationship to his head and shoulders. The source photograph was a publicity shot provided by the Frank Driggs Archives.

Count Basie's portrait, showing the bandleader's head and smiling face in profile, was the only one to win the family's unconditional approval, although one relative had originally asked that a picture of Basie wearing a Hawaiian shirt and sailor hat be used on the stamp. USPS declined. "We wrote back," said Terrence McCaffrey, "stressing the dignity of the series and how the other subjects would be shown in suits." The source photo came from Archive Photos, but no information on it is available.

Basie's image, seen as part of the block of four, is much larger than the others. This is unusual for the Legends of American Music series, whose previous sets all have contained portraits of the same relative size.

Nelson provided soft pastel-colored backgrounds for his portraits. The

In this early version of the Dorsey brothers stamp design, the Dorseys are wearing tuxedo jackets and their heads are on the same level and close together. CSAC members thought the treatment, with the black of the jackets merged into one shape, made the brothers look like Siamese twins. So Bill Nelson revised the portraits, giving them white dinner jackets and putting more distance between them.

names of the subjects appear on the stamps in the same style as on previous sets in the Legends series. They are in white Helvetica compressed capital letters, either dropped out of the design itself or on black panels that suggest torn ticket stubs. The descriptive lines in small black Helvetica type up the left side read "Pianist and Bandleader," "Trombonist and Bandleader," "Clarinetist and Bandleader," and, in the case of the Dorseys, simply "Bandleaders," because of lack of room to mention their instruments.

First-Day Facts

Michael S. Coughlin, deputy postmaster general, dedicated the Big Band Leaders and Songwriters stamps in a ceremony at New York City's Shubert Alley, which is a byway in Manhattan off West 44th Street between Broadway and Eighth Avenue, near the Shubert Theater.

The event marked the beginning of what USPS called American Music Stamp Festival 1996. Other events were held in locations around the country beginning the next day. The final event was a "Big Band Extravaganza" and stamp dedication ceremony October 18-19 at Mackinac Island, Michigan.

At Shubert Alley, Stan Martin, vice president and station manager of WQEW radio, was master of ceremonies, and Paul Shaffer, leader of the CBS Orchestra, gave the welcome and introduced the guests.

Those participating in the unveiling of the Big Band Leaders stamps were Rosemary Matthews and Aaron A. Woodward III, daughter and son of Count Basie; Jane Dorsey and Steve Dorsey, widow and son of Tommy Dorsey; Eugene Goodman and Shirley Deeter, Benny Goodman's brother and stepdaughter; Irene Miller Wolfe, Glenn Miller's sister; and Jonnie Dee Miller and Steven D. Miller, Glenn Miller's daughter and son.

Honored guests included Joan J. Woodward, daughter-in-law of Count Basie; Aaron A. Woodward IV, the Count's grandson; Ali S. Vann, his great-grandson; Gloria Goodman, Benny Goodman's sister-in-law; Wynne Miller Bernatschke, Glenn Miller's niece; Rudolph Bernatschke, his nephew-in-law; and Welby Wolfe, his brother-in-law.

32¢ SONGWRITERS (4 DESIGNS)
LEGENDS OF AMERICAN MUSIC SERIES

Date of Issue: September 11, 1996

Catalog Numbers: Scott 3100-3103, single stamps; 3103a, block or strip of 4

Colors: black, cyan, magenta, yellow, blue (PMS 287), red (PMS 1935)

First-Day Cancel: New York, New York

First-Day Cancellations: 1,235,166 (includes Big Band Leaders stamps)

Format: Panes of 20, horizontal, 4 across, 5 down. Offset printing plates of 120 subjects (12 across, 10 down).

Overall Stamp Size: 1.56 by 1.225 inches; 39.6mm by 31.1mm

Perforations: 11.1 by 10.9

Selvage Inscription: "LEGENDS OF AMERICAN MUSIC SERIES/Songwriters."

Selvage Markings: "© USPS/1995." ".32/x20/$6.40." "PLATE POSITION" and diagram. "The American Music/Stamp Festival" logo.

Designer: M. Gregory Rudd of Fairfield, Connecticut

Typographer: Tom Mann, Mann and Mann Graphics, Warrenton, Virginia

Selvage Typographer: Julian Waters of Gaithersburg, Maryland

Modeler: Joseph Sheeran, Ashton-Potter (USA) Ltd.

Art Director: Howard Paine

Project Manager: Terrence McCaffrey, USPS

Stamp Manufacturing: Stamps printed by Ashton-Potter (USA) Ltd., Williamsville, New York, on offset portion of a Stevens Varisize Security Documents webfed 6-color offset, 3-color intaglio press. Stamps perforated, processed and shipped by Ashton-Potter.

Quantity Ordered and Distributed: 92,100,000

Plate Number Detail: 1 set of 6 offset plate numbers preceded by the letter P in selvage next to each corner stamp

Plate Number Combinations Reported: P111111, P222222

Paper Supplier:

Tagging: phosphored paper

The Stamps

The second set of four stamps in the Legends of American Music series to be issued in New York City on September 11 honored writers of popular songs. Two were composers, Harold Arlen and Hoagy Carmichael, and the other two were lyricists, Johnny Mercer and Dorothy Fields (although Mercer also wrote his own tunes on occasion).

As originally planned, the group comprised five individuals, with Frank Loesser as the fifth. However, officials decided that Loesser, who wrote the songs for such musical shows as *Guys and Dolls* and *The Most Happy Fella*, should be held for inclusion in a Broadway Composers set to be issued in some later year.

This block of four was taken from the Songwriters pane.

The Songwriters set originally included Frank Loesser, but Loesser was withdrawn and moved to a set to be issued later honoring Broadway composers. This is Greg Rudd's pencil sketch for the abandoned Loesser stamp. It shows the treble clef that the artist planned to paint behind each songwriter's portrait. However, art director Howard Paine preferred that the backgrounds be plain white.

In fact, however, the distinction between Songwriters and Broadway Composers was an arbitrary one. All four individuals honored in the Songwriters set — Arlen, Mercer, Fields and Carmichael — wrote songs for the Broadway stage during their careers. Arlen, in fact, was the composer for more major stage musicals and revues (seven) than the man who was bumped to the Broadway group, Frank Loesser (five).

The Songwriters stamps, like the four Big Band Leaders stamps issued on the same day, were offset-printed by Ashton-Potter (USA) Ltd. and are arranged in blocks of four on 20-stamp panes. A set of plate numbers appears in the selvage next to each of the four corner stamps on the pane. Scott's U.S. specialized catalog lists a plate block of four from either lower corner and a horizontal plate block of eight with the top selvage, or header, attached.

The four craftsmen shown on the stamps were no strangers to each other's work. Mercer collaborated with both Arlen and Carmichael to create some of America's most enduring songs. With Arlen, he wrote *Blues in the Night*, *Come Rain or Come Shine*, *That Old Black Magic* and *Accent-tchu-ate the Positive*, and his output with Carmichael included *Lazybones* and *Skylark*. Fields and Arlen teamed up to create the scores for two musical films in the 1950s, *Mr. Imperium* and *The Farmer Takes a Wife*.

The name of Harold Arlen (1905-1986) is relatively unfamiliar to the general public, but many experts believe he should be ranked alongside the American Big Five of popular song (Jerome Kern, Irving Berlin, George Gershwin, Richard Rodgers and Cole Porter). His biographer, Edward Jablonski, calls him "the most versatile, original and superlatively endowed of contemporary American composers," possessing a "unique gift of melody ... sensitive harmonic sense ... (and a powerful) rhythmic pulse." One of his lyricists, E.Y. (Yip) Harburg, adds: "An Arlen song is completely individual, completely uninfluenced by anyone else."

Arlen was born Hyman Arluck in Buffalo, New York, the son of a cantor. In his early teens, he sang and played piano at local clubs and on lake steamers. His work as a pianist, vocalist and arranger for a dance orchestra called the Buffalodians took him to New York, where he became a Broadway pit pianist and began composing.

His first hit song, written with Ted Koehler, was *Get Happy*. With Koehler he wrote songs for revues at Harlem's famed Cotton Club, several of which became standards, including *Between the Devil and the Deep Blue Sea*, *I Love a Parade*, *I've Got the World on a String*, *Stormy Weather* and *Ill Wind*. This work paved the way for his later successes in Hollywood and on Broadway.

Arlen's scores for two great Judy Garland films were among his finest: *The Wizard of Oz*, written with Yip Harburg, featuring the popular classic *Over the Rainbow*, and *A Star is Born*, with Ira Gershwin, whose big number was *The Man That Got Away*. Among his stage musicals were the bluesy *St. Louis Woman*, with an all-black cast, and *House of Flowers*, with book and lyrics by Truman Capote.

Hoagy Carmichael (1899-1981) is best remembered for one enduring song, *Stardust*, which he wrote in 1927 as an instrumental; the lyrics were added later by Mitchell Parish. Carmichael composed many other standards, however, including *Little Old Lady*, *Small Fry*, *Two Sleepy People*, *Heart and Soul*, *I Get Along Without You Very Well*, *The Nearness of You* and *Ole Buttermilk Sky*.

He was born Hoagland Howard Carmichael in Bloomington, Indiana. He taught himself to play piano and, as a pre-law student at Indiana University, led student bands. In 1922 he met trumpeter Bix Beiderbecke, and composed one of his first works, *Riverboat Shuffle*, for Beiderbecke's group, the Wolverines.

Eventually Carmichael quit law school to make a career in music. In New York, he mixed with the jazz community, playing piano, singing and learning from such gifted musicians as Louis Armstrong, Benny Goodman, Glenn Miller, Gene Krupa, the Dorsey brothers and Jack Teagarden. These friends recorded several of his compositions, such as *Rockin' Chair*, *Georgia on My Mind*, *Lazy River* and *Lazybones*. Later, in Hollywood, he was a staff songwriter for Paramount and went on to act in several movies.

As a singer, Carmichael's intonation was uncertain and his vocal range limited, but he sang with an amiable simplicity and a sure sense of rhythm. His stature is secure as one of America's most inventive and melodic "pure" popular composers, who wrote a song at a time rather than complete film or theater scores.

Johnny Mercer (1909-1976), singer, songwriter, radio performer and recording executive (he co-founded Capitol Records), was born in Savannah, Georgia, the scion of an old colonial family. As a youth he moved to New York and worked in a variety of jobs before placing one of his first songs, *Out of Breath and Scared to Death of You*, in a Broadway show.

For more than three decades, Mercer wrote lyrics, mostly for movies, working with some of the top composers in the business: Arlen, Carmichael, Richard Whiting, Jerome Kern, Harry Warren, Arthur Schwartz, Jimmy Van Heusen, Duke Ellington, Gordon Jenkins and Henry Mancini. Among the best-known of his more than 1,000 songs are *I'm an Old Cowhand*; *Too Marvelous For Words*; *Hooray for Hollywood*; *Jeepers Crepers*; *P.S. I*

Love You; *Goody Goody*; *You Must Have Been a Beautiful Baby*; *And the Angels Sing*; *Day In, Day Out*; *Personality*; *GI Jive*; *Tangerine*; *I Remember You*; *I'm Old-Fashioned*; *Dearly Beloved*; *Fools Rush In*; *Laura*; *One for My Baby*; *Something's Gotta Give*; *Autumn Leaves*; *The Summer Wind*; *On The Atchison, Topeka and the Santa Fe*; *In the Cool, Cool, Cool of the Evening*; *Moon River*; and *Days of Wine and Roses*. The last four mentioned won Academy Awards. His Broadway musical credits include *St. Louis Woman* (with Arlen) and *Li'l Abner* (with Gene DePaul).

Mercer was casual and easygoing, with an engaging personality. He also was a meticulous craftsman whose literate, witty lyrics had a flowing naturalness that made frequent use of the vernacular.

Dorothy Fields (1905-1974) has no competitor for the distinction of America's best woman songwriter. She was born in Allenhurst, New Jersey, into a show-business family. Her father was Lew Fields, who won fame as a member of the comedy duo Weber and Fields and later became a successful Broadway impresario. Her two older brothers, Joseph and Herbert, also made their mark on Broadway as writers.

Dorothy wrote poetry for her school's literary magazine and later, as an avocation, for popular periodicals. In 1926 she met composer and song-plugger Jimmy McHugh, with whom she wrote a series of memorable theater and film songs: *I Can't Give You Anything But Love, Diga Diga Doo, Exactly Like You, On the Sunny Side of the Street* and *I'm in the Mood for Love*. In Hollywood, where she spent the 1930s, she also collaborated with Jerome Kern on several film musicals, creating such songs as *Lovely to Look At, I Won't Dance, A Fine Romance, Pick Yourself Up* and *The Way You Look Tonight* (winner of the 1936 Academy Award).

In 1939 Fields returned to New York, where she collaborated with her brother Herbert on the books for several Broadway musicals, the most successful of which was *Annie Get Your Gun*, with lyrics and music by Irving Berlin. She wrote songs for the stage with Arthur Schwartz, Sigmund Romberg, Albert Hague and Cy Coleman.

During her 48-year career, Fields co-wrote more than 400 songs and worked on 15 musicals and more than 25 movies. Her lyrics were known for their strong characterization, clarity of language and humor. An amateur pianist and lover of classical music, she was highly conscious of the melodic line and tailored her words to float freely over it.

The Designs

To paint the portraits for the Songwriters set, art director Howard Paine chose M. Gregory Rudd of Fairfield, Connecticut. These were Rudd's first designs in the Legends of American Music series. His previous stamp assignments had been Francis Ouimet (1988), Ernest Hemingway (1989), Marianne Moore (1990) and Dorothy Parker (1992). As with the earlier portraits, he painted the new ones in oil on a rag-board panel that he had prepared with a gesso coating.

Rudd produced paintings of all five of the individuals originally chosen for the Songwriters group. However, when Frank Loesser was withdrawn and held for inclusion in the later Broadway Composers set, Rudd's painting of him was put aside. Because another illustrator has been chosen for Broadway Composers, the Loesser stamp, when it appears, will have a different look.

One of Paine's consistent instructions to artists working on the Legends of American Music series has been to show the subjects in an active mode. To depict several dozen faces simply staring at the viewer would make a boring series, Paine felt. In the case of musical performers, this requirement hasn't been difficult to meet. Singers could be shown from below, as from an audience, with their mouths open and, in some cases, with microphones. Instrumentalists could be playing or holding their horns or guitars. Songwriters, however, who create rather than perform, were another matter.

"We wanted the stamps to be very theatrical," Paine said. "But you don't write a song on stage. So for the Songwriters set, we tried to convey the theatricality in different ways."

He and Rudd decided to use pencils as visual props. Mercer, Fields, Arlen and Loesser each was given a pencil in the right hand (after it was carefully determined that all four were right-handed). In Loesser's case, both hands were raised, as if he was conducting a band and using the pencil as a baton.

With Carmichael, the designers thought they had a better solution. They found a photograph of the composer at a piano keyboard, his right hand lifted as if in a flourish after striking an arpeggio. His eyes are lowered, but he is smiling as though he is pleased with what he has just played. Rudd based his painting on this photograph, and USPS staff members and

This is Greg Rudd's original painting of Hoagy Carmichael and the photograph of the composer at the piano on which he based it. However, Carmichael's son objected strongly to the painting, calling it unflattering and uncharacteristic. As a result, the Postal Service scrapped the design, and Rudd started over.

202

the Citizens' Stamp Advisory Committee liked it.

Unfortunately, Carmichael's son, Hoagy Bix Carmichael, didn't. The son, of Brewster, New York, spends much of his time on what he calls "the Carmichael industry" and is president of Amsong, an association of songwriters and heirs seeking to extend copyright protection for songs. He reacted strongly and negatively when he saw the proposed design. It didn't help that the preliminary mockup of the stamp that was shown to him bore the words "American Lyricist," which of course was inaccurate.

Carmichael telephoned Terrence McCaffrey, head of stamp design, and complained emphatically. He accused McCaffrey and his colleagues of knowing and caring nothing about his father. The pose shown on the stamp, he said, was unflattering and uncharacteristic. He demanded a new portrait, one that would show the laid-back Hoagy Carmichael of his movie persona.

It is Postal Service policy to satisfy the subject's family whenever possible, and McCaffrey agreed to order a new painting. In preparing it, Greg Rudd used two other photographs of Carmichael. The basic photograph showed Carmichael with his fedora tipped back on his head. However,

These are the two photographs of Hoagy Carmichael, from the Michael Ochs Archives, that Greg Rudd used as reference for his revised painting, also shown here. One photo was used for the smiling face; the other for the pose, hat, shirt and tie. To convey the songwriter's characteristic casualness, Rudd removed the jacket and gave him suspenders over his tattersall shirt.

Harold Arlen's stamp portrait was based on this photograph that was published in Edward Jablonski's biography of the composer, Happy With the Blues. *The photograph was taken January 10, 1956, in Spasso House, Moscow, residence of U.S. Ambassador Charles Bohlen, at the party to celebrate the Moscow premiere of George Gershwin's opera* Porgy and Bess. *Horace Sutton, who was covering the opera's Soviet tour for* Saturday Review of Literature, *took the picture. Arlen was clean-shaven during this period, although he wore a moustache from time to time, and Greg Rudd gave him a moustache in his painting for the stamp.*

the son wanted the face to be smiling, so Rudd "borrowed" a smile from another photo. To complete the informal look, he removed the jacket and added a pair of suspenders over the tattersall shirt. The result was a portrait with no action or prop that would hint at Carmichael's vocation. Nevertheless, it does convey the idea of a likable personality, and the songwriter's son pronounced himself pleased with it.

The most unusual portrait of the four — and Rudd's own favorite — is of Harold Arlen. Rudd based the painting on a photograph made in the Soviet Union in 1956, at a party following the Moscow debut of the Gershwin opera *Porgy and Bess.* The photograph is published in Edward Jablonski's 1961 biography of Arlen, *Happy With the Blues.*

The camera caught the composer with a quizzical look on his face. The look may also have reflected fatigue; Arlen had flown to the Soviet capital earlier in the day from Helsinki, where he had been obliged to stay over to await his visa. To Rudd, the expression was one of a creative artist "staring into space," somewhere in "the mystical, ethereal area of creativity." In the photograph, Arlen was clean-shaven. However, he wore a moustache at various times in his career, and Rudd gave him one for the stamp. "A moustache seemed liked his signature, and I thought it added a lot of character to him," Rudd explained.

The Johnny Mercer stamp portrait was based on this Capitol Records publicity photograph from the Michael Ochs Archives. A USPS consultant dated the photo to the mid-1930s.

The portrait of a smiling Johnny Mercer was based on a Capitol Records publicity photograph of the singer-songwriter standing at a radio microphone. In the photograph, the gap between Mercer's two front teeth — a visual trademark — is quite prominent, but Rudd modified it in his final version of the painting.

Rudd depicted his subject seated at a piano, with the corner of its music stand visible at the right. In the first version, he depicted Mercer making a thumb-and-forefinger "OK" sign with his left hand, "as if he was simply enjoying what he was doing," the artist said. "Again, it was an attempt to create something that would suggest activity. He seemed like an outgoing, gregarious, sanguine personality, and I thought, a guy like that might make that gesture because he's enthusiastic." However, a Postal Service consultant said Mercer wouldn't have made such a gesture, and Rudd painted it out. On the consultant's advice, Rudd also changed the bow tie he had given Mercer to a four-in-hand.

Rudd's painting of Dorothy Fields was also based on a photograph of 1930s vintage. In it, she is smiling broadly, and her large eyes look directly at the viewer. For the stamp, Rudd gave Fields a turtleneck sweater and crossed her hands in front of her, the pencil in her right hand, a piece of sheet music in her left.

In the photograph, Fields' nose is somewhat more prominent than it appears in Rudd's painting. "I bobbed it just a bit," he said. "I played plastic surgeon. No one seemed to object." The resulting portrait, he thought, came out well. "I liked her kind eyes, and she had a great smile," Rudd said. "She seemed not like a star, but like somebody who was very real."

CSAC's initial reaction to the Fields painting, however, as well as to

Greg Rudd's original Johnny Mercer painting showed the lyricist giving the "OK" sign with his left hand and wearing a bow tie. On the advice of USPS consultants, Rudd eliminated the "OK" sign and changed the tie to a four-in-hand. The corner of a piano's music stand at the lower right, as well as the pencil in Mercer's right hand, are meant to suggest his vocation. This and other early versions of the designs included a song title along the left side, an idea that USPS later abandoned.

the others, was that they were too harsh and hard-edged. At the committee's request, Rudd softened the lines, added warmth to the colors and reduced the amount of contrast between the lights and shadows on the subjects' faces. "They (the committee members) seemed to like them much more that way, and I think they were right," Rudd said.

In his early sketches, Rudd gave each portrait a backdrop of a treble clef with a time signature and a few notes. However, Paine informed him that another illustrator, Tom Blackshear, was using a similar symbolic

Greg Rudd used this photograph of Dorothy Fields as visual reference for his stamp painting. It was taken in the mid-1930s, according to the Postal Service's consultant. In the painting, Rudd made the lyricist's prominent nose slightly smaller.

This is Greg Rudd's first version of a Dorothy Fields portrait, with hard edges and strong highlights on her face. For the final painting he softened the edges, diminished the highlights and used somewhat warmer colors. He did the same with his other three paintings.

device — a piano keyboard — for the Jazz Musicians set that was then in preparation. Paine told him to eliminate the clef and show the songwriters against a plain white background. No previous set in the Legends of American Music series had presented its subjects that way.

Otherwise, however, the Songwriters designs were consistent with those of previous Legends stamps. Each subject's name was in white Helvetica compressed capital letters dropped out of the portrait or on stylized panels suggestive of ticket stubs. The descriptive wording — "American Composer" or "American Lyricist" — was in small black Helvetica type running up the left side of the stamp. Here the word "American" was an afterthought, added to lengthen the line of type for better balance.

CSAC had suggested that this line on the left side be filled out with the title of the songwriter's best-known piece of music. The preliminary choices were *Over the Rainbow* for Arlen, *Stardust* for Carmichael, *Moon River* for Mercer and *The Way You Look Tonight* for Fields. "Talk about being subjective!" Terrence McCaffrey said. "No two experts could agree on what songs should be named. We discussed it between meetings and decided it was a bad idea, that we were leaving ourselves wide open to second-guessing." The song titles came off.

First-Day Facts

General information on the first-day ceremony in New York's Shubert Alley for the Big Band Leaders and Songwriters stamps can be found in the preceding chapter.

Taking part in the unveiling of the Songwriters stamps at the ceremony were Hoagy Bix Carmichael; Samuel Arlen, Harold Arlen's nephew, whom the songwriter had adopted as his own son a few months before his death; David Lahm and Eliza Brewster, son and daughter of Dorothy Fields; and Bart M. Hackley, executive director of the Johnny Mercer Foundation. Honored guests included Joan Arlen, Harold Arlen's niece-in-law; Sam Brewster, Dorothy Fields' son-in-law; and Benjamin Carmichael.

The earliest-known prerelease use of a Songwriters stamp was a Dorothy Fields stamp on a cover postmarked Montgomery, Alabama, September 6, five days ahead of schedule.

207

23¢ F. SCOTT FITZGERALD
LITERARY ARTS SERIES

Date of Issue: September 27, 1996

Catalog Number: Scott 3104

Colors: cyan, magenta, yellow, black

First-Day Cancel: St. Paul, Minnesota

First-Day Cancellations: 150,783

Format: Panes of 50, horizontal, 5 across, 10 down. Gravure printing cylinders of 200 subjects (10 across, 20 around).

Overall Stamp Size: .99 by 1.56 inches; 25.1mm by 39.6mm

Perforations: 11.1 (REMY stroke perforator)

Selvage Markings: "© USPS 1995." ".23 x 50 = $11.50." "PLATE/POSITION" and diagram.

Designer: Michael Deas of New Orleans, Louisiana

Typographer: John Boyd, Anagraphics, Inc., New York, New York

Modeler: Clarence Holbert, Bureau of Engraving and Printing

Art Director: Phil Jordan

Project Manager: Terrence McCaffrey, USPS

Stamp Manufacturing: Stamps printed by BEP on the 7-color Andreotti webfed gravure press (601)

Quantity Ordered and Distributed: 300,000,000

Cylinder Number Detail: 1 set of 4 gravure cylinder numbers in selvage next to 1 upper corner and 1 lower corner stamp on same side

Cylinder Number Combination Reported: 1111

Paper Supplier: Westvaco/Ivex

Tagging: phosphored paper

The Stamp

On September 27, the Postal Service commemorated the 100th anniversary of the birth of F. Scott Fitzgerald, novelist and chronicler of the Jazz Age, by issuing a stamp at his birthplace, St. Paul, Minnesota.

The stamp bore a 23¢ denomination, to cover the rate for the second ounce and each additional ounce of first-class mail. It was the first commemorative in many years to be issued for this particular postal purpose. In fact, when the design of the stamp was made public in November 1995, some collectors assumed at first that the stamp was a 32-center that somehow had gotten its numbers transposed.

"In the past 18 months, we've received a lot of customer feedback asking that we incorporate some exciting and interesting subject matter and designs on stamps that are 'workhorses,' " Azeezaly S. Jaffer, manager of stamp services for USPS, told *The Washington Post*'s Bill McAllister. He cited the current Love stamps as "a good example," with both the one-ounce and two-ounce rate stamps carrying similar cherub designs.

"When the demand for 23¢ (second-ounce) stamps increased, we recommended to the (Citizens' Stamp Advisory) Committee the F. Scott Fitzgerald stamp as an opportunity to fill the need of our customers, mail users and collectors," Jaffer said. "Unlike serious collectors who make a clear distinction between commemoratives and definitives, the American people care for appealing subjects and designs on all stamps.

"As we move into the next few years, it is reasonable to say that we will recommend subject matter to the committee for second-ounce and international rates that have relevant subject matter and design."

Apparently the Fitzgerald's 23¢ denomination caused some confusion, however. A letter to *Linn's Stamp News* from Joseph E. Boling of Federal Way, Washington, reported that shortly after the stamp was issued his local stamp clerk "was flabbergasted and embarrassed" to notice the denomination because she had sold some for 32¢ each. Moreover, Boling said, he had just received a back issue of *Linn's* franked with six Fitzgeralds and a 1¢ stamp, although for the weight of the item *Linn's* mailroom should have used — and the post office should have required — six 32¢ stamps plus a 1¢ stamp.

The Fitzgerald stamp was the 13th in a somewhat arbitrary grouping of commemoratives that USPS calls the Literary Arts series, which began with a John Steinbeck stamp in 1979. Like its immediate predecessor (Tennessee Williams, 1995), the Fitzgerald was designed by Michael Deas and was horizontally arranged, with a head-and-shoulders portrait of the subject on one side and a background scene evocative of his work on the other. But whereas the Williams stamp was offset-printed by Ashton-Potter (USA) Ltd. and issued in panes of 20, the Fitzgerald stamp was produced by the Bureau of Engraving and Printing by the gravure method and issued in panes of 50.

Fitzgerald had been on CSAC's approved list for a Literary Arts stamp for a long time. In 1986, the late Bradbury Thompson, a Postal Service stamp designer and typographer, mocked up a vertical stamp design based on a profile photograph of Fitzgerald. The stamp, had it been issued, would have been similar to engraved stamps in the series honoring Herman Melville, T.S. Eliot and William Faulkner. However, it never came to pass.

Francis Scott Key Fitzgerald wrote five novels and 160 short stories. Born in St. Paul September 26, 1896, he was named for the author of *The Star-Spangled Banner*, a distant relative. He entered Princeton University in 1913, where he spent much of his time writing lyrics for Triangle Club theatrical productions. He left college without graduating, served in the Army in World War I and later made Princeton the setting for his first novel, *This Side of Paradise* (1920).

"It was perfect literary timing," wrote Thomas Fleming in a biographical sketch. "The '20s were beginning to roar, bathtub gin and flaming youth were on everyone's lips, and the handsome, witty Fitzgerald seemed to be the ideal spokesman for the decade. With his stunning southern wife Zelda, he headed for Paris and a mythic career of drinking from hip flasks, dancing until dawn, and jumping into outdoor fountains to end the party.

"Behind this facade was a writer struggling to make enough money to match his extravagant lifestyle and still produce serious work. His second novel, *The Beautiful and the Damned* (1922), which recounted an artist's losing fight with dissipation, was badly flawed. His next, *The Great Gatsby* (1925), the story of a gangster's pursuit of an unattainable rich girl, was close to a masterpiece."

Fitzgerald's ascent to literary fame soon was touched by tragedy. He became an alcoholic, and Zelda, jealous of his fame (or in some versions, thwarted by it), collapsed into mental illness. Home in an America in the grip of the Depression, they found readers no longer interested in flaming youth. The novel with which he had struggled for years, *Tender is the Night*, about a psychiatrist destroyed by his wealthy wife, was published

in 1934 to lukewarm reviews and poor sales. Fitzgerald retreated to Hollywood, where he made a precarious living as a scriptwriter and struggled to control his alcoholism. He found the energy to begin another novel, *The Last Tycoon* (1941), about a complex, gifted movie producer. He had finished about one-

The late Bradbury Thompson prepared this design for a proposed F. Scott Fitzgerald stamp in the Literary Arts series in 1986. Based on a profile photo of Fitzgerald, the stamp would have been similar to other commemoratives of the period that honored Melville, Eliot and Faulkner.

third of it when he died of a heart attack, December 21, 1940.

Not until the 1950s did critical interest in Fitzgerald revive. Today he is highly regarded as, in Fleming's words, "a writer with an acute sense of history, an intellectual pessimist who had grave doubts about Americans' ability to survive their infatuation with the bitch goddess success" who, nevertheless, "conveyed in his best novels and short stories the sense of youthful awe and hope America's promises created in many people."

The Design

Michael Deas' portrait of Fitzgerald, done in oil on paper, is based primarily on a photograph made in 1920, although he referred to other photographs as well. The picture shows the writer, then only 24, at his desk, a serious expression on his face. He wears a tweed coat and necktie. His hair is parted in the middle in the fashion of the times.

The background of the painting consists of a red sea and sky with the Long Island shore dimly visible in the distance. A boat floats offshore; a single green light casts its reflection on the water. It is the green light at the end of Daisy Buchanan's dock, which Jay Gatsby, protagonist of Fitzgerald's best-known work, could see from his own lawn. The light represented Gatsby's unattainable dream that once had "seemed so close that he could hardly fail to grasp it." With the boat, it evokes the familiar closing lines of the novel:

"Gatsby believed in the green light, the orgiastic future that year by year recedes before us. It eluded us then, but that's no matter — tomorrow we will run faster, stretch out our arms farther ... And one fine morning —

"So we beat on, boats against the current, borne back ceaselessly into the past."

"When you're condensing a person's life and work into an image less than one square inch, you have to have a motif that will speak in a fairly loud way," Michael Deas explained. "I didn't want to use a cliche, like dancing flappers or antique cars. If any one motif from

Michael Deas based his portrait of F. Scott Fitzgerald on this photograph made in 1920, when the writer was 24, shortly after the publication of his first novel, This Side of Paradise.

This design is one of two that Michael Deas painted before creating the final version that appeared on the stamp. In it, the coastal scene in the background is more distinct than on the final version, and two boats are visible instead of one. The portrait is slightly smaller relative to the whole, the eyes are more prominent and the part in Fitzgerald's hair is more to the side than it is on the stamp. Note that in this version of the typography, there is no period after the initial F; one was later added. The "32" denomination indicates that the Postal Service had in mind a conventional first-class-rate stamp instead of the second-ounce-rate stamp that actually was issued.

Fitzgerald's work comes to mind, it's that green light." Deas tried to make the scene "dreamlike," he added, to suggest the "lyricism" of Fitzgerald's prose.

Deas, whose admirers at the Postal Service uniformly describe him as a "perfectionist," painted the whole picture at least three times before he was satisfied. In the process, he made numerous subtle changes, including softening the background and making the details less clear-cut; in one version, there are two boats, but in the final painting only one is visible.

"It was mostly trying to get the likeness (of Fitzgerald)," Deas said. "He was a tough likeness to get. He looks very different in different periods of his life. He had a very tough life and it shows in his features later on. As a young man he was extremely handsome ... I was trying to get a look that was representative of him in between those periods."

The stamp, printed on BEP's old Andreotti gravure press, suffers by comparison with its predecessor in the Literary Arts series, the offset-printed Tennessee Williams stamp, and some postal officials expressed disappointment with it. The Williams printed image is much crisper, clearer and truer to the original art than the Fitzgerald. A telling point of comparison is the typography; although the type on the two stamps is from the same Times Roman family, the letters and numerals are more graceful on the Williams stamp, and the contrast between the thinner and heavier lines is considerably more striking.

First-Day Facts

Michael S. Coughlin, deputy postmaster general, dedicated the stamp at the Landmark Center in St. Paul as part of a week-long celebration of the centennial of Fitzgerald's birth.

Speakers were Eleanor Lanahan, the author's granddaughter; William J. Brown, vice president for Midwest area operations of USPS; and Page Cowles of the Fitzgerald Committee. Norm Coleman, mayor of St. Paul, gave the welcome.

The earliest-known prerelease use of a Fitzgerald stamp was on a cover postmarked Cody, Wyoming, September 18, nine days early.

32¢ ENDANGERED SPECIES (15 DESIGNS)

Date of Issue: October 2, 1996

Catalog Numbers: Scott 3105a-3105o (single stamps); 3105 (pane of 15)

Colors: black, cyan, magenta, yellow

First-Day Cancel: San Diego, California

First-Day Cancellations: 941,442 (includes 5,000 Endangered Species postal cards)

Format: Panes of 15, horizontal, 3 across, 5 down. Offset printing plates of 90 subjects (9 across, 10 down).

Overall Stamp Size: 1.56 by 1.225 inches; 39.6mm by 31.1mm

Perforations: 11.1 by 10.9 (Wista and Gammeler stroke perforator)

Selvage Inscription: "Endangered Species." "National Stamp/Collecting Month/ 1996 highlights/these 15 species/to promote aware-/ness of endangered/ wildlife. Each/generation must/work to protect the/delicate balance of/na- ture, so that/future generations/may share a sound/and healthy planet."

Selvage Markings: "© USPS 1995." ".32 X 15 = $4.80." "PLATE/POSITION" and diagram.

Designer (Photographer): James Balog of Boulder, Colorado

Typographer and Art Director: Richard Sheaff

Modeler: Joseph Sheeran, Ashton-Potter (USA) Ltd.

Project Manager: Terrence McCaffrey, USPS

Stamp Manufacturing: Stamps printed for Ashton-Potter (USA) Ltd., Williamsville, New York, by Sterling Sommer, Tonawanda, New York, on an Akiyama 628 6-color sheetfed offset press. Stamps perforated, processed and shipped by Ashton-Potter.

Quantity Ordered and Distributed: 223,650,000

Plate Number Detail: 1 set of 4 offset plate numbers preceded by the letter P in selvage next to upper and lower corner stamp on left side

Plate Number Combinations Reported: P1111, P2222, P3333, P4444

Paper Supplier: Coated Papers

Tagging: block tagging applied over stamps

The Stamps

On October 2, the Postal Service launched National Stamp Collecting Month with a pane of 15 stamps bearing photographs of different American animal species that are threatened with extinction. The Citizens' Stamp Advisory Committee had approved the set at the request of USPS marketing officials, who believed that the subject would have a special appeal to children and teenagers.

The stamps were sold nationwide on the first day of issue. The official dedication ceremony was held at the San Diego Zoo, home of one of the world's largest animal collections, on the zoo's 80th birthday.

On the same day, Mexico issued a pane of 24 stamps to promote awareness of its own endangered species. Although not a joint issue with the United States, the Mexican stamps were dedicated at the San Diego ceremony along with the U.S. stamps, and a similar ceremony for both nations' stamps was held in Mexico City. Mint panes of the Mexican stamps were sold through the USPS Philatelic Fulfillment Service Center for $6.

The species shown on the U.S. stamps are the black-footed ferret, Schaus swallowtail butterfly, brown pelican, San Francisco garter snake, ocelot, Gila trout, Hawaiian monk seal, thick-billed parrot, California condor, Wyoming toad, woodland caribou, Florida manatee, Florida panther, piping plover and American crocodile. All are on the U.S. Fish and Wildlife Service's List of Endangered and Threatened Wildlife and Plants, which currently includes 431 animal species.

The Endangered Species stamps were offset-printed for Ashton-Potter (USA) Ltd. by Sterling Sommer and have the extra-wide pictorial selvage that USPS is using with increasing frequency. Their designs were based on photographs by James Balog of Boulder, Colorado.

214

Originally, CSAC and the project's art director, Richard Sheaff, had intended to follow the usual practice of commissioning an illustrator to paint the images for the stamps. They changed their minds, however, after learning of Balog's work as a photographer of endangered species from CSAC member Richard Brock. Brock, a graphic designer, had helped Balog design a text-and-picture book titled *Anima*, and he convinced his associates that the photographer could make camera portraits of the selected animals that would work effectively in stamp designs.

As part of its promotion effort for the Endangered Species set, USPS sent a kit including teacher lesson plans and student guides, posters and "Stamper" cards to more than 65,000 classrooms and libraries nationwide to help educators generate awareness of endangered species. The glossy cards, 15 to a set, carried photographs of the animals featured on the stamps and a place on each card to affix the stamp in a plastic mount. In addition, an educational video focusing on six of the species was distributed to more than 20,000 schools.

The American Zoo and Aquarium Association (AZA) joined the Postal Service in sponsoring the 1996 National Stamp Collecting Month, with

Mexico's pane of 24 Endangered Species stamps and the U.S. pane of 15 were jointly issued at ceremonies in San Diego and Mexico City. The Mexico pane — 12 1.80-peso values and 12 2.70p values — pictures one large scene and includes a label at the top reading "Conservemos las especies de Mexico" (Conserve the species of Mexico).

its theme "Collect and Protect." "Using stamps to heighten the awareness of endangered wildlife is a great way to keep conservation on the minds of the public," said Sydney J. Butler, AZA's executive director.

Some collectors, and even some USPS officials, thought in retrospect that more could have been done to make the theme of the stamps explicit. In 1979, when the Postal Service issued four stamps depicting rare American wildflowers, the words "Endangered Flora" appeared on each stamp. Since then, however, CSAC and USPS staff have adopted a minimalist policy toward stamp typography, and on this issue the only place where the words "Endangered Species" appear is on the selvage.

"We wanted to keep the stamps clean and uncluttered," said Terrence McCaffrey, the stamps' project manager. "We were hoping people would save the entire pane as a collectible, so we decided not to label each one."

However, CSAC member Mary Ann Owens said she had to agree with those who thought each stamp should have been labeled. "Sometimes you don't see the forest for the trees," she said. "On the extra-large issues, we don't look at the stamps individually as much as we should ... We might learn from this and do it differently next time."

As an additional promotion for National Stamp Collecting Month, the Postal Service furnished a pictorial machine cancel die hub to the country's 10 highest-volume letter mail processing sites for use beginning October 1. The die hub, which is the part of a machine cancel that actually cancels the stamp or stamps on a letter, showed four stylized animals — a caribou, toad, fish and parrot — and the words: "Collect & Protect Endangered Species. 1996 National Stamp Collecting Month."

Ironically, heavy pictorial die hubs such as this one tend to obliterate stamps and make them undesirable to collect as used specimens. Their only value to collectors, as one writer pointed out, would be in serendipitous combinations with the designs of unrelated stamps, such as Popeye socking a fish or Marilyn Monroe with a parrot's beak.

Of all the animals on the pane, the one with the strongest public support for stamp honors was the Florida manatee. The principal credit for that belongs to a third-grade schoolteacher and her students.

In 1992, the teacher, Sylvia Wood, and her class at Westfield Area Elementary School in Westfield, Pennsylvania, did a research project on manatees. The students became concerned about the future prospects for the species, and at the suggestion of Wood, a stamp collector, they de-

This is the National Stamp Collecting Week machine die hub postmark, intended to promote the Endangered Species stamp pane and stamp collecting in general. Critics say such pictorial die hubs tend to make used stamps uncollectible.

cided to try to persuade the Postal Service to issue a manatee stamp.

The children drafted letters to CSAC, the postmaster general, and newspapers and magazines around the country; the latter, when published, generated more letters. Each child had a personal computer disk in the school's computer center and used it to send out multiple letters simply by changing the date and address.

Using Love stamps, the students wrote "We" to the left of the stamp and printed a rubber-stamp manatee to its right so the envelopes' message was "We love the manatee." They kept track of where the responses originated on a classroom map. The next year the new third-grade students picked up the campaign, and so did the third-grade class after that.

"They got a lot of skills out of this project," Wood told *Stamp Collector.* "They set a long-term goal and were able to achieve it, realizing that results are not always instantaneous."

Writing to the school after the Endangered Species stamps were announced, Mark D. Weinberg, manager of marketing communications and special events for USPS, said the children's efforts "helped make possible" the inclusion of the manatee stamp in the set. In recognition of their efforts, the Postal Service sent 21 members of Sylvia Wood's original third-grade class, now seventh-graders, along with Wood and five other chaperones, to SeaWorld in Orlando, Florida, home of the country's leading manatee research facility.

Their chartered bus, "The Manatee Express," left Westfield October 3 and made stops at tourist attractions in Washington, D.C., and Atlanta, Georgia, before arriving in Orlando, where they were honored October 7 at what USPS called "a manatee stamp celebration." The Postal Service paid for transportation and lodging for the trip.

Black-footed ferret (Mustela nigripes). This nocturnal member of the weasel family, 20 to 24 inches in length, once ranged throughout the North American plains. It is dependent on prairie dogs for both prey and habitat, living in burrows dug by the creatures it hunts. With the dwindling of prairie dog populations its own numbers fell catastrophically, and today it is the rarest mammal on the continent. It can be found in the wild as experimental populations in Wyoming, Montana and South Dakota.

Thick-billed parrot (Rhynchopsitta pachyrhyncha). When flying, this

bird, up to 16 inches in length, displays conspicuous yellow stripes on its underwings, and its piercing screeches can be heard for up to three miles. The parrot nests in tree cavities and feeds on pine nuts, acorns and juniper berries. It is primarily a resident of Mexico. A few reintroduced parrots are struggling to survive in southeast Arizona and southwest New Mexico, where the bird flourished until it was wiped out early in the century by min-

Thick-billed parrot
32
USA

ers, loggers and soldiers who hunted it and destroyed its forest habitat.

Hawaiian Monk Seal (Monachus schauinslandi). The largely solitary, sedentary monk seals rest and give birth under the hot sun on coral atolls in the northwest waters of the Hawaiian archipelago, but spend most of their days and nights at sea, diving deep for fish, lobster and octopus. Humans have put this species on the endangered list; as early as 1837, shipwrecked sailors ate monk seals to survive, and later they were exploited for fur and oil.

American Crocodile (Crocodylus acutus). This reptile lives in the salty marshes of the Everglades and the Florida keys. Despite their reputation, American crocodiles aren't aggressive toward humans. That trait belongs to the more numerous American alligators, which live in adjacent, less saline habitats. Crocodiles can be distinguished from alligators by their longer, more tapered jaws and triangular snouts with protruding teeth. Adult crocodiles have dull, scaly hides and may measure 12 feet in length. Crocodiles have been known to live well over 50 years.

Ocelot (Felis pardalis). Ocelots are so shy and reclusive, spending their nights hunting and their days hidden in thick brush, that even the biologists devoted to their recovery know little about their habits in the wild. They are found in southermost Texas, as well as Mexico and Central America. The beauty of this small but muscular cat has helped make it scarce; until a few years ago, European furriers bought ocelot skins for as much as $4,000 apiece. Protected from hunting by the Endangered Species Act, it suffers now from loss and fragmentation of the dense brushland that is its preferred habitat.

Schaus Swallowtail Butterfly (Heraclides aristodemus ponceanus). The Schaus butterfly is large, with wings up to five inches from tip to tip. Its distinctive half-diamond pattern of yellow stripes on the top of the dark brown wings helps distinguish it from other butterflies. It lives no longer than three weeks after emerging from its pupa. In 1992 Hurricane An-

Hawaiian monk seal
32
USA

32
USA
American crocodile

drew devastated its habitat in the Florida keys and nearly finished off the species. Today only a tiny population survives in Key Biscayne National Park.

Wyoming Toad (Bufo hemiophrys baxteri). This amphibian is a glacial relic. Its ancestors moved south ahead of the Ice Age glaciers, and when the ice retreated, they remained isolated around a series of ponds in southeast Wyoming's Laramie Basin. Over the next 12,000 years, the Wyoming toad evolved into a distinct subspecies, with a unique crown atop its head. It was believed extinct until about 150 individuals were found in 1987, and biologists have managed to keep the population from disappearing. Unlike other toads, the Wyoming toad spends most of its time in or around water. It eats insects, larvae and other small organisms.

Brown Pelican (Pelecanus occidentalis). This bird can weigh up to eight pounds and have a wingspan over seven feet. There are two similar subspecies: the California, which mainly lives on the southern California coast, and the Eastern, which inhabits areas along the southern Atlantic and Gulf coasts. Pelicans are rarely far from sea. They often nest on offshore islands, and eat fish almost exclusively. Both subspecies have suffered sharp declines in population from the pesticide-induced problem of thin eggshells.

California Condor (Gymnogyps californianus). With a wingspan of more than nine feet, the California condor is North America's largest flying bird. A triangular patch of white on the underside of each wing is visible only in flight. A scavenger like other vultures, the condor feeds on

animal carcasses, which it spots from high in the sky. The last wild condor was taken into captivity in 1987, when the species numbered only 27 individuals, and a captive-breeding and reintroduction program was begun. In 1992 the first captive pair were freed in the mountains northwest of Los Angeles. Others followed, including six fledglings released in December 1996 in Arizona, north of the Grand Canyon. The ultimate goal is to restore three separate populations of 150 birds each.

Gila Trout (Oncorhynchus gilae). Iridescent sides and gill covers distinguish the Gila trout from its relatives. It settles in deep pools of clearwater streams, feeding on insects and other invertebrates. It was formerly common throughout the Gila and San Francisco rivers and streams in New Mexico, and in Arizona's Agua Fria and Verde waterways, but its numbers and range have decreased substantially.

San Francisco Garter Snake (Thamnophis sirtalis tetrataenia). This small snake, which grows to just over four feet long, is harmless to humans and typically flees if disturbed. Striped in yellow, red and black, with red on the top of its head, it ranks with the most vividly colored American serpents. In recent years it has lost much of its marshy habitat in the San Francisco area to urban developers and roadbuilders, and only small populations remain in scattered colonies around reservoirs. Its diet includes frogs, toads and small fish. Biologists breed adults and release the young in their native areas.

Woodland Caribou (Rangifer tarandus caribou). The harsh mountainous terrain of the Washington-Idaho border is home to the lower United

States' "endangered" woodland caribou. Healthier populations exist in Alaska and British Columbia. Dense forests provide the animal with food and shelter. Caribou are closely related to reindeer. Unlike other deer, the females as well as the males grow antlers.

Florida Panther (Felis concolor coryi). This member of the cat family once ranged throughout the southeastern United States, but its population of 50 or so animals now is confined to south Florida. It prefers subtropical swamps and forest lands, far from humans. A single adult male needs a territory of 25 to 300 square miles to survive, depending on the variety and density of its prey. Deer and armadillo are its primary diet, but it also eats wild hogs, raccoons and other small animals. With a captive-breeding program begun in 1991, scientists hope to build up its numbers, but its fate is entwined with that of its vulnerable habitat.

Piping Plover (Pharadrius melodius). Most piping plovers nest along the Atlantic Ocean or above inland rivers in the Great Plains, but a few raise their families along the Great Lakes. A stocky bird, about 6½ inches long, it was nearly hunted to extinction early in this century, before passage of the Migratory Bird Treaty Act in 1918 led to a resurgence of its numbers. But it has come under renewed attack by less intentional but harder-to-regulate threats: waterfront development and off-road vehicles that disrupt its habitat.

Florida or West Indian Manatee (Trichechus manatus). This gentle mammal, sometimes called the sea cow, is large and blimplike, with two flippers forward and a fleshy paddle aft. It can reach more than 12 feet in length and weigh a ton and a half. Its habitat is the streams and brackish estuaries of Florida, where it floats just under the surface, browsing for aquatic plants, of which it devours 80 to 150 pounds a day. The few surviving manatees are protected from hunting, but are constantly menaced by the propellers of big power boats, and most surviving specimens show scars from these encounters.

Two of the 15 species had made previous appearances on U.S. stamps. The California condor was shown on one of four varieties issued in 1971 in a previous stamp promotion for the conservation of wildlife (Scott 1430). And the black-footed ferret was one of 50 North American Wildlife species painted by Chuck Ripper for a 1987 pane of stamps (Scott 2333). Ripper depicted his ferret in a pose much like the one that Balog captured in his photograph for the Endangered Species pane.

The Designs

When the project began in 1993, art director Richard Sheaff commissioned Leslie Evans, a Massachusetts illustrator, to prepare some sketches for the stamps. Because some types of animal would be more suitable graphically for a horizontal stamp and others would fit better in a vertical, Sheaff experimented with different pane layouts in which the stamps varied not only in orientation but in size and even shape.

Among the layouts of Evans' sketches that Sheaff showed CSAC was one consisting of 14 conventional four-sided stamps and one round stamp at the top, into which the butterfly image would fit. "I've always loved New Zealand's round kiwi stamp," Sheaff said. "As long as we were using a custom perforating die anyway, which we would have had to do with that layout, we could also have included a circle-shaped stamp at the top of the pane."

However, after Michael Brock and like-minded members of CSAC persuaded the design team to use photographs rather than illustrations for the set, Evans' sketches were put aside, along with the idea of giving the

Two animals from the Endangered Species pane had made previous appearances on U.S. stamps: the California condor, in Stanley W. Galli's design for a 1971 Wildlife Conservation stamp (Scott 1430), and the black-footed ferret, which Chuck Ripper painted, in a pose much like the one in James Balog's photograph, for the North American Wildlife issue of 1987 (Scott 2333).

stamps different sizes and shapes.

When James Balog was commissioned to make the photographs, postal officials weren't certain how many stamps would comprise the pane. For that reason, and to provide some flexibility in the selection process, Balog was asked to photograph several more animals than the 15 that ultimately ended up on stamps.

Balog and Sheaff worked from a list provided by the Fish and Wildlife Service that originally contained 50 species. Among those that didn't make the initial cut were such exotic animals as the Key Largo cotton mouse, the Point Arena mountain beaver, the Delmarva Peninsula fox squirrel, the blunt-nosed leopard lizard, the unarmored threespine stickleback and the Tooth Cave spider.

In deciding which species Balog would pursue with his camera, the designers' main consideration was to select animals that could be located and photographed in a reasonable period of time. Other factors were the need for biological and geographical diversity; the set, they decided, should include mammals, birds, fish, reptiles and insects, and should represent all major geographic areas.

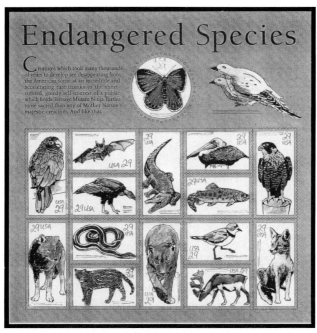

**Art director Richard Sheaff's original concept for the En-
dangered Species pane was of a set of 15 stamps of dif-
fering sizes and shapes, including a round stamp, with
artwork by illustrator Leslie Evans. Sheaff made this layout, with Evans' sketches and a text block of nonsense
prose for placement purposes, to show the Citizens' Stamp
Advisory Committee what he had in mind.**

"For me," Balog said, "the real issue, the aesthetic issue, was to create pictures that satisfied me in terms of bringing across some sort of emotional connection with the animal but yet were strong enough to play well at that tiny scale.

"I had never shot anything that was intended to be as small as a postage stamp in its primary presentation, and I was a little bit put off at first by having to make the pictures so small. Then I realized that this was the same kind of challenge that faced the artists in the Middle Ages who did Persian miniatures, and that it was possible to make tiny pieces of art that are aesthetically rewarding. You just had to think a little differently."

After Balog and Sheaff completed their preliminary planning, the photographer and his staff at Jupiter Pictures in Boulder began preparations for his photographic odyssey. Much of the basic work — locating the animals at zoos and other institutions, convincing the curators to let him photograph their wards, and scheduling his travel — was done by his studio manager, a woman named Sport ("That's the sum total of the name she goes by," Balog said). It was a project that would consume six months in 1995 and take him and his equipment — a Mamiya medium-format camera with normal and macro lens and Comet strobe lighting — more than 20,000 miles, from Hawaii to Florida with many stops in between.

For two of the species, however, Sheaff decided not to require Balog to take new pictures. One was the brown pelican, which Balog had photographed some time earlier at the Sun Coast Seabird Sanctuary in St. Petersburg, Florida. The other species was destined to give the Postal Service its biggest design headache of the entire project. It was the manatee.

Balog's existing portfolio included a photograph he had made at Sea World in Orlando, Florida, in 1989 of a seven-year-old female manatee named Marina. In this unusual picture, which had been published in Balog's book *Survivors: A New Vision of Endangered Wildlife*, Marina is out of the water, nose in the air, wrinkled belly facing the viewer.

"She is gentle and quiet," Balog had written, "happy to loll at pool's edge and feel me scratch her skin, talk to her, and shake her blubber. Her snout is soft leather, like deerskin, but the rest of her body has the rough tautness of a football made from sandpaper. She sleeps, then blinks an eye open and slips back beneath the waves as unexpectedly as she came."

Because shooting a new manatee picture would add to Balog's already-full schedule and require him to make an underwater dive, the design team and CSAC decided that his existing shot of Marina, although unconventional, would be suitable for the stamp. However, after the Postal Service released the design of the pane, including the manatee stamp, on November 7, 1995, it became obvious that many people disagreed with that view.

In early February 1996, *Florida Today*, a daily newspaper in Brevard County, Florida, printed a picture of the stamp and asked readers to telephone in their feelings about it. The response, as described by writer Billy Cox in an article published February 10, was strongly negative.

"I think it's the ugliest thing I've seen in my life," one reader commented. Manatees "have their own charm," another said, "and this doesn't show it."

Cox told *Linn's Stamp News* that the treatment of the manatee is an important issue in Brevard County. Even so, he said, he was surprised at the number of calls the newspaper received, beginning shortly after 5 a.m. on the day the picture was published.

"We got so many calls we had to clear the (voice mail) files, and clear the files, and clear the files," he said. "That's pretty unusual. People don't call unless it directly affects them, but I guess this directly affected them."

Linn's also received letters critical of the stamp. One writer thought the manatee looked like Jabba the Hutt in the *Star Wars* movies; another likened it to an accordion.

A Florida-based organization called the Save the Manatee Club urged the Postal Service to change the design. Judith Valle, director of the club, told James Tolbert and Terrence McCaffrey of the Postal Service that the animal shown on the stamp, with its overlapping folds of fat, was a disturbing reminder to her of dead manatees she had seen, their bodies slashed by motorboat propellers.

Tolbert and McCaffrey at first intended to hold firm. However, corporate relations and environmental officials of the Postal Service became alarmed at the criticism and insisted that a different picture be found. They were worried, among other things, that musician Jimmy Buffett, a co-founder of the Save the Manatee Club, would boycott a scheduled ceremony to promote the stamps if the design wasn't revised.

Because printing of the stamps hadn't yet begun, the design team was able to give in without causing major complications. Balog made a quick trip to Lowry Park Zoo in Tampa, Florida, with his scuba gear and underwater photography equipment, and dove in among the manatees to get some alternative pictures. Of these shots, Sheaff chose one that showed a pair of the mammals placidly swimming in the blue depths to use on the replacement stamp.

On April 15, USPS unveiled the revised manatee stamp. The accompanying press release only hinted that there had been any controversy. In the release, Judith Valle said: "We had some concerns about the initial design, but this final design really captures the gentle nature and unique

Manatee lovers protested when the Postal Service unveiled this design for the Manatee stamp, calling it ugly and an unnatural pose. The photograph, made by James Balog in 1989, was of a seven-year-old female manatee named Marina and had been previously published without stirring controversy. USPS bowed to the protests and had Balog make new manatee photos.

Balog made this alternative shot of a swimming manatee at Lowry Park Zoo in Tampa, Florida, but it was passed over in favor of his picture of a pair of manatees.

beauty of the manatees." Postmaster General Marvin T. Runyon was quoted as saying: "We appreciated the input we received from the Save the Manatee group and valued their suggestions as we finalized the design for this stamp."

None of the other 14 designs produced any notable public reaction.

For Balog, some of the photographs were more difficult to get than others, but he was able to draw on years of experience to smooth the process.

"It's a matter of knowing how to play this game, and how to ask the right questions of the animal keepers and schedule your photographic activity at the key time of day," he said. An example was his crocodile photograph, which showed the reptile with its jaws agape. "The trainers told me that if I wanted interesting action, I had to be there at 3:30 p.m., feeding time, and he'd open his mouth," Balog said. "So we timed our trip to make sure we'd be there in Tampa at 3:30. It was quite simple.

"You always have some anxiety when you fly 3,000 miles to shoot a picture, wondering whether for reasons completely out of your control — let's say, a hurricane — the whole situation will come apart on you and you won't get anything. But by and large I felt comfortable with the project, and it went pretty much as planned."

The closest thing to a mishap occurred after Balog had finished a long photo shoot with the Florida panther at the Wildlife Rescue shelter, also in Tampa. "The cat was lying on the ground and I was crouched behind him, while my assistant shot a picture of the two of us together," Balog recalled. "I had shorts on and my bare thigh was right behind the cat's head, and the cat kept looking back up at me. I had a feeling something was wrong — I was either too close to him, or he didn't like the fact that I was above him and he was taking it as a dominance gesture.

"All of a sudden he turned around, opened his mouth and slapped his jaws around my thigh. I can still feel the imprint of his fangs in my leg. He wasn't really trying to attack me, and he didn't break the skin, but he gave me a good squeeze. It was just a way to say that I was in his face and that I needed to back off and leave him alone. Which I did."

In contrast with that experience was what Balog called the "sweet" moment when Schaus swallowtail butterflies hatched from their chrysalises before his eyes at the University of Florida in Gainesville. The breeding center had notified him by phone that the insects were due to emerge, and the photographer entered the room just as it was happening. "It was incredible," Balog said. "These little shells were cracking apart and the butterflies would walk out of them and sit there with their wings all folded up in accordion-style pleats. Over the course of a couple of minutes they would unfurl the wings, and then they would have to wait for about an hour while the wings dried and became stiff enough to fly."

The California condor photograph, made at the San Diego Zoo, "drove me crazy," Balog admitted. "I had it fixed in my mind that I had to have a picture of the bird with its wings spread out. I was thinking of that classic Native American-style drawing of a condor sitting there with wings out to the side. I shot for two and a half days — it was physically very grueling because the weather was so hot — and I never got what I wanted. But as we went along, I did get the head shot that ended up on the stamp.

"I was despondent when we were through with the shooting, but when I got home I realized, hey, this one isn't so bad. It turned out I had something after all."

One of the most striking designs in the set shows two San Francisco garter snakes as graceful sinuous lines against a stark white background. "It was a real bonus when we got there (a zoo in Seattle, Washington) and discovered that we had more than one snake to work with," Balog said. On the same trip, Balog stopped in nearby Tacoma, Washington, at a preserve called Northwest Trek to photograph the woodland caribou, only to find that the animals had shed their antlers. He had to return several months later when they had grown new ones.

The ferret and ocelot pictures were made at the Cheyenne Mountain Zoo in Colorado Springs, Colorado. Because both animals were so active and lively, Balog came away with relatively few usable frames. He photographed the Gila trout through the glass wall of a tank at a Fish and Wildlife Service facility in Mescalero, New Mexico. He found his Wyoming toad in a Fish and Wildlife station in that state; he placed the creature on a sheet of clear plexiglas over white paper to get the reflection effect he wanted.

The parrot was photographed at a zoo in Fresno, California. The two piping plovers were found at Lincoln Park Zoo in Chicago, and the monk seal was in a facility in Honolulu, Hawaii.

While on the Hawaii trip, Balog also photographed two other creatures, the Oahu tree snail and the Hawaiian stilt. Sheaff worked both pictures up as stamp designs, but they were left out of the final 15. Including them, Sheaff said, would have made the pane too Hawaii-heavy.

Sheaff and Balog, as well as some of the members of CSAC, wanted to include a bat in the set of stamps. It didn't happen, but not for want of effort on Balog's part. In a remote cave on Cherokee Indian territory in Oklahoma, guided by a team of experts conducting a bat census, the photographer found himself stalking the Ozark big-eared bat.

Richard Sheaff mocked up James Balog's photographs of the gray bat, the Hawaiian stilt and the Oahu tree snail as stamps, but none made the final cut for the pane.

"We were literally crawling on our bellies in this limestone cave in the dark," he recalled. "We couldn't put flashlights on because it would flip the bats out. We went inside the earth for a ways, and we could hear them — they have a very high-pitched squeak — and then we turned on a light with a red filter, so it wouldn't aggravate them, and there they were, a pair of these incredibly rare bats hanging from the ceiling. They were so tiny that I had to shoot with a macro lens, and they would fly away if you got too close. But I got a fairly decent picture of them."

The group then went to another cave a few miles away where the biologists were conducting their species count by netting bats as they emerged

These Balog photographs of a red wolf were mocked up as stamp designs, including one in vertical format. However, newly reported questions about whether the red wolf was a distinct species, plus the unpopularity of the wolf in some sections of the West, led to a decision not to include the animal on the pane.

from the entrance at sunset. Most of these were gray bats, also an endangered species but not as rare as the Ozark big-eared variety. "We set up a little photo studio there in the oak trees," Balog said. "They would very gingerly carry one of these bats over to us and we'd take its picture and they would let it go. Later we went inside the cave, and it was wild — bats all over the place, fluttering around and squeaking, with their wings beating as they went by our faces. We shot pictures inside until about 1 o'clock in the morning."

Out of this group of photographs, Sheaff chose one of a gray bat hanging upside down to test as a stamp design. The final verdict of USPS staff and CSAC was that the dark, rather curiously shaped form in the picture wouldn't make a satisfactory stamp, and the bat stamp, to the regret of all, fell by the wayside.

Another animal that had strong support within CSAC was the red wolf. However, two factors were decisive in keeping it off the final list. One was political: the fact that many Western sheep ranchers harbor a strong anti-wolf sentiment. The other was technical. Before the list was finalized, *Scientific American* published in its July 1995 issue a timely article, "The Problematic Red Wolf," reporting that new genetic evidence has led some scientists to believe that the red wolf isn't a distinct species after all, but a long-established hybrid of the coyote and the gray wolf. This provided a scientific rationale for dropping the animal.

The 15 stamps on the pane are arranged three across by five down and are contained in a white block that is surrounded by the color photograph comprising the selvage artwork. The photograph, meant to represent a generic wildlife habitat, is one that Richard Sheaff himself had made in Vermont and kept in his files.

The Florida panther stamp, in the lower-left corner, is the only one in which an image breaks out of its borders. The panther's forelegs cross the bottom row of perforations as well as the white margin and enter the selvage illustration. "It was a vertical image, and there was no way to crop it and do it justice," said Terrence McCaffrey. "So we decided to let it bleed off the edge. Of course, that made it necessary to keep the panther in the bottom row of stamps when Dick (Sheaff) was laying out the pane."

The words "Endangered Species" are stretched across the top part of the selvage. All the typography on the pane, including the inscriptions on the stamps, is in a font called American Typewriter. The text block in the

This is an unused alternative design for the Gila Trout stamp that emphasizes the fish's head and dorsal fin.

229

selvage was set in a heavier weight to ensure its legibility when printed over the photograph.

First-Day Facts

Virginia Noelke, chairperson of CSAC, dedicated the U.S. Endangered Species stamps at the San Diego Zoo ceremony, attended by several hundred area schoolchildren. C.P. Carlos Montijo Soto of the Mexican Postal Service dedicated Mexico's stamps.

Azeezely S. Jaffer, USPS manager of stamp services, welcomed the guests. Speakers were David Sidoni of Nickelodeon TV and Joan Embery, the zoo's goodwill ambassador.

A long list of honored guests included Zhang Zhihe, president of the China National Stamp Corporation, and five other CNSC officials; Bill L. Fox, president of the zoo's board of trustees, and Douglas Myers, the zoo's executive director; several members of the Citizens' Stamp Advisory Committee, which was meeting in San Diego; San Diego Postmaster Glenn Crouch; and stamp photographer James Balog.

Rusty and Nelson, two of the zoo's sea lions; Pelona, an Andean condor; and Nokona, a North American timber wolf, also were on hand.

In Mexico City, Tirso del Junco M.D., chairman of the USPS Board of Governors, and James Grubiak, USPS vice president for international business, joined Mexican officials to dedicate the two countries' stamps.

Other zoos around the country hosted their own educational programs in conjunction with the Endangered Species stamps, including Lincoln Park Zoo in Chicago and Busch Gardens in Tampa, Florida.

32¢ COMPUTER TECHNOLOGY

Date of Issue: October 8, 1996

Catalog Number: Scott 3106

Colors: black, cyan, magenta, yellow (offset); green (PMS 347), red (PMS 185) (intaglio)

First-Day Cancel: Aberdeen Proving Ground, Maryland

First-Day Cancellations: 153,688

Format: Panes of 40, vertical, 8 across, 5 down. Offset printing plates of 160 subjects (10 across, 16 around). Intaglio printing plates of 160 subjects (10 across, 16 around).

Overall Stamp Size: 1.23 by 1.56 inches; 31.09mm by 39.59mm

Perforations: 10.9 by 11.1 (Wista and Gammeler stroke perforator)

Selvage Markings: "© USPS 1996." ".32 x 40 = $12.80." "PLATE/POSITION" and diagram.

Designer: Nancy Skolos and Tom Wedell of Charlestown, Massachusetts

Typographer: Nancy Skolos

Modeler: Joseph Sheeran, Ashton-Potter (USA) Ltd.

Engraver: lettering photochemically engraved

Art Director: Richard Sheaff

Project Manager: Vance Harris, USPS

Stamp Manufacturing: Stamps printed by Ashton-Potter (USA) Ltd., Williamsville, New York, on a Stevens Varisize Security Documents webfed 6-color offset, 3-color intaglio press. Stamps perforated, processed and shipped by Ashton-Potter.

Quantity Ordered and Distributed: 93,612,000

Plate Number Detail: 1 set of 4 offset plate numbers preceded by the letter P and 2 intaglio plate numbers in selvage above or below each corner stamp

Plate Number Combinations Reported: P1111-11, P2222-11

Paper Supplier: Coated Paper

Tagging: phosphored paper

The Stamp

The 50th anniversary of ENIAC (Electronic Numerical Integrator and Calculator), the world's first general-purpose electronic digital computer and the prototype of most computers in use today, occurred in 1996. On October 8, the Postal Service marked the occasion with a stamp commemorating the role of computers in modern life.

Officials at the University of Pennsylvania, where ENIAC was conceived and assembled, had wanted USPS to single out their specific computer for postal honors. However, because many individuals and institutions had played important roles in the development of the computer, the Postal Service decided to make the stamp a general salute to computer technology, and give the ENIAC anniversary special recognition through the design unveiling and first-day ceremonies.

This solution was similar to one USPS had arrived at earlier in the year when it issued a stamp commemorating the sport of marathoning in general but dedicated it in Boston in connection with the 100th running of the world's oldest distance race, the Boston Marathon.

"I would have liked a stamp that said, 'The University of Pennsylvania — On to the 21st Century!' " Barbara Beck, Penn's director of news and public affairs, said laughingly. "But I think the Postal Service was wise and generous, and the stamp they came up with was not only beautiful but really got the message across that computing is and will be a major part of our lives."

The stamp's design was unveiled February 14, 1996, at a dinner in Philadelphia co-sponsored by the university to honor the scientists who developed ENIAC. Representing USPS were Loren Smith, chief marketing officer and senior vice president, and S. David Fineman of the Board of Governors. The October 8 first-day ceremony was held at the Army Research Laboratory at Maryland's Aberdeen Proving Ground, a military facility that played a key role in ENIAC's development.

At the Philadelphia ceremony, Loren Smith used a light wand to launch the first-ever laser unveiling of a U.S. postage stamp design. In his remarks, the executive stressed the role of the computer and technology in the evolution of the modern Postal Service. Largely because of computers, Smith said, USPS now delivers 181 billion pieces of mail a year, twice as much as it delivered in the mid-1970s, and handles it "with virtually the same number of employees on the rolls today as we had 20 years ago."

The accompanying news release noted that even the design and production of stamps — including the one Smith unveiled that day — involves computer technology. "Virtually every stamp design now is prepared for presentation and production on computers," the release said. "The majority of stamp designs sent to production are forwarded in the form of a digital electronic file, meaning printers may never even see the original artwork."

The Computer Technology stamp was printed by Ashton-Potter (USA) Ltd. by a combination of offset and intaglio. A semijumbo in format, it was issued in panes of 40.

ENIAC had its origin in a top-secret military joint project of the Moore School of Electrical Engineering at Penn and the ballistic research laboratory (BRL) at Aberdeen. At the outset of World War II, the BRL prepared firing and bombing tables for the Army and Army Air Corps using the Bush differential analyzer, which has been acknowledged as the world's first analog computer. But a swifter way of doing the thousands of necessary computations was needed.

At the Moore School, the problem was put to Dr. John W. Mauchly, a professor of electrical engineering. He decided that the project called for an electronic digital machine. Teamed with a 23-year-old engineer named J. Presper Eckert Jr., Mauchly submitted a proposal in August 1942 with a detailed design specification for such a machine, and $400,000 in federal funding was approved. The project wasn't completed until after the war, but in February 1946 ENIAC was assembled and switched on.

ENIAC was massive, like all early computers. It weighed more than 30 tons and measured 10 feet in height and 80 feet in width. With its 18,000 vacuum tubes, it had a huge appetite for electricity and presented a major cooling problem. At a press demonstration, ENIAC dazzled onlookers by multiplying the number 97,367 by itself 5,000 times in less than half a second.

In January 1947, ENIAC was installed at Aberdeen. Despite its capabilities, this pioneering machine also had significant shortcomings. Its computing power, by today's standards, was minute; it was comparable, as Vice President Al Gore noted during a 1996 speech at Penn, to the microprocessors used to create musical tunes in today's novelty greeting cards. While programmable in principle, ENIAC could be switched from one kind of task to another only with great difficulty. To change a program, one literally had to rewire part of the machine.

It took the Moore School's next major computer, EDVAC, to incorporate the concept of the stored program — the major single factor that allowed computers to advance far beyond the capabilities of ENIAC and its contemporaries.

The Design

The idea of unconventionally shaped stamps had intrigued art director Richard Sheaff and other members of the Postal Service's stamp design team for some time. As reported in previous chapters, Sheaff originally

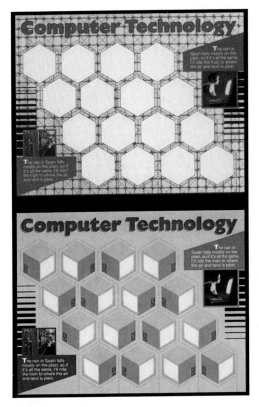

proposed that one of the stamps on the 1996 Endangered Species pane be in the form of a circle, and another art director, Carl Herrman, had created a set of triangular designs for the 1996 Olympic Games centennial only to find that they couldn't be used because of production difficulties.

In one brainstorming session, CSAC members and art directors discussed such unorthodox stamp shapes as hexagons and even octagons. Later, when the committee first was considering a stamp dealing with computers, Sheaff thought he saw an opportunity to turn the talk into action.

"One of the things I noticed was that a six-sided shape is also the shape of a cube, as seen from an angle, which could also be the shape of a computer monitor," Sheaff said. He worked up some designs for panes incorporating hexagonal stamps, with various kinds of pictorial selvage with images related to computers.

Nothing came of this concept, however. Later, when the committee addressed a specific proposal — a Computer Technology stamp linked to the ENIAC anniversary — the key question wasn't what shape the stamp should be but what should be the theme of its design. The committee members didn't know what they wanted the stamp to "say." In order to offer them some approaches they could discuss, Sheaff commissioned several designers and illustrators to prepare sketches.

"One thing that made some sense to the committee was the idea of miniaturization — the idea of components becoming smaller and smaller, but more and more powerful," Sheaff said. "Then, as they got into it, they also liked the idea of presenting the computer as an extension of human capabilities and senses, which is the direction that many of the designers' concepts ended up going."

The designers avoided literal images, such as pictures of a large mainframe computer or an individual operating a personal computer at home. Instead, they submitted graphic and abstract designs of the kind favored

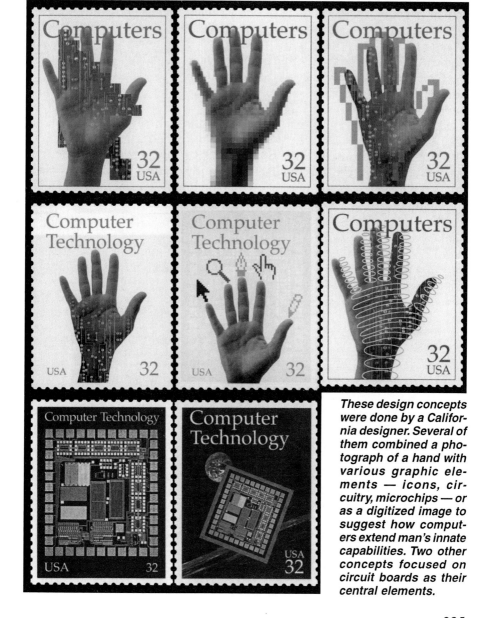

These design concepts were done by a California designer. Several of them combined a photograph of a hand with various graphic elements — icons, circuitry, microchips — or as a digitized image to suggest how computers extend man's innate capabilities. Two other concepts focused on circuit boards as their central elements.

by some of the newer members of CSAC, particularly Meredith Davis, head of graphic design at the North Carolina State University School of Design, and Phil Meggs, a Richmond, Virginia, graphic designer. Most of their proposals consisted of combinations of visual elements related to computers, such as icons, microchips, circuitry and binary-code numbers. The designers who took the "human extension" approach made their point by including parts of the body whose power was enhanced by the computer: the hand, the eye and the brain.

In the end, it was a series of designs featuring the brain that the committee favored. These were the work of Nancy Skolos and Tom Wedell, a husband-and-wife team from Boston. Skolos is a designer and Wedell a photographer, and together they created a computerized montage of a human brain — scanned into their computer from an engraving in a 19th-century anatomy textbook — partially covered by small photographed cubes. Some of the cubes were blank, while others contained parts of circuit boards and binary language.

Skolos and Wedell refined their design through several stages. Even after the formal unveiling February 14, they made further modifications at the request of the art director and USPS staff, so that the stamp as issued varied in some of its details from the illustration that first was made public. The effect of the last-minute changes was to make the design a little simpler, with fewer and larger elements. Officials hoped, by thus making the design easier to "read," to avoid a repeat of a recent unfortunate experience.

In 1995, the Postal Service had issued a stamp marking the 75th anniversary of Woman Suffrage with a contemporary design by April Greiman featuring a montage of photographs and graphic elements. However, the design, at stamp size, was difficult to decipher, and the problem was com-

A Pennsylvania illustrator whose clients include software firms prepared these two concept sketches, one of a globe inside a computer monitor, the other a hand with computer icons and other images, both against backgrounds of binary-code numbers.

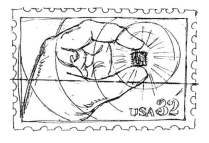

A Texas illustrator created these concept sketches, two as rough sketches that focused on a computer chip, the other a montage of graphic elements in finished-design form.

A husband-and-wife team who operate a design institute in Michigan created these rather far-out concepts. CSAC quickly decided they weren't what it had in mind for the Computer Technology stamp.

These design concepts, including one with the profile of Benjamin Franklin, were prepared by Nancy Skolos and Tom Wedell as they worked toward creating the design that ultimately was approved for the ComputerTechnology stamp.

pounded by a less-than-satisfactory printing job on a new press. Numerous critics — including some CSAC members — labeled the stamp an incomprehensible mishmash.

For this reason, once officials had made the decision to risk a photomontage approach again, they resolved to do their best to make the elements at least recognizable.

"We realized that the final version would probably be challenging also," Sheaff said, "but we wanted to improve the readability as much as possible. So I went back to Nancy Skolos, and she was very amenable to reworking it."

"It's another radically contemporary stamp design," added Terrence McCaffrey, the project manager. "It's something that not everybody is going to like ... I think it's an interesting design; I think it works.

"We need to take some new approaches in design ... to bring some balance to the program. Not all stamps are going to look like this one, and not all are going to be conventional and engraved. We're trying to appeal to a wide audience ...

"Designs such as this are being very well received in the graphic design community. We'll continue to explore such designs, but we'll try to simplify them so they read well at stamp size."

The stamp, as issued, is a semijumbo, vertically arranged. The brain and its superimposed cubes are a pale blue in color and the long shadows cast by the cubes are a darker blue. The words "Computer Technology," in an Adobe typeface called OCRB, stretch across the stamp near the

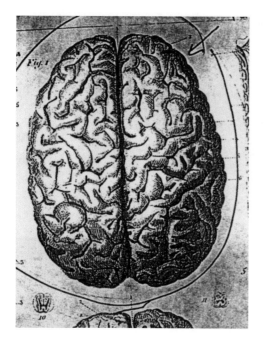

This drawing of a human brain from a 19th-century anatomy textbook was the source of the brain image on the accepted design for the Computer Technology stamp.

center. A large "32," in staggered gold numerals on a blue panel, is in the upper-left corner. The only intaglio portions of the design are the word "Computer," in red, and the "USA," in green.

First-Day Facts

The Computer Technology stamp was dedicated by Gerald McKiernan, USPS vice president of legislative affairs, at a ceremony at the Army Research Laboratory's "Top of the Bay Club" in Building 30 at Aberdeen Proving Ground.

Featured speakers included Representative Robert L. Ehrlich Jr., Republican of Maryland; Major General Robert D. Shadley, commander, U.S. Army Ordnance Center and School; and Dr. John W. Lyons, director of the research laboratory.

The earliest-known prerelease use of a Computer Technology stamp was on a cover postmarked in Fayetteville, North Carolina, October 3, five days before the stamp's dedication.

50¢ CYCLING (2 DESIGNS)

Date of Issue: November 1, 1996

Catalog Numbers: Scott 3119 (full pane); 3119a-b (individual stamps)

Colors: yellow, magenta, cyan, black

First-Day Cancel: New York, New York, and Hong Kong

First-Day Cancellations: 290,091

Format: Panes of 2, horizontal, 2 across. Gravure printing cylinders of 18 panes containing 36 stamp subjects (3 panes across, 6 around) manufactured by Armotek Industries, Palmyra, New Jersey.

Overall Stamp Size: 1.56 by 0.99 inches; 25.1mm by 39.6mm

Pane Size: 5.25 by 3.5 inches; 133.35mm by 88.9mm

Perforations: 11.1 (APS rotary perforator)

Selvage Markings: "CYCLING." "© USPS 1996."

Designer and Typographer: McRay Magleby of Provo, Utah

Modeler: Richard C. Sennett

Art Director: Carl Herrman

Project Manager: Terrence McCaffrey, USPS

Stamp Manufacturing: Stamps printed for Stamp Venturers by J.W. Fergusson and Sons, Richmond, Virginia, on Champlain webfed gravure press 1. Stamps perforated, processed and shipped at Stamp Venturers, Fredericksburg, Virginia.

Quantity Ordered and Distributed: 20,000,000 panes (40,000,000 stamps)

Cylinder Number Detail: No numbers

Paper Supplier: Paper Corporation U.S./Brown Bridge

Tagging: block tagging only on the colored portions of the stamps

The Stamps

The final U.S. commemoratives of 1996 were two 50¢ stamps saluting the sport of cycling. The stamps — one of each — were contained in a miniature pane, which USPS referred to as a souvenir sheet. They were issued November 1 in two cities: New York, site of the American Stamp Dealers Association Postage Stamp Mega-Event, and Hong Kong, where the Tour of China 96 cycling race began on that date.

The Postal Service's purpose in issuing the pane was to have an item it could sell at international cycling meets in which the USPS Pro Cycling Team competed, to help defray the team's $1 million annual subsidy. The 50¢ denomination of each stamp covered the international postal card rate, and the $1 total face value made a convenient selling price.

Collectors generally were unable to buy the stamps at U.S. post offices, except for those with philatelic windows. Orders also could be placed with the Philatelic Fulfillment Service Center in Kansas City, Missouri.

The stamps were a late addition to the 1996 commemorative stamp program. The designs still were being finalized in early May 1996, a few days before Deputy Postmaster General Michael Coughlin unveiled them May 21 at China 96, the Ninth Asian International Philatelic Exhibition in Beijing, China.

"America's commemorative stamp program has celebrated many important themes," Coughlin said. "Not the least of these, this year, is professional cycling. It is one of the world's most popular sports, and is viewed each year by more than 60 million spectators."

When the Citizens' Stamp Advisory Committee first learned that USPS marketing officials were pushing for a pair of cycling stamps, its members were less than enthusiastic. But they knew the project had the endorsement of Loren E. Smith, at the time the Postal Service's senior vice president and chief marketing officer and the man whose idea it was to organize a cycling team as a way of promoting USPS internationally.

"They felt it was something that would eventually get the approval of the postmaster general anyhow," one official explained. "They saw the handwriting on the wall and said, 'This is an internal initiative and we'll support it.'"

Terrence McCaffrey, head of stamp design, and his art directors were able to establish some guidelines for the stamps in discussions with Richard Arvonio, manager of operations and direct marketing for Stamp Services, and other marketing officials. The marketing people specified that the inscription on the stamps should be simply "cycling," and the design

241

should show generic racing cyclists, rather than identifiable members of the Postal Service team.

The miniature panes were gravure-printed by Stamp Venturers in sheets of 18 panes (36 stamps). The two stamps were arranged se-tenant horizontally in the lower-right corner of the pane. They were perforated, although the perfs didn't extend to the edges of the pane; postal clerks were expected to sell entire panes, not individual stamps. No plate numbers appeared on the panes, and the only selvage text, other than the word "CYCLING" in large letters, was a small black copyright line ("© USPS 1996") next to the left-hand stamp.

The most recent comparable philatelic item issued by USPS was the Norman Rockwell Four Freedoms pane of 1994, which contained a block of four stamp varieties. Like the Cycling stamps, the Four Freedoms stamps bore the 50¢ denomination and were available only in the miniature-pane format. However, the Rockwell pane did contain explanatory text in its selvage; the Cycling pane did not.

A Melbourne, Australia, stamp dealer named Max Stern arranged to have 100,000 Cycling panes overprinted in gold ink with a map of the Tour of China 96 race, the phrase "Tour of China '96" and Chinese characters. The overprinting was on the selvage and not the stamps. The item wasn't sanctioned by USPS and has no catalog status.

Stern told *Linn's Stamp News* that he arranged the overprinting in conjunction with a Taiwanese dealer who was in charge of the distribution and marketing of the panes. The design and overprinting were done in China, Stern said. He priced the panes at $2 Australian (approximately $1.60 in U.S. currency).

USPS announced that the Cycling stamp images would be displayed on the jerseys worn by members of the Postal Service's Pro Cycling Team when they competed in 1997 cycling races in the United States, Europe and Asia. The team's goal was to compete in the 1997 Tour de France.

The Tour de France is rated the world's third largest sporting event, with more than 20 million spectators and television coverage in 120 countries. American Greg LeMond's three victories in this prestigious race have been credited with significantly increasing U.S. awareness of the sport of professional cycling. More than four million spectators watch cycling races annually in this country.

Bicycles on stamps constitutes a popular topical, and several U.S. stamps and stamped envelopes showing bicycles have been issued since the first one, the 10¢ Special Delivery stamp of 1902.

Bicycle racing was depicted on a 6¢ Olympic Games stamp of 1972, a 35¢ Olympic Games airmail stamp of 1983 and one of the 20 32¢ Atlanta Centennial Olympic Games stamps of 1996. The U.S. Transportation coil series included a 5.9¢ stamp in 1982 showing a high-wheel bicycle of the 1870s, a 6¢ stamp in 1985 depicting an 1880s tricycle, and a 24.1¢ stamp in 1988 featuring a tandem bike. One of the four 6¢ Christmas antique toys stamps of 1970 showed a mechanical tricycle. A 15¢ stamped envelope of 1980 displayed a high-wheeler on its indicium stamp and a racing bicycle in its cachet area.

The Designs

To design these last two commemorative stamps of 1996, USPS turned to the same illustrator who had designed the year's first commemorative, for Utah statehood: McRay Magleby of Provo, Utah.

Magleby is a cyclist, although he favors mountain bikes rather than racing bikes. "I like to pick people who have a passion for the subject," said art director Carl Herrman. "I was looking for a design that would be nice, clean and simple, and Mac turned out to be the perfect choice.

"Mac is famous for his posters, and these stamps and pane really have that look — the look of a great poster."

Magleby created the stamp and selvage images by the same method he had used for the Utah project. He made pencil outlines of the figures, scanned them into his computer, and then filled in the colors, using the Adobe Illustrator program. For pictorial reference, Magleby used color photographs of the USPS cycling team supplied by Richard Arvonio.

CSAC, in giving its reluctant approval to the project, had proposed that the issue be limited to a single stamp, but Arvonio and other marketing officials insisted on two stamps in order to maximize revenue. Someone then suggested that the same design be used for both stamps, but with different colors. Terrence McCaffrey vetoed that idea.

"I said, if we're going to have two different stamps, let's make them look different," McCaffrey said. "I want different colors AND different

This is one of several color photographs of the USPS Pro Cycling Team that McRay Magleby used for reference. The team member shown here closely resembles the cyclist Magleby drew for the first of the two stamps on the pane.

poses."

Each of Magleby's two stamps showed a side view of a bicycle racer against a plain background, but in conformance with McCaffrey's instructions, the images differ slightly, with the second stamp showing more of a frontal view of the cyclist. On the first stamp, the background gradates from a dark brownish orange on the left to a lighter orange on the right; on the second one, the gradation is from blue-violet to aqua.

The two stamps are surrounded by a narrow white border, outlined in black. This separates their designs from the large selvage design, which depicts a team of three riders pedaling side by side against a plain background that shades from maroon to violet. The word "CYCLING," in plain block dropout-white capitals, runs up the left edge of the pane. On each stamp the same word, also in dropout white but in smaller letters, runs up the left edge, and "USA 50" is in the upper-right corner.

Magleby's cyclists are stylized, with bodies and features defined by simple lines and shapes. Their faces are white, with heavy black shadows

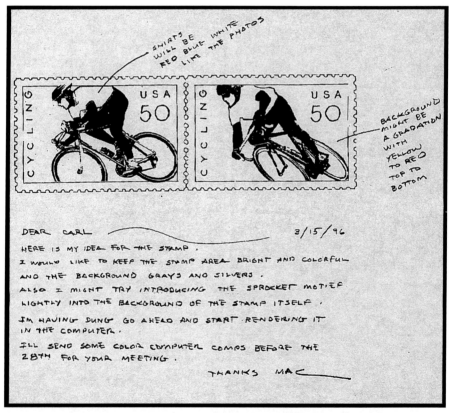

McRay Magleby sent Carl Herrman this sketch of the designs that ultimately were used on the two stamps, along with his suggestions for the color scheme. "Dung," whom Magleby refers to in his note, is a colleague and assistant to the artist.

244

beneath the helmets and on their necks and throats. Their uniform jerseys are red, white and blue, similar to those of the Postal Service team but without the wording and corporate logos that cover the team uniforms.

The design team settled on the basic stamp designs fairly quickly. However, finding a suitable design for the selvage part of the pane was more complicated.

Magleby's first approach was to create a graphic pattern consisting of enlarged pedals and sprocket wheels with the word "CYCLING" repeated several times. "We liked it, because it emphasized the stamps and played down the background," McCaffrey said. "Unfortunately, Rick (Arvonio) and those above him didn't like it. They thought it was too cold."

Carl Herrman then mocked up a pane using a color photograph of a bicycle race, with the racers and background blurred by the speed of the

These two proposed selvage designs incorporate graphic images of bicycle gears and sprockets, and the word "CYCLING" repeated several times.

Carl Herrman mocked up this color action photo as a potential selvage illustration, but officials decided it didn't work effectively with Magleby's posterlike stamp designs.

In the process of developing the multiple-image selvage design, Magleby made these six sketches for Carl Herrman's consideration.

In this version of the selvage design, the cyclist's image on the first stamp is enlarged and projected behind the pair of stamps.

action. However, officials decided that the photo and Magleby's stamp art were an unsatisfactory match of styles. An alternative, and more promising, concept was to fill the selvage with an enlargement of one of the two stamp images, or a portion thereof. In the end, the problem was solved by having Magleby create a new design — the three cyclists racing in formation — just for the selvage area.

"It gave very much of a family look to the stamps and the selvage," Herrman said.

Because the project demanded such fast work, CSAC and its design subcommittee, which normally would be closely involved in the development of the design, didn't see the final product until after the computer disk containing the electronic design file had been sent to Stamp Venturers. "We said a little prayer that the committee would buy the design," McCaffrey said. "When they saw it, the design subcommittee really liked it. They said it was very strong, that we'd done a good job. Subsequently the full committee blessed it as well."

First-Day Facts

Mary Ann Owens of the Citizens' Stamp Advisory Committee dedicated the Cycling stamps in a ceremony prior to the second day of the Postage Stamp Mega-Event, held in New York City's Jacob Javits Center.

Owens, a well-known collector of topical stamps, listed for the audience all the U.S. stamps that have pictured bicycles, tricycles and motorcycles. She included the bicycle Mail Route local stamp for service from Fresno to San Francisco, California, in July 1894. It's the only local to show a bicycle, she said, adding: "Most locals were issued before there were bicycles."

Featured speakers were Mike Greehan, publisher of *Bicycling* magazine, and Randy Neil, president of the American Philatelic Society. Phil Bansner, president of the American Stamp Dealers Association, gave the welcome. Three members of the USPS Pro Cycling Team were honored guests: Darren Baker, George Hincapie and Marty Jemison.

Robert F. Rider of the Postal Service Board of Governors dedicated the stamps in Hong Kong November 1 at the start of the Tour of China 96 race.

A cover bearing the Cycling pane is known with a Fort Myers, Florida, Cape Coral South branch handstamp dated October 29, three days before the dedication date.

Special Stamps

Special stamps are issued to convey certain generic messages on the part of the mailer. They customarily are printed in greater quantities than commemoratives and are on sale for longer periods.

Thirteen special stamps were issued in 1996: one Love stamp, 10 Christmas stamps, one self-adhesive stamp with a winter holiday theme for vending through automatic teller machines, and a self-adhesive celebrating Hanukkah. The Hanukkah stamp, the first U.S. stamp marking a religious holiday other than Christmas, was a joint issue with Israel. Its issuance launched a new series USPS is calling "Special Celebration."

For the first time, a Madonna and Child Christmas stamp was issued as a self-adhesive as well as with water-activated gum. For the first time since 1988, there was no conventional booklet version of the traditional and contemporary Christmas stamps.

32¢ LOVE (SELF-ADHESIVE)

Date of Issue: January 20, 1996

Catalog Number: Scott 3030 (single stamp), 3030a (pane of 20)

Colors: yellow, magenta, cyan, black (offset); red (intaglio) (stamps); special red, black (covers)

First-Day Cancel: New York, New York

First-Day Cancellations: 57,639 (includes 1¢ Kestrel coil and 32¢ Flag Over Porch self-adhesive in pane of 10)

Format: Panes of 20 stamps plus 1 non-stamp label, vertical, arranged vertically 3 across by 7 down, with 2 horizontal peel-off strips, one below horizontal row 3, the other below horizontal row 6. Offset printing plates and intaglio printing plates printed 300 stamps plus 15 labels per revolution.

Overall Stamp Size: 0.87 by 0.982 inches; 22.09mm by 24.94mm

Perforations: Die-cut simulated perforations. Die-cut circles and lines on non-stamp label.

Front Markings: On first peel-off strip: "© USPS 1994 • Peel here to fold • Self-adhesive stamps • DO NOT WET." On second peel-off strip: "• Peel here to fold • Self-adhesive stamps • DO NOT WET •" and offset and intaglio plate numbers. On nonstamp label: "TIME TO/REORDER/THIS BLOCK/IS NOT VALID/POSTAGE."

Liner Markings: "SELF-ADHESIVE (A) DO NOT WET" in a repeat pattern. (A) is trademark for Fasson laminated paper. (Later printings will not have liner markings.)

Back Markings: "Twenty/Self-adhesive Stamps," "First-Class/Letter Rate," "$6.40," "UNITED STATES/POSTAL SERVICE./We Deliver For You." USPS logo. Universal Product Code (UPC), promotion for *Stamps etc.* catalog, all on backing paper.

Designer, Art Director and Project Manager: Terrence McCaffrey, USPS

Typographer: Thomas Mann, Mann & Mann Graphics, Warrenton, Virginia

Engraver and Modeler: Banknote Corporation of America (BCA)

Stamp Manufacturing: Stamps printed by BCA at Browns Summit, North Carolina, on 6-color Goebel offset press and 4-color Epikos intaglio press. Stamps processed by BCA at Browns Summit.

Quantity Ordered and Distributed: 2,550,000,000

Plate Number Detail: 1 set of 4 offset plate numbers preceded by the letter B and 1 intaglio plate number on second horizontal peel-off strip

Plate Number Combinations Reported: B1111-1, B1111-2, B2222-1, B2222-2

Paper Supplier: Westvaco/Brown Bridge

Tagging: phosphored paper

The Stamp

On January 20, the Postal Service issued a self-adhesive version of its current 32¢ Love stamp depicting an angel from Raphael's 16th-century painting *Sistine Madonna*. The self-adhesive format allowed customers "to save their kisses for loved ones — not their stamps," a whimsical USPS news release explained.

The stamp, in a pane of 20, was dedicated at the American Postage Stamp Show in New York City along with a 32¢ Flag Over Porch self-adhesive in a 10-stamp pane and a 1¢ American Kestrel coil stamp.

Its angel design had been used on an earlier self-adhesive stamp, as well as a conventional stamp with water-activated gum. However, those varieties, which were issued in February 1995, were nondenominated, having been printed before the recent first-class rate change from 29¢ to 32¢ had been confirmed. In May 1995, a 32¢ denominated version of the conventional stamp appeared in two forms, sheet and booklet. The variety that was issued January 20, 1996, was both self-adhesive and denomi-nated, and "completed" the set.

Like its nondenominated counterpart of the year before, the new 32¢ Love self-adhesive was printed by Banknote Corporation of America by a combination of offset (the image) and intaglio (the word "LOVE"). Each of the panes, which the Postal Service calls "convertible booklets," con-tains two peel-off strips and a nonstamp label bearing a "Time to Reor-der" reminder.

The stamp and pane differ from those of the nondenominated version in certain physical details, however. The die-cuts that separate the stamps are serpentine, to simulate perforations, instead of straight, as they were on the 1995 stamp. And the Time to Reorder label has an internal die-cut pattern (the Postal Service calls it a "kiss-cut") of the kind the Postal Service began using on other self-adhesives late in 1995 to deter custom-ers from trying to remove the label, which is tagged like a stamp, and use it on mail. The pattern consists of three concentric circles and four short lines extending diagonally from the outer circle almost to the corners.

As with previous self-adhesive stamps, the pane carried the message "SELF ADHESIVE • DO NOT WET" in a repeat pattern on the liner beneath the stamps. However, the Postal Service announced March 21, 1996, that beginning the following month, "in order to reduce turnaround times and costs associated with the production of self-adhesive stamps," it no longer would require printers to include this wording on the liners. This would cut the lead time for paper procurement by two to three weeks and also reduce paper costs, USPS said.

The significance to collectors was that future printings of the 32¢ Love stamp would have blank liners, as would future printings of any of the current definitive issues in the self-adhesive format. The "self-adhesive, do not wet" message would continue to be printed on the peel-off strips, USPS said.

The Design
The design of the stamp features a detail from the Raphael painting and shows one of the two winged child-figures who are leaning on the coffin of Pope Julius II beneath the Virgin Mary and the infant Jesus. (The other child-figure was shown on a 55¢ two-ounce-rate Love stamp of 1995, issued in two formats, self-adhesive and lick-and-stick.) Although the

Postal Service described the figures as "cupids" to justify their use on Love stamps, art historians say they actually are "putti," good spirits assigned to attend the soul of the recently deceased pope.

The design is identical to that of its nondenominated counterpart of 1995 with two exceptions: the inscription "32 USA" appears in place of the "USA 1995" on the earlier stamp, and the tiny date beneath the design at the left reads "1996" instead of "1995."

The backside of the liner, which is also the "cover" of the convertible booklet, bears an enlarged reproduction of the stamp, as did the cover of the 1995 nondenominated Love self-adhesive. Except for the differences in these stamp designs, the two covers are virtually identical.

First-Day Facts

The Postal Service held no official first-day ceremony for the three stamps that made their debuts at Metropolitan Expositions' American Postage Stamp Show in New York City's Holiday Inn Crowne Plaza.

The earliest-reported prerelease use of the 32¢ Love self-adhesive stamp was on a cover postmarked in Oshkosh, Wisconsin, December 18, 1995, more than a month before the stamp's dedication.

Date of Issue: October 8, 1996

Catalog Numbers: Scott 3108-3111 (single stamps), 3111a (block or strip of 4)

Colors: black, cyan, magenta, yellow

First-Day Cancel: North Pole, Alaska

First-Day Cancellations: 884,339 (includes self-adhesive Family Scenes and Skaters stamps)

Format: Panes of 50, vertical, 10 across, 5 down. Offset printing plates of 200 subjects (10 across, 20 around).

Overall Stamp Size: 0.91 by 1.19 inches; 23.11mm by 30.26mm

Perforations: 11.3 by 11.2 (Wista and Gammeller perforator)

Selvage Markings: "© USPS 1995." ".32 x 50 = $16.00." "PLATE/POSITION" and diagram.

Designer: Julia Talcott of Newton, Massachusetts

Typographer and Art Director: Richard Sheaff

Modeler: Joseph Sheeran, Ashton-Potter (USA) Ltd.

Project Manager: Elizabeth A. Altobell, USPS

Stamp Manufacturing: Stamps printed by Ashton-Potter (USA) Ltd., Williamsville, New York, on offset portion of a Stevens Varisize Security Document webfed 6-color offset, 3-color intaglio press. Stamps perforated, processed and shipped by Ashton-Potter.

Quantity Ordered: 225,900,000

Quantity Distributed: 225,916,000

Plate Number Detail: 1 set of 4 offset plate numbers preceded by the letter P above or below each corner stamp

Plate Number Combinations Reported: P1111, P2222, P3333, P4444

Paper Supplier: Westvaco/Ivex

Tagging: phosphored paper

The Stamps

On October 8, the Postal Service marked what it called "the official start of the holiday season" by issuing its 1996 contemporary, or secular, Christmas stamps. The stamps came in two formats: panes of 50, with conventional water-activated gum (lick-and-stick), and panes of 20, as a self-adhesive. For the first time since 1988, there was no lick-and-stick booklet version.

As often has been the case in recent years, the contemporary Christmas issue consisted of multiple designs. Four different cartoonlike images, arranged in se-tenant blocks, depicted "family scenes": a family, complete with dog, seated by a decorated fireplace; a father lifting his child on his shoulders to place a star atop a Christmas tree; a little girl dreaming of Santa Claus coming down the chimney with his bag of gifts; and a mother and her daughter carrying wrapped gifts through the snow.

Both the lick-and-stick and self-adhesive versions were printed by the offset process, but by different contractors. Ashton-Potter (USA) Ltd., produced the former version, and Banknote Corporation of America printed the latter.

To dedicate the stamps, a group of high-ranking USPS officials, including Postmaster General Marvin T. Runyon and four members of the Board of Governors, flew to North Pole, Alaska, a community of some 700 people near Fairbanks. The selection of the site and the unusual number of dignitaries who attended were evidence of how much importance the Postal Service places on its relations with Capitol Hill.

The 1995 contemporary Christmas stamps had been dedicated in another town called North Pole, but in New York, in the home district of a congressman influential in postal matters, Representative John M. McHugh. According to *Washington Post* stamp writer Bill McAllister, "No one in Washington seemed more upset" over that choice of venues than Senator Ted Stevens, R-Alaska. "Long a key player on postal issues on Capitol Hill, Stevens argued that the ceremony should really be in North Pole, Alaska, a community that, after all, is much closer to the real North Pole," McAllister wrote. At the next opportunity the Postal Service gave Stevens his wish, and topped it off by inviting him to be the principal speaker at the first-day ceremony.

Late in 1996, it was disclosed that one of the water-activated contemporary Christmas stamps was used so far in advance of its issue date that the U.S. Postal Inspection Service launched an investigation.

According to the semiannual report of the Postal Service's chief postal

These four concept sketches by Julia Talcott for the contemporary Christmas stamps showed a crowd of people with their breaths showing in the cold weather, a pajamas-clad figure looking out over the city, a family sitting by the fireplace and a family decorating their Christmas tree. The last two sketches evolved into designs that were used on the Family Scenes block of four.

inspector, released in December, someone at one of the stamp printing contractors made off with 1,600 Christmas stamps, probably during the time they were being manufactured or printed.

An alert window clerk at the Buffalo, New York, general mail facility was credited with spotting in August what the report called "a first-class mail piece bearing a 32¢ Christmas stamp that was not scheduled for sale to the public until October 16."

No Christmas stamps were issued October 16. *Linn's Stamp News* reported, however, that the stamp the mail clerk saw was one of the stamps issued October 8. It was one of the water-activated stamps bearing the Christmas tree design. The printer of the stamps, Ashton-Potter, is located in Williamsville, New York, a Buffalo suburb.

According to Buffalo postal inspector Michelle Siwinski, the stamp, on a number 6¾ envelope, was found in the mailstream August 9. The uncanceled piece was removed from the mail and put aside, she said. It was the only one of the stolen stamps known to have been circulated.

These four concept sketches incorporated an unusual architectural approach depicting four scenes in Talcott's hometown of Boston, Massachusetts: a Beacon Hill doorway, the Massachusetts State House, Trinity Church and a doorway on Commonwealth Avenue, all decorated for Christmas.

Postal inspectors identified a suspect in the case and prosecution was pending, the chief postal inspector's report said. As of this writing, there has been no announcement of any further action.

The Designs

The four stamp illustrations were the work of Julia Talcott, 38, a Newton, Massachusetts, commercial artist. In 1994 she was commissioned to submit some designs by art director Richard Sheaff, who was attempting to build up the Postal Service's inventory of Christmas stamp images.

"She has a very light, contemporary, fun sort of style, and the (Citizens' Stamp Advisory) committee liked her work," Sheaff said.

Talcott faxed Sheaff a series of rough sketches incorporating ideas for holiday-related designs: shopping, gift-wrapped packages, tree decorating, sleeping children. From these sketches and ensuing discussion evolved the four pictures seen on the stamps.

She executed her finished art in cut colored paper. The linework — the

These are four more of Talcott's concept sketches: a mother and daughter shopping, which evolved into one of the finished stamp designs; a holiday street scene; shopping commuters boarding a train; and a public Christmas tree being decorated.

outlines of the figures, the motion lines to indicate that the dog is wagging its tail, the jagged lines in the fireplace suggesting flames — were done on a transparent overlay. Richard Sheaff then scanned the images and lines into his computer, touched them up electronically, added the "32 USA" to each stamp in a typeface called Gill sans-serif, and output the finished images.

Sheaff's computer revisions of the art included smoothing the cut edges of the paper figures where necessary and removing any signs of paper texture or layering. But he also made some minor changes in the design of the stamp that shows a mother and daughter shopping.

In the design of that stamp as it was released to the public in October 1995, the ribbons on the gift-wrapped packages were crossed in a plus-sign configuration, and the pompon on the child's cap had three points or lobes, like a crown. On the stamp as issued, the crossed ribbons on the packages have been turned into X's and the pompon is a round one.

Four more Talcott concept sketches: a child and its teddy bear in bed, deaming of the symbols of Christmas; wrapped gifts turning into buildings; a pile of gift-wrapped packages; and four faces around a candle. The child's-dream concept, with Santa Claus as the object of the dream, became the fourth of the approved designs.

The design of the stamp showing a mother and daugher shopping was revised after it first was made public in October 1995. The original version is shown here. The shapes of the ribbons on the packages were changed from crosses to Xs, and the pompon on the child's hat was converted to a round one.

Reportedly, these design details were changed because someone in postal management thought the crossed ribbons looked too much like Christian crosses and the pompon could be interpreted as a diabolical symbol.

First-Day Facts

Postmaster General Marvin T. Runyon dedicated the Family Scenes and Skaters stamps in a ceremony in the North Pole High School auditorium.

Speakers were U.S. Senator Ted Stevens, Alaska Lieutenant Governor Fran Ulmer, and Mike Miller, a member of the Alaska Senate. Fairbanks Postmaster Raymond E. Clark presided (the North Pole postal facility is a substation of the Fairbanks Post Office), and Lute Cunningham, mayor of North Pole, gave the welcome.

Honored guests were members of the Postal Service Board of Governors: chairman Tirso del Junco, Susan E. Alvarado, LeGree S. Daniels and Robert F. Rider.

32¢ CHRISTMAS FAMILY SCENES
(4 DESIGNS, SELF-ADHESIVE)

Date of Issue: October 8, 1996

Catalog Numbers: Scott 3113-3116 (single stamps), Scott 3116a (pane of 20)

Colors: yellow, magenta, cyan, black (stamps); black, special red (cover)

First-Day Cancel: North Pole, Alaska

First-Day Cancellations: 884,339 (includes water-activated Family Scenes and self-adhesive Skaters stamps)

Format: Panes of 21 (20 stamps and 1 nonstamp label), vertical, arranged horizontally 7 across by 3 down, with 2 vertical peel-off strips, 1 to the right of vertical row 3, the other to the right of vertical row 6. Gravure printing cylinders of 315 subjects (15 across, 21 around).

Overall Stamp Size: 0.91 by 1.19 inches; 23.11mm by 30.23mm

Overall Pane Size: 6.75 by 3.57 inches; 171.45mm by 90.68mm

Perforations: die cut in simulated perforation shape. Nonstamp label has die cuts in concentric circles and diagonal lines on its face. (Innotech rotary equipment)

Front Markings: On first peel-off strip: "• Peel here to fold • Self-adhesive stamps • DO NOT WET" and plate numbers. On second peel-off strip: "© USPS 1995 • Peel here to fold • Self-adhesive stamps • DO NOT WET." On nonstamp label: "TIME TO/REORDER/THIS BLOCK/IS NOT VALID/POSTAGE."

Liner Markings: none

Back Markings: "Holiday Greetings," "Four Different/Holiday Designs," "Twenty 32¢/Self-adhesive/Stamps/$6.40," "UNITED STATES/POSTAL SERVICE ™," Universal Product Code (UPC), promotion for USPS free catalog, all on backing paper.

Designer: Julia Talcott of Newton, Massachusetts

Typographer and Art Director: Richard Sheaff

Project Manager: Elizabeth A. Altobell, USPS

Stamp Manufacturing: Stamps printed by Banknote Corporation of America (BCA), Browns Summit, North Carolina, on Muller-Martini Progress model offset press. Stamps die-cut, processed and shipped at BCA.

Quantity Ordered: 1,805,250,000

Quantity Distributed: not available

Plate Number Detail: 1 set of 4 offset plate numbers preceded by the letter B on first peel-off strip

Plate Number Combinations Reported: B1111, B2222, B3333

Paper Supplier: Paper Corporation of America/Brown Bridge

Tagging: phosphored paper

The Stamps

Banknote Corporation of America produced the self-adhesive version of the four Christmas Family Scenes stamps on its offset press.

The stamps were sold in panes of 20. BCA used the same layout that Avery Dennison had used the year before when it printed the self-adhesive versions of the four se-tenant Christmas Children and Santa stamps. The vertically arranged stamps are laid out sideways, seven across by three down. The 21st "stamp" on the pane, located in the lower-right corner, is a nonpostage dummy label bearing a "Time to Reorder" reminder. There are two peel-off strips to facilitate folding the pane into a booklet shape.

The four designs appear in sequence on the horizontal rows of the pane, in this order: fireplace scene, Christmas tree, Santa dream, shopping scene, repeat the sequence. Each design appears twice on two horizontal rows and once on the third. The sides of the pane are straight-edged, and the stamps are separated from each other by serpentine die-cutting to simulate conventional perforations. Individual stamps from the pane have straight edges in the following locations:

Fireplace scene: top and left, top only, bottom only. Christmas tree: top only, right side only, bottom only. Santa dream: top only, top and right, left and bottom, bottom only. Shopping scene: top only, left side only, bottom only. In addition, five stamps from the interior of the pane have the "perfs" on all four sides: two fireplace scene and one each of the other three designs.

The Designs

Although the basic designs of both the conventional and self-adhesive versions are the same, the matching stamps of the two categories can be told apart in several ways.

The easiest way to distinguish one from another is by examining the edges. The self-adhesives have simulated perfs, all of which are exactly equal in length, and except for the five stamps from the middle of the pane each has at least one straight edge. The conventional stamps have normal perforations, with normal variations in length, and the perforations are on all four sides.

Both printers used the four standard process colors, yellow, cyan, magenta, and black, to reproduce the colors of Julia Talcott's cut-paper illustrations. However, the end result is that BCA's self-adhesive stamps are somewhat lighter in color than Ashton-Potter's water-activated products. This is particularly noticeable in the blue areas, which have a grayer tone on the self-adhesives, and in the green of the wreath and Christmas tree.

Because of a slight difference in cropping, the self-adhesive version of the "shopping" stamp has three more snowflakes at the top of the design than does its conventional counterpart. On the self-adhesives, the year date "1996" beneath the lower-left corner of each design is much smaller than on the water-activated stamps, and only can be read with a good magnifying glass.

The back side of the pane's backing paper, which serves as a cover when the pane is converted to a booklet, is printed in two colors, red and black. Beneath the words "Holiday Greetings" it reproduces the four stamp designs in an overlapping fashion, without the type.

Varieties

At least two panes of the Christmas Family Scenes self-adhesive stamps with no die cutting were bought at post offices in December 1996.

Linn's Stamp News reported that Dave Miller, a collector in Tennessee, bought such a pane at a local Tennessee post office while purchasing stamps for postage. The pane has plate number combination B2222. Miller said he looked for similar panes at the same post office but found no more.

Stamp Collector reported that Warren W. Vache Sr. of Rahway, New Jersey, also purchasing stamps for postage, bought an imperforate pane December 20 at the Colonia branch of the Rahway post office. His pane has a B1111 plate number combination. He called the error to the attention of the clerk, who immediately checked his stack of at least 50 other panes but found all of them to be normal, Vache said.

First-Day Facts

Information on the first-day ceremony at North Pole, Alaska, can be found in the preceding chapter.

32¢ HOLIDAY SKATERS (SELF-ADHESIVE, ATM-VENDED)

Date of Issue: October 8, 1996

Catalog Numbers: Scott 3117 (single stamp), 3117a (pane of 18)

Colors: yellow, magenta, cyan, black (stamps); yellow, red, blue, black (cover)

First-Day Cancel: North Pole, Alaska

First-Day Cancellations: 884,339 (includes water-activated and self-adhesive Family Scenes stamps)

Format: Panes of 18, vertical, arranged vertically 3 across by 6 down, with horizontal peel-off strip in center. Gravure printing cylinders of 30 panes (5 across, 6 around).

Overall Stamp Size: 0.87 by 0.982 inches; 22.08mm by 24.92mm

Perforations: straight die cuts (Comco Commander rotary equipment)

Front Markings: On peel-off strip: "• Peel here to fold • Self-adhesive stamps • DO NOT WET •" and cylinder numbers

Back Markings: "Eighteen/Self-adhesive/Stamps," "$5.76," "© UNITED STATES POSTAL SERVICE 1996," Universal Product Code (UPC), promotion for USPS free catalog, disclaimer of any amount charged over stamps' face value, all on backing paper.

Designer: Julia Talcott of Newton, Massachusetts

Art Director and Typographer: Richard Sheaff

Project Manager: Elizabeth A. Altobell, USPS

Stamp Manufacturing: Stamps printed by Avery Dennison Security Printing Division, Clinton, South Carolina, on an 8-color Dai-Nippon Kiko webfed gravure press. Stamps lacquer coated, front and back, die cut, processed and shipped by Avery Dennison.

Quantity Ordered and Distributed: 495,504,000

Cylinder Number Detail: 1 set of 4 gravure cylinder numbers preceded by the letter V printed on selvage strip

Cylinder Number Combinations Reported: V1111, V2111

Paper Supplier: Consolidated/Fasson

Tagging: phosphor added to lacquer coating applied to front of panes

The Stamp

Each year, beginning in 1992, USPS has issued a self-adhesive stamp with a winter theme in panes designed to be vended through automatic teller machines, or ATMs. The 1996 stamp had its first-day sale October 8 in North Pole, Alaska, along with the Christmas Family Scenes block of four varieties.

The designs of the first two seasonal ATM stamps, in 1992 and 1993, were adaptations of designs used on the contemporary Christmas stamps of those years. But the banks that participate in the ATM stamp program wanted a stamp that would be appropriate through the entire winter. So in 1994 and each subsequent year the Postal Service has provided a distinctive design for the ATM stamp that wasn't specifically tied to the holiday.

The 1996 design, like those of the four Family Scenes Christmas stamps, was a cartoonlike image based on a piece of cut-paper artwork by Julia Talcott of Newton, Massachusetts. Depicting a pair of ice skaters, it was made public by the Postal Service in mid-March.

The stamps were gravure-printed by Avery Dennison and distributed in panes with the length, width and thickness of a dollar bill. The panes contained 18 stamps. Like all panes of self-adhesives, this one had a narrow strip that the customer could peel off to facilitate folding the pane in half.

JuliaTalcott put these four winter sports design ideas into sketch form: figure skating, sledding, skiing and snowshoeing.

Unlike self-adhesive stamps made for over-the-counter and vending-machine sales, the ATM stamps were separated by straight die cuts rather than serpentine cuts made to simulate perforations. Some collectors reported that the stamps on this particular pane were unusually difficult to remove from their backing paper.

The Postal Service ordered 495 million Skaters stamps, more than five times the 90 million seasonal ATM stamps (Children Sledding) it had ordered in 1995.

The Design

Julia Talcott's design shows a female figure skater skating backward, one leg in the air, the skate on the ice tracing a double loop. Her male companion stands in the foreground watching her, a skate hanging over his shoulder.

Like the Christmas Family Scenes stamps, the artist created this one by cutting colored paper and adding the heavy linework on an overlay. Art director Richard Sheaff then scanned the images into his computer and

After Talcott and Richard Sheaff had settled on an ice-skating theme for this stamp, the artist made this rough in colored pencil of an alternative design showing a single skater.

This is Talcott's original pencil sketch that eventually was translated into the finished cut-paper design.

added a black "32 USA" in Gill sans-serif type.

Talcott made sketches of several different ideas for the seasonal stamp for the consideration of Sheaff and the Citizens' Stamp Advisory Committee before the final design was chosen. These included skiers, a sledder, snowshoers and a single skater.

The back of the backing paper reproduced an enlarged replica of the stamp in full color.

First-Day Facts

Information on the first-day ceremony at North Pole can be found in the chapter on the Christmas Family Scenes stamps.

32¢ HANUKKAH (SELF-ADHESIVE)
HOLIDAY CELEBRATION SERIES
JOINT ISSUE

Date of Issue: October 22, 1996

Catalog Number: Scott 3118

Colors: yellow, magenta, cyan, black, pink

First-Day Cancel: Washington, D.C.

First-Day Cancellations: 179,355

Format: Panes of 20, horizontal, 4 across, 5 down, on backing paper. Gravure printing cylinders of 200 (10 across, 20 around).

Overall Stamp Size: .99 by 1.56 inches; 25.146mm by 39.624mm

Perforations: Die-cut simulated perforations that penetrate backing paper. Backing paper on each stamp has vertical curved die-cut to facilitate its removal. Comco rotary die cutter used.

Selvage Markings: "© 1995 USPS." ".32 x 20 = $6.40." "PLATE/POSITION" and diagram.

Designer and Typographer: Hannah Smotrich of Washington, D.C.

Art Director: Derry Noyes

Project Manager: Elizabeth A. Altobell, USPS

Stamp Manufacturing: Stamps printed by Avery Dennison Security Printing Division, Clinton, South Carolina, on an 8-color Dai Nippon Kikko webfed gravure press. Stamps processed by Avery Dennison.

Quantity Ordered and Distributed: 103,520,000

Cylinder Number Detail: 1 set of 5 gravure cylinder numbers preceded by the letter V in selvage above or below each corner stamp

Cylinder Number Combination Reported: V11111

Paper Supplier: Westvaco/Consolidated/Fasson

Tagging: phosphored paper

The Stamp

On October 22, the Postal Service launched a new series of what it called "Holiday Celebration" stamps with a stamp commemorating Hanukkah, the Jewish Festival of Lights. The stamp was a joint issue with Israel, the first between the two countries, and dual first-day ceremonies were held in Washington and Jerusalem.

The Citizens' Stamp Advisory Committee had considered requests for a Hanukkah stamp for many years, and always had turned down the idea. Committee members had feared that to issue such a stamp would be to invite pressure for a new version of the stamp each year, like the Christmas stamps that have been issued annually since 1962, as well as demands from other religious groups for similar recognition. "We didn't want to open Pandora's box," one member recalled.

However, the committee, with the encouragement of USPS management, has been placing increasing emphasis on reflecting the diversity of the American people in the U.S. stamp program. Ultimately, the decision was made to produce a Hanukkah stamp, but as part of a series that would honor a different cultural or religious holiday annually. In this way, officials hoped to head off requests for new Hanukkah stamps in the future. (The 1997 entry in the Holiday Celebration series, unveiled in October 1996, will be the nonreligious African-American holiday Kwanzaa.)

As a further hedge, CSAC members suggested that as long as the first-class rate stayed at 32¢, the Postal Service could keep the Hanukkah stamp available and reprint it if necessary, just as it reprinted the 1996 Midnight Angel self-adhesive stamp for use in the 1997 Christmas season.

Although no one specific request from the public led to the decision to issue the Hanukkah stamp, a few of its recent advocates were singled out for credit in the press.

One was Ronald J. Scheiman, a window clerk in the Holbrook, New York, post office, who told *Stamp Collector* that he had been asking for the stamp since January 1993 and called its approval "a dream come true." And *The Los Angeles Times* reported that it was the "heartfelt letters" to the Postal Service from 300 students at the Kadima Hebrew Academy in Woodland Hills, California, that "led to the creation" of the stamp. The local post office acknowledged the students' efforts at a ceremony at the school October 23, the second day of issue, by providing a special cancel reading: "You Can Make a Difference. Hanukkah Stamp Station."

"Having this stamp is important," sixth-grader Tali Shousterman told the newspaper, "because it helps people know there isn't just one religion in this country. There are many."

The stamp was a self-adhesive, printed by gravure and distributed in panes of 20. Like the panes of self-adhesive Riverboat commemoratives issued just two months earlier, the Hanukkah panes were given die-cut simulated perforations that penetrated the peelable backing paper to make possible the purchase of individual stamps, and serpentine die cuts on the backing paper to facilitate its removal.

270

The Israel version of the Hanukkah stamp bears a 2.50-shekel denomination and has tabs attached to the four bottom stamps on the pane of 20. The tabs depict three spinning toys known as dreidels, along with Hebrew words meaning: "A great miracle occurred here."

Israel's Hanukkah stamp also was a self-adhesive, the first for that country. It had a denomination of 2.50 shekels and could be purchased by American collectors through the Philatelic Fulfillment Service Center for $16 for a pane of 20.

Both countries used the same design — a stylized menorah with nine colored candles, created by Hannah Smotrich of Washington, D.C. — and the same printer, Avery Dennison of Clinton, South Carolina. No previous Israeli stamp had been printed outside Israel.

Postmaster General Marvin T. Runyon unveiled the Hanukkah stamp design March 5, 1996, at the B'nai B'rith Klutznick National Jewish Museum in Washington. The design actually had been released to the press two months earlier, in anticipation of a scheduled January 9 unveiling, but that event was canceled because of a January 7 snowstorm that paralyzed much of the East Coast.

Featured speakers at the March 5 ceremony included S. David Fineman of the Postal Service Board of Governors; U.S. Representative Benjamin A. Gilman, Republican of New York; Tommy P. Baer, president of B'nai B'rith International; Ori Soltes, director of the National Jewish Museum; and Rabbi Jack Allen Luxemburg, president of the Washington Board of Rabbis.

Baer praised the Postal Service "for recognizing the important contributions of religious groups in this country by issuing the Holiday Celebration stamps."

"We are proud that B'nai B'rith has been chosen as the site of the unveiling of the first Hanukkah stamp," he said. "For more than 150 years, we have promoted tolerance, diversity and understanding. Hanukkah, a celebration of freedom, represents victory over tyranny, and is therefore meaningful for all Americans."

Hanukkah's origins can be traced back some 2,160 years to 164 B.C., when Judah the Maccabee and his followers liberated Jerusalem from the Syrian Greeks and set about to purify and rededicate the city's ancient temple.

However, when the time came to light the menorah, only one jar of pure olive oil could be found, enough to burn for a single day. Miracu-

For a while, officials considered issuing the Hanukkah stamp without the word "Hanukkah" in the design, but focus-group responses helped convince them to include it.

lously, the light burned for eight days and nights, long enough to prepare a supply of fresh consecrated oil.

Today Hanukkah is celebrated for eight days, beginning on the 25th of the Hebrew month Kislev. Each night the family gathers around the menorah, exchanges gifts, chants blessings and lights candles — one the first night, two the second night, and so on, until eight candles are lit the final night. The ninth candle in the menorah is called the Shamash, meaning "helper," and is used to light the other candles.

Because the name of the holiday is spelled in various ways, including "Chanukkah" and "Chanukah," PhotoAssist, the Postal Service's consultant firm, turned to numerous reference works and authorities for guidance in how to spell it on the stamp. It concluded: "There is no official spelling of the holiday. Different organizations and books cite preferred spellings, but concur that Hanukkah, Hanukah or Hanukhah are acceptable. The predominant choice is 'Hanukkah.' They all suggest that the word begin with H rather than CH."

The fact that Israel also opted to use the "Hanukkah" spelling (along with its Hebrew equivalent) was a confirmation that the Postal Service had made the right choice.

The Design

Hannah Smotrich saves pieces of colored paper for use in creating special cards for family members and friends, and she dipped into this accumulation to make her simple cut-paper stamp design. It shows nine candles, each of a different color and with a flickering flame at the top, side by side on a horizontal gold bar against a plain white background. The slate-green Shamash candle in the center, taller than the rest, stands in a small

This is Hannah Smotrich's first cut-paper design for the Hanukkah stamp. CSAC asked her to add a horizontal gold bar across the bottom, and a holder for the central (Shamash) candle, to make it more clear that the candles were fastened to a menorah. Note that in setting the type, Smotrich inadvertently misspelled "Hanukkah."

red candleholder. Across the top of the stamp are the word "HANUK-KAH," in red Lithos type, and "USA 32" in black.

Smotrich, 31, is a graphic designer who serves corporate and nonprofit, educational and cultural clients and teaches at the Corcoran School of Art in Washington. The Hanukkah stamp's art director, Derry Noyes, knew of her work — both women had attended the Yale Graduate School of Graphic Design — and knew she had grown up observing the Jewish holidays in her own home, had spent a year in Israel and had studied Hebrew. "I thought this was a good match, and that if anyone should be doing the stamp, it was Hannah," Noyes said.

In an interview with Daniel Keren of *Global Stamp News*, Smotrich said her first thought when she was invited to submit a Hanukkah stamp design was to find a way to "communicate the essence of the holiday." Thinking a menorah and candles might be too obvious as symbols, she considered alternative designs such as dreidels (four-sided toys that can be spun like tops). She finally decided, however, that the candle image was most appropriate and recognizable as representing Hanukkah.

She offered Noyes two completely different design approaches for CSAC's consideration. One was a literal treatment, for which she hired a professional photographer to take color photographs of menorahs from her own collection. The other was her graphic cut-paper design, her personal favorite.

The photographic project was "very time-consuming," Smotrich said, "whereas the cut-paper composition, although it took a number of hours to work out the color relationships, was a very spontaneous and quick process."

Although some members of CSAC preferred the realistic designs, the majority liked what Derry Noyes called "the more abstract, upbeat, colorful approach." "The photographs were dark and dull in comparison," Noyes said.

In Smotrich's original design, the candles "floated" against the white background, but Noyes asked her to add the horizontal bar to make it clear the candles were attached to a menorah. "Everybody was afraid it would look like a Happy Birthday stamp otherwise," Noyes said.

Before USPS gave final approval to Smotrich's design, it had it focus-

Hannah Smotrich offered USPS these two photographic images of decorative menorahs as alternatives to her cut-paper design.

group tested with traditional, reform and unaffiliated Jews in large and small Jewish communities around the country. Elizabeth A. Altobell, the stamp's project manager, reported back on the reactions of the focus groups:

"The design is largely seen as joyful, pretty, colorful, simple, elegant and straightforward. It is viewed not only as joyous, but as conveying images of hope and giving which are consistent with the December holiday season."

Because the Postal Service had omitted the word "Christmas" from the 1995 Madonna and Child stamp, officials considered leaving the word "Hanukkah" off the Hanukkah stamp, and alternative versions of Smotrich's design were prepared without it. However, the focus groups wanted the word included. They felt that "not everyone would know this is a menorah," Altobell reported, "and many were concerned that we be up front about what this stamp is celebrating or it would have no meaning."

The focus groups' reaction also eased any concern on the part of USPS officials that some branches of American Judaism, particularly the orthodox and ultra-orthodox, might object to the "lightheartedness" of the design. In fact, the groups were shown Smotrich's photographic treatment of a menorah and found it much less appealing than her stylized version.

The biggest problem encountered by the design team — Smotrich, Noyes and John Boyd of Anagraphics Inc., a computer graphics specialist — was getting a computer printout with colors that exactly matched the nine different colors of paper Smotrich had selected for her candles. Although they finally obtained a print that satisfied them, the finished stamp, which was produced in the standard four process colors by Stamp Venturers, fell short of a match in some respects.

For example, a comparison of Smotrich's original cut-paper design with the printed stamp shows that the candle on the left, which is maroon on the original, is a red-violet on the stamp, and the third candle, for which Smotrich used purple paper, came out blue.

The Israeli version of the Hanukkah stamp had labels, called tabs, attached to the four bottom stamps on the pane. These tabs — which Smotrich also designed — showed three dreidels and a bar containing the message in Hebrew: "A great miracle occurred here."

The Israeli stamp had printing on its backing paper, unlike the U.S. stamp. The printing formed an image of two oil jugs, mirror images of each other.

Hannah Smotrich gave a slide presentation on her Hanukkah stamp design October 31 at the Postage Stamp Mega-Event at the Jacob Javits Convention Center in New York City. Her appearance was sponsored by the Israel Philatelic Agency.

First-Day Facts

Postmaster General Marvin T. Runyon dedicated the U.S. stamp and Amos Mar-Haim, chairman of the Israel Postal Authority Board of Direc-

The Israeli stamp had printing on its backing paper. The printing formed mirror images of two oil jugs.

tors, dedicated the Israeli stamp in the U.S. first-day ceremony for the joint issue at the Adas Israel Congregation in Washington.

Rabbi Jeffrey A. Wohlberg of Adas Israel Congregation gave the welcome, and Rabbi Jack Moline, the recently installed president of the Washington Board of Rabbis, gave the invocation. Dr. Eliahu Ben-Elissar, Israel's ambassador to the United States, was the principal speaker. Honored guests were Yinon Beiln and Yitzhak Granot of the Israel Philatelic Service; Ori Soltes, director of the B'Nai B'rith Klutznick National Jewish Museum; and stamp designer Hannah Smotrich.

In Jerusalem, Postal Service Governor S. David Fineman was joined by Israeli Prime Minister Benjamin Netanyahu and President Ezer Weizman at a private stamp dedication ceremony in the president's official residence.

Rabbi Ephraim Buchwald, director of the National Jewish Outreach Program in New York, flew to Washington October 22 to purchase the first 20,000 U.S. Hanukkah stamps. He said he intended to "create 20,000 first-day covers for my friends who see in this stamp an incredible opportunity to communicate the value of Judaism in our day and age."

Buchwald, who, according to *Linn's Stamp News*, is known in the American Jewish community as a "pied piper" to a generation of Jews who are disconnected with their heritage, gave a check for the stamps to Postmaster General Runyon, who praised NJOP's use of the Hanukkah stamp as "a wonderful educational tool." Ambassador Ben-Elissar also accepted a check from Buchwald for Israeli Hanukkah stamps.

32¢ CHRISTMAS MADONNA AND CHILD

Date of Issue: November 1, 1996

Catalog Number: Scott 3107

Colors: magenta, yellow, cyan, black (offset), black (intaglio)

First-Day Cancel: Richmond, Virginia

First-Day Cancellations: 164,447 (includes self-adhesive)

Format: Panes of 50, 10 across by 5 down, 300-subject plates (15 across, 20 around), 600 subjects printed per revolution.

Overall Stamp Size: 0.91 by 1.19 inches; 23.1mm by 30.2mm

Perforations: 11.2

Selvage Markings: "© USPS 1995." "50 x .32 = $16.00." "PLATE/POSITION" and diagram.

Designer, Typographer and Art Director: Richard Sheaff of Norwood, Massachusetts

Modeler: Peter Cocci, Bureau of Engraving and Printing

Engraver: Dixie March, BEP

Project Manager: Elizabeth A. Altobell, USPS

Stamp Manufacturing: Stamps printed by BEP on Giori offset-intaglio F press (801).

Quantity Ordered: 243,575,000

Quantity Distributed: not available

Plate/Sleeve Number Detail: 1 set of 4 offset plate numbers and 1 intaglio sleeve number above or below each corner stamp

Plate/Sleeve Number Combinations Reported: 1111-1, 1112-1, 1212-1, 2222-1

Paper Supplier: Westvaco/Ivex

Tagging: phosphored paper

The Stamp

On November 1, USPS issued its annual traditional Christmas stamp reproducing a painting of the Madonna and infant Jesus from an American art gallery. The image chosen for the 1996 stamp was a detail from Paolo de Matteis' 18th-century masterwork, *Adoration of the Shepherds*, which hangs in the Virginia Museum of Fine Arts in Richmond.

Like the contemporary Christmas stamps that were issued October 8, the Madonna stamp came in two formats: panes of 50, with water-activated gum, and panes of 20, as a self-adhesive. The self-adhesive version, the first for a Madonna, replaced the conventional 20-stamp booklet version of the stamp that had been issued each year since 1989. Both versions were printed by the Bureau of Engraving and Printing by a combination of offset and intaglio.

The de Matteis design was one of a group of Madonna stamp designs that were developed by USPS art director Richard Sheaff in 1995, after a plan by officials of Stamp Services to use a design other than a Madonna for that year's "religious" Christmas stamp was reversed on orders of Postmaster General Marvin T. Runyon. Runyon's action, taken in response to pressure from politicians, religious groups and the White House, made it clear to the Postal Service that a Madonna stamp would be expected each year for the foreseeable future. Accordingly, Sheaff designed — and the Citizens' Stamp Advisory Committee approved — enough Madonna designs to carry the Postal Service through the year 2003.

Even after a Madonna stamp had been hurriedly inserted into the 1995 program, however, not all the critics were satisfied. Sheaff chose a somewhat different design style than had been used for previous Madonna stamps, omitting the word "CHRISTMAS" across the top and opening up more space for the image. The absence of the word from the 1995 stamp displeased some people, who saw it as an attempt by the Postal Service to distance itself from the religious underpinning of the season. They made their opinions known. As a result, the 1996 stamp — although its design was unveiled in October 1995 minus the "CHRISTMAS" inscription — had the word in place by the time the final version of the design was made public in July.

That final version was different in another significant respect from the design that originally was made public. The difference had to do with the anatomy of the infant Jesus.

Di Matteis' painting, like many early nativity scenes, unashamedly depicted the genitalia of the naked child. But Postal Service officials, already gun-shy over criticism of their decisions regarding Christmas stamps, were afraid that prudish patrons would be offended if they copied this feature literally onto their stamp.

The fact that the infant's penis would be so tiny at stamp size that it would require a magnifying glass to detect didn't ease their initial concern. Some veteran employees claimed to remember that there had been an earlier controversy over an equally tiny naked Christ child on a Christmas stamp. Apparently their reference was to the 1978 stamp, which reproduced a terra-cotta sculpture by Andrea della Robbia; this was the only previous image in the 30-year history of Madonna stamps on which the genitals were distinguishable.

In other past instances, the Postal Service had discreetly censored its Madonna paintings by cropping them at the infant's waist, but that wasn't a practical option with the di Matteis. Instead, officials ordered the artwork electronically modified so as to neuter the infant image. But then, according to Terrence McCaffrey, head of stamp design, the officials had second thoughts. In preventing one imagined offense, indecency, they had committed another — tampering with an art masterpiece.

"We tried to be politically correct," McCaffrey said. "But when we briefed our corporate relations people, they insisted that we put the baby back the way he was. They said they would fight any battle that might develop with the public over it. So we reproduced the painting uncensored, and I think it was the right thing to do."

"It was ridiculous," another official said of the original decision. "We were talking about a fuzzy light area on the stamp, involving a few halftone dots, and by the time it's printed out

This reproduction of most of Paolo de Matteis' masterwork The Adoration of the Shepherds *is from a picture postal card sold by the Virginia Museum of Fine Arts, which owns the painting.*

of register it doesn't really matter."

Although most of the Madonna paintings reproduced on Christmas stamps have been from the collection of the National Gallery of Art in Washington, in recent years the Postal Service has sought out paintings from other museums for this honor. The di Matteis painting in the Virginia gallery was brought to the attention of CSAC by one of its members, Philip Meggs, who lives in Richmond and teaches design history at Virginia Commonwealth University.

As a youth, Paolo de Matteis (1662-1728) studied under Luca Giordano, the dominant Neapolitan artist of the late 17th century. During this period, he also worked in Rome, attracting the attention of the Spanish ambassador, the Marchese del Carpio.

That early sojourn in Rome was the first of many that de Matteis made outside Naples, including three years in Paris working at the court of Louis, heir to the French throne. However, the artist produced most of his works in Naples, where many of them are still to be seen.

He painted *Adoration of the Shepherds* in 1712 for the Duchess of Laurenzano, one of Naples' leading patrons of art. A typical example of the late Baroque, or early Rococo, style of Naples, it is a large oil on canvas, 79½ inches high by 70 inches wide.

The painting and a companion painting titled *Annunciation* came to the auction market in 1906 in Vienna, Austria, as part of the collection of Prince Henry of Bourbon-Parma, Count of Bardi. The *Annunciation* is in the St. Louis Art Museum in St. Louis, Missouri. The Virginia museum acquired *Adoration of the Shepherds* in 1979 with money from the Adolph D. and Wilkins C. Williams Fund.

The portion of the painting reproduced on the stamp is the center, in which the hooded Mary holds the naked infant on a bed of straw; the glow emanating from the child illuminates her face and bosom. The other figures in the painting are cropped out of the stamp design. They are, overhead, a nude cherub with a ribbon bearing the words "Excelsis Deo," and,

The design of the 1996 Madonna and Child stamp as first unveiled by the Postal Service showed a neutered image of the Christ child and left off the word "CHRISTMAS." Both omissions were corrected on the stamp as issued.

gathered around the central figures, Joseph, a man, a woman, two children and an ox and donkey. The painting is signed and dated on a rock in the foreground, Paulus de' Mattei ft. 1712.

The Design

Richard Sheaff's design is dominated by the central figures of the di Matteis painting within a rectangular frame. The word "CHRISTMAS," in black serif capitals, crosses the top of the stamp above the frameline. "USA 32," in Sabon type, is dropped out of the dark background in the upper-left corner of the picture. Beneath the picture, in small uppercase and lowercase lettering, is the identifying line: "Paolo de Matteis Va. Mus. of Fine Arts."

Sheaff would have preferred not to abbreviate the gallery's name, but because of its length an abbreviation was necessary. Museum officials were given their choice between "Virginia MFA" and "Va. Mus. of Fine Arts" and opted for the latter.

This line of small type is the only engraved element on the stamp. The picture and the word "CHRISTMAS" are printed by offset.

First-Day Facts

The two varieties of the Madonna and Child stamp were dedicated by Henry Pankey, USPS vice president for mid-Atlantic area operations, in a ceremony in the Great Hall of the Virginia Museum of Fine Arts. Virginia Governor George Allen was the featured speaker, and the welcome was given by W. Taylor Reveley III, president of the museum's board of trustees.

Harry F. Barnett Jr., Richmond postmaster, presided. Honored guests were Philip Meggs and C. Douglas Lewis of CSAC and Joseph J. Rein

32¢ CHRISTMAS MADONNA AND CHILD (SELF-ADHESIVE)

Date of Issue: November 1, 1996

Catalog Numbers: Scott 3112 (single stamp), Scott 3112a (pane of 20)

Colors: magenta, yellow, cyan, black (stamp, offset); black (stamp, intaglio); black, red (cover)

First-Day Cancel: Richmond, Virginia

First-Day Cancellations: 164,447 (includes water-activated version)

Format: Panes of 21 (20 stamps and 1 nonstamp label), vertical, arranged horizontally 7 across by 3 down, with 2 vertical peel-off strips, 1 to the right of vertical row 3, the other to the right of vertical row 6. 720 subjects printed per revolution (20 across, 36 around).

Overall Stamp Size: 0.91 by 1.16 inches; 23.1mm by 29.5mm

Overall Pane Size: 6.77 by 3.5 inches; 172mm by 88.9mm

Perforations: die cut in simulated perforation shape.

Front Markings: On first peel-off strip: "© USPS 1995 • Peel here to fold • Self-adhesive stamps • DO NOT WET." On second peel-off strip: "• Peel here to fold • Self-adhesive stamps • DO NOT WET •" and plate numbers. On non-stamp label: "TIME TO/REORDER/THIS BLOCK/IS NOT VALID/POSTAGE."

Liner Markings: none

Back Markings: "Season's Greetings," "Twenty/32 Cent/Self-adhesive Stamps $6.40," 32¢/Self-adhesive/Stamps/$6.40," "© UNITED STATES POSTAL SERVICE 1995," Universal Product Code (UPC), promotion for USPS free catalog, "May the/season bring/joy and/peace to you/this year/Best wishes/from your/Postal Service," "UNITED STATES/POSTAL SERVICE ™" and USPS logo, all on backing paper.

Designer, Typographer and Art Director: Richard Sheaff of Norwood, Massachusetts

Modeler: Peter Cocci, Bureau of Engraving and Printing

Engraver: Dixie March, BEP

Project Manager: Elizabeth A. Altobell, USPS

Stamp Manufacturing: Stamps printed by BEP on Giori offset-intaglio F press (801).

Quantity Ordered: 847,750,000

Quantity Distributed: not available

Plate Number Detail: 1 set of 4 offset plate numbers and 1 intaglio sleeve number on second peel-off strip

Plate Number Combinations Reported: 1111-1, 1211-1, 2212-1, 2222-1, 2323-1, 3323-1, 3333-1, 3334-1, 4444-1, 5544-1, 5555-1, 5556-1, 5556-2, 5656-2, 6656-2, 6666-1, 6666-2, 6766-1, 7887-1, 7887-2, 7888-2, 7988-2

Paper Supplier: Glatfelter/Brown Bridge

Tagging:

The Stamp

The 1996 Madonna and Child stamp was the first in the Madonna series to be issued as a self-adhesive in addition to the conventional lick-and-stick version. Like the lick-and-stick, it was made by the Bureau of

Engraving and Printing.

The 20 self-adhesive stamps on the pane are separated from each other and from the two peel-off strips by the usual serpentine die-cutting that simulates perforation teeth on the individual stamps. The pane's four sides are straight. Thus, on each pane there are five stamps with straight edges at the top only, five with "perfs" all around, five with straight edges at the bottom only, and one each with straight edges at the top and left, top and right, bottom and left, left only, and right only. There is no stamp with straight edges at the bottom and right; that space on the pane is occupied by a "Time to Reorder" label.

This label, like its counterpart on other recent self-adhesive panes, has internal die cuts to prevent the tagged label from being removed intact from the backing paper and used as postage. The cuts are in a new kind of pattern, similar to a tic-tac-toe game, with two serpentine vertical cuts and two serpentine horizontal cuts to divide the label into nine pieces.

The Design

BEP used the same press and colors to print both the self-adhesive and water-activated versions of the Madonna stamp, and the printed portions of the two varieties are identical. They can be easily told apart by looking at the edges.

A self-adhesive Madonna, with its simulated perfs of precise regularity, square corners and, in the majority of cases, at least one straight edge, is impossible to confuse with a lick-and-stick, which has conventional perfs on all four sides. In addition, the overall height of the self-adhesive is slightly less than that of the water-activated stamp, although the width of the two stamps is the same.

The back of the backing paper, which formed the cover of the convertible booklet, displayed a circular medallion containing an enlarged detail from the stamp design, showing the Virgin Mary, the Christ Child and one of the worshipping shepherd children. The image was discreetly cropped at the nude infant's waist. The two colors in which the cover was printed, black and red, were blended to give a sepia tone to the medallion picture.

First-Day Facts

Details about the first-day ceremony can be found in the preceding chapter.

The earliest-known use of a 1996 Madonna stamp was on a cover postmarked Anaheim, California, October 28, four days before the official issue date.

Definitives

Twenty-four definitive stamps were issued in 1996, which was a high number for a year in which there was no rate change. Most of them were new versions of previous issues. Only four bore original designs: the 2¢ Red-Headed Woodpecker, 50¢ Jacqueline Cochran, nondenominated Mountain Scene and 32¢ Cal Farley. The last-mentioned was the year's only entry in the long-running Great Americans series.

The year saw the first true booklets of self-adhesive stamps (prefolded, with separate panes inside). Three of these (Flag Over Porch and two Yellow Rose booklets) contained stamps printed from plates that were laid out specifically for that purpose. Several others, however, were improvised booklets, made for vending-machine sales and containing self-adhesive stamps cut from printing sheets that had been configured for other formats. Other improvised booklets that showed up during 1996 contained water-activated commemorative stamps taken from regular post office panes. Keeping track of these makeshift products, and finding them, proved to be somewhat of a challenge to collectors.

The first self-adhesive coil stamps created for sale to the general public appeared in 1996. These coils, attached to backing paper, were a transitional issue, paving the way for the linerless coil stamps that were scheduled to make their debut in early 1997. Another first for 1996 was booklet stamps bearing plate numbers. In the booklets of 15-stamp and 30-stamp Yellow Rose self-adhesives that appeared late in the year, one stamp per booklet had a set of plate numbers beneath the design.

1¢ AMERICAN KESTREL COIL

Date of Issue: January 20, 1996

Catalog Number: Scott 3044

Colors: black, yellow, cyan, magenta

First-Day Cancel: New York, New York

First-Day Cancellations: 57,639 (includes 32¢ Love self-adhesive and 32¢ Flag Over Porch self-adhesive in pane of 10)

Format: Coils of 500 and 3,000. Offset printing plates of 432 subjects (18 across, 24 around).

Overall Stamp Size: 0.87 by 0.96 inches; 22.1mm by 24.4mm

Perforations: 9.8 (Huck stroke perforator)

Designer: Michael Matherly of Cambridge City, Indiana

Typographer: John Boyd of Anagraphics Inc., New York, New York

Modeler: Clarence Holbert, Bureau of Engraving and Printing

Art Director: Joe Brockert (USPS)

Project Manager: Vance Harris, USPS

Stamp Manufacturing: Stamps printed by BEP on the offset stations of the 6-color offset, 3-color intaglio webfed D press (902)

Quantity Ordered and Distributed: 350,000,000 (50,000,000 in coils of 500 and 300,000,000 in coils of 3,000)

Plate Number Detail: 1 group of 4 plate numbers on every 24th stamp

Plate Number Combination Reported: 1111

Paper Supplier: Westvaco/Ivex

Tagging: untagged

The Stamp

At one time 1¢ coil stamps were frequently used, to carry postcards or, in small multiples, to pay the postage on first-class letters. As rates have climbed in recent decades, the need for small-denomination stamps in all formats has declined. The Postal Service now uses 1¢ coils primarily as change-makers in its coil-stamp vending machines.

In 1995, supplies ran low. USPS could have ordered additional quantities of the 1¢ Omnibus coil stamp that first was issued in 1983 as part of the Transportation series. But this would have required the Bureau of Engraving and Printing to manufacture new intaglio sleeves, a relatively expensive proposition. Instead, the Postal Service opted for a cheaper solution. It asked BEP to prepare a new variety — a coil version of the offset-printed American Kestrel stamp that the Bureau already was making in sheet form. This new coil stamp was issued January 20, 1996, in rolls of 500 and 3,000.

The Kestrel design actually had made its debut in 1991 on a sheet stamp printed by the American Bank Note Company. On that stamp, the denomination was shown as "01," which was the prescribed style at that time for denominations of 9¢ and below. When another printing was needed, the job went to BEP and the denomination was changed to "1¢," the present style. This second version of the sheet stamp was issued May 10, 1995. Thus, the 1996 Kestrel coil represents the third use of the same basic design.

The coil originally had been scheduled to be printed on BEP's Optiforma web offset presses, which had been used to produce the sheet version. But a change in the type of plates and plate-mounting mechanism was pending for the Optiformas, and so the job was moved to the offset stations of the combination offset-intaglio D press.

Later, according to *Linn's Stamp News*, additional Kestrel coil stamps were printed on the Optiforma presses but were believed not to have been immediately issued. As of this writing there has been no report that Optiforma-printed Kestrel coils have been sold to the public.

Some *Linn's* readers reported finding markings on the stamps that appeared as scratches, dashes, hairlines or wisps of color. The publication said the lines might be from dirt particles or dust that eventually worked its way out of the press, or they might be from flaws in press blanket cylinders (the cylinders that accept the ink from the plates and transfer it to the stamp paper). Other readers reported Kestrel strips with lines, resembling joint lines, printed over the perforations between some stamps. These probably were seam lines caused by ink picked up by the worn edges of an offset plate, *Linn's* said.

The Design

The design of the coil stamp and that of the previous year's sheet stamp are identical, with one exception. The year date, printed in small black numbers below the design on the left side, is "1996" on the coil and "1995" on the sheet version. The design is based on Michael Matherly's acrylic painting of an American kestrel, or sparrow hawk, sitting on a cedar branch.

First-Day Facts

There was no first-day ceremony for the American Kestrel coil stamp, which was issued at the Holiday Inn Crowne Plaza in New York City in conjunction with the American Postage Stamp Show. On the same day, January 20, the 32¢ Love self-adhesive stamp and the 32¢ Flag Over Porch self-adhesive in panes of 10 also made their debut at the show.

For a brief time, the Philatelic Fulfillment Service Center offered uncacheted first-day covers of the new coil stamp for 53¢ each. The covers bore a pair of the Kestrel coils and a 30¢ Cardinal stamp to cover the first-class rate.

Date of Issue: January 20, 1996

Catalog Number: Scott 2920d, individual stamp; 2920e, pane of 10

Colors: gold, red, dark blue, light blue, black (stamp); black (cover)

First-Day Cancel: New York, New York

First-Day Cancellations: 57,639 (includes 32¢ Love self-adhesive and 1¢ Kestrel coil)

Format: Pane of 10 vertical stamps, arranged vertically, 2 across by 5 down, with 3 horizontal selvage strips: wide strip at top, narrow (peel-off) strip below horizontal row 2, narrow strip below horizontal row 5. Gravure printing cylinders printing 22 panes per revolution (2 across by 9 around) manufactured by North American Roto Engravers, Wadsworth, Ohio

Overall Stamp Size: 0.87 by 0.982 inches; 22.09mm by 24.94mm

Perforations: Die-cut simulated perforations. Die-cut concentric circles and lines on wide selvage strip at top. (Comco Commander die-cutter)

Front Markings: "UNITED STATES/POSTAL SERVICE./We Deliver For You./© USPS 1994" on top selvage strip. "Peel this strip and fold here" on narrow peel-off strip. Gravure color circles on each peel-off strip.

Liner Markings: "SELF-ADHESIVE (A) DO NOT WET" in a repeat pattern. (A) is trademark for Fasson laminated paper.

Back Markings: "Ten/Self-adhesive/Stamps/$3.20" on front of convertible booklet cover. Promotion for *Stamps etc.* catalog and Universal Product Code (UPC) on back of convertible booklet cover.

Designer: Dave LaFleur of Derby, Kansas

Art Director and Typographer: Richard Sheaff

Project Manager: Terrence McCaffrey, USPS

Stamp Manufacturing: Stamps printed by Avery Dennison Security Printing Division at Clinton, South Carolina, on Chesnut gravure press. Stamps processed by Avery Dennison.

Quantity Ordered and Distributed: 788,760,000

Cylinder Number Detail: 1 set of 5 gravure cylinder numbers preceded by the letter V on wide selvage strip at top

Cylinder Number Combinations Reported: V11111, V12111, V23222, V31121, V32111, V32121, V44444, V55555

Paper Supplier: Westvaco/Fasson

Tagging: phosphored paper

The Stamp

On January 20, the Postal Service issued a pane of 10 self-adhesive 32¢ stamps with the same Flag Over Porch design it had used in 1995 for seven different varieties. In its utilization of this design, USPS was only getting started; the pane turned out to be the first of five additional Flag Over Porch varieties issued in 1996.

The new item was printed by Avery Dennison by the gravure process, and was the first U.S. self-adhesive to be sold in units as small as 10.

Avery Dennison had also produced two of the 1995 Flag Over Porch stamps, a 20-stamp pane and a 5,000-stamp coil, in the self-adhesive format.

The stamps on the new pane of 10 are arranged in a vertical configuration, two across by five down. There are three pieces of selvage; a wide strip at the top, bearing the Postal Service logo and slogan, six color dots and the five-digit plate number; a narrow peel-off strip at the center, which can be removed to facilitate folding the pane into a booklet configuration; and another narrow strip, with color dots, at the bottom.

The stamps are separated by serpentine die-cuts that create the now-familiar simulated perforations. Each stamp has a straight edge at either the left or right. The wide selvage at the top of the pane is internally die-cut with a double set of concentric circles and diagonal lines to discourage customers from removing it and using it as a stamp. (Because the paper of the selvage, like that of the stamps, is prephosphored, an envelope bearing the label wouldn't be rejected by the Postal Service's facer-canceler machines.)

The Design

The design is based on Dave LaFleur's acrylic-and-colored-pencil picture of a portion of an American flag waving over a Victorian-era front porch. Avery Dennison used the same combination of colors to print the stamp that it used on its 1995 version: gold, red, dark blue, light blue and black. The back of the liner, which doubles as the cover when the pane is converted to a booklet, is printed in black and bears an enlarged reproduction of the stamp.

The stamp has a small blue "1996" year date beneath the design on the left. This enables collectors to readily distinguish it from any of the seven Flag Over Porch varieties of the year before, including one from the Avery Dennison pane of 20. Another difference between the two Avery Dennison-produced stamps is the size and number of the "perforations." The company's 1996 stamp has 12 and 13 teeth along its vertical sides instead of the 9 and 10 teeth that are on its 1995 version.

First-Day Facts

The new Flag Over Porch made its debut at the American Stamp Show at the Holiday Inn Crowne Plaza in New York City along with a 32¢ self-adhesive Love stamp and a 1¢ American Kestrel coil stamp. USPS held no official first-day ceremony.

The earliest-reported prerelease use of this stamp was on a cover machine-canceled in Atlanta, Georgia, January 12, eight days before the official release date.

VARIABLE DENOMINATION COIL (BEP)

Date of Issue: January 26, 1996

Catalog Number: Scott 33 (Computer Vended Postage section)

Colors: red (PMS 185C), blue (PMS 295C). Denominations printed in black.

First-Day Cancel: Arlington, Virginia

First-Day Cancellations: 17,423

Format: Coils of 3,000. Gravure printing cylinders of 432 subjects (18 across, 24 around).

Overall Stamp Size: .87 by .96 inches; 22.1mm by 24.4 mm

Perforations: 9.8 (Huck stroke perforator)

Designer, Typographer and Art Director: Richard Sheaff of Norwood, Massachusetts

Modeler: Peter Cocci, Bureau of Engraving and Printing

Project Manager: Joe Brockert, USPS

Stamp Manufacturing: Stamps printed by BEP on 7-color Andreotti webfed press (601).

Quantity Ordered: 4,450,000

Quantity Distributed: 3,312,000

Cylinder Number Detail: 1 group of 2 numbers on every 24th stamp

Cylinder Number Combination Reported: 11

Paper Supplier: Westvaco/Ivex

Tagging: phosphored paper

The Stamp

On January 26, the Postal Service issued its third variable-rate coil (VRC) stamp for use in the coin-operated, computerized stamp-dispensing systems it calls Postage and Mailing Centers (PMCs).

The new stamp, like its two predecessors, carries no denomination. The denomination selected by the buyer is printed on the stamp by the PMC at the time of purchase.

The stamp was printed by the Bureau of Engraving and Printing on its Andreotti gravure press in rolls of 3,000. It features the same design as the first two VRC stamps: a red, white and blue shield with draped bunting.

PMCs are 24-hour, self-service units designed to increase the number of potential customer-service locations, increase the speed of retail servicing and expand the hours during which customers can obtain rate information and stamps.

A PMC weighs individual mail pieces and automatically computes and displays postage rates and fees based on destination ZIP codes and class of service. The stamps it dispenses can be printed in denominations from 20¢ to $20.

PMCs first went into use on an experimental basis in 1992 with machines manufactured by the ECA GARD company of Chicago, Illinois. These dispensed a VRC stamp that was oriented horizontally with perforations at top and bottom. The stamp was printed by the Bureau of Engraving and Printing by the intaglio process.

Later, a different kind of machine, manufactured by Unisys, was added to the system. The Unisys equipment required a stamp that was vertically arranged, with perforations at the sides. Such a stamp, gravure-printed by the American Bank Note Company, was issued in 1994.

But ABNC's contract to produce stamps for the Postal Service wasn't renewed. So when supplies of Unisys stamps ran low, USPS turned again to BEP to provide replacements.

At the time the new stamp was issued, 11 post offices in Northern Virginia were equipped to dispense it: Preston King station (Arlington), Eads station (Arlington), Merrifield branch, Trade Center station (Alexandria), Community branch (Alexandria), McLean main post office, West McLean branch, and the Woodbridge, Sterling, Manassas and Herndon post offices. Only the Preston King station got supplies on January 26, USPS said. At the other offices, the new stamp was placed into service only when existing supplies of the previous PMC stamp were exhausted.

Collectors could obtain the new VRC stamp, in the 32¢ denomination only, from the Philatelic Fulfillment Service Center in Kansas City, Missouri.

The Scott catalogs list VRC stamps in a separate category called "Computer Vended Postage."

The Design

The BEP stamp would be difficult to distinguish from its ABNC predecessor, except for one important feature. The BEP stamp has a small red "1996" printed beneath the design on the left side; the ABNC stamp has no year date.

A side-by-side comparison of the stamps shows only very subtle differences. The red and blue colors on the ABNC stamp are slightly darker, and the lettering and security lathework, which the Scott catalog calls a moire pattern, is crisper, than on the BEP version.

First-Day Facts

No official first-day ceremony was held January 26 at the Preston King postal station in Arlington, where first-day postmarks on the new stamp were available on a handback basis only.

However, the Graebner Chapter of the American First Day Cover Society sponsored an unofficial ceremony on that date at the Swanson Middle School in Arlington. At the ceremony, the chapter distributed a free printed program that bore one first-day-canceled 32¢ example of the new stamp.

Collectors requesting first-day cancellations by mail were instructed to send self-addressed envelopes bearing the new stamp to the Philatelic Fulfillment Service Center in Kansas City by April 25, 1996. The Service Center also offered uncacheted first-day covers bearing 32¢ VRC stamps for sale at 53¢.

2¢ RED-HEADED WOODPECKER

Date of Issue: February 2, 1996

Catalog Number: Scott 3032

Colors: black, yellow, cyan, magenta, light tan (PMS 155)

First-Day Cancel: Sarasota, Florida

First-Day Cancellations: 37,319

Format: Panes of 100, 10 across, 10 down. Offset printing plates of 400 subjects (20 across, 20 around)

Overall Stamp Size: 0.84 by 0.99 inches; 21.336mm by 25.146mm

Perforations: 11.2 by 11.1 (Eureka stroke perforator)

Selvage Markings: "© USPS 1996." "100 x .02 = $2.00." "PLATE/POSITION" and diagram.

Designer: Michael Matherly of Cambridge City, Indiana

Typographer: John Boyd, Anagraphics Inc., New York, New York

Modeler: Peter Cocci, Bureau of Engraving and Printing

Art Director: Joseph Brockert, USPS

Project Manager: Vance Harris, USPS

Stamp Manufacturing: Stamps printed by BEP on Optiforma webfed 6-color offset press

Quantity Ordered: 310,500,000

Quantity Distributed: 308,400,000

Plate Number Detail: 1 set of 5 offset plate numbers in selvage next to 1 upper corner stamp and 1 lower corner stamp on the same side

Plate Number Combinations Reported: 11111, 11121, 22222

Paper Supplier: Westvaco/Ivex

Tagging: untagged

The Stamp

On February 2, in Sarasota, Florida, the Postal Service issued the third in a series of low-value definitive stamps picturing birds. The 2¢ stamp, distributed in panes of 100, depicted a red-headed woodpecker.

The previous stamps in the group were the 1¢ American Kestrel and the 3¢ Eastern Bluebird, both first issued in 1991. Only 13 days before the Woodpecker stamp appeared, USPS had issued the Kestrel in coil form (see separate chapter).

Like the Kestrel coil, the Woodpecker stamp was produced by offset lithography by the Bureau of Engraving and Printing, but on a different webfed press. The Woodpecker was printed on BEP's Optiforma press, while the Kestrel coil came from the offset stations of the combination offset-intaglio D press.

The bird stamps are intended to gradually replace stamps of the same denominations in the Great Americans (sheet) and Transportation (coil) series. In the case of the Woodpecker, the stamp it is slated to replace is the 2¢ Mary Lyon of the Great Americans set, which has been in the postal inventory since 1987. A new supply of the Lyon was distributed to post offices late in 1995.

The Postal Service considers multicolor stamps featuring wildlife to be more popular with the general public than the monochromatic stamps of the older series. Furthermore, being printed by offset lithography rather than intaglio, they are considerably cheaper to produce.

With the new stamp, the red-headed woodpecker (Melanerpes erythrocephalus) made its first appearance on U.S. postage. The bird measures up to 10 inches long, with a wingspread of 16 to 18 inches. Its entire head, neck and upper breast are a bright red, with bluish-black wings and tail. The large areas of white on the rear part of the wings and the upper rump are especially noticeable in flight. The sexes are identical in appearance, and the female, unlike females of other woodpecker species, is an active aggressor in taking over a nest cavity from competing starlings and in its subsequent defense.

Although redheads are found throughout all the central and eastern United States, they aren't the common sight they once were. They favor mature, isolated stands of oak and hickory, elms and sycamores, along streams and bottomlands. Such habitat is in dwindling supply. Telephone poles, which once provided myriad nest sites for this open-country bird, now are treated with creosote, which poisons woodpecker nestlings. Acorn crops, a staple in redheads' winter diet, often fail, and when that happens the bird's population drops.

In the summer, redheads switch to insects, of which beetles, grasshoppers and ants make up the bulk. Less inclined to drill for food than other woodpeckers, redheads often fly down to the ground to capture bugs, bluebird-style, or make flycatcherlike pursuits of winged prey. In late summer and fall, berries and grain round out a predominantly vegetarian diet.

The Design

The acrylic painting on which the Red-Headed Woodpecker stamp design was based was one of several wildlife paintings that Michael R. Matherly, a Cambridge City, Indiana, artist and magazine illustrator, had done in a group for USPS. Other Matherly paintings were used for the American Kestrel and Eastern Bluebird stamps of 1991, the 45¢ Pumpkinseed Sunfish stamp of 1992 and the 29¢ Red Squirrel self-adhesive of 1993.

The image on the new stamp is of a woodpecker seated on a bare near-horizontal tree limb against a light-tan background. The words "Red-Headed Woodpecker," in black italics, appear in the lower-left corner, and the year, 1996, appears in black below the design on the left side. The background color was produced with a separate ink; the bird, limb and typography were created with the four standard process colors, black, yellow, cyan and magenta.

First-Day Facts

USPS district manager Robert Davis dedicated the Red-Headed Woodpecker stamp on the opening day of the Sarasota National Stamp Exhibition at the Sarasota Municipal Auditorium. Sarasota Postmaster Peter Fernandez presided at the ceremony. The three-day show was sponsored by the Sarasota Philatelic Club.

For a limited time, the Philatelic Fulfillment Service Center offered uncacheted first-day covers of the Red-Headed Woodpecker stamp for sale at 53¢ each. The covers bore one of the new stamps and a 30¢ Cardinal stamp of 1991.

The earliest-known prerelease use of a Red-Headed Woodpecker stamp was on a cover postmarked January 23 at New Haven, Indiana. A 30¢ Cardinal stamp made up the balance of the 32¢ first-class rate.

50¢ JACQUELINE COCHRAN

Date of Issue: March 9, 1996

Catalog Number: Scott 3066

Colors: magenta, yellow, cyan, black (offset); black (intaglio)

First-Day Cancel: Indio, California

First-Day Cancellations: 30,628

Format: Panes of 50, horizontal, 5 across, 10 down. Offset printing plates of 300 subjects (20 across, 15 around); intaglio printing sleeves of 600 subjects (20 across, 30 around).

Overall Stamp Size: 1.19 by 0.91 inches; 30.2mm by 23.1mm

Perforations: 11.2 (Eureka stroke perforator)

Selvage Inscriptions: "Like to see other great/stamps and products offered/by the Postal Service? Send." "for our free catalog USPS/FREE CATALOG OFFER/NCSC, 6060 PRIMACY PKWY." "SUITE 101, MEMPHIS, TN/38188-0001. Offer good while supplies last."

Selvage Markings: "©USPS 1996." "50 x .50 = $25.00." "PLATE/POSITION" and diagram.

Designer: Davis Meltzer of Huntingdon Valley, Pennsylvania

Typographer and Art Director: Phil Jordan

Modeler: Clarence Holbert, Bureau of Engraving and Printing

Engraver: Photoengraved by BEP

Project Manager: Terrence McCaffrey, USPS

Stamp Manufacturing: Stamps printed by BEP on Goebel offset-intaglio D press (902).

Quantity Ordered and Distributed: 314,175,000

Plate/Sleeve Number Detail: 1 set of 4 offset plate numbers and 1 intaglio sleeve number above and below each corner stamp

Plate/Sleeve Number Combinations Reported: 1111-1, 2111-1, 2212-1, 2222-1, 3232-1, 4242-1, 4244-1, 5345-1, 5353-1, 6353-1, 6363-1, 7777-1

Paper Supplier: Guardbridge/CPL, England

Tagging: phosphored paper

The Stamp

On March 9, USPS issued a 50¢ stamp in its Pioneers of Aviation series picturing Jacqueline Cochran, one of the nation's most famous pilots and the first woman to fly faster than sound. The stamp was dedicated at the Indian Palms Resort in Indio, California, the site of the ranch where Cochran lived for many years with her husband, Floyd Odlum.

The denomination of the stamp corresponded to the international postcard rate that took effect in 1995. All first-class mail now is carried by air, and so the stamp didn't bear the "airmail" wording it would have had if it had been issued earlier.

Although not so designated, the Cochran stamp was part of the Postal Service's Pioneers of Aviation series, which has honored more than a dozen early flyers and designers and builders of aircraft since it was launched in 1978 with a se-tenant pair picturing the Wright brothers. The most recent previous stamp in the series was the 60¢ Eddie Rickenbacker stamp, issued in 1995 to cover the international letter rate.

The Rickenbacker and Cochran stamps were planned and designed at the same time in anticipation of the 1995 rate change. "We knew there would be a need for two new international-rate stamps," said Terrence McCaffrey, the project manager. "Rickenbacker was long overdue. We wanted to get another woman into the series as well, and we thought Cochran was perfect. She had been on the (Citizens' Stamp Advisory Committee's) approved list for a number of years."

The *Postal Bulletin* of February 1, 1996, reported that unfilled requisitions for the 50¢ Chester Nimitz stamp of the Great Americans series would be filled with 50¢ Jacqueline Cochrans. The Postal Service's Robin Wright told Great Americans specialist Stephen G. Esrati that the Cochran stamp replaced the Nimitz. The Nimitz would not be reprinted, although it would remain on sale as long as supplies lasted, Wright said.

Like the Rickenbacker stamp, the stamp honoring Cochran was printed by the Bureau of Engraving and Printing in the "special" size previously reserved for Love and Christmas stamps. But whereas the Rickenbacker was vertically oriented and printed by gravure, the Cochran was a horizontal stamp and was printed by a combination of offset (picture) and intaglio (black lettering).

The stamp was announced by USPS February 20, 18 days before its issue date.

Jacqueline Cochran never knew who her parents were. She was born in northern Florida around 1906 and raised by a poor foster family in the confines of what she called "Sawdust Road," the sawmill camps where laboring families endured an impoverished day-to-day existence.

From early childhood she was determined to free herself from poverty. At 8 she was working full time in a mill. At 11 she had apprenticed herself to a hairdresser. By 14, self-trained, she had selected the name "Cochran" out of a Pensacola telephone book and set out alone to make her fortune. At 19, in New York, she was working at Antoine's salon at Saks Fifth Avenue.

Here she met Floyd Odlum, a millionaire investor. A few years later Odlum divorced his wife and married Jacqueline Cochran. She took up flying in 1932 on a dare from Odlum, earning her license in three weeks, and found in aviation a lifetime passion.

Within two years she became the first woman to compete in the prestigious Bendix transcontinental air race. In 1938 she became the first woman to win it, flying a P-35 pursuit plane designed by Major Alexander P. de Seversky from Burbank, California, to Cleveland, Ohio, in 8 hours and 10 minutes.

When World War II broke out, Cochran became the first woman to ferry a bomber across the Atlantic Ocean. In 1943 she founded the Women's Air Force Service Pilots (WASP) program, which trained more than 1,000 women, and was awarded the Distinguished Service Medal in 1945. She served in the Air Force Reserve from 1948 to 1970, retiring with the rank of colonel.

In 1953, under the tutelage of her friend, test pilot Chuck Yeager, Cochran broke the sonic barrier in a Canadian F-86 Sabrejet. In 1964 she piloted another jet aircraft at 1,429 mph, more than twice the speed of sound.

She won the Harmon Trophy, awarded to the year's outstanding female pilot, 15 times. She won many other trophies and awards, and in 1971 she became the first living woman elected to the Aviation Hall of Fame. She had a distinguished parallel career in business, as head of Jacqueline Cochran Cosmetics, and flew 90,000 miles a year selling her products. Associated Press editors voted her Woman of the Year in Business in 1953 and 1954.

At the time of her death August 9, 1980, Jacqueline Cochran held more speed, altitude and distance records than any other pilot, male or female, in aviation history.

The Design

Illustrator Davis Meltzer and art director Phil Jordan, the design team that produced the Eddie Rickenbacker stamp, also was responsible for the Jacqueline Cochran stamp. Both are experts in aeronautical art; Jordan is the long-time design director of *Air and Space* magazine.

For both stamps, Meltzer first created a design in commemorative size that featured a head-and-shoulders portrait of the flyer along with a picture of an appropriate aircraft. For Cochran, the artist and art director decided at the outset that the plane should be the P-35 in which she won

These are two of Davis Meltzer's unused concept sketches in commemorative size for the Jacqueline Cochran stamp, showing different portraits of the aviator with her P-35 de Seversky pursuit plane and a Bendix Trophy race pylon in the background.

the Bendix race and that it should be shown rounding a pylon from that race.

Meltzer made three concept sketches, each with a different portrait of Cochran. The sketch chosen by the Citizens' Stamp Advisory Committee to be made into finished art showed the flyer with her head turned slightly, her collar opened and her goggles pushed up on her helmet, which is unbuckled. The plane sweeps past the pylon behind her right shoulder, while a white cumulus cloud billows into a blue sky in the distance. Meltzer based the portrait on a Bettman Archive photograph that reportedly was made immediately after Cochran had won the Bendix Trophy.

In preparing Meltzer's finished acrylic painting for the printer, a computer graphics specialist at Dodge Color in Washington, D.C., made some adjustments using Adobe PhotoShop software. Following Jordan's instructions, the specialist enlarged Cochran's portrait and moved the airplane, which was touching the side of her face, a slight distance away. To fill the resulting empty space, portions of the cloud and pylon and the plane's horizontal stabilizer were electronically "cloned" from the painting. These changes were kept in the design when the stamp format was reduced from commemorative size to the so-called special size shortly before the two airmail stamps were scheduled to go to press.

Jordan selected a typeface called News Gothic for the intaglio black lettering "Jacqueline Cochran Pioneer Pilot" and a condensed Franklin Gothic for the dropped-out "50 USA."

Varieties

Specimens of the Cochran stamp were found with the intaglio lettering missing. The first to report the error was Chris Christiansen, a North Carolina collector, who bought a block of 10 stamps in a shrink-wrapped package at a postal store June 11. Five days later he inspected his purchase and noticed that none of the stamps contained the words "Jacqueline Cochran Pioneer Pilot," which should have been there. The single black intaglio plate number also was absent from the attached top selvage, although the four offset plate numbers were in their normal position.

Shown here are two versions of Davis Meltzer's finished design for the Jacqueline Cochran stamp, both in the commemorative size. A comparison of the two shows how a computer-graphics specialist, working with Meltzer's painting, enlarged Cochran's portrait and moved the plane slightly away from her face, "cloning" a portion of the clouds and pylon to fill in the resulting gap. Later the revised artwork was cropped to fit the smaller special-stamp format. The word "airmail" was omitted from the finished stamp.

Shown here is a photographically cropped portion of one of the blocks of Cochran stamps found in North Carolina with the black intaglio words "Jacqueline Cochran Pioneer Pilot" missing from the lower left. Nothing was wrong, however, with the black offset printing, which produced the tiny "1996" below the bottom-left frameline and also helped create the tones in the picture.

The next day, Christiansen returned to the postal store and was able to buy nine more packages containing 10 error stamps each, which, including his original purchase, gave him a total of 100 stamps. Like the first block he bought, each of the other nine was an upper-right position plate block with attached selvage.

Later reports of similar finds came from collectors in Syracuse and New York, New York, and in California. Most of them, like Christiansen's find, were in prepackaged blocks purchased at postal stores.

First-Day Facts

Michael Coughlin, deputy postmaster general, dedicated the Cochran stamp at the ceremony in Indio. Speakers were Marty Wyall, president, Women Air Force Service Pilots; Ann Wood-Kelly of the British Air Transport Auxiliary; and Beverly Hansen Sfingi, a friend of Jacqueline Cochran. Danny Jackson, USPS district manager for customer service and sales, presided and introduced the guests, and Indio Mayor Marcos Lopez gave the welcome.

NONDENOMINATED (5¢) MOUNTAIN NONPROFIT RATE COIL (BEP) AMERICAN SCENES SERIES

Date of Issue: March 16, 1996

Catalog Number: Scott 2903

Colors: magenta, light blue (PMS 305C), yellow, purple (PMS 2725C), dark purple (PMS 2745U).

First-Day Cancel: San Jose, California

First-Day Cancellations: 28,064 (includes Stamp Venturers version)

Format: Coils of 500 and 3,000. Gravure printing cylinders of 432 subjects (18 across, 24 around).

Overall Stamp Size: 0.87 by 0.96 inches; 22.1mm by 24.4mm

Perforations: 9.8 (Huck stroke perforator)

Designer: Tom Engeman of Carbondale, Colorado

Art Director and Typographer: Phil Jordan

Modeler: Peter Cocci, Bureau of Engraving and Printing

Project Manager: Vance Harris, USPS

Stamp Manufacturing: Stamps printed by BEP on the 7-color Andreotti webfed gravure press (601)

Quantity Ordered and Distributed: 825,000,000 (750,000,000 in coils of 3,000; 75,000,000 in coils of 500)

Cylinder Number Detail: 1 group of 5 numbers on every 24th stamp

Cylinder Number Combination Reported: 11111

Paper Supplier: Westvaco/Ivex

Tagging: untagged

NONDENOMINATED (5¢) MOUNTAIN NONPROFIT RATE COIL (STAMP VENTURERS) AMERICAN SCENES SERIES

Date of Issue: March 16, 1996

Catalog Number: Scott 2904

Colors: yellow, magenta, cyan

First-Day Cancel: San Jose, California

First-Day Cancellations: 28,064 (includes Bureau of Engraving and Printing version)

Format: Coils of 10,000. Gravure printing cylinders of 616 subjects (22 across, 28 around) manufactured by Armotek Industries, Palmyra, New Jersey

Overall Stamp Size: 0.87 by 0.96 inches; 22.1mm by 24.4mm

Perforations: 9.8 (APS rotary perforator)

Designer: Tom Engeman of Carbondale, Colorado

Art Director and Typographer: Phil Jordan

Modeler: Richard C. Sennett, Sennett Enterprises

Project Manager: Vance Harris, USPS

Stamp Manufacturing: Stamps printed for Stamp Venturers by J.W. Fergusson and Sons, Richmond, Virginia, on Champlain webfed gravure press 1. Stamps perforated and processed by Stamp Venturers, Fredericksburg, Virginia.

Quantity Ordered and Distributed: 150,000,000

Cylinder Number Detail: 1 group of 3 numbers preceded by the letter S on every 14th stamp

Cylinder Number Combination Reported: S111

Counting Number Detail: 1 5-digit counting number printed by dot-matrix printer in magenta or black on back of every 10th stamp. Numbers advance from right to left.

Paper Supplier: Coated Paper Unlimited, Bollington, England

Tagging: untagged

The Stamps

On March 16, USPS issued two versions of a nondenominated coil stamp depicting a mountain scene. The stamps, made for use by nonprofit organizations on mass mailings, sold for 5¢ each. Users were required to pay the difference between the 5¢ cost and the actual per-piece mailing cost at the time of mailing.

The two versions were by two different printers: the Bureau of Engraving and Printing, which produced the stamp in coils of 500 and 3,000, and Stamp Venturers, which produced it in coils of 10,000. Both versions were printed by the gravure process.

At the time of issuance, USPS announced that a self-adhesive version of the stamp would be issued later (see separate chapter).

The Mountain stamp was the second nondenominated coil stamp depicting a colorful landscape scene to be issued for use by nonprofit mailers in a little over a year. On March 10, 1995, USPS had inaugurated what it called its "American Scenes series" with a stamp depicting a series of Western buttes silhouetted against the sky. It also sold for 5¢.

The Butte stamp would continue to be available, and the Mountain stamp would give mailers a choice of noncontroversial designs — "comfortable" images, as one USPS official put it.

In preparing designs for the American Scenes series, the Postal Service decided to create four regional images, representing the West, the mountains, the Northeastern coast and the South. The latter two remained in reserve for future use.

BEP's version of the stamp has a set of five gravure cylinder numbers centered below the design on every 24th stamp. On the Stamp Venturers version, there are three numbers preceded by the letter S that occur on every 14th stamp, beneath the lower-right corner of the design.

The Stamp Venturers stamps have counting numbers on the back of every 10th stamp, printed in magenta or black-violet by a dot-matrix process over the gum. The company began this practice with the G first-class rate (32¢) coil stamps that were issued in 1994.

The Design

Tom Engeman, who had designed the previous year's Butte coil stamp and the previous month's Smithsonian Institution commemorative, provided the acrylic painting on which the Mountain stamps' image was based.

Engeman's painting is of a generic mountain range, with three peaks silhouetted against a blue sky. Sunlight falls on the left slopes, creating patches and streaks of yellow, orange and red, and leaving the rest of the range in deep shadow. This contrast between light and shade is an Engeman trademark, present on all his artwork for the Postal Service, including the

Butte and Smithsonian stamps.

An important requirement of the illustrations made for the nondenominated bulk-rate stamps has been that they allow the inclusion of easily readable service inscriptions without encroaching on the designs. On both the Mountain and Butte stamps, the words "USA" and "NONPROFIT ORG." in condensed News Gothic capitals were dropped out of the design at the bottom.

The two printers of the Mountain stamp employed different color combinations. BEP used five inks: magenta, light blue (PMS 305C), yellow, purple (PMS 2725C) and dark purple (PMS 2745U). Stamp Venturers used only three colors: yellow, magenta and cyan.

This difference causes the two stamps to look quite different when placed side by side. On the BEP stamp, the sky is light blue and the shadowed portions of the mountains are purple. The Stamp Venturers stamp has a darker sky and the shadows are dark blue. The lettering on the BEP version is outlined in purple; the Stamp Venturers letters have no outlines.

The purple year date "1996" beneath the design of the BEP stamp is about half the size of its cyan counterpart on the Stamp Venturers product.

First-Day Facts

The Mountain stamp was issued at the Filatelic Fiesta, held at the San Jose Scottish Rite Center in San Jose, California. The annual Fiesta, sponsored by the San Jose Stamp Club, began in 1933 and is one of the oldest stamp shows in the United States. The decision to hold the stamp dedication ceremony there "reflects the Postal Service's commitment to bring new collectors to the hobby by supporting major stamp shows," USPS said in a news release.

James H. Aanenson, San Jose district manager of the Postal Service, dedicated the stamp. Marshall Burde, chairman of the Fiesta, was the principal speaker, and Rigo Chacon, Southbay bureau chief of KGO-TV, gave the welcome. Also attending were Charolette Power, a San Jose councilwoman, and Jeannie Schmelzer, community relations vice president for the United Way. San Jose Postmaster Suzanne C. Chaille presided.

Collectors were given 90 days after the issue date, rather than the usual 30, to submit prestamped covers to the San Jose postmaster for first-day postmarks. The stamps weren't available at most post offices, and the extra grace period allowed ample time to obtain them from the Philatelic Fulfillment Service Center.

For a limited time, the center sold uncacheted first-day covers bearing both versions of the Butte stamp: a strip of four of the Stamp Venturers version and a strip of three of the BEP variety. The cost was 56¢, representing the face value of the stamps plus 21¢.

3¢ EASTERN BLUEBIRD, REDESIGNED

Date of Issue: April 3, 1996

Catalog Number: Scott 3033

Colors: black, yellow, cyan, magenta, light tan (PMS 155c)

First-Day Cancel: Washington, D.C.

First-Day Cancellations: 23,405

Format: Panes of 100, 10 across, 10 down. Offset printing plates of 400 subjects (20 across, 20 around)

Overall Stamp Size: 0.84 by 0.99 inches; 21.3mm by 25.1 mm

Perforations: 11.2 by 11.1 (Eureka stroke perforator)

Selvage Markings: "© USPS 1996." "100 x .03 = $3.00." "PLATE/POSITION" and diagram.

Designer: Michael Matherly of Cambridge City, Indiana

Typographer: John Boyd, Anagraphics Inc., New York, New York

Modeler: Clarence Holbert, Bureau of Engraving and Printing

Art Director and Project Manager: Joseph Brockert, USPS

Stamp Manufacturing: Stamps printed by BEP on Optiforma webfed 6-color offset press

Quantity Ordered: 317,000,000

Quantity Distributed: 317,330,000

Plate Number Detail: 1 set of 5 offset plate numbers in selvage next to 1 upper corner stamp and 1 lower corner stamp on the same side

Plate Number Combination Reported: 11111

Paper Supplier: Westvaco/Ivex

Tagging: untagged

The Stamp

The increase in the first-class postage rate from 29¢ to 32¢ on January 1, 1995, created a demand for 3¢ stamps to pair with leftover 29¢ stamps. In due time this demand exhausted the Postal Service's supply of the 3¢ Eastern Bluebird sheet stamp that it had issued in 1991. The original printer, the American Bank Note Company, no longer was under contract to produce stamps, so USPS turned to the Bureau of Engraving and Printing to create an additional 317 million Bluebird stamps. The new stamp was placed on sale April 3 in Washington, D.C.

Because new offset plates had to be made, USPS specified that the design be modified to conform to its current policy regarding stamp denominations. When the first Eastern Bluebird stamp was issued, the policy called for denominations of less than 10¢ to be expressed with a zero in front of the single digit, and no "¢" sign. In 1995, USPS abandoned this practice. It dropped the superfluous zero and restored the "¢," with the complete virgule (vertical stroke), for low-value stamps. So the Bureau-printed Eastern Bluebird stamp is inscribed "USA 3¢" instead of "USA 03" as was the prototype.

A similar metamorphosis had taken place with the 1¢ American Kestrel stamp, which, like the 3¢ Bluebird, first was issued in 1991. When supplies of the ABNC-printed Kestrel sheet stamp ran low in 1995, BEP was called on to provide a new supply, with the original "01" denomination changed to "1¢." Early in 1996 the Postal Service issued a coil version of the Kestrel stamp, also printed by BEP (see separate chapter).

The Design

The design used for both the original and revised Eastern Bluebird stamps was based on an acrylic painting of a bluebird sitting on a flowering crab apple tree branch. It was the third stamp variety issued in 1996 to use artwork by Michael R. Matherly of Cambridge City, Indiana. The others were a coil version of the 1¢ American Kestrel stamp mentioned above, issued January 20, and a 2¢ Red-Headed Woodpecker sheet stamp, issued February 2 (see separate chapters).

Once again, as had been the case with the two printings of the American Kestrel sheet stamp, BEP produced a much better printed product than ABNC had done. A comparison of the original and revised Eastern Bluebird stamps shows some dramatic differences in appearance.

BEP used finer screens, which resulted in details of greater clarity. The improvement is particularly noticeable in the bird's eye and feathers and the leaves on the branch. The colors on the BEP stamp are deeper, and the blossoms are orange on the BEP version, rather than pink as on the ABNC stamp. ABNC used only the four standard process colors, magenta, yellow, cyan and black, while BEP used these plus a light tan self-color for the background.

The BEP stamp has a small black "1996" below the design on the left side. The ABNC version has no date, having been produced before the

The Bureau of Engraving and Printing produced a much better printed stamp (right) than the earlier, American Bank Note Company version.

Postal Service began year-dating its stamp designs.

First-Day Facts

No first-day ceremony was held for the new Eastern Bluebird stamp.

For a limited time, the Philatelic Fulfillment Service Center offered uncacheted first-day covers for sale for 53¢. The covers bore a block of four Bluebird stamps and one 20¢ Blue Jay booklet stamp of 1995.

32¢ CAL FARLEY
GREAT AMERICANS SERIES

Date of Issue: April 26, 1996

Catalog Number: Scott 2934

Color: green (PMS 3435)

First-Day Cancel: Amarillo, Texas

First-Day Cancellations: 109,440

Format: Panes of 100, 10 across, 10 down. Intaglio printing plates of 400 subjects (20 across, 20 down) printing 800 stamps per pass.

Overall Stamp Size: 0.84 by 0.99 inches; 21.336mm by 25.146mm

Perforations: 11.2 by 11.1 (Wista stroke perforator)

Selvage Markings: "© USPS 1995." ".32/X 100/$32.00." "PANE POSITION" and diagram.

Designer: Dennis Lyall of South Norwalk, Connecticut

Typographer: Tom Mann, Mann & Mann Graphics, Warrenton, Virginia

Engraver: Martin Morck

Art Director: Howard Paine

Project Manager: Vance Harris, USPS

Stamp Manufacturing: Stamps printed by BCA on a T.A. sheetfed intaglio press in Browns Summit, North Carolina

Quantity Ordered and Distributed: 150,000,000

Plate Number Detail: 1 intaglio plate number preceded by the letter B in selvage next to 1 upper corner stamp and 1 lower corner stamp on the same side

Plate Number Reported: B1

Paper Supplier: Ivex

Tagging: phosphored paper

The Stamp

On April 26, the Postal Service issued a 32¢ stamp in the Great Americans series honoring Cal Farley, founder of a foster-home operation near Amarillo, Texas, called Cal Farley's Boys Ranch.

The design bore the identifying inscription "Humanitarian." Postal patrons wishing to find out anything more about Farley had a difficult task, because he is unlisted in any standard encyclopedia or biographical reference work.

The Farley stamp was the second Great Americans stamp in eight months to depict a benefactor of young people. The previous September, another 32¢ stamp in the series had honored Milton Hershey, who founded a school in Pennsylvania bearing his name for orphans and other disadvantaged children.

Like the Hershey stamp, the Farley stamp was approved only after it was endorsed by a member of the Postal Service Board of Governors, which oversees the agency. In the Hershey campaign, the governor who took up the cause was LeGree Daniels; for Farley, it was J. Sam Winters, the Austin, Texas, lawyer who chaired the board.

As Bill McAllister of *The Washington Post* told it, the campaign for a Cal Farley stamp was launched some 10 years earlier by a group of Texans. It was going nowhere until 1995, when business executive Wales Madden Jr., a Boys Ranch director, called on Winters for help. Winters had lived in Amarillo and recalled Farley's efforts to create the ranch for children in need.

"We have to salute J. Sam Winters," Madden said. "Mr. Winters took up the standard on this. He believed in this project. He knew Cal Farley as a young man."

On November 8, 1995, Postmaster General Marvin T. Runyon announced plans to issue the stamp in 1996, and 20 days later chairman Winters unveiled the design at Cal Farley's Boys Ranch. Farley's daughter, Gene Farley Harriman, was quoted as saying: "This is a dream come true — seeing my dad honored on a national level."

The stamp was the 59th face-different variety in the Great Americans series, which began in 1980. It was intaglio-printed by Banknote Corporation of America and issued in panes of 100.

The plate position diagram that appears on each pane was placed in the selvage opposite the fourth row of stamps from the top, even on panes from the lower half of the printing sheet. Plate block collectors who wanted the diagram had to collect blocks of eight.

Great Americans specialist Stephen G. Esrati noted that in the Cal Farley

311

selvage, BCA turned the multiplication formula (.32 x 100/$32.00) sideways. On all previous Great Americans stamps with this information, the formula is upright, oriented in the same direction as the stamps.

Cal Farley was born in Iowa in 1895. An athlete, he went to Amarillo after World War I to play semiprofessional baseball with the Amarillo Gassers. He also was a Greco-Roman and freestyle wrestler.

He became a department-store owner and civic leader in Amarillo. In 1934, during the Depression, Farley helped organize the city's Maverick Club to keep neglected boys off the street through athletics. Today, more than 1,500 boys and girls are Maverick Club members.

Farley's concern for such youth became a lifelong calling in 1939 when a rancher gave him 150 acres of land on which to build Boys Ranch. He based his project on the proposition: "Furnish a boy with a shirttail to hang on to, and you'll never have to furnish him a room in the reformatory." Starting out with only nine boys, Boys Ranch has grown into a modern community of 441 boys (and girls since 1992). It has provided homes, education and opportunities for success to more than 4,000 young people since its inception.

In 1945, Farley established Kids Inc. to provide athletic programs for Amarillo children, many of whose families were broken or separated during World War II. Now the recreation provided by Kids Inc. is enjoyed by 17,000 boys and girls each year.

Cal Farley and his wife Mimi, affectionately known as "Mom and Pop" Farley, often dipped into their own pockets to meet the needs of growing youngsters.

Farley's dream of helping troubled boys has continued since his death February 19, 1967. Today there are two affiliates of Cal Farley's Boys Ranch; these are Girlstown, U.S.A., located in Whiteface, Texas, and Cal Farley's Family Program, which serves preschool and elementary-age children in Borger, Texas.

The Design

To design the Cal Farley stamp, art director Howard Paine called on artist Dennis Lyall, who had also designed the 32¢ Milton Hershey and 23¢ Mary Cassatt Great Americans stamps as well as several commemoratives.

The Farley family provided several photographs, and in August 1995 Lyall sent Paine pencil sketches based on three of them. Although the photos showed Farley with a necktie, Lyall removed the tie and opened the collar to give the subject a more informal look. "I didn't want another head on a stamp with a tie and a suit," said Paine. "Farley had founded a boys' ranch and was obviously an outdoors type. That's what I wanted to convey."

The sketch chosen by the Citizens' Stamp Advisory Committee to be made into a finished India-ink drawing for use on the stamp was a three-quarters portrait that was based on a 1946 photograph of Farley standing

This is the 1946 photograph of Cal Farley and his daughter Gene Farley on which artist Dennis Lyall based his portrait of the philanthropist.

beside his daughter Gene and squinting into the sun. CSAC and postal officials wanted Farley's eyes behind his spectacles to be more open on the stamp, but instead of asking Lyall to revise his artwork, they instructed BCA to have its engraver make the necessary changes, using the other photographs of Farley for guidance. The same procedure had been used for the previous year's Milton Hershey stamp, which also was based on a photograph of the subject looking toward the sun.

The job of creating an intaglio stamp portrait is an exacting one and subject to close supervision. After BCA's engraver, Martin Morck, made his first engraving, a proof was pulled from the unhardened die and reviewed both by BCA officials and Terrence McCaffrey, head of design at USPS.

Dennis Lyall's India-ink line-and-wash drawing of Farley showed him squinting, as he was doing in the photo. On the instructions of USPS, the engraver opened the subject's eyes when translating Lyall's artwork onto the steel die.

BCA's experts made these comments on the proof: "Collar: light left-to-right line on his left, top of collar. Forehead: lines seem strong. Ear: inside of lobe too dark, lacks detail and softness. Background under chin: darker area seems to follow contour of jaw. Top of hair: looks a little flat. Background under right lens extends too far. Spot on left jaw. Glasses frame: his left side seems a little intense. Under the nose: soften shadow. Teeth: soften lines between each tooth." McCaffrey added further instructions. "The eyes didn't seem to go together," he recalled. "The right eye looked larger than the left, and it wasn't rounding right — it was sticking out too far. I marked on the proof 'Eye too buggy.' Also, the nose was too large and the left nostril was too flared. The printer and I thoroughly marked up the proof, and the engraver made the changes we wanted."

The typeface chosen for the wording was the familiar Galliard font used on previous Great Americans stamps.

As Paine recommended, the stamp was printed in a forest green color to further convey the idea that Farley was an outdoorsman.

These are two alternative sketches of Farley made by Dennis Lyall, along with the photographs on which they were based.

First-Day Facts

Sam Winters, a member of the USPS Board of Governors, dedicated the stamp at the first-day ceremony in Amarillo. Representative Larry Combest of the U.S. House of Representatives and Gene Farley Harriman, daughter of Cal Farley, were the principal speakers. Other participants were Amarillo Mayor Kel Seliger and Amarillo Postmaster James C. Pridmore. Music was provided by the varsity glee choir and concert band of Cal Farley's Boys Ranch, and honored guests included the family of Cal and Mimi Farley and the officials and young people of Cal Farley's Boys Ranch and Girlstown, U.S.A.; Kids Inc.; and the Maverick Club.

NONDENOMINATED (10¢) EAGLE AND SHIELD BULK RATE COIL (SELF-ADHESIVE)

Date of Issue: May 21, 1996

Catalog Number: Scott 2907

Colors: metallic gold, brown, green, blue, red

First-Day Cancel: Washington, D.C.

First-Day Cancellations: 54,102 (includes 32¢ Flag Over Porch self-adhesive booklet of 20 and self-adhesive coil)

Format: Coils of 10,000. Gravure printing cylinders of 252 subjects (12 across, 21 around) manufactured by Armotek Industries, Palmyra, New Jersey

Overall Stamp Size: 0.87 by 0.96 inches; 22.1mm by 24.4mm

Perforations: die-cut simulated perforations (Comco custom die cutter)

Designer: Chris Calle of Ridgefield, Connecticut

Typographer: John Boyd of Anagraphics Inc., New York, New York

Art Director and Project Manager: Terrence McCaffrey, USPS

Modeler: Richard C. Sennett, Sennett Enterprises

Stamp Manufacturing: Stamps printed for Stamp Venturers by J.W. Fergusson and Sons, Richmond, Virginia, on Champlain webfed gravure press 1. Stamps perforated and processed by Stamp Venturers, Fredericksburg, Virginia.

Quantity Ordered and Distributed: 450,000,000

Cylinder Number Detail: 1 group of 5 numbers preceded by the letter S on every 21st stamp

Cylinder Number Combination Reported: S11111

Counting Number Detail: 1 5-digit counting number printed by dot-matrix printer in magenta on back of liner paper behind every 10th stamp.

Paper Supplier: Nichimen/Kanzaki

Tagging: untagged

The Stamp

On May 21, the Postal Service issued a nondenominated 10¢-value self-adhesive coil stamp with the Eagle and Shield design it first had used in 1991. The new version, made in rolls of 10,000, was placed on sale in Washington, D.C., along with the 32¢ Flag Over Porch stamp in two new self-adhesive formats, booklet and coil.

USPS originally had planned to issue its new Eagle and Shield stamp June 15 at Texpex 96 in San Antonio, Texas, along with six other self-adhesive coil stamps produced in rolls of 10,000. On April 26 it announced the change in plans.

The stamp was printed by Stamp Venturers by the gravure process. It was the fourth coil stamp to use this particular Eagle and Shield design, but the first to be a self-adhesive.

The design made its debut in 1991 on a stamp printed by the American Bank Note Company in rolls of 500, 3,000 and 10,000. In 1993, USPS ordered additional supplies of the Eagle and Shield stamp from two different printers: rolls of 3,000 from the Bureau of Engraving and Printing, and rolls of 10,000 from Stamp Venturers. The three suppliers' versions have differences in inscriptions and colors that make them readily distinguishable from each other.

The Eagle and Shield stamp is used by third-class bulk-mail users who prefer to use stamps rather than imprinted envelopes or postage meters. Rates vary widely for such mail, depending on the degree to which the customer presorts his envelopes. The user of the stamp, at the time of mailing, pays a sum representing the difference between the 10¢ cost of each stamp and the actual rate for mailing each letter.

The "Bulk Rate" service inscription on the stamp is considered a precancel by USPS. Mail bearing the stamps bypasses post office canceling machines.

The self-adhesive Eagle and Shield stamps have die-cut simulated perforations on the vertical sides and straight edges at the top and bottom, mimicking traditional coil stamps. Excess stamp paper (matrix) was stripped away in the production process, leaving the individual stamps spaced slightly apart from each other on their backing paper, with portions of the backing visible between the stamps and above and below each one. Gravure cylinder-number combinations can be found on every 21st stamp. The counting numbers that Stamp Venturers prints on its coil stamps appear in black or magenta on the back of the backing paper behind every

317

10th stamp.

The rolls of 10,000 stamps are approximately 10 inches in diameter. Because they contain backing paper as well as stamps, the diameter is a few inches greater than that of a 10,000-stamp roll of water-activated coils.

The Design

The stamp features the artwork (by Christopher Calle) and typography (by John Boyd) that were developed for the 1991 Eagle and Shield prototype and adapted for the 1993 reprints. It was printed with the same combination of colors Stamp Venturers used for its 1993 coil version: metallic gold, brown, green, blue and red.

The printed areas of the two Stamp Venturers products differ from each other in one important way. The self-adhesive has the small year date "1996" in blue beneath the design at the left, whereas the 1993 stamp has no date. In addition, the metallic gold color of the eagle is lighter on the new stamp than on the older one.

First-Day Facts

No first-day ceremony was held. Collectors were given 90 days to submit covers bearing the new stamp for first-day cancellation.

For a limited time, the Philatelic Fulfillment Service Center offered uncacheted first-day covers bearing one new Eagle and Shield stamp, two conventionally gummed Eagle and Shield coil stamps of 1993, and one Automobile Tail Fin coil stamp of 1995, for 56¢.

32¢ FLAG OVER PORCH BOOKLET OF 20 (SELF-ADHESIVE, BEP)

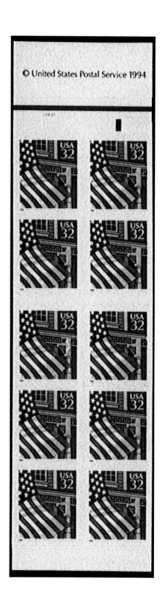

Date of Issue: May 21, 1996

Catalog Number: Scott 2921 (single stamp), 2921a (booklet pane of 10)

Colors: tan (PMS 722C), blue (PMS 300C), blue (PMS 294C), red (PMS 186C), brown (PMS 1545C)

First-Day Cancel: Washington, D.C.

First-Day Cancellations: 54,102 (includes 32¢ Flag Over Porch self-adhesive coil and nondenominated Eagle and Shield self-adhesive coil)

Format: 2 panes of 10 self-adhesive stamps each, vertical, arranged vertically on backing paper, 2 across by 5 down, with scored peel-off strip between second and third horizontal rows. Gravure printing cylinders of 480 subjects (20 across, 24 around).

Overall Stamp Size: 0.87 by 0.96 inches; 22.1mm by 24.4 mm

Perforations: die-cut simulated perforations

Selvage Markings: gravure cylinder numbers on each binding stub. Narrow or wide cross-register lines, color blocks, other markings on some binding stubs.

Cover Markings: "© United States Postal Service 1994" or "©USPS 1994"on inside of front cover. Universal Product Code (UPC) and recycled-paper information with recycling symbol on outside of back cover. Promotion for *Stamps etc.* catalog on inside of back cover.

Liner Markings: none

Designer: Dave LaFleur of Derby, Kansas

Art Director and Typographer: Richard Sheaff

Modeler: Peter Cocci, Bureau of Engraving and Printing

Project Manager: Terrence McCaffrey, USPS

Stamp Manufacturing: Stamps printed by BEP on 7-color Andreotti gravure press (601) and processed into booklets on Goebel booklet-forming machine.

Quantity Ordered and Distributed: 1,680,000,000

Cylinder Number Detail: 1 set of 5 gravure cylinder numbers on each pane binding stub

Cylinder Number Combinations Reported: 11111, 13111, 21221, 22221, 22222, 44434

Paper Supplier: Paper Corporation, New York/Brown Bridge

Tagging: phosphored paper

The Stamps

On May 21, the Postal Service issued two stamps in previously unused self-adhesive formats, using its familiar Flag Over Porch design. One of the formats was a booklet of 20 stamps with two folded panes of 10 stamps each. These are like conventional booklets containing stamps with water-activated gum, except for the fact that the panes have backing paper. The other was a coil of 100.

Both versions were printed by the Bureau of Engraving and Printing. They were the first self-adhesive stamps since the experimental Christmas Weathervane stamp of 1974 to be made by BEP. All recent self-adhesives prior to these had been produced by private firms.

The booklet stamps were gravure-printed on BEP's Andreotti press and the booklets were assembled on the Goebel booklet-forming machine. This was the same equipment BEP had used in 1995 to produce 10-stamp and 20-stamp booklets of Flag Over Porch stamps with water-activated gum.

The self-adhesive stamps of 1996 are arranged vertically on the 10-stamp pane, two across by five down, and are separated from each other and from the binding tab at the top by serpentine die-cuts that produce simulated perforation teeth on the stamps. Like conventional booklet panes, a pane from this booklet has a straight edge along the sides and across the bottom. A narrow strip of selvage separates the second and third horizontal pairs of stamps on the pane, and this is where the pane is folded, along a scored line. Unfolded single panes were offered to collectors through the Philatelic Fulfillment Service Center.

Booklet specialist Michael Perry, writing in *Linn's Stamp News*, reported that although the top pane in each booklet looks the same except for the different plate number combinations on the binding tab, the bottom panes offer 15 collectible varieties of tab. Because of the near-impossibility of removing these bottom panes intact from the booklets, the only practical way to collect them is as unfolded single panes. Three different plate number combinations are known on the never-folded panes and six different combinations on the folded ones (see accompanying checklists).

Obtaining examples of all the marginal markings wasn't an easy task, Perry wrote. The only way to get them was by placing multiple orders to Philatelic Fulfillment or visiting the philatelic counter at USPS headquarters in Washington.

"Finding position panes through mail-order is like playing the lottery," Perry wrote. "The Kansas City fulfillment center fills orders on a random basis. Half of all panes (24 of the 48 pane positions in the printed web) are generic position 2 panes with a cross register line (thick line running across many tabs) and length register mark in the tab (the short bar in many tabs), and about another 20 percent (10 positions) will have tabs without any register marks (position 1).

"Only about 30 percent of panes (14 per 48) will have the most desirable markings on their tabs. Thus, the odds are stacked against any single collector working alone ever obtaining all the positions. Trading with other collectors or buying from dealers is almost a requirement."

The inside back cover of the booklet carries an address for ordering a free copy of the Postal Service's *Stamps etc.* mail-order catalog. When the booklets first were issued, the address given was in Memphis, Tennessee. Late in the year specimens of the booklet were found in which the address was one in Grand Rapids, Minnesota. Both the addresses are used by the Postal Service for request fulfillment.

In addition, some of the covers with the Grand Rapids address bear the

$6.40 SELF-STICK FLAG OVER PORCH BOOKLET PANE LAYOUT

This drawing represents a web segment printed from a set of gravure cylinders used for the $6.40 self-stick 20-stamp booklets made by the Bureau of Engraving & Printing in 1996. While similar to the layout for regular gummed lick 'n' stick booklet panes, the BEP had to make new cylinders to accomodate the peel strip located where the panes are folded. Panes from the right half of the web are inverted in relation to panes from the left half.

DARK BROWN TRIANGLE
RED TRIANGLE
DARK BLUE TRIANGLE
LIGHT BLUE TRIANGLE
TAN TRIANGLE

Five "CC1" squares at right side of tab with gravure color registration "+" cross

Part of two "CC1" squares at left side of tab with thin brown "+" register mark.

Five "CC1" squares at left side of tab with gravure color registration "+" cross

Part of two "CC1" squares at right side of tab with thin brown "+" register mark.

TAN color density blocks
LIGHT BLUE color density blocks
DARK BLUE color density blocks
RED color density blocks
DARK BROWN color density blocks

Brown half of Color Ladder at left of tab.
DARK BROWN
RED
BLUE
TAN
Color Ladder at right edge of tab.

Dashed lines represent "cut" lines for panes.

© 1996 Michael O. Perry   Revised 1/18/97

Large numbers represent arbitrary booklet pane positions.

322

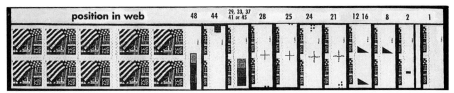

position in web				48	44	29, 33, 37 41 or 45	28	25	24	21	12 16	8	2	1

These 11 overlapped, never-folded Flag Over Porch self-adhesive booklet panes show the 16 tab varieties (including color varieties) that can appear on the panes. The chart below describes the different colors for the arrows or squares on each.

copyright notice "© USPS 1994" on the inside of the front cover. On others, "United States Postal Service" is spelled out in the copyright line.

The Design

The printed portion of the stamp is identical to that on the Flag Over Porch stamps that BEP produced in conventional coil and booklet form in 1995, with one exception: The small red year date printed beneath the design on the left side reads "1996."

* LEFT/RIGHT DIE CUT VARIETIES: The following only applies to unfolded panes, and not panes found in booklets. The horizontal wavy die cut at the left or right of the vertical "perfs" can start with either a "valley" or a "hill" - panes from the left half of the web have a "valley" at the left while panes from the right half of the web have the "valley" at the right. Thus, position 1 and 4 (and position 2 and 3) panes can be differentiated. This can also be useful in identifying position 25 and 28 panes that don't show part of the two CC1 squares at the edges of the panes.

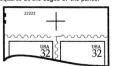

Position 25 - Brown Register Mark with 2 partial CC1 squares at left. Note the "Valley" at begining of horizontal "perforations" at LEFT side of the vertical "perforations".

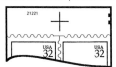

Position 28 - Brown Register Mark with 2 partial CC1 squares at right. Note "Valley" at begining of horizontal "perforations" at RIGHT side of the vertical "perfs".

NOTE: There are three cover varieties on this booklet. The inside back covers have been found with either a Memphis, Tennessee ("TN") or Grand Rapids, Minnesota ("MN") address on the cover; Grand Rapids books exist with either "© United States Postal Service 1994" or "© USPS 1994" on the inside cover.

Unfolded FOP Self-Stick Panes from $6.40 booklet				
POS	IDENTIFYING SELVAGE (TAB) MARKINGS	21221	22221	22222
1*	Plain - plate number at left ("valley" at left*)			
2*	CRL and LRM - (die cut perf "valley" at left*)			
3*	CRL and LRM - (die cut perf "valley" at right*)			
4*	Plain - plate number at left ("valley" at right*)			
8	Dark Brown Triangle over right stamp			
12	Dark Blue and Red Triangles			
16	Tan)and Light Blue Triangles			
21	Color Register "+", 5 CC1 squares at right			
24	Color Register "+", 5 CC1 squares at left			
25	Brown "+" Mark, two CC1 squares at left			
28	Brown "+" Mark, two CC1 squares at right			
29	Tan "color density blocks" over right stamp			
33	Light Blue "density blocks" over right stamp			
37	Dark Blue "density blocks" over right stamp			
41	Red "color density blocks" over right stamp			
44	Portion of Brown color ladder at left edge			
45	Dark Brown "density blocks" over right stamp			
48	Tan, Blue, Red, and Brown color ladder at right			

NOTE: Position 33 and 37 panes are hard to tell apart - the "light" and "dark" blue density blocks are similar. The $4.80 FOP books issued in 1997 also have similar 10-subject unfolded panes with the same register markings, but the BEP processed those panes so the marks were located in different positions

Michael Perry developed this checklist for the tab varieties for the three plate number combinations known on never-folded Flag Over Porch panes. (Copyright 1996 by Michael O. Perry.

323

First-Day Facts

No first-day ceremony was held for the two Flag Over Porch stamps or for a self-adhesive version of the Eagle and Shield nondenominated coil stamp, which also was issued May 21. First-day cancellations for the three varieties were provided at Washington, D.C. Collectors were given 90 days to send envelopes with the new stamps affixed to the Washington postmaster for servicing.

32¢ FLAG OVER PORCH COIL (SELF-ADHESIVE, BEP) (2 VARIETIES)

Date of Issue: May 21, 1996

Catalog Numbers: 2915A (serpentine die cut 9.7); 2915C (serpentine die cut 10.9)

Colors: tan (PMS 722C), blue (PMS 300C), blue (PMS 294C), red (PMS 186C), brown (PMS 1545C)

First-Day Cancel: Washington, D.C.

First-Day Cancellations: 54,102 (includes 32¢ Flag Over Porch self-adhesive booklet of 20 and nondenominated Eagle and Shield self-adhesive coil)

Format: Coils of 100 self-adhesive stamps abutting on liner paper. Gravure printing cylinders of 480 subjects (20 across, 24 around).

Overall Stamp Size: 0.87 by 0.96 inches; 22.1mm by 24.4mm

Perforations: die-cut simulated perforations, 2 varieties: gauge 9.8 and gauge 10.9.

Liner Markings: none

Designer: Dave LaFleur of Derby, Kansas

Art Director and Typographer: Richard Sheaff

Modeler: Peter Cocci, Bureau of Engraving and Printing

Project Manager: Terrence McCaffrey, USPS

Stamp Manufacturing: Stamps printed by BEP on 7-color webfed Andreotti gravure press (601)

Quantity Ordered: 7,344,000,000

Quantity Distributed: 2,900,000,000

Cylinder Number Detail: 1 group of 5 gravure cylinder numbers on every 24th stamp

Cylinder Number Combinations Reported: 66666, 78777, 87888, 87898, 88888, 88898, 89878, 89888, 89898, 97898, 98878, 99999 (Scott 2915A); 55555, 66666 (Scott 2915C)

Paper Supplier: Paper Corporation/Brown Bridge

Tagging: phosphored paper

The Stamps

On May 21, along with the booklet of self-adhesive Flag Over Porch stamps described in the preceding chapter, the Postal Service issued a coil version of Flag Over Porch self-adhesives in 100-stamp rolls. Like the booklet, the coil was produced by the Bureau of Engraving and Printing.

This was the first U.S. self-adhesive coil stamp mass-produced for sale over post office counters. Previous self-adhesive coil stamps were byproducts of the manufacture of self-adhesives in panes, and basically were made for the convenience of the Postal Service in preparing first-day covers and other products that required stamps to be affixed.

Those earlier self-adhesive coil stamps had been attached to their backing paper at intervals, with a small space between individual stamps and above and below each stamp. On this one, however, the stamps abut each other with their die-cut simulated perforation teeth interlocking. No backing paper is visible from the front.

Collectors soon discovered that there are two distinctly different gauges for the simulated vertical perforations. One is approximately gauge 9.7, with 10 or 11 teeth on the vertical side. The other is gauge 10.9, with 11 or 12 teeth on the side. Stamps from cylinder-number combination 66666 were found with both gauges. All other combinations are known in only one type of "perf": 55555 in gauge 10.9, the others in gauge 9.7.

Late in the year, dealer-columnist Robert Rabinowitz wrote in *Linn's Stamp News* that the Postal Service, in printing the 1996 Flag Over Porch self-adhesive coil stamp, had broken what he called "a covenant" with collectors that had been in effect since 1981.

In that year, Rabinowitz noted, USPS began a new system of plate numbering that included, for the first time, printing numbers on coil stamps and booklet-pane stubs. Because there wasn't room in these small areas to print the actual multidigit number assigned to each different color plate, sleeve or cylinder used in producing a stamp, the Postal Service substituted a single-digit number. Each single digit on a coil stamp (or the selvage of a booklet or sheet stamp) was a stand-in for the actual number of the plate for that color. In creating this system, Rabinowitz wrote, officials made a commitment to collectors to change the stand-in number each time an actual plate, sleeve or cylinder was replaced.

However, he wrote, a review of a plate-activity report produced by the

Postal Service in October 1996 showed that the Flag Over Porch coil stamps printed by BEP between June 3 and July 25, 1996, used two different tan, light blue, blue and brown cylinders. In each case, however, the different cylinders were designated on the stamps by the same printed digit, a 9.

Rabinowitz speculated that BEP did this because it didn't consider it feasible to advance to double-digit numbers as new cylinders were required — even though a previous contractor for U.S. stamps, American Bank Note Company, had done so successfully with the nondenominated Eagle and Shield water-activated coil stamp.

"The coded plate number system is only of value when it is used properly without deception, with one code number signifying one and only one actual cylinder, plate or sleeve," Rabinowitz wrote. "If (USPS) allows the current practice to continue, plate numbers will become nothing more than a collectible souvenir, as has been the case for decades with U.S. official first-day-of-issue cancels."

Another, less serious collector concern was deciding how to save strips of mint Flag Over Porch coil stamps with their interlocking "perfs." Dealer Stephen G. Esrati, preparing plate number strips of five for his customers, cut the strips just beyond the simulated perfs at either end. The trimming was done by Esrati's wholesaler, Al Haake, using a guillotine made for cutting Showgard mounts. This rendered the two stamps on either side of a plate strip of five unfit for collecting, of course, but they remained usable for postage.

The Design

The printed image on the stamp is identical to that of the BEP-produced conventional coil stamp with water-activated gum that was issued in 1995. The only exception is that the small red year date below the left side of the design on the new stamp is "1996."

Robert Rabinowitz, in another *Linn's* article, reported that BEP used

The 32¢ Flag Over Porch self-adhesive coil stamp exists with two distinctly different gauges of die cutting: gauge 10.9 (left) and gauge 9.7 (right).

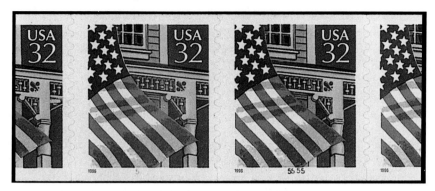

The tan cylinder number on the stamp on the left should be with the other numbers on the stamp on the right. The images on the two stamps look normal because the misregistration of the tan is shifted the width of one stamp.

some of the same cylinders to print the self-adhesive that it had used for the lick-and-stick stamp. None of the red cylinders could be reused, however, because they had to be remade to incorporate the new year date.

Varieties

An unusual cylinder number shift was found on five pairs of Flag Over Porch stamps from a roll of 100 that was printed with the 55555 combination of numbers. On the affected pairs, the stamp on the left has a single tan "5" at the bottom and the stamp on the right has the remaining "5555." All five cylinder numbers should be on one stamp, of course, with the tan number leading the sequence.

The variety was caused by a misregistration of the cylinder that applied the tan ink, Michael Schreiber reported in *Linn's Stamp News*. Although this cylinder was misregistered when the stamps were printed on BEP's webfed Andreotti gravure press, the colors of the stamp align normally because the misregistration was off by almost exactly the width of a stamp. The tan ink on each stamp really should be on the stamp to its right.

The misregistration was noticed later and fixed because proper 55555 stamps exist, with all five cylinder numbers printed where they belong.

A BEP spokesman told *Linn's* the misregistration occurred because of a combination of human error and new technology, namely, the new Bobst registration system on the 26-year-old Andreotti press. It can quickly register the colors from web markings, even though the cylinders may have been engaged out of register. The Bureau said probably two large rolls of paper were printed with the tan cylinder numbers located on the wrong stamps, creating about 360,000 numbered strips.

The roll reported by *Linn's* was consigned to the Jacques C. Schiff Jr. auction firm. Schiff sold a strip of six containing the divided cylinder numbers at his November 15-16 public auction for $130 plus the 10-percent buyer's commission.

First-Day Facts

The 32¢ BEP Flag Over Porch self-adhesive coil stamp was used well before its May 21 issue date, according to Stephen G. Esrati. Collector Joan Lenz received one on cover dated April 23. She learned that the stamp came from a roll with the plate-number combination 66666, Esrati wrote.

Linn's reported that specimens of the stamp were sold as early as mid-April in at least one New York City post office. A collector sent some of these to *Linn's*, which illustrated them in color in its May 13 issue.

The publication speculated that the stamp was sold early because USPS originally had announced April 3 as its date of issue. That date was changed to an undetermined date in late spring and then to May 21.

32¢ FLAG OVER PORCH COIL (SELF-ADHESIVE, STAMP VENTURERS)

Date of Issue: June 15, 1996

Catalog Number: Scott 2915B

Colors: yellow, magenta, cyan, dark blue, gray

First-Day Cancel: San Antonio, Texas

First-Day Cancellations: 87,400 (includes nondenominated Butte, Mountain, Automobile, Tail Fin and Jukebox coils)

Format: Coils of 10,000 self-adhesive stamps placed at intervals on backing (liner) paper. Gravure printing cylinders of 252 subjects (12 across, 21 around) manufactured by Armotek Industries, Palmyra, New Jersey

Overall Stamp Size: 0.87 by 0.96 inches; 22.1mm by 24.4mm

Perforations: die-cut simulated perforations

Liner Markings: none

Designer: Dave LaFleur of Derby, Kansas

Art Director and Typographer: Richard Sheaff

Modeler: Richard Sennett, Sennett Enterprises

Project Manager: Terrence McCaffrey, USPS

Stamp Manufacturing: Stamps printed for Stamp Venturers by J.W. Fergusson and Sons, Richmond, Virginia, on Champlain webfed gravure press. Stamps die-cut, processed and shipped by Stamp Venturers, Fredericksburg, Virginia.

Quantity Ordered: 300,000,000

Quantity Distributed: 330,000,000

Cylinder Number Detail: 1 group of 5 gravure cylinder numbers preceded by the letter S on every 21st stamp

Cylinder Number Combination Reported: S11111

Counting Number Detail: 1 5-digit counting number printed by dot-matrix process in black on back of liner paper behind every 10th stamp. Numbers progress from right to left.

Paper Supplier: Kanzaki

Tagging: phosphored paper

The Stamp

On June 15, in San Antonio, Texas, the Postal Service issued a Flag Over Porch self-adhesive coil stamp printed by Stamp Venturers and distributed in rolls of 10,000. Earlier, on May 21, USPS had released a Flag Over Porch in the same format, but printed by the Bureau of Engraving and Printing and sold in rolls of 100.

Like BEP's version, the Stamp Venturers stamps have die-cut simulated perforations on each vertical side and straight edges at top and bottom. Unlike the BEP stamps, however, they are spaced out on their backing paper and have a small amount of the backing showing above and below each stamp. The BEP stamps interlock with each other with no backing paper showing from the front.

Stamp Venturers' Flag Over Porch stamp was one of six self-adhesive coil stamps issued on the second day of Texpex 96, a stamp show sponsored by the San Antonio Philatelic Association. The other five were non-denominated stamps created for bulk mailers (see succeeding chapters).

The Design

As with the two Flag Over Porch stamps printed by Stamp Venturers in 1995 — a sheet and a coil stamp, both with water-activated gum — the year date beneath the design of the new coil stamp is in blue. It reads "1996," which distinguishes it from the earlier coil stamp made by Stamp Venturers. Otherwise, the printed areas are identical. Both were made with the same five colors: yellow, magenta, cyan, dark blue and gray.

Plate numbers appear on every 21st stamp in the roll, and black counting numbers can be found on the reverse side of the backing paper of every 10th stamp.

First-Day Facts

No official first-day ceremony was held at Texpex for the six stamps issued June 15.

NON-DENOMINATED (5¢) BUTTE NONPROFIT RATE COIL (SELF-ADHESIVE)
AMERICAN SCENES SERIES

Date of Issue: June 15, 1996

Catalog Number: Scott 2902B

Colors: yellow, red, blue

First-Day Cancel: San Antonio, Texas

First-Day Cancellations: 87,400 (includes 32¢ Flag Over Porch and nondenominated Mountain, Automobile, Tail Fin and Jukebox self-adhesive coils)

Format: Coils of 10,000 self-adhesive stamps at intervals on backing (liner) paper. Gravure printing cylinders of 252 subjects (12 across, 21 around) manufactured by Armotek Industries, Palmyra, New Jersey

Overall Stamp Size: 0.87 by 0.96 inches; 22.1mm by 24.4mm

Perforations: die-cut simulated perforations

Liner Markings: none

Designer: Tom Engeman of Carbondale, Colorado

Art Director and Typographer: Phil Jordan

Modeler: Richard Sennett, Sennett Enterprises

Project Manager: Elizabeth A. Altobell, USPS

Stamp Manufacturing: Stamps printed for Stamp Venturers by J.W. Fergusson and Sons, Richmond, Virginia, on Champlain webfed gravure press. Stamps die-cut, processed and shipped by Stamp Venturers, Fredericksburg, Virginia.

Quantity Ordered and Distributed: 550,000,000

Cylinder Number Detail: 1 group of 3 gravure cylinder numbers preceded by the letter S on every 21st stamp

Cylinder Number Combination Reported: S111

Counting Number Detail: 1 5-digit counting number printed by dot-matrix process in magenta on back of liner paper behind every 10th stamp. Numbers progress from right to left.

Paper Supplier: Nichimen/Kanzaki

Tagging: untagged

The Stamp

On June 15, the Postal Service issued five nondenominated coil stamps for use on various categories of bulk mail. The stamps were self-adhesives and bore designs that first were used in 1995 on conventional stamps with moisture-activated gum.

The stamps were sold in rolls of 10,000, complete with backing paper. This made a roll approximately 10 inches in diameter, somewhat wider than a 10,000-stamp roll of conventional coil stamps.

The new self-adhesives had their first-day sale in San Antonio, Texas, on the second day of Texpex 96, a stamp show sponsored by the San Antonio Philatelic Association. No official first-day ceremony was held.

A sixth self-adhesive coil stamp, also made in rolls of 10,000, was issued on the same occasion. It was a 32¢ denominated definitive with the Flag Over Porch design (see previous chapter).

Two of the nondenominated stamps were inscribed for use by nonprofit organizations and sold for 5¢. The cost of the additional postage per piece, which depended on the degree to which the mailing had been presorted, was paid when it was brought to the post office.

One of these stamps depicted a generic Western scene showing a series of buttes silhouetted against a yellow sky. The original artwork, painted in acrylic by Tom Engeman, was inspired by two buttes called East Mitten and West Mitten, located in the Arizona part of Monument Valley Navajo Tribal Park.

The Butte stamp was gravure-printed by Stamp Venturers, which produced the earlier water-activated version (in rolls of 3,000 and 10,000). It has die-cut simulated perforations on the two vertical sides. Individual stamps are attached to the backing paper at intervals, with about one-eighth of an inch of backing showing between stamps and about one-sixteenth of an inch showing above and below each stamp.

The printed area of the stamp is identical to that of the 1995 conventional coil version except that the small year date printed below the left side of the design reads "1996" instead of "1995."

First-day covers were offered by the Philatelic Fulfillment Service Center for 56¢. They bore two Butte stamps and one Jukebox coil stamp.

NONDENOMINATED (5¢) MOUNTAIN NONPROFIT RATE COIL (SELF-ADHESIVE) AMERICAN SCENES SERIES

Date of Issue: June 15, 1996

Catalog Number: Scott 2904A

Colors: pink, yellow, orange, violet, light blue, dark blue

First-Day Cancel: San Antonio, Texas

First-Day Cancellations: 87,400 (includes 32¢ Flag Over Porch and nonde-nominated Butte, Automobile, Tail Fin and Jukebox self-adhesive coils)

Format: Coils of 10,000 self-adhesive stamps at intervals on backing (liner) paper. Gravure printing cylinders of 135 subjects (9 across, 15 around).

Overall Stamp Size: 0.87 by 0.982 inches

Perforations: die-cut simulated perforations

Liner Markings: none

Designer: Tom Engeman of Carbondale, Colorado

Art Director and Typographer: Phil Jordan

Modelers: Gary Charles of Avery Dennison and North American Roto Engravers

Project Manager: Vance Harris, USPS

Stamp Manufacturing: Stamps printed by Avery Dennison Security Printing Division, Clinton, South Carolina, on a 6-color Chesnut webfed gravure press. Stamps die-cut, processed and shipped by Avery Dennison.

Quantity Ordered and Distributed: 150,000,000

Cylinder Number Detail: 1 group of 6 gravure cylinder numbers preceded by the letter V on every 15th stamp

Cylinder Number Combinations Reported: V222222, V333323, V333333, V333342, V333343

Counting Number Detail: 1 5-digit counting number printed by dot-matrix process in cyan on back of backing paper behind every stamp. Numbers progress from left to right or right to left.

Paper Supplier: for stamps, Westvaco; for liner, Otis; converter, Fasson

Tagging: untagged

The Stamp

Of the six self-adhesive coil stamps in rolls of 10,000 that USPS issued in San Antonio June 15, the only one not printed by Stamp Venturers was the nondenominated (5¢) stamp showing a generic mountain scene. It was made by Avery Dennison.

The Mountain stamp was one of two in the group that were intended for bulk mailings by nonprofit organizations. The other depicted several Western buttes (see previous chapter).

Avery Dennison was the third printer to produce a coil stamp using the mountain design. On March 16, 1996, USPS issued two conventional coil stamps with water-activated gum that used the design. One was manufactured by the Bureau of Engraving and Printing, the other by Stamp Venturers (see separate chapter).

The self-adhesive Mountain stamp has serpentine die-cuts on the vertical sides to simulate perforations, and straight edges at the top and bottom. The stamps are attached at intervals to their backing paper and are slightly shorter than the backing.

Plate number combinations appear on every 15th stamp in the roll. They consist of six digits — one for each color used on the stamp — preceded by the letter V.

Avery Dennison printed counting numbers on the back of the stamps (actually, the back of the backing paper), just as Stamp Venturers had been doing on its coil stamps since 1994. The Avery Dennison numbers appear on every stamp, however, instead of every 10th stamp, as was the case with the Stamp Venturers products.

Dealer Robert Rabinowicz, writing in *Linn's Stamp News*, reported that the counting numbers on the Mountain self-adhesives can be found running in both directions. On all rolls except those with plate number combination V222222, the back numbers begin with 10,000 and count down as the roll is unwound. On V222222, however, the counting numbers are upside down in relation to the stamp design, and they run low to high, which is the mode used on previous back-numbered coil stamps.

This picture shows a strip of five Mountain self-adhesive coil stamps from plate V333333, front and back. Every stamp has a counting number on the back of its backing paper, with the numbers progressing from left to right. Previous U.S. coil stamps with back numbers had every 10th stamp numbered, with the numbers progressing from right to left.

In an event that may have been related to the numbering inconsistency, USPS ordered a recall early in May 1996 of 5,000 rolls of the self-adhesive Mountain stamps that had been shipped to large post offices April 15. The rolls, totaling 50 million stamps, were recalled because they had been wound in the wrong direction and fed off the roll to the right instead of the left when the stamps were viewed right side up. Post offices with the affected rolls were told to ship them by registered mail to the Avery Dennison plant in Clinton, South Carolina.

The design, like that of the two conventional coil stamps issued earlier in the year, is based on an acrylic painting by Tom Engeman. The simplest way to distinguish a used single of the self-adhesive from one of the earlier stamps is by the "perforation teeth," which are die-cut and uniform on the self-adhesive. However, there are some subtle differences in the printed portions as well.

For example, the inscription ("USA/NONPROFIT ORG.") is less indented on the self-adhesive. The letters are outlined, as they are on the BEP version, but in blue rather than purple, and not as bold. The "1996" year date below the design is larger and clearer on the self-adhesive than it is on either of the conventional stamps.

First-day covers were offered by the Philatelic Fulfillment Service Center for 56¢. They bore two Mountain stamps and one Jukebox coil stamp.

NONDENOMINATED (10¢) AUTOMOBILE BULK RATE COIL (SELF-ADHESIVE) AMERICAN TRANSPORTATION SERIES

Date of Issue: June 15, 1996

Catalog Number: Scott 2906

Colors: light brown, black, dark brown

First-Day Cancel: San Antonio, Texas

First-Day Cancellations: 87,400 (includes 32¢ Flag Over Porch and nondenominated Butte, Mountain, Tail Fin and Jukebox self-adhesive coils)

Format: Coils of 10,000 self-adhesive stamps at intervals on backing (liner) paper. Gravure printing cylinders of 252 subjects (12 across, 21 around) manufactured by Armotek Industries, Palmyra, New Jersey

Overall Stamp Size: 0.87 by 0.96 inches; 22.1mm by 24.4mm

Perforations: die-cut simulated perforations

Liner Markings: none

Designer: Robert Brangwynne of Boston, Massachusetts

Art Director and Typographer: Richard Sheaff

Modeler: Richard Sennett, Sennett Enterprises

Project Manager: Terrence McCaffrey, USPS

Stamp Manufacturing: Stamps printed for Stamp Venturers by J.W. Fergusson and Sons, Richmond, Virginia, on Champlain webfed gravure press. Stamps die-cut, processed and shipped by Stamp Venturers, Fredericksburg, Virginia.

Quantity Ordered and Distributed: 450,000,000

Cylinder Number Detail: 1 group of 3 gravure cylinder numbers preceded by the letter S on every 21st stamp

Cylinder Number Combination Reported: S111

Counting Number Detail: 1 5-digit counting number printed by dot-matrix process in magenta on back of liner paper behind every 10th stamp. Numbers progress from right to left.

Paper Supplier: Nichemen/Kanzaki

Tagging: untagged

The Stamp

Among the five nondenominated self-adhesive coil stamps issued June 15 for use on various categories of presorted mail was a stamp intended for use on regular third-class bulk mail and selling for 10¢. Like the others, it was made in rolls of 10,000.

Its design was one that had been used the year before on a conventional coil stamp with water-activated gum. The design featured a graphic rendition, in flat colors, of the front of a generic pre-World War II automobile. It is credited to Robert Brangwynne, based on a concept by Paul Meehan.

The stamp's issuance gave bulk-mail users a second nondenominated (10¢) self-adhesive in a 10,000-stamp roll to choose from. A few weeks earlier, on May 21, USPS had issued the Eagle and Shield stamp with the same format, purpose and price.

The Automobile stamp was gravure-printed by Stamp Venturers, which produced the earlier water-activated version (in rolls of 500, 3,000 and 10,000) and also printed the Eagle and Shield self-adhesive. It has die-cut simulated perforations on the two vertical sides. Individual stamps are attached to the backing paper at intervals, with about one-eighth of an inch of backing showing between stamps and about one-sixteenth of an inch showing above and below each stamp.

Cylinder-number combinations appear on every 21st stamp in the roll. Dot-matrix-printed counting numbers are on the back of the backing paper behind every 10th stamp.

The printed area of the stamp is identical to that of the 1995 conventional coil version except that the small year date printed below the left side of the design reads "1996" instead of "1995."

First-day covers were offered by the Philatelic Fulfillment Service Center for 56¢. They bore two Automobile stamps and one Automobile Tail Fin coil stamp.

NONDENOMINATED (15¢) TAIL FIN
FIRST-CLASS POSTCARD PRESORT RATE COIL
(SELF-ADHESIVE)
AMERICAN CULTURE SERIES

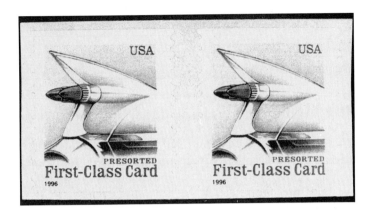

Date of Issue: June 15, 1996

Catalog Number: Scott 2910

Colors: yellow, magenta, cyan, black, dark aqua

First-Day Cancel: San Antonio, Texas

First-Day Cancellations: 87,400 (includes 32¢ Flag Over Porch and nondenominated Butte, Mountain, Automobile and Jukebox self-adhesive coils)

Format: Coils of 10,000 self-adhesive stamps at intervals on backing (liner) paper. Gravure printing cylinders of 252 subjects (12 across, 21 around) manufactured by Armotek Industries, Palmyra, New Jersey

Overall Stamp Size: 0.87 by 0.96 inches; 22.1mm by 24.4mm

Perforations: die-cut simulated perforations

Liner Markings: none

Designer: Bill Nelson of Richmond, Virginia

Typographer: John Boyd, Anagraphics Inc., New York, New York

Art Director: Carl Herrman

Project Manager: Terrence McCaffrey (USPS)

Stamp Manufacturing: Stamps printed for Stamp Venturers by J.W. Fergusson and Sons, Richmond, Virginia, on Champlain webfed gravure press. Stamps die-cut, processed and shipped by Stamp Venturers, Fredericksburg, Virginia.

Quantity Ordered and Distributed: 450,000,000

Cylinder Number Detail: 1 group of 5 gravure cylinder numbers preceded by the letter S on every 21st stamp

Cylinder Number Combination Reported: S11111

Counting Number Detail: 1 5-digit counting number printed by dot-matrix process in magenta on back of liner paper behind every 10th stamp. Numbers progress from right to left.

Paper Supplier: Nichimen/Kanzaki

Tagging: untagged

The Stamp

One of the five nondenominated self-adhesive coil stamps issued June 15 in San Antonio was intended for use on presorted postcards. It sold for 15¢ and, like the other stamps issued that day, was made in rolls of 10,000.

The design was the same one found on two conventional coil-stamp varieties that were issued for the same purpose in 1995. It was based on Bill Nelson's colored-pencil drawing of a closeup of the tail fin on a 1959 Cadillac, the stylistic high point of Detroit's tail fin era.

The Tail Fin self-adhesive was gravure-printed by Stamp Venturers, which had produced one of the two 1995 conventional versions, also in rolls of 10,000. It has die-cut simulated perforations on the two vertical sides. Individual stamps are attached to the backing paper at intervals, with about one-eighth of an inch of backing showing between stamps and about one-sixteenth of an inch showing above and below each stamp.

Cylinder-number combinations appear on every 21st stamp in the roll. Dot-matrix-printed counting numbers are on the back of the backing paper behind every 10th stamp.

The printed area of the stamp is similar to that of Stamp Venturers' 1995 conventional coil version except that the small black year date printed below the left side of the design reads "1996" instead of "1995."

First-day covers were offered by the Philatelic Fulfillment Service Center for 56¢. They bore one Automobile Tail Fin coil stamp, one Automobile coil and one Eagle and Shield coil stamp.

NONDENOMINATED (25¢) JUKEBOX FIRST-CLASS PRESORT RATE COIL (SELF-ADHESIVE) AMERICAN CULTURE SERIES

Date of Issue: June 15, 1996

Catalog Number: Scott 2912A

Colors: yellow, magenta, cyan, black, teal (PMS 3155)

First-Day Cancel: San Antonio, Texas

First-Day Cancellations: 87,400 (includes 32¢ Flag Over Porch and nondenominated Butte, Mountain, Automobile and Tail Fin self-adhesive coils)

Format: Coils of 10,000 self-adhesive stamps at intervals on backing (liner) paper. Gravure printing cylinders of 252 subjects (12 across, 21 around) manufactured by Armotek Industries, Palmyra, New Jersey

Overall Stamp Size: 0.87 by 0.96 inches; 22.1mm by 24.4mm

Perforations: die-cut simulated perforations

Liner Markings: none

Designer: Bill Nelson of Richmond, Virginia

Typographer: John Boyd, Anagraphics Inc., New York, New York

Art Director: Carl Herrman

Project Manager: Terrence McCaffrey (USPS)

Stamp Manufacturing: Stamps printed for Stamp Venturers by J.W. Fergusson and Sons, Richmond, Virginia, on Champlain webfed gravure press. Stamps die-cut, processed and shipped by Stamp Venturers, Fredericksburg, Virginia.

Quantity Ordered and Distributed: 550,000,000

Cylinder Number Detail: 1 group of 5 gravure cylinder numbers preceded by the letter S on every 21st stamp

Cylinder Number Combination Reported: S11111

Counting Number Detail: 1 5-digit counting number printed by dot-matrix process in magenta on back of liner paper behind every 10th stamp. Numbers progress from right to left.

Paper Supplier: Nichemen/Kanzaki

Tagging: untagged

The Stamp

The last of the five nondenominated self-adhesive coil stamps issued June 15 in San Antonio was intended for use on presorted first-class mail. It sold for 25¢ and, like the other stamps issued that day, was made in rolls of 10,000.

The design was the same one found on two conventional coil-stamp varieties that were issued for the same purpose in 1995. It was based on Bill Nelson's colored-pencil drawing of a Wurlitzer Model 1015 jukebox of 1946, the best-known and most popular jukebox ever made.

The Jukebox self-adhesive was gravure-printed by Stamp Venturers, which had produced one of the two 1995 conventional versions, also in rolls of 10,000. It has die-cut simulated perforations on the two vertical sides. Individual stamps are attached to the backing paper at intervals, with about one-eighth of an inch of backing showing between stamps and about one-sixteenth of an inch showing above and below each stamp.

Cylinder-number combinations appear on every 21st stamp in the roll. Dot-matrix-printed counting numbers are on the back of the backing paper behind every 10th stamp.

The printed area of the stamp is similar to that of Stamp Venturers' 1995 conventional coil version except that the small black year date printed below the left side of the design reads "1996" instead of "1995." In addition, the areas of color on the self-adhesive stamp appear somewhat darker and better-defined than on the earlier Stamp Venturers product.

First-day covers were offered by the Philatelic Fulfillment Service Center for 56¢. They bore one Jukebox stamp, one Butte coil and one Mountain coil.

20¢ BLUE JAY (SELF-ADHESIVE PANE OF 10)

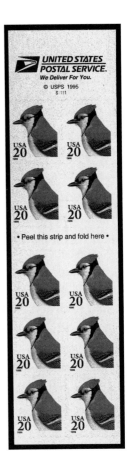

Date of Issue: August 2, 1996

Catalog Number: Scott 3048, single stamp; 3048a, pane of 10

Colors: yellow, magenta, cyan, black

First-Day Cancel: St. Louis, Missouri

First-Day Cancellations: 32,633 (includes Blue Jay self-adhesive coil)

Format: Pane of 10 vertical stamps, arranged vertically, 2 across by 5 down, with 3 horizontal selvage strips: wide strip at top, narrower (peel-off) strip below horizontal row 2, narrowest strip below horizontal row 5. Gravure printing cylinders of 280 subjects (10 across, 28 around), manufactured by Armotek Industries, Palmyra, New Jersey.

Overall Stamp Size: 0.87 by 0.982 inches; 22.09mm by 24.94 mm

Perforations: die-cut simulated perforations (Comco custom die-cutter)

Front Markings: "UNITED STATES/POSTAL SERVICE./We Deliver For You./© USPS 1995" and cylinder numbers on top selvage strip. "• Peel this strip and fold here •" on peel-off strip. No markings on bottom selvage strip.

Liner Markings: "SELF-ADHESIVE (K) DO NOT WET" in a repeat pattern. (K) is a trademark for Kanzaki laminated paper.

Back Markings: "Ten/Self-adhesive/Stamps/for Postcards," "$2.00," on front of convertible booklet cover. Universal Product Code (UPC) and promotion for *Stamps etc.* catalog on back of convertible booklet cover.

Designer: Robert Giusti of New Milford, Connecticut

Typographer: John Boyd of Anagraphics Inc., New York, New York

Modeler: Richard C. Sennett of Sennett Enterprises

Art Director: Derry Noyes

Project Manager: Terrence McCaffrey, USPS

Stamp Manufacturing: Stamps and backing paper printed for Stamp Venturers by J.W. Fergusson and Sons, Richmond, Virginia, on Champlain webfed gravure press 1. Stamps processed by Stamp Venturers, Fredericksburg, Virginia.

Quantity Ordered and Distributed: 490,770,000

Cylinder Number Detail: 1 group of 4 gravure cylinder numbers preceded by the letter S printed on top selvage strip.

Cylinder Number Combination Reported: S1111

Paper Supplier: Westvaco/Kanzaki

Tagging: phosphored paper

20¢ BLUE JAY (SELF-ADHESIVE COIL)

Date of Issue: August 2, 1996

Catalog Number: Scott 3053

Colors: yellow, magenta, cyan, black

First-Day Cancel: St. Louis, Missouri

First-Day Cancellations: 32,633 (includes Blue Jay self-adhesive pane of 10)

Format: Coils of 100. Gravure printing cylinders of 364 subjects (13 across, 28 around) manufactured by Armotek Industries, Palmyra, New Jersey

Overall Stamp Size: 0.87 by 0.98 inches; 22.09mm by 24.89mm

Perforations: die-cut simulated perforations

Designer: Robert Giusti of New Milford, Connecticut

Typographer: John Boyd of Anagraphics Inc., New York, New York

Modeler: Richard C. Sennett, Sennett Enterprises

Art Director: Derry Noyes

Project Manager: Terrence McCaffrey, USPS

Stamp Manufacturing: Stamps printed for Stamp Venturers by J.W. Fergusson and Sons, Richmond, Virginia, on Champlain webfed gravure press 1. Stamps perforated and processed by Stamp Venturers, Fredericksburg, Virginia.

Quantity Ordered and Distributed: 330,000,000

Cylinder Number Detail: 1 group of 4 numbers preceded by the letter S on every 14th stamp

Cylinder Number Combination Reported: S1111

Counting Number Detail: no counting numbers

Paper Supplier: Nichimen/Kanzaki

Tagging: phosphored paper

The Stamps

On August 2, the Postal Service issued yet another stamp in self-adhesive form that it previously had issued with water-activated gum. This time the stamp was the 20¢ Blue Jay, which had made its debut in 1995 in conventional booklets of 10. It now reappeared in two new self-stick varieties: as a "convertible booklet" stamp in panes of 10, and as a coil stamp in rolls of 100.

The 20¢ denomination covered the current postcard rate. The Blue Jay was the first postcard-rate stamp to be produced as a self-adhesive.

USPS originally intended to issue the two varieties in Washington, D.C., without a ceremony. Plans were changed in April and the stamps were dedicated in St. Louis, Missouri, at Americover 96, the annual meeting and exhibition of the American First Day Cover Society.

Both the pane and coil varieties, like the 1995 booklet version, were gravure-printed by Stamp Venturers. The pane of stamps has three horizontal selvage strips, at the top, center and bottom. The center strip is meant to be peeled off so the pane can be folded into a booklet configuration. The stamps on the pane are separated from each other by serpentine die cuts that simulate perforations. Each stamp has a straight edge on the left or right side and simulated perfs on the remaining three sides.

The coil stamps also are separated from each other by die-cut simulated perfs, with straight edges at top and bottom. Unlike previous self-adhesive coil stamps made by Stamp Venturers, the Blue Jays aren't spaced out on their backing paper, but abut each other with no backing paper showing, like the Bureau of Engraving and Printing's Flag Over Porch self-adhesive coil stamp that was issued May 21.

The simulated perfs on the pane and coil stamps are of different gauges. The coil stamp has 14 "teeth" on its vertical sides, compared to 13 on the pane version.

The Design

The design used on the two stamps is the same one used on the conventional booklet stamp of 1995. It is based on Robert Giusti's acrylic painting of the head and neck of a blue jay, seen in profile. The picture was the third in a series of bird paintings by Giusti to appear on U.S. definitive stamps. The first two, showing a wood duck and a cardinal, were used on stamps issued in 1991.

The printed portions of the pane and coil versions of the Blue Jay stamp are virtually identical to each other and also to the conventional booklet version of 1995. The latter can be distinguished from the self-adhesives by the fact that it has actual perforations, and also by the small year date printed in black beneath the design, which is "1996" on the new varieties. The paper of the self-adhesives appears whiter than the paper of the booklet stamp.

On the self-adhesive pane, the back of the backing paper, which becomes the cover of the convertible booklet when the peel-off strip is re-

346

moved and the pane is folded, is printed in blue and bears an enlarged replica of the stamp with the customary diagonal "cancellation" line across the denomination.

First-Day Facts

Catherine V. Caggiano, manager of stamp acquisition for USPS, dedicated the Blue Jay stamps in the ceremony at the St. Louis Airport Marriott, site of the American First Day Cover Society's 41st annual convention.

The principal speaker was Carol Kershner, president of Wild Bird Rehabilitation Inc. Thomas L. Foust, president of the AFDCS, gave the welcome, and Larry Wood, St. Louis postmaster, presided. Honored guests were Steven M. Ripley, national chairman of Americover 96; E. William Anderson, president of the American Ceremony Program Society, and Grace E. Marchese, meeting coordinator, American Society of Philatelic Pages and Panels.

As Wayne Youngblood reported in *Stamp Collector*, the first-day program prepared by the Postal Service should have borne a specimen of each of the two varieties of Blue Jay stamp, but didn't. Each program contained two pane singles rather than a pane and a coil example. As Youngblood wrote, the firm that produces the ceremony programs, Minnesota Diversified, probably didn't know the difference between the varieties.

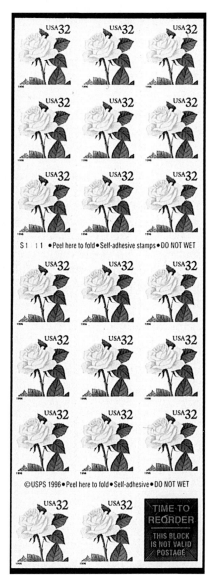

Date of Issue: October 24, 1996

Catalog Number: Scott 3049 (single stamp), 3049a (pane of 20)

Colors: green, yellow, warm red, black (stamps); yellow, green, black (back of backing paper)

First-Day Cancel: Pasadena, California

First-Day Cancellations: 7,849

Format: Pane of 20 stamps plus 1 nonstamp label, vertical, arranged vertically 3 across by 7 down, with 2 horizontal peel-off strips, one below horizontal row 3, the other below horizontal row 6. Gravure printing cylinders of 315 subjects (15 across, 21 around) manufactured by Armotek Industries, Palmyra, New Jersey.

Overall Stamp Size: 0.87 by 0.98 inches; 22.1mm by 24.9mm

Perforations: Die-cut simulated perforations. Die-cut circles and lines on non-stamp label.

Front Markings: On first peel-off strip: "• Peel here to fold • Self-adhesive stamps • DO NOT WET" and gravure cylinder numbers. On second peel-off strip: "© USPS 1996 • Peel here to fold • Self-adhesive • DO NOT WET •." On non-stamp label: "TIME TO/REORDER/THIS BLOCK/IS NOT VALID/POSTAGE."

Back Markings: "Twenty/Self-adhesive Stamps," "$6.40," "UNITED STATES/ POSTAL SERVICE./We Deliver For You." USPS logo. Universal Product Code (UPC). Promotion for *Stamps etc.* catalog. "SALUTING THE/108TH TOUR-NAMENT OF ROSES ® PARADE/&/83RD ROSE BOWL GAME ®/The Granddaddy of Them All ®/PASADENA, CALIFORNIA, USA," all on backing paper.

Designer: Gyo Fujikawa of New York, New York

Typographer: John Boyd, Anagraphics Inc., New York, New York

Modeler: Richard C. Sennett

Art Director: Joseph Brockert, USPS

Project Manager: Elizabeth A. Altobell, USPS

Stamp Manufacturing: Stamps printed for Stamp Venturers by J.W. Fergusson & Sons, Richmond, Virginia, on Champlain webfed gravure press 1. Stamps die-cut, processed and shipped by Stamp Venturers, Fredericksburg, Virginia.

Quantity Ordered and Distributed: 2,900,000,000

Cylinder Number Detail: 1 set of 4 gravure cylinder numbers preceded by the letter S on first horizontal peel-off strip

Cylinder Number Combinations Reported: S1111, S2222

Paper Supplier: Glatfelter/Brown Bridge

Tagging: phosphored paper

Date of Issue: early December 1996

Catalog Number: Scott 3049 (single stamp), 3049b (booklet of 15)

Colors: green (PMS 106), yellow, warm red, black (stamps); yellow, green, black (cover)

First-Day Cancel: none

Format: Pane of 5 stamps plus 1 nonstamp label, vertical, arranged vertically 2 across by 3 down, and pane of 10 stamps, arranged vertically 2 across by 5 down, with gap between horizontal rows 2 and 3 where pane is folded along scored line to form booklet. Gravure printing cylinders of 384 subjects (16 across, 24 around) manufactured by Armotek Industries, Palmyra, New Jersey.

Overall Stamp Size: 0.87 by 0.98 inches; 22.09mm by 24.94mm

Perforations: Die-cut simulated perforations. Die-cut circles and lines on non-stamp label.

Front Markings: On nonstamp label: "TIME TO/REORDER/THIS BLOCK/IS NOT VALID/POSTAGE."

Back Markings: "Fifteen/Self-adhesive Stamps," "$4.80," "UNITED STATES/POSTAL SERVICE./We Deliver For You," USPS logo, Universal Product Code (UPC), "© USPS 1996," promotion for *Stamps etc.* catalog, all on booklet cover. "You can own a/Masterpiece./Collect U.S./Commemorative/Stamps" on back of backing paper for 5-stamp pane.

Designer: Gyo Fujikawa of New York, New York

Typographer: John Boyd, Anagraphics Inc., New York, New York

Modeler: Richard C. Sennett

Art Director: Joseph Brockert, USPS

Project Manager: Elizabeth A. Altobell, USPS

Stamp Manufacturing: Stamps printed for Stamp Venturers by J.W. Fergusson & Sons, Richmond, Virginia, on Champlain webfed gravure press 1. Stamps die-cut, processed and shipped by Stamp Venturers, Fredericksburg, Virginia.

Quantity Ordered: 240,000,000

Quantity Distributed: 242,085,000

Cylinder Number Detail: 1 set of 4 gravure cylinder numbers preceded by the letter S on bottom left stamp on 5-stamp pane.

Cylinder Number Combination Reported: S1111

Paper Supplier: Paper Corporation of the United States/Brown Bridge

Tagging: phosphored paper

32¢ YELLOW ROSE PREFOLDED PANE OF 30 (SELF-ADHESIVE)

Date of Issue: December 24, 1996 (earliest-known sale)

Catalog Number: Scott 3049 (single stamp), 3049c (pane of 30)

Colors: green (PMS 106), yellow, warm red, black (stamps); yellow, green, black (cover)

First-Day Cancel: none

Format: pane of 30 stamps, vertical, arranged vertically 2 across by 15 down, attached to backing paper in 5 blocks of 6 stamps each, with gap between each pair of blocks where backing paper is folded along a scored line to form booklet. Gravure printing cylinders of 360 subjects (15 across, 24 around) manufactured by Armotek Industries, Palmyra, New Jersey.

Overall Stamp Size: 0.87 by 0.98 inches; 22.09mm by 24.94mm

Perforations: Die-cut simulated perforations (Comco die cutter).

Front Markings: none

Back Markings: "Thirty/Self-adhesive Stamps," "$9.60," "UNITED STATES/ POSTAL SERVICE./We Deliver For You," USPS logo, Universal Product Code (UPC), "© USPS 1996," promotion for *Stamps etc.* catalog, all on booklet cover.

Designer: Gyo Fujikawa of New York, New York

Typographer: John Boyd, Anagraphics Inc., New York, New York

Modeler: Richard C. Sennett

Art Director: Joseph Brockert, USPS

Project Manager: Elizabeth A. Altobell, USPS

Stamp Manufacturing: Stamps printed for Stamp Venturers by J.W. Fergusson & Sons, Richmond, Virginia, on Champlain webfed gravure press 1. Stamps die-cut, processed and shipped by Stamp Venturers, Fredericksburg, Virginia.

Quantity Ordered: 270,000,000

Quantity Distributed: 274,050,000

Cylinder Number Detail: 1 set of 4 gravure cylinder numbers preceded by the letter S on bottom right stamp.

Cylinder Number Combination Reported: S1111

Paper Supplier: Paper Corporation of the United States/Brown Bridge

Tagging: phosphored paper

The Stamp

On October 24, the Postal Service issued the third version of a self-adhesive stamp with a design featuring a single rose blossom. The two previous versions, in 1993 and 1995, had depicted red and pink roses, respectively. The new rose is yellow. Like its predecessors, it was gravure-printed by Stamp Venturers.

The stamp was dedicated in Pasadena, California, where it was available on that day in panes of 20. Pasadena is the home of the Rose Bowl, and the back of the pane's liner, which serves as a cover when the pane is folded, carried a salute to the forthcoming 108th Tournament of Roses Parade and the 83rd Rose Bowl game on January 1.

The decision to change the color of the rose a second time was made by the stamp acquisition section rather than the design section, which registered a mild objection that the rose design was being "worn out." The first color change, to pink, had accompanied an increase in the stamp's denomination from 29¢ to 32¢ to match the increase in the first-class rate. The change to yellow coincided with a decision to reissue the 32¢ stamp in some new formats.

"I think they've run out of colors," Terrence McCaffrey, head of stamp design, said with a laugh. "The only rose left is a white rose, and that wouldn't work very well against a white background."

The "convertible booklet" pane of 20 yellow rose stamps that was available at the October 24 dedication was the same format that USPS used for the pink rose stamp of the year before.

Then, in December 1996, the yellow rose turned up in two hitherto-unseen formats: a booklet of 15 and a prefolded pane of 30. Unlike the October 24 pane of 20, the booklet and the larger pane were placed on sale without an official issue date, a first-day ceremony or first-day cancellation.

The two new formats, selling for $4.80 and $9.60 respectively, were created to facilitate change-making in post office vending machines. The $3.20 (10-stamp) and $6.40 (20-stamp) booklets that had previously filled these machines caused them to empty of change too rapidly. Until custom-designed $4.80 and $9.60 vending-machine booklets could be produced, the Postal Service improvised booklets to sell for those prices out of existing stamp stock (see separate chapter).

The two new yellow rose formats provided collectors with another novelty: booklet-stamp plate number singles. Neither the 15-stamp booklet nor the 30-stamp prefolded pane contains selvage or a peel-off strip on which the cylinder number combination could be printed. Instead, the numbers are printed on one stamp in each booklet or pane, as is done with coil stamps.

The creation of booklet-stamp plate number singles was first announced by Joe Brockert of USPS at a seminar at the Postage Stamp Mega-Event show in New York City November 1. Brockert explained that the Postal Service intended to reduce the selvage on self-adhesive panes, or do away with it completely, because of environmental considerations.

On the 20-stamp pane of October 24, the stamps are arranged vertically, three across by seven down, with a "Time to Reorder" label occupying the bottom right stamp position. There are two peel-off strips. The cylinder number combination — an S followed by four digits — appears on the upper strip.

The 15-stamp booklet of December consists of a pane of 10 stamps, arranged vertically on their liner, two across by five down, with a gap between the second and third horizontal pairs. The liner is folded along a scored line in this gap, with its back forming the cover of the booklet.

Glued to the top of the pane, above the first horizontal pair, is a second pane consisting of five stamps, two across by three down, with a "Time to Reorder" label in the lower-right stamp position. The bottom left stamp on this second pane bears the cylinder number combination, in tiny figures, below the design on the right side.

On both panes, the stamps are separated from each other by serpentine die-cutting to create simulated perforations. Each stamp has a straight edge on either the left or right side. The plate number stamp on the inner pane also has a straight edge at the bottom.

The 30-stamp pane is long and narrow, two stamps across by 15 stamps down. The stamps are grouped on the liner in blocks of six with gaps between the blocks and scored lines across the gaps where the pane is folded in four places to create a booklet. The bottom right stamp bears the cylinder number combination. Twenty-six of the 30 stamps have straight edges on the left or right side only; the two top stamps also have straight edges at the top, and the two bottom stamps, including the plate number stamp, have straight edges at the bottom.

Apparently on the assumption that the public now is accustomed to self-adhesive stamps, the Postal Service did not include anywhere on the 15-stamp booklet or the 30-stamp prefolded pane the customary admonition "Do not wet." It had stopped requiring printers of self-adhesives to include that message on the liner paper earlier in 1996.

Plate number singles from the two panes can be told apart from the location of the straight edge on the side. If it's on the left, the stamp comes from a 15-stamp booklet; if from the right, it's from the 30-stamp pane. Otherwise, individual stamps from the 20-stamp pane, 15-stamp booklet and 30-stamp pane are indistinguishable.

Stamp Venturers officials say they print the cylinder numbers on stamps and selvage only because their contract with the Postal Service requires them. The company doesn't use the numbers in monitoring production.

The tie-in between the yellow rose stamps and the Tournament of Roses Association, which oversees the annual parade and Rose Bowl game, was the result of a USPS initiative. The association paid no fee for the prominent mention of its parade and football game on the back of the 20-stamp pane.

Robin Wright, a Postal Service spokesman, told *Linn's Stamp News* that the linkage was done for publicity for USPS. It was an attempt to connect stamps with popular, well-known events to help expose stamps as collectibles, Wright said.

Wright noted that USPS employees had a float in the 1996 Tournament of Roses parade and that the float won an award. The Postal Service also is recognized as the Tournament of Roses Association's official expedited delivery service, he said.

The Design

The design common to the red, pink and yellow rose stamps was based on a color sketch in gouache done in 1987 by artist Gyo Fujikawa of New York City. It was one of seven sketches of roses that Fujikawa, who was then 79, had made at the Postal Service's request for possible use in the future as a Love stamp.

At that time she wasn't asked to do a finished version of any of them. Four years later, however, Jack Williams of USPS asked her to make a finished painting based on one of the sketches for use in producing a self-adhesive definitive stamp. By then, however, her eyesight had been damaged by glaucoma and she could no longer paint. She had to turn down the request.

However, postal officials decided that the sketch itself, with the word LOVE deleted, was good enough to use in making the color separations, and the 29¢ red rose stamp was issued.

Both the red rose and the 32¢ pink rose that replaced it were printed in only three colors: green, black, and red or pink. On these stamps, the black color was used to give shading and detail to the blossom and leaves. The yellow rose stamp, however, was printed in four colors. Instead of using black to define the yellow blossom, Stamp Venturers used a color it called warm red, creating a softer, more pleasing effect.

First-Day Facts

Tirso del Junco M.D., chairman of the USPS Board of Governors, dedicated the yellow rose stamp at the October 24 dedication ceremony at the Tournament House in Pasadena, home of the Tournament of Roses Association.

William S. Johnstone Jr., president of the Tournament of Roses, gave the welcome, and Pasadena Postmaster Robert M. Mysel officiated. The 79th Rose queen and her court were honored guests.

The 15-stamp yellow rose booklets first were sold at post offices in Salt Lake City, Utah, December 5, and Cupertino, California, December 9. They were stocked by the philatelic window at Salt Lake City December 11. The 30-stamp prefolded panes first were sold in Tucson, Arizona, December 24.

Because plate number singles were available only on those two configurations, and collectors were given only 30 days after the official October 24 first-day-sale date to submit stamped covers to the Pasadena postmaster for first-day cancellations, it would have been impossible — at least in theory — to obtain a plate number single on a first-day cover.

Revised Definitives

1¢ Omnibus

A new version of the 1¢ Omnibus coil stamp of the Transportation series, with shiny gum, turned up in January. It was printed from intaglio sleeve 3 by the Bureau of Engraving and Printing. All previous Omnibus stamps have had dull gum.

The shiny-gum variety also was found on paper with surface taggant. Visible under shortwave ultraviolet light, the taggant has a uniform but finely speckled (rather than smooth) appearance. Use of the phosphored paper on this stamp is an error because USPS no longer issues stamps on phosphored paper or with tagging if their denominations are lower than 10¢.

The previous Omnibus varieties, also produced by BEP, were:

Scott 1897, issued August 19, 1983, with a small "1c." Overall tagging, dull gum, sleeve numbers 1, 2, 3, 4, 5, 6. Issued August 19, 1983.

Scott 2225, issued November 26, 1986, with a large "1." Block tagging, dull gum, sleeve numbers 1, 2.

Scott 2225a, first appeared in March 1991. Untagged, dull gum, sleeve numbers 2, 3.

The shiny-gum variety is listed below Scott 2225a in the 1997 *Specialized Catalogue of United States Stamps*, but is not given a separate number designation.

In addition to these varieties, all sleeve numbers of the overall-tagged and block-tagged Omnibus stamps exist as untagged errors, according to the 1995 *Plate Number Coil Catalog* published by Nazar Publications.

2¢ Mary Lyon

Linn's Stamp News, in its February 5, 1996, edition, reported the finding of intentionally untagged 2¢ Mary Lyon stamps of the Great Americans series. The stamps appeared some time in late 1995, probably in the fall, *Linn's* said.

They were printed from sleeve 3, which was needed because cylinders 1 and 2 were made for the Bureau of Engraving and Printing's abandoned A press.

The 1996 Scott U.S. specialized catalog had listed an intentionally untagged Lyon stamp, giving it the number 2169a. However, *Linn's* said it had examined the stamp on which Scott based that listing and found it to contain traces of tagging.

When the Lyon stamp originally was issued February 28, 1987, it had block tagging. Since then, specimens have been found with tagging omitted, but these are errors resulting from the tagging blocks being shifted down one stamp row so that the top row was untagged, *Linn's* said.

$3 Challenger Priority Mail

What USPS called a mistake by the printer, Ashton-Potter (USA) Ltd., caused the creation of a new face-different variety of the $3 Challenger definitive stamp that was issued in 1995 to cover the basic rate for Priority Mail.

When the stamp was sent back to press early in 1996, Ashton-Potter changed the tiny offset-printed year date that appears below the design on the left side from "1995" to "1996." The company did so on its own, without prior approval or authorization from the Postal Service, USPS said.

In all other respects, the reprinted stamp is identical to the original stamp that was issued June 22, 1995. The image is based on a photograph of the *Challenger* space shuttle taken in orbit during a 1984 mission. *Challenger* later was lost, along with its crew of seven astronauts, when it blew up shortly after launch January 28, 1986.

Plate number combinations reported for the new printing are P4444-2 and P5555-2.

Collectors on the Philatelic Fulfillment Service Center's mailing list received notification of the variety by mail in a letter dated "March 1996" and signed by Azeezaly S. Jaffer of USPS. Jaffer is manager of stamp services.

Ashton-Potter's mistake was discovered about halfway through the 52.1 million stamp press run, Barry Ziehl, a USPS spokesman, told *Stamp Collector*. USPS officials decided to continue the press run with the variety rather than order destruction of the stamps already printed, he said.

USPS doesn't know when or where the 1996 Challenger stamp first was used. It provided no first-day cancels and didn't prepare any first-day covers of its own. Ziehl and Robin Wright, another USPS spokesman, told *Stamp Collector* that supplies of replenishment stock were shipped in late February as planned for use at some post offices in March.

Scott Publishing Company didn't mention the variety in its 1997 U.S. specialized catalog. The Scott number for the original stamp is 2544.

For a period of time, the Philatelic Fulfillment Service Center offered collectors a choice of the original and the revised stamp. Later it listed only the revised variety in its catalog.

Some collectors were offended and suspicious over this seemingly casual creation of an expensive stamp. "Wasn't it fortunate that Ashton-Potter could hand the Postal Service such a high-priced collectible variety along with their admission of unauthorized tampering with the printing plates of a U.S. security?" Janet F. Allen of Michigan City, Indiana, wrote to *Linn's Stamp News*. "This lucky turn of events will probably save the printer from being barred from future contracts."

IMPROVISED VENDING-MACHINE BOOKLETS

Late in the winter of 1996 the Postal Service introduced a new kind of stamp product for vending-machine sales. These were improvised booklets containing various definitive, special and commemorative stamps that originally were created for sale in other formats. The stamps included self-adhesives, which previously had been unavailable in any type of self-service arrangement other than automatic teller machines (ATMs).

Collecting the booklets turned out to be a challenge, however. They were issued without prior announcement, were available at post offices only on a hit-or-miss basis, and couldn't be purchased through the Philatelic Fulfillment Service Center.

The booklets contain 15 32¢ stamps and sell for $4.80, or 30 32¢ stamps for $9.60. The Postal Service created them in those configurations to minimize the number of coins required in vending machines to make correct change. At the end of 1996, the first "planned" 15-stamp and 30-stamp booklets appeared, containing Yellow Rose stamps (see separate chapter).

Minnesota Diversified Industries of St. Paul, Minnesota, a USPS contractor, assembled the makeshift booklets from specially cut panes of self-adhesives or ordinary pane stock of water-activated stamps. With the self-adhesives, the peel-off strips that are found on regular panes were stripped away during production so the panes could be folded inside the booklets.

Each booklet has a distinctive dark blue and white cardboard cover to which the panes inside are affixed with a small spot of glue. A die-cut stamp-shaped window on the front cover enables the buyer to see a portion of the stamps inside. On the back is a white panel that carries a printed text identifying the contents and giving a Postal Service item number and the price of the booklet.

Linn's Stamp News first reported in March on the existence of this new product. A reader had purchased $4.80 booklets of 15 1995 Pink Rose self-adhesive stamps in Salt Lake City, Utah, on or before March 1. The Salt Lake City post office told *Linn's* the booklets had arrived there February 27.

The actual test site chosen by the Postal Service for the booklets was Albuquerque, New Mexico, according to Gregg Greenwald, writing in *Stamp Collector*. The booklets used were the $4.80 Pink Rose booklet, with one pane of 15 stamps, and a $9.60 Pink Rose booklet with panes of 16 and 14 stamps.

These first booklets were shrink-wrapped, but the wrapping reportedly caused problems with the vending-machine operations, and it was removed and replaced with a round sticker to hold the booklets together. Few wrapped booklets were saved, and some collectors now will pay a premium for them. In February 1997, dealer Michael M. Karen advertised unwrapped 30-stamp Pink Rose booklets for $18 and wrapped ones for $45.

Booklet of 30 Pink Rose stamps shown open. One pane is glued to the cover and has the other pane glued to it. Both 15-stamp panes have one blank location where a stamp was removed during manufacturing.

Soon, vending machine clerks elsewhere began receiving stocks of booklets, which included not only Pink Roses but 32¢ Love Cherub self-adhesives (in 15-stamp and 30-stamp booklets) and water-activated Utah Statehood and Fulbright Scholarship commemoratives (15 stamps per booklet).

By the end of 1996, collectors had found booklets containing these additional 32¢ stamps:

Water-activated: Georgia O'Keeffe (15 stamps); James Dean (15); Olympic Games Discus Thrower (15); Tennessee Statehood (15); Folk Heroes (15); Indian Dances (15); Iowa Statehood (15); Rural Free Delivery (30); Endangered Species (15); 1996 Christmas Madonna (15). The sale of Utah, Tennessee and Iowa Statehood stamp booklets was largely limited to vending machines in their respective states.

Front and back of a 15-stamp booklet of Pink Rose self-adhesive stamps shrink-wrapped in plastic. The identification of the contents, item number and price are on a label stuck onto the plastic, rather than printed on the back of the cover itself, as is the case with unwrapped booklets.

Self-adhesive: 1995 Midnight Angel (15 and 30); Flag Over Porch (15 and 30); Riverboats (15); and Hanukkah (15). In addition, the self-adhesive 20¢ Blue Jay was found in folded vending-machine panes of 10, shrink-wrapped in plastic but without a cardboard cover.

The Midnight Angel booklets were made from an additional printing of 222 million stamps ordered by the Postal Service from Banknote Corporation of America during the summer of 1996. Nearly 218 million of the stamps from this order were shipped to Minnesota Diversified Industries between August 19 and September 6 for processing into booklets of 15 and 30.

The remainder of the order — 202,488 panes of 20, or slightly more than 4 million stamps — was sent to the Philatelic Fulfillment Service Center to be sold to collectors. These panes were of interest to plate number specialists because they bore a new offset plate number combination: B3333. Midnight Angel stamp panes issued in 1995 had plate numbers B1111 or B2222.

In the improvised booklets of self-adhesive Pink Rose, Love Cherub, Flag Over Porch and Midnight Angel stamps, the 15-position panes are cut from sheets that were laid out in panes of 20. Thus, the stamps in the booklets of 15 or 30 have backing paper with printing that straddles at least two pane-of-20 covers and often carries an incorrect $6.40 price instead of $4.80 or $9.60. This seemingly miscut backing is folded inside the booklets.

Some self-adhesive panes have a Time to Reorder label plus 15 stamps, but others have 15 stamps with a 16th stamp removed. The reorder label can be in one of four specific positions on a pane; the removed stamp can be from one of two positions. Reorder labels in the improvised booklets have simulated perforations along the bottom, and some have straight edges on their left sides. Thus they differ from their counterparts on the regularly issued panes of 20 stamps, which always are located in the lower-right corner and therefore have straight edges on the bottom and right sides.

The pane-stock (water-activated) stamp booklets are made from ordinary post office panes, with one or two blocks of 15 stamps removed from the pane, folded accordion-style and spot-glued into the booklet.

Improvised vending-machine booklets exist in a large number of variations, offering booklet collectors as much opportunity to specialize as their time, patience and funds will allow.

For example, Pink Rose booklets of 30 are found in three forms: with panes of 16 and 14 stamps and no reorder labels, with two panes of 15 plus reorder labels, and with two panes of 15 with a 16th stamp removed from each. This doesn't include the shrink-wrapped and unwrapped variations.

There are variations in the product identification printed on the booklet covers. Booklets with the same USPS item number can be found with or without an X after the number. The X indicates that the booklets were

This is the cover of a 15-stamp Midnight Angel booklet, with the folded backing paper extended. One can see how the sheets of printed stamps and backing paper, which were laid out for regular 20-stamp panes, were cut to produce makeshift 15-stamp booklets panes.

packaged in a crisscross fashion for use in older gravity-activated vending machines that require this kind of stacking so only one booklet at a time will drop through. Also, on some booklets, the item number is preceded by the abbreviation "No." and in others it is preceded by a "#" sign. And on the booklets that came with plastic wrapping, the printing isn't on the cover at all, but on a sticker fastened to the outside of the wrap.

Love Cherub and Flag Over Porch booklets have been reported with upside-down panes. The repeat message "Self Adhesive • Do Not Print" that is printed on the backing paper beneath the stamps on some booklets is found reading in two different directions. The Time to Reorder labels can be found with and without die-cut concentric circles.

The water-activated stamps taken from pane stock also offer a wide range of variations. Booklet specialist Michael Perry estimates that there could be thousands of combinations of different Rural Free Delivery selvage blocks affixed to booklets. This stamp has nine different plate number combinations and six different pane-position diagrams, and the blocks of 15 in the booklets can be from the left or right sides of the regular panes of 20.

(As a practical matter, however, no one is likely to attempt this challenge because, as Perry notes, the folded RFD stamps generally are so dry their folded perforations are falling apart.)

The Scott *Specialized Catalogue of United States Stamps* listed a few of the improvised booklets in its 1997 volume. Panes of 15 with the Time to Reorder label are identified as Scott 2492b (Pink Rose), 2920f (Flag Over Porch) and 3030b (Love Cherub). The Scott booklet numbers are BK178A, BK227 and BK235, respectively.

Later, Scott assigned numbers to additional improvised panes and booklets for inclusion in its 1998 catalog.

$15 MIGRATORY BIRD HUNTING (DUCK) STAMP 1996-97

Date of Issue: June 27, 1996

Catalog Number: Scott RW63

Colors: magenta, yellow, cyan, black (offset); black, green (intaglio); black (flexography, back of stamp)

First-Day Cancel: June 27, 1996, Washington, D.C.; June 29, 1996, Basking Ridge, New Jersey

Format: Panes of 30, horizontal, 5 across, 6 down. Offset printing plates of 120 subjects (10 across, 12 around); intaglio printing sleeves of 240 subjects (10 across, 24 around); flexographic back plate of 120 subjects (10 across, 12 around).

Perforations: 11.2 by 11.1

Selvage Markings: none

Gum-Side Inscription: "INVEST IN AMERICA'S FUTURE/BUY DUCK STAMPS/SAVE WETLANDS/SEND IN ALL BIRD BANDS/IT IS UNLAWFUL TO HUNT WATERFOWL OR USE THIS STAMP/AS A PASS TO A NATIONAL WILDLIFE REFUGE UNLESS/YOU SIGN YOUR NAME IN INK ON THE FACE OF THIS STAMP."

Stamp Artist: Wilhelm J. Goebel of Somerset, New Jersey

Stamp Design, Typography and Modeling: Brian Thompson, Bureau of Engraving and Printing

Engravers: Gary Chaconas, BEP (vignette); John Smith, BEP (lettering)

Stamp Manufacturing: Stamps printed by BEP on the 4-color offset, 3-color intaglio webfed F press (801)

Quantity Ordered: 4,000,000

Sleeve Number: 1 6-digit intaglio sleeve number printed in selvage above or below corner stamp

Sleeve Number Reported: 195744

Tagging: untagged

The Stamp

The 1996-97 Migratory Bird Hunting and Conservation Stamp, better known as the duck stamp, depicted two surf scoters, a male and female, flying along the New Jersey coastline. In the background is the historic Barnegat Lighthouse on Long Beach Island.

The design — the first in the history of the duck stamp to show a recognizable landmark — was based on an oil painting by 35-year-old Wilhelm J. Goebel of Somerset, New Jersey. Goebel's art was judged the best among 453 entries in the annual Department of the Interior duck stamp competition, held November 6-8, 1995, in the department's auditorium in Washington, D.C.

The runner-up was Daniel Smith of Bozeman, Montana, a two-time winner of the contest, who submitted an acrylic painting of two Barrow's goldeneye drakes on water. Third place went to Robert Steiner of San Francisco, California, who painted a single Barrow's goldeneye, also in acrylic.

The 1996-97 duck stamp is the 63rd in a continuing annual series. Each year the current stamp must be purchased by waterfowl hunters over 16 years of age. The first stamp, issued in 1934, had a face value of $1. Since then the price has increased in increments to the present $15.

Ninety-eight cents of each duck stamp dollar goes to buy wetlands habitat for the National Wildlife Refuge System. To date, nearly half a billion dollars raised from duck stamp sales have been used to acquire more than 4.2 million acres of wetlands for the system.

Duck stamps also are popular with stamp collectors, wildlife artists and conservationists. Purchases by non-hunters have risen from 3 to 10 percent of all duck stamp sales in the last few years, the U.S. Fish and Wildlife Service reports.

The 1996-97 duck stamp, like all the stamps in the series since 1970, was printed by a combination of offset and intaglio by the Bureau of Engraving and Printing. It was produced on BEP's four-color offset, three-color intaglio F press, the first time that press has been used for a duck stamp.

Duck stamp dealer and expert Bob Dumaine, writing in *Linn's Stamp News*, reported seeing numerous examples of the stamp on which the thin inner frameline, which is part of the engraved portion, is broken or incomplete. The amount of frameline missing varies from about 10 percent to 75 percent, Dumaine wrote. He found flawed stamps in panes from all four positions on the printing sheet.

Dumaine contacted Leonard Buckley, design foreman at BEP, who told him: "A review here at the BEP shows that we lost the fine line on the inside border of the printing sleeve because of excess wiping pressure on a portion of the run. Unfortunately this was missed by (the) examining (department). The entire run, however, was not affected."

Besides the surf scoter and Barrow's goldeneye, the species of waterfowl eligible for portrayal in the contest for the 1996-97 stamp were the black scoter and mottled duck. Each year, the contest entrants are given a list of the species from which they can choose their subjects. In alternate years, as on this occasion, the list consists of the dwindling number of American species that never have appeared on a duck stamp. In the other years, the list comprises more common waterfowl.

Of the artists who entered the 1996-97 stamp contest, 285 painted the Barrow's goldeneye, 103 the surf scoter, 37 the mottled duck and 28 the black scoter. "Many stamp and duck art collectors considered the contest a competition of ugly ducks," Bob Dumaine wrote in *Linn's*. "All but the goldeneye are considered unattractive ducks and are very difficult for artists to depict favorably."

Winners of the duck stamp contest receive no cash award, but winning boosts the reputation of even a previously unknown artist to the top of the profession. Contest winners can look forward to earning hundreds of thousands of dollars from the sale of limited-edition prints of their duck stamp design.

Judges for the duck stamp competition are chosen from among specialists in wildlife, art, hunting, philately and conservation. The judges for the 1996-97 stamp contest were: Jane Alexander, chairman of the National Endowment for the Arts; Ben Cerven of Sunbury, Pennsylvania, whose organization, White Deer, helps support aspiring wildlife artists; Nick Oglesby, founding president of the National Duck Stamp Collectors society; Mary Ann Owens, a philatelic judge and a member of the Citizens' Stamp Advisory Committee since 1979; and Kelly Seibels, one of

This is Wilhelm J. Goebel's winning painting of two surf scoters with the Barnegat Lighthouse in the background.

Close-ups of two 1996 duck stamps showing broken inner border lines (arrows). The flaws are nonconstant and appear in various locations on all four panes of the printing sheet.

North America's leading waterfowl taxidermists.

Mary Ann Owens, describing in *Linn's* her experience as a judge, explained that the judges were told beforehand not to discuss the merits or demerits of any of the entries with each other. They were instructed to vote independently without any outside influences, including from members of the audience.

"The three gentlemen on the panel were duck experts, especially in regard to correct anatomy and coloration," Owens wrote. "On the other hand, I knew that I was on the panel primarily looking for art that would reproduce to a good-looking stamp in its reduced size.

"In fact, we were all furnished with reduction glasses that look just like magnifying glasses but perform the opposite. I had never heard of such glasses before, but they were very helpful."

Wilhelm Goebel's victory in the competition was a powerful testimonial to perseverance. He had entered the contest every year since 1978, when he was a biology major at Ithaca College in Ithaca, New York. In 1990 he placed second with a painting of black scoters.

Goebel's professional work consists primarily of wildlife paintings for sale through galleries, but his pictures also have has been published in such magazines as *Outdoor Life, National Wildlife, Bird Watchers' Digest, U.S. Art, Wildlife Art News* and *Sporting Classics*. He designed the 1994 New Jersey duck stamp, and after winning the federal contest, he received commissions for state duck stamps for New Jersey, Alaska, North Dakota and Virginia, all for 1996, and North Carolina for 1997.

The artist has made numerous field trips to Canada, the West Indies and various U.S. national parks to study wildlife. "I spend a lot of time in the field observing birds," he said. "I prefer to watch them and get to know them that way rather than trying to get a lot of photographs. I feel I can learn far more observing them and seeing how they hold their heads when they're swimming, or how they fly — things like that, which photographs don't always tell you."

Among the products created by Goebel's publisher, Sport'en Art, for sale to collectors in connection with the 1996-97 duck stamp were numbered and signed prints, a gold-plated medallion replica of the stamp, and a hand-carved surf scoter decoy. For $975, a collector could obtain one of a limited edition of 50 artist proof prints complete with a color remarque hand-painted by Goebel, showing a male surf scoter floating on the water, plus a medallion and decoy.

Shortly after winning the contest, Goebel encountered a problem no previous duck stamp artist had faced. In December 1995 the federal government shut down for three weeks because of the budget stalemate between Congress and the White House. "We were all pulling our hair out," Goebel said. "I needed my painting to get my print program going; the Bureau wanted it to get going on the stamp; and everything was sort of in limbo. The painting got caught up in the bureaucracy in Washington, and it took us six weeks to finally get it back."

The surf scoter, a diving duck, is sometimes called the "surf coot." It breeds in northern Canada and Alaska and winters along both coasts of the United States and Canada. Its habitat is large lakes, marine bays and shores, and it feeds on molluscs and vegetation.

The male is black with large white patches on the forehead and at the nape of the neck. Its most distinctive feature is the oversized bill, which has a variegated pattern of white, red, grayish blue and yellow. It has orange-red feet and its eyes are white. The female is dark brown with white patches on the head and has a gray bill.

The Remarque

Goebel created a hand-painted remarque showing a surf scoter, like this one, on each of the 550 "executive edition" lithographs of his duck stamp artwork that his publisher offered for sale to collectors.

One authority on game birds, Walter H. Rich, has written of the surf scoter: "They are unusually tough customers either in life or at the table. Most of our cooks believe it impossible to so prepare this bird as to make it decent food for any but a starving man."

The other design element, the Barnegat Lighthouse, is the second such structure to appear on a duck stamp. The first, a generic lighthouse, was shown on the 1963 stamp, designed by Edward J. Bierly and featuring a pair of brant about to land. Barnegat was completed in 1858, and its great red and white tower has stood guard over the Atlantic coast ever since.

The Design

Goebel's painting and the stamp show the male surf scoter in the fore-ground, flying low over the waves, while the female is just behind and above. The lighthouse, with its distinctive red upper half, is seen in the distance at the right. The time is early morning, with the clouds glowing a pinkish-orange and the east side of the lighthouse illuminated by the ris-ing sun.

"I thought right away of choosing the scoter to paint because they're fairly common off the New Jersey coast in the winter months, and it was a bird I was familiar with," Goebel said. "I've seen them numerous times and I know a lot about them.

"I knew a majority of the artists would opt to do the goldeneye, be-cause it's easier to get reference for, and I felt that if I did a good enough scoter piece, it might stand out among them. When you have 20 or 30 paintings up on the board and 15 of them are goldeneyes, the odd ones tend to stand out."

Goebel did use some photographs of surf scoters to verify such details as the size and color of the bills. "But it's basically a black bird. It's not real colorful, or one that has unique feather patterns," he said. "So in that sense it was quite a simple bird to do.

"I think I had a harder time composing the background and getting a pleasing color to the sky and water than doing the birds."

Goebel realized he might be taking a chance by including a lighthouse in the painting. "I knew that most entries tend to keep man-made struc-tures out and focus more on just the bird," he said. "But I was working with a sea duck, and I wanted to convey in some way that this was the ocean — that you weren't just looking at a lake. One of the best ways to convey that, I felt, was to put some kind of coastal structure in there.

"Then, right away, I realized that the colors in that drake's bill sort of echoed the Barnegat Lighthouse here on the Jersey coast. I thought, gee, that would be sort of a neat play on color. So I put the Barnegat Light-house in. And of all the five judges I've spoken to, four of them noticed that correlation and liked it. My planning paid off there, I guess."

(As luck would have it, at least one of the judges, Mary Ann Owens, had a special affinity for lighthouses, having visited several such struc-tures on Lake Huron less than five months earlier while en route to

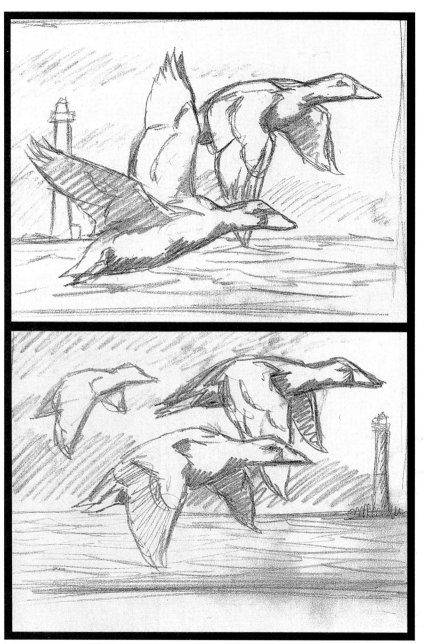

These are two of Wilhelm Goebel's preliminary pencil sketches that he made in the process of developing the composition of his surf scoters painting.

Cheboygan, Michigan, for the first-day ceremony for the Great Lakes Lighthouses booklet stamps. In the final round of voting, Owens, along with two other judges, gave Goebel's painting the maximum score of 5.)

Goebel used artistic license in depicting the Barnegat Lighthouse. "It probably looks (in the painting) more like it did 70, 80, 90 years ago, compared to today," he said. He deleted some of the surrounding artifacts, including outbuildings, a chain-link fence and rock jetties reaching into the sea. "If you put in little dinky details like that, you tend to be penalized in the judging," he explained. "You have to sort of edit certain things out.

"I learned that back when I came in second (in 1990). I had basically the same type of design, flying birds, but they were black scoters. Then down in the water I had three little scoters swimming. Afterward, when I spoke to the judges, they all said they liked the painting, but they felt those three little birds would disappear on the stamp, and I had points deducted for that. That's one reason I tended to keep this one very simple and not get into minutiae."

The artist spent most of the summer of 1995 working on the painting, "off and on, not constantly. I spent about two months painting it, then several weeks just looking at it and touching it up here and there, and then sent it out the very last day it was due."

On the finished stamp, the engraved portion consists of the detail work on the ducks' bodies, wings and heads; all the lettering and numerals; and the outer and inner framelines, including the wider top and bottom panels, which contain words in dropout white. The ducks' feathers and the identification "Surf Scoter," in small italic letters, are in black. The remaining intaglio printing is in green. All other elements of the design — ocean, sky, lighthouse, and the colored portions of the ducks — are offset-printed.

In addition to the problem with broken framelines mentioned earlier, some color shifting has been noted with this stamp. In a few specimens, the black intaglio printing on the male duck has moved so far upward that it obliterates the white patch on the back of the bird's head. "It gives the duck a kind of skinny-necked appearance, because half of its neck is missing," said Goebel.

First-Day Facts

The first-day ceremony for the 1996-97 duck stamp was held at the National Postal Museum in Washington June 27 to coincide with the public opening of the museum's permanent federal duck stamp exhibit, titled "Artistic License: The Duck Stamp Story." The exhibit was funded with a gift from Jeanette Cantrell Rudy of Nashville, Tennessee, a waterfowl hunter and prominent collector of duck stamps. The Postal Service provided a hand cancellation for this event that showed a surf scoter in flight with the words "Duck Stamp Station." Two days later, the traditional second-day ceremony in the artist's hometown was held. In this case, al-

DUCK STAMP STATION
Washington, DC 20066
June 27, 1996

USPS provided this hand cancellation for the duck stamp first-day ceremony.

though Basking Ridge, New Jersey, isn't Goebel's place of residence, he chose as the location the Somerset County Park Commission Environmental Education Center in Basking Ridge, adjacent to the Great Swamp National Wildlife Refuge, for its significance to local residents, including himself. The hand cancellation for this ceremony depicted a surf scoter afloat on the water and was inscribed "Surf Scoter Station."

Among those taking part in the Basking Ridge ceremony were U.S. Senator Frank R. Lautenberg, D-New Jersey; John Rogers, acting director of the U.S. Fish and Wildlife Service; Ron Lambertson, regional director of the Fish and Wildlife Service; and local postmasters.

The duck stamp was issued nationwide July 1.

Postal Stationery

The Postal Service issued 38 postal cards and two stamped envelopes in 1996. Thirty-five of the postal cards were accounted for by two sets: Centennial Olympic Games (20) and Endangered Species (15). Both sets were associated with sets of stamps that featured the same basic designs.

These picture postal cards were the first tangible results of a change in postal stationery policy by USPS. They were created by the stamp and product marketing office rather than the stamp development office, which meant that the Postal Service considered them primarily a product rather than security paper, which stamps, stamped envelopes and postal cards always had been considered in the past. In keeping with their changed status, the cards were marketed in a novel format — bound as complete sets in colorful booklets — and sold for unprecedentedly high markups over their face value of 20¢ apiece.

20¢ WINTER SCENE POSTAL CARD
SCENIC AMERICA SERIES

Date of Issue: February 23, 1996

Catalog Number: Scott UX241

Colors: yellow, magenta, cyan, black

First-Day Cancel: Watertown, New York

First-Day Cancellations: 11,764

Format: Cards printed in 80-subject press sheets but available only as single-cut cards. Offset printing plates of 80 subjects (8 across, 10 down).

Size: 5½ by 3½ inches

Marking: "© 1996 USPS." "recycled" and recycled symbol.

Designer and Art Director: Howard Paine, Delaplane, Virginia, based on a painting by Dale Nichols

Typographer: Tom Mann, Mann & Mann Graphics, Warrenton, Virginia

Project Manager: Terrence McCaffrey, USPS

Card Manufacturing: Cards printed by the Government Printing Office in Washington, D.C., on an offset 5-color MAN Roland sheetfed press. Cards processed and shipped by GPO.

Quantity Ordered: 18,000,000

Quantity Distributed: 20,000,000

Tagging: vertical bar to right of stamp

The Postal Card

The Postal Service's first postal card of 1996 depicted a winter farm scene in Nebraska. It was issued February 23 in another part of the country that, like Nebraska, is familiar with long winters and heavy snowfalls: upstate New York.

The city chosen for first-day honors, Watertown, is in the congressional district of Representative John M. McHugh, the Republican who chaired the House Postal Service Subcommittee in the 104th Congress. It was the second such ceremony the influential congressman had obtained for his district in five months; the first, in North Pole, New York, had featured the 1995 contemporary Christmas stamps.

The picture on the postal card "could be representative of thousands of family farms in New York and the Northeast," McHugh said in announcing that the card would be issued in Watertown.

The Winter Scene card was the second in a Scenic America series that USPS had launched a year earlier with a postal card depicting a red barn amid green grass and leafy trees. The new card also showed a red barn, although in an altogether different setting.

Most art used on stamps and postal stationery is commissioned by the Postal Service, but in this case the artwork was adapted from an existing painting. The painting is *John Comes Home for Christmas*, a 40- by 30-inch oil on canvas done in 1937 by a painter and illustrator named Dale Nichols.

Art director Howard Paine had known of Nichols' work, and when postal officials suggested a winter scene for the new card, he volunteered to look for an appropriate piece by the artist. "His paintings were hard-edged, clean kinds of scenes, and I thought I could find one that would serve,"

Dale Nichols (1904-1995) in a photograph made in 1988.

Paine recalled.

In January 1995, after making numerous telephone calls, Paine located Nichols' niece, Ruth Nichols of David City, Nebraska. Ruth, a painter and sculptor herself, had studied art with her uncle. From her, Paine learned that the 90-year-old Nichols was in poor health and living in a nursing home in Sedona, Arizona.

Ruth Nichols sent Paine some catalogs of Dale Nichols' paintings, along with a Christmas card that reproduced *John Comes Home for Christmas*. When he saw the picture, Paine knew it was the one he wanted for the postal card.

The Christmas card, made in 1990 by Joy Creations Company, Omaha, Nebraska, offered this information on the back:

"Dale Nichols was born and raised on a farm near David City, Nebraska. Much of his work features rural life. 'These paintings are not just pictures of farms,' he has written. 'All are re-creations of farm life. In painting these canvases I felt again the vastness of endless skies; experienced again the penetrating cold of Nebraska winters; lived again as farmers live.' The light of the sun is an important feature in Nichols' work ...

"Best known for his painting, Nichols spent many years as a fashion illustrator in Chicago. In 1943 he succeeded Grant Wood as art editor for *The Encyclopedia Britannica*. His works were featured on the covers of national publications, including *The Saturday Evening Post*.

"*John Comes Home for Christmas* represents Nichols at a younger age returning home to visit his family. In 1943 he gave this painting to Father Edward Flanagan, the founder of Boys Town (Nebraska), and to the youth

This is Dale Nichols' 1937 painting John Comes Home for Christmas *that was adapted for use on the Winter Scene postal card. Art director Howard Paine cropped the painting at the top and bottom to make it fit into the elongated indicium-stamp space.*

of Boys Town."

The painting today hangs in the reference area in the Hall of History at Boys Town. The Postal Service obtained permission from the institution to adapt the painting for use on the postal card.

Dale Nichols died in late 1995, and apparently never was aware that his nearly 60-year-old painting was about to get such widespread circulation.

The card was printed by the Government Printing Office, using color separations made by Dodge Color in Washington, D.C. In the past, GPO had contracted out its own color-separation work, but beginning with the Red Barn card of 1995, USPS has had Dodge Color make the separations for its postal cards.

Because the Postal Service had a request pending for a 21¢ postcard rate before the Postal Rate Commission at the time the Winter Scene card was being prepared, two sets of separations were made and sent to the GPO, one with the 20¢ denomination, the other reading 21¢. When the rate increase was turned down, the 21¢ set was discarded.

The Design

Nichols' painting depicts a sleigh drawn by two horses turning off a road into a driveway leading to a farm house and outbuildings, as a dog runs excitedly alongside. A driver stands in the front of the sleigh, and a passenger — obviously the homecoming John — is seated behind him, waving a greeting to a figure standing beside the driveway. A late afternoon sun causes the waiting figure, the dog, the sleigh and a roadside mailbox to cast long shadows on the snow. The predominant color of the picture is blue; contrast is provided by the red expanse of the barn and touches of red on the two chimneys of the farmhouse.

To fit the picture into the long image area of the postal card, Howard Paine had to crop sky and treetops at the top of the picture and some of the shadowed foreground at the bottom.

The Winter Scene was the first postal card to be imprinted with the word "recycled" and the three-arrow recycling symbol. USPS has included those items on its stamped envelopes since 1992.

Varieties

Linn's Stamp News reported the existence of a Winter Scene postal card on which two of the process colors, magenta and yellow, appear to be missing, leaving only the blue and black. However, using 30-power magnification, *Linn's* writer Michael Schreiber found minute traces of magenta ink in the area of the side of the barn. This would indicate that the item was a freak rather than a true color-missing error.

Schreiber was unable to find any trace of yellow, but he cautioned that the card would have to be examined by experts before it could be said with certainty that all the yellow was missing. "This may be difficult to determine," he added, "because yellow on stamps often is tricky to recognize and because of how it is used on the card as an underlying color that is covered by darker ones."

First-Day Facts

Representative McHugh was the featured speaker at the dedication ceremony in the Jefferson Community College gymnasium in Watertown. Anderson Hodges, USPS district manager, and Warren A. Johnson, Watertown postmaster, delivered opening and closing remarks.

A total of 1,100 Winter Scene postal cards were used in Cincinnati, Ohio, February 9, two weeks before the card's official first-day sale. The cards were machine-addressed and had a printed message on the back advertising a February 15-22 sale at a local toy store. An inquiry by *Linn's Stamp News* revealed that a clerk at Cincinnati's Anderson branch post office had mistakenly comingled the Winter Scene cards with 20¢ Red Barn postal cards and had sold 1,125 of them to the retailer.

32¢ SAVE OUR ENVIRONMENT ENVELOPE

Date of Issue: April 20, 1996

Catalog Number: Scott U640

Colors: yellow, magenta, cyan, black (offset, patch); blue (PMS 321) and yellow (PMS 109) (flexography, envelope)

First-Day Cancel: Chicago, Illinois

First-Day Cancellations: 9,921

Size: number 10, no window

Paper: 100 percent recycled

Markings: "© USPS 1996" under flap; "PRINTED ON RECYCLED PAPER/IN KEEPING WITH OUR COMMITMENT TO THE ENVIRONMENT" and recycling symbol on back at bottom

Designer, Typographer and Art Director: Richard Sheaff of Norwood, Massachusetts

Project Manager: Vance Harris, USPS

Envelope Manufacturing: Envelopes die cut, stamp patch affixed and formed by Westvaco Envelope Division in Williamsburg, Pennsylvania, on VH-3 machine. Envelopes printed front and back by flexography. Stamp patches printed in rolls by Amgraph Inc., North Versailles, Connecticut, on an offset press.

Quantity Ordered and Distributed: 21,575,000

Tagging: vertical bar to right of patch

The Envelope

On April 20, in connection with the 20th anniversary of Earth Day, the

378

Postal Service issued a 32¢ stamped envelope with an outdoor scene and the message: "Save Our Environment" in the stamped area. The picture portion is on a four-color, offset-printed paper patch affixed to the inside of the envelope so it can be seen through a square window cut out of the upper-right corner.

The use of this window-and-patch method of manufacture enables USPS to mate a high-quality image with standard envelope paper. The format was introduced with the 25¢ Space Station hologram envelope of 1989 and since then has been used for three other hologram envelopes and several envelopes featuring multicolored offset pictures.

Among the latter was an earlier Environment envelope, also issued as part of an Earth Day celebration. It was the 29¢ "Protect the Environment" envelope of 1992 (Scott U627), which depicted on the patch a branchful of Hillebrandia blossoms and bore the additional message: "Save the Rain Forests."

The new Save Our Environment envelope was available only as a number 10 plain and sold for 38¢ apiece and $175 for a box of 500.

USPS billed the envelope as "made from 100 percent recycled materials, 20 percent of which is provided by Postal Service recycling efforts." It explained that this 20 percent comes from undelivered bulk business mail. Although all stamped envelopes issued since 1992 have carried the recycling symbol imprinted beneath the flap, this one has the symbol in the open on the back, accompanied by the wording: "Printed on recycled paper in keeping with our commitment to the environment."

The Postal Service noted in its news release that in 1995 the White House had awarded it seven "Closing the Circle" awards for waste prevention. "A leader in environmental efforts, the USPS has the nation's largest compressed natural gas delivery fleet, recycles an estimated one million tons of material per year, and uses recycled material for many of its stamps, retail and philatelic products," the release said.

Designer Richard Sheaff offered CSAC an alternative image featuring ferns, which also was based on a photograph he had taken.

In the design first released to the public, the words "Save Our Environment" were in what designer Richard Sheaff described as a "funky birchbark kind of type." It was replaced by a Lithos Bold typeface to match the "USA 32."

The Design

The Save Our Environment envelope was designed by Richard Sheaff, a Postal Service art director from Norwood, Massachusetts. For the four-color image on the patch, Sheaff reproduced a photograph he had taken several years earlier on the Pacific coast of Oregon; he doesn't remember the exact location, Sheaff said. The photograph shows a sandy white beach in the foreground, a freshwater stream running over rocks toward the ocean, a hillside with a cave entrance, and, in the background, wooded hills and blue sky.

Sheaff gave the Citizens' Stamp Advisory Committee an alternative photograph filled with ferns. "They felt that the image we used was better because it does have the right elements in it: fresh water flowing toward salt water, forest, sky," he said. "It's got a lot of the aspects of the natural environment in one picture, and that seemed appropriate."

The rest of the indicium design is printed on the envelope itself. The "USA 32" and "SAVE OUR ENVIRONMENT" are greenish-blue and in a Lithos Bold typeface. An earlier version of the "SAVE OUR ENVIRONMENT" type, which was part of the design that was first released to the public, was in "a kind of funky birchbark kind of type," Sheaff said.

A sun symbol, printed in yellow, completes the design. The sun actually is a pictogram-type character in a type font called Poptics One on Sheaff's computer.

First-Day Facts

The envelope was dedicated at Garfield Park in Chicago, Illinois, by Rufus Porter, USPS district manager for customer service and sales. Speakers were Fran McPoland, federal environmental executive; Forrest Claypool, general superintendent, Chicago Park District; and Erma Tranter, executive director, Friends of the Parks. Charlie Bravo, USPS manager of environmental policy, presided.

Date of Issue: May 2, 1996

Catalog Number: Scott U641

Colors: red (PMS 032), blue (PMS 286), gold (PMS 131), black

First-Day Cancel: Washington, D.C.

First-Day Cancellations: 1,807,316 (includes Centennial Olympic Games stamps and picture postal cards)

Size: number 10, no window

Paper: recycled

Markings: "© USPS 1996" under flap; "RECYCLED" and recycling symbol on back at bottom

Designer and Typographer: Brad Copeland of Atlanta, Georgia

Art Director: Carl Herrman

Project Manager: Vance Harris, USPS

Envelope Manufacturing: Envelopes printed by Westvaco, Williamsburg, Pennsylvania, by offset and flexography on VH-3 machine.

Quantity Ordered and Distributed: 16,500,000

Tagging: vertical bar to right of stamp

The Envelope

On May 2, the Postal Service issued a stamped envelope honoring the 1996 Atlanta Paralympic Games for physically or visually impaired athletes, which were scheduled to take place later in the year in Atlanta, Georgia, after the close of the Centennial Olympic Games.

The envelope was dedicated in Washington, D.C., along with the pane of 20 Centennial Olympic Games commemorative stamps and the matching 20 Centennial Olympic picture postal cards.

Paralympics Games officials originally asked the Postal Service for a commemorative stamp for the Atlanta event. Because of the large number of stamps they were planning for the Olympics, USPS officials turned down the stamp request, but offered a stamped envelope instead, and the counterproposal was quickly accepted.

The designs of the envelope and of the 20 Centennial Olympic Games stamps were unveiled by USPS chief marketing officer Loren Smith February 1 at Sport Summit 96 in Atlanta, the longest-running and largest trade show and conference in the sports business.

The envelope was a number 10 without window. It sold for 38¢ apiece, or 35¢ in quantities of 500 ($175).

The Paralympic Games provide the ultimate in competition for elite athletes with disabilities. The philosophy guiding the movement is that such individuals should have opportunities and experiences equivalent to those afforded nondisabled athletes. The first Paralympic Games were held in Rome in 1960, and they have been held every Olympic year since then, usually in the city or country hosting the Olympic Games.

The Paralympics are recognized by the International Olympic Committee and governed by the International Paralympic Committee. Participants represent four international federations: Cerebral Palsy International Sports and Recreation Association, International Blind Sports Association, International Stroke-Mandeville Wheelchair Sports Federation and the International Sports Organization for the Disabled. To compete, each

These are the obverse sides of the two silver $1 coins issued by the U.S. Mint specifically to honor and help fund the 10th Paralympic Games. They were part of a larger set of 16 coins issued in 1995 and 1996 to commemorate the Centennial Olympic Games in Atlanta. The 1995 design features a blind tethered runner and the Paralympic logo; the 1996 coin shows a wheelchair athlete competing in a track event. On both coins, the word "spirit" is minted in Braille. Both designs are by Jim Sharpe, who previously designed the 12 U.S. stamps in the Performing Arts series.

athlete must meet strict qualifying standards and be selected for his national team.

At the 10th Paralympic Games in Atlanta, more than 100 nations were represented during 10 days of competition from August 16 through 27, 1996. Some 4,000 athletes took part in 17 sports, 14 of which were Olympic events, and two demonstration sports. Supporting them were 1,000 coaches and team staff members, 1,500 officials and technical personnel and 15,000 volunteers. These figures made the games the second-largest sporting event in the world, roughly one-third the size of the Olympic Games.

The Design

For the indicium design, art director Carl Herrman adapted the official "Starfire" logo of the 1996 Atlanta Paralympic Games, which was designed by Brad Copeland of Atlanta.

The logo features a blue star with one white point, a series of concentric arcs in blue and gold suggesting a wheelchair wheel, a flickering red flame, and the words "1996 ATLANTA PARALYMPIC GAMES" in a single line of black serif capitals. Herrman stacked the typography in two lines to the left of the star and added a red "USA 32" in the same typeface to the right.

Copeland was quoted by the Postal Service as saying that his logo was "designed to represent the fulfillment of the athlete's dreams. The star is the athlete; the fire is the passion that burns in the heart."

"We don't normally like to use logos, and if we had done this as a stamp we probably wouldn't have used it, because logos on stamps just don't work well," said Terrence McCaffrey, head of stamp design for USPS. "They seem to work better on envelopes. This one was such a strong graphic that everyone on the (Citizens' Stamp Advisory) Committee loved it. It was one of the easiest projects of the year."

Unlike most first-class-rate envelopes, this one had no special security feature, such as embossing, a die-cut window or a wraparound design element. Officials discussed embossing the red flame portion of the design, but decided against it. "I think our fear of counterfeiting has relaxed a little bit," said McCaffrey. "Tagging is one security feature that's always there. We don't feel a need to build in excessive amounts of security."

First-Day Facts

The envelope was dedicated at the Washington ceremony by Gail G. Sonnenberg, USPS vice president for human resources. Aimee Mullins, national 100- and 200-meter record holder in the women's amputee division, was the principal speaker. A double below-knee amputee from birth, Mullins runs on two prosthetic devices and trains with the Georgetown University nondisabled track team.

Honored guests were Mike Kraft, Washington representative of the Atlanta Paralympic Organizing Committee, and Kirk Bauer, executive director, Disabled Sports, USA. For further details on the ceremony, see the chapter on the Centennial Olympic Games stamps.

Although the 20 Olympic stamps were available in both Washington and Atlanta on May 2, the envelope was available only in Washington on that day.

The Philatelic Fulfillment Service Center offered uncacheted first-day covers of the Paralympics envelope for 48¢.

20¢ CENTENNIAL OLYMPIC GAMES
PICTURE POSTAL CARDS (20 DESIGNS)
CLASSIC COLLECTIONS SERIES

For more than a thousand years at Olympia, in ancient Greece, a sprint race was held every four years in honor of Zeus, and the winner was crowned with an olive wreath. Other sports were soon added to this quadrennial event—including the four-horsed chariot race and the pancration, a violent contest in which two men engaged in no-holds-barred combat until one of them quit. The Olympic Games were banned in the fourth century A.D. by the Roman emperor Theodosius II, who outlawed all non-Christian rituals.

Over 1,500 years later, a Frenchman named Pierre de Coubertin revived the tradition. De Coubertin was not much more than five feet tall, and weighed only 100 pounds, but was nonetheless greatly interested in sports. The first Modern Games were held in Athens, Greece, in 1896. More than 100,000 spectators watched 311 athletes from 13 countries compete in nine sports: cycling, gymnastics, fencing, wrestling, track and field, tennis, swimming, weightlifting, and shooting. Today more than 10,000 men and women from nearly 200 countries around the world take part in the Games, competing in a wide variety of sports.

Set records for speed and distance with these pre-stamped, gold medal quality postal cards. Just write your message, address the card, and drop it in the mail!

Date of Issue: May 2, 1996

Price: $12.95 per set

Catalog Numbers: Scott UX242-UX261 (individual cards); UX261a (booklet of 20 cards)

Colors: tan, yellow, magenta, cyan, black

First-Day Cancel: Washington, D.C.

First-Day Cancellations: unavailable (cancellations applied by Philatelic Sales Division, Kansas City, Missouri, after which cards were returned to manufacturer for binding)

Format: Cards bound into booklets of 20 different varieties by rouletted tabs. Cards printed on 20-subject plates, 4 each of 5 designs per plate.

Size of Cards: $5^{29}/_{32}$ by 4¼ inches

Size of Booklet: $6^{21}/_{32}$ by 4¼ inches

Card Markings: Description of each subject, in same wording and punctuation as inscriptions on back of Centennial Olympic Games stamps, with two exceptions. On women's diving card, inscription reads "Platform diving is performed from 10 meters above the water" instead of "Platform diving is performed from a board 10 meters above the water." On women's sailboarding card, period is omitted at the end of the text. Also: "Stamps etc. • US POSTAL SERVICE • PO BOX 57 • GRAND RAPIDS MN 55744-0057." "36 USC 380."

Booklet Markings, Front Cover: "Centennial Olympic Games/The U.S. Postal Service/Ready-to-Mail Postal Cards."

Booklet Markings, Back Cover: USPS logo and "UNITED STATES/POSTAL SERVICE ®." "© 1996 U.S. Postal Service. All Rights Reserved." Promotional sentence for *Stamps etc.* catalog. "36 USC 380." On spine of booklet: "The Centennial Olympic Games Postal Card Collection."

Booklet Markings, Inside (on first page): "For more than a thousand years at Olympia, in ancient Greece, a sprint race was held every four years in honor of Zeus, and the winner was crowned with an olive wreath. Other sports were soon added to this quadrennial event — including the four-horsed chariot race and the pancration, a violent contest in which two men engaged in no-holds-barred combat until one of them quit. The Olympic Games were banned in the fourth century A.D. by the Roman emperor Theodosius II, who outlawed all non-Christian rituals.

"Over 1,500 years later, a Frenchman named Pierre de Coubertin revived the tradition. De Coubertin was not much more than five feet tall, and weighed only 100 pounds, but was nonetheless greatly interested in sports. The first Modern Games were held in Athens, Greece, in 1896. More than 100,000 spectators watched 311 athletes from 13 countries compete in nine sports: cycling, gymnastics, fencing, werestling, track and field, tennis, swimming, weightlifting, and shooting. Today more than 10,000 men and women from nearly 200 countries around the world take part in the Games, competing in a wide variety of sports.

"Set records for speed and distance with these pre-stamped, gold medal quality postal cards. Just write your message, address the card, and drop it in the mail!"

Stamp Designer: Richard Waldrep of Sparks, Maryland

Stamp Typographer: John Boyd, Anagraphics Inc., New York, New York

Stamp Art Director: Carl Herrman

Card and Booklet Designer: Supon Design Group, Washington, D.C.

Card Project Manager: Kathryn Miller, USPS

Card Manufacturing: Cards printed by the Art Litho Company, Baltimore, Maryland, on Planeta 5-color offset press. Cards processed, bound and shipped by Art Litho.

Quantity Ordered and Distributed: 3,300,000 (165,000 each of 20 designs)

Tagging: vertical bar to right of stamp

The Cards

On May 2, the Postal Service issued a set of 20 picture postal cards that reproduced, on their picture sides and their indicium stamps, the designs of the 20 stamps of the Centennial Olympic Games pane that made their debut the same day. The cards bore the 20¢ postcard-rate denomination.

The issuance of matching picture postal cards is one of the distinctive features of the Postal Service's Classic Collections stamp series, of which the Centennial Olympic Games stamps were a part. The Olympic Games cards were sold only in sets, like the first three groups of Classic Collections cards, Legends of the West (1993), Civil War (1994) and Comic Strip Classics (1994). But they differ significantly from these cards and, in fact, are unlike any previous U.S. postal card.

At $5^{29}/_{32}$ inches long by 4¼ inches deep, the Olympic Games cards are much larger than normal U.S. postal cards, which measure 5½ by 3½ inches, and are the maximum size permitted for the 20¢ postcard rate. Instead of being packaged as separate items, the 20 cards are bound into a booklet, each card attached along one side by a binding stub that is scored to facilitate the card's removal. The booklet has a colorful front and back cover. An inside page contains a brief history of the Olympic Games and a paragraph promoting the use of the postal cards for mailing.

Finally, the price was unprecedentedly high: $12.95, compared to the $7.95 USPS had charged for its Civil War and Comic Strip Classics sets of the previous year. This worked out to just under 65¢ a card, or 45¢ more than face value.

Like the first three Classic Collections postal cards sets, the Centennial

Olympic Games set was manufactured by Art Litho Company of Baltimore, Maryland. The printed and bound cards then were sent to Minnesota Diversified Industries in St. Paul, Minnesota, to be shrink-wrapped.

However, unlike the previous sets, the Olympic Games cards were produced entirely by the stamp and product marketing section of Stamp Services, headed by Valoree S. Vargo. The earlier Classic Collections postal cards had been created by the stamp development section, headed by James Tolbert, in consultation with the marketing section. The transfer of responsibility showed that Stamp Services considered the cards to be primarily a "product" rather than a postage item, even though each card bore live postage and was, in effect, a government security.

Supon Design Group of Washington, D.C., designed the cards and the booklet in which they were bound. The firm, whose creative director is Thai-born Supon Phornirunlit, had done previous design work on USPS products, but this was its first assignment involving items of postage.

The cards were sold at post office philatelic windows, postal retail stores, and the Olymphilex 96 stamp show in Atlanta, and by mail from the Philatelic Fulfillment Service Center in Kansas City, Missouri. But the Postal Service was slow getting them to these distribution points. Delays in getting final design approval for the stamps and cards from the U.S. Olympic Committee contributed to the problem, postal officials said.

Even at the first-day ceremony in Washington, D.C., May 2, only 1,000 booklets of bound cards were available. To get them there on time, the Postal Service had them sent directly from the printer, without shrink-wrapping.

For several weeks thereafter, collectors had only two opportunities to buy the cards, and these were limited and unpublicized ones. Five hundred booklets were sent to Pittsburgh, Pennsylvania, to be sold May 26, and another 500 were sent to Philadelphia, Pennsylvania, to be sold June 9. Both occasions marked the participation of the Postal Service's cycling team in local races. It wasn't until late July, about the time of the Games themselves, that the Philatelic Fulfillment Service Center obtained 22,000 sets of the cards and began filling its several thousand back orders from collectors and dealers.

As was noted in the chapter on the Centennial Olympic Games stamps, the issuance of the postal cards gave the Postal Service the opportunity to correct a technical mistake in the informational text on the back of one of those stamps.

The stamp depicting women's diving carried the sentence: "Platform diving is performed from a board 10 meters above the water." In the text on the card, the words "a board" have been deleted. Otherwise, the wording and punctuation on the cards is the same as that on the stamps, with

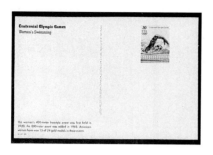

Centennial Olympic Games
Women's Swimming

The women's 400-meter freestyle event was first held in 1920; the 800-meter event was added in 1968. American women have won 15 of 24 gold medals in these events.

Centennial Olympic Games
Men's Swimming

The backstroke event was first included in the Games of 1900. There are now two events: the 100 meters, which is two lengths of the pool, and the 200 meters, which is four lengths.

Centennial Olympic Games
Men's Shot Put

The shot put has been included in all Games since 1896. A shot is a 16-pound ball of iron or brass. The United States has won 15 of 22 gold medals.

Centennial Olympic Games
Freestyle Wrestling

Wrestling has 10 weight divisions. It is the only sport with a maximum weight limit: wrestlers must be less than 286 pounds. The United States has earned more medals than any other nation.

Centennial Olympic Games
Women's Sailboarding

The first sailboarding contest was included in the 1984 Los Angeles Games. A separate women's event was added in 1992.

Centennial Olympic Games
Men's Rowing

There will be 14 rowing events contested at the 1996 Games: 8 for men and 6 for women. For the first time, lightweight events will be included for men under 160 lbs. and for women under 130 lbs.

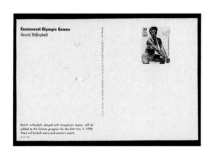

one minor exception: On the women's sailboarding card, the final period has been inadvertently omitted from the text.

Robert C. Bellinger of Long Beach, California, writing to *Stamp Collector*, compared his experiences in obtaining postally used sets of the Centennial Olympic Games cards and previous picture postal card sets.

With the Legends of the West, Bellinger wrote, he had to use about one and one-half sets to get one undamaged set complete. But the next two sets, Civil War and American Comic Classics, "seemed to be printed on a very soft card stock, which does not stand up under the Postal Service's high-speed equipment," he wrote. He had to use two Civil War sets to complete one set, "and even then some are damaged ... Most of the rejects were pretty nearly destroyed and are useless." With the Comics, he continued, "out of a half set (10 cards), only one arrived undamaged, and some were torn in half or totaled."

"Better news are the Atlanta Olympic cards," Bellinger concluded. "Those are printed on a heavier card stock than the previous two sets and are coming through 95 percent OK."

The size of the cards, the weight of the stock and the booklet format all were chosen with the potential buyer in Atlanta in mind, according to Kathryn Miller, project manager for the postal cards. "We thought this would be something people would buy and use or take home with them,

and that they should be bound so they wouldn't fall apart," she said. "By using the larger size we would get the full benefit of the design, and the heavier stock would hold up better."

The issuance of the 1996 Olympic postal cards more than tripled the total number of U.S. postal stationery items issued for the Olympic Games over the years. USPS had issued six previous postal cards, three each for the 1980 and 1984 winter and summer Olympics; one stamped envelope, for the 1980 Games; and one aerogram, for the 1984 Games.

The Designs

Because of the large size of the cards, Richard Waldrep's action-packed artwork shows to much greater advantage on their picture sides than it does on their companion postage stamps.

A comparison of the cards' picture sides and the stamps shows that, although the images had to be cropped slightly at the sides and bottom to fit the different proportions of the cards, each card actually shows slightly more of its picture at the top than does the equivalent stamp. Most of this "bonus" is in the one-eighth inch of the artwork that is on the binding tab rather than on the card itself.

As for the cards' indicium stamps, the major difference between them and the postage stamps is the denomination, 20¢ instead of 32¢. The

indicium stamps also lack the black frame line of the postage stamps, and are slightly smaller: 1 inch by 1¼ inch compared to 1¹/₁₆ inch by 1¹³/₃₂ inch.

The cover of the booklet containing the cards reproduces Waldrep's paintings of the male cyclist and shot putter.

First-Day Facts

Details on the first-day ceremony for the Centennial Olympic Games stamps and postal cards can be found in the chapter on the Centennial Olympic Games stamps.

Because of the delay in filling orders for the postal cards, the Postal Service extended the grace period for submitting cards for first-day cancels from the normal 30 days to 90 days.

The printer, Art Litho, sent sets of unbound cards to the Philatelic Fulfillment Service Center in Kansas City, Missouri, to be canceled with the May 2 first-day postmark, after which they were returned for binding. The Postal Service then offered these first-day booklets for sale for $14.95.

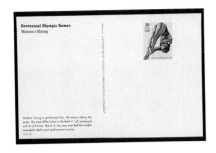

Centennial Olympic Games
Women's Diving

Platform diving is performed from 10 meters above the water. The most difficult dive is the back 3 1/2 somersault with 4 1/2 twists. The U. S. has won over half the medals awarded in both men's and women's events.

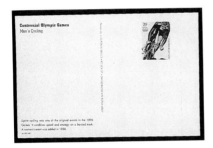

Centennial Olympic Games
Men's Cycling

Sprint cycling was one of the original events in the 1896 Games. It combines speed and strategy on a banked track. A women's event was added in 1988.

Centennial Olympic Games
Women's Soccer

Although men's soccer has been a part of the Games since 1900, a women's tournament will be held for the first time in 1996. Eight teams will take part.

20¢ McDOWELL HALL POSTAL CARD
HISTORIC PRESERVATION SERIES

St. John's College, Annapolis, Maryland

Date of Issue: June 1, 1996

Catalog Number: Scott UX262

Colors: yellow, magenta, cyan, black

First-Day Cancel: Annapolis, Maryland

First-Day Cancellations: 8,793

Format: Cards printed in 80-subject press sheets but available only as single-cut cards. Offset printing plates of 80 subjects (8 across, 10 down).

Size: 5½ by 3½ inches

Marking: "© 1996 USPS." "recycled" and recycled symbol.

Designer: Harry Devlin of Mountainside, New Jersey

Typographer: Tom Mann, Mann and Mann Graphics, Warrenton, Virginia

Art Director: Howard Paine

Project Manager: Vance Harris, USPS

Card Manufacturing: Cards printed by the Government Printing Office in Washington, D.C., on an offset 5-color MAN Roland sheetfed press. Cards processed and shipped by GPO.

Quantity Ordered and Distributed: 20,000,000

Tagging: vertical bar to right of stamp

The Postal Card

On June 1, USPS commemorated the 300th anniversary of St. John's College in Annapolis, Maryland, with a postal card depicting the school's historic McDowell Hall. St. John's is the third oldest college in the nation after Harvard University and the College of William and Mary.

The card was issued in conformance with the criterion for subject selection of the Citizens' Stamp Advisory Committee that reads: "Requests for commemoration of significant anniversaries of universities and other institutions of higher education shall be considered only in regard to Historic Preservation Series postal cards featuring an appropriate building on the campus."

Less than a year earlier, however, the Postal Service had deviated from this policy by issuing a 32¢ stamp for the 150th anniversary of the U.S. Naval Academy — also located, coincidentally, in Annapolis, on land adjoining the St. John's College campus. CSAC justified the stamp on grounds that the service academies had special national significance and therefore should be in a separate category.

Much earlier, in 1949, the city of Annapolis itself was honored on its 300th anniversary with a 3¢ commemorative stamp depicting an early map of the city (Scott 984). That stamp was designed by F. Townsend Morgan, an artist in residence at St. John's College.

St. John's College is a direct descendant of the King William School, a grammar and secondary institution that was established in 1696 by an act of the Maryland General Assembly for "Propagation of the Gospel and the Education of the Youth of this Province in Good Letters and Manners." The alumni of St. John's include Francis Scott Key and George Washington's step-grandson and two nephews.

Work on the building that now is McDowell Hall began in 1742, when Governor Thomas Bladen started construction of a new home to serve as his mansion. Originally conceived to have a central section with a wing on either side, the building soon proved to be too expensive for the colony to complete. Roofless, its unfinished walls exposed to the elements, the hulk became known as Bladen's Folly. It sat for more than 40 years before the site was given to a new college — St. John's College — chartered in the new state of Maryland in 1784. All the property and endowment of the King William School, including its library, were conveyed to the new college.

St. John's, with Washington College, became the first University of Maryland. Among the founders were four signers of the Declaration of Independence: William Paca, Charles Carroll, Thomas Stone and Samuel Chase. Five years after receiving its charter, St. John's began accepting students.

In 1789 the state completed reconstruction of the unfinished Bladen building for use as the main hall of the college and named it for the first president of St. John's, John McDowell. Until 1837, McDowell Hall was the only building on campus, and served as a dormitory, library, dining hall and classroom structure.

During the Civil War, the building was a headquarters for the Union Army Medical Corps, which used it as a hospital for exchanged prisoners. On February 20, 1909, the building was gutted by fire. In 1952 another fire, confined to the basement, brought about the replacement of the original wooden beams, which had been in place since 1744.

In 1989 the building was renovated to appear as it had when first completed in the late 18th century.

McDowell Hall was the only building at St. John's to be considered for depiction on the postal card. It is the third oldest academic building in continuous use in the United States, following the Sir Christopher Wren Building at William and Mary (which was shown on a Historic Preservation postal card in 1993) and Massachusetts Hall at Harvard.

Since 1937, St. John's has provided a unique unified all-required program built around the reading and discussion of more than 130 of the "great books" of the Western tradition, including the Bible and works by writers ranging from Euclid to Einstein, from Tacitus to Twain. The great books seminars are supplemented by mathematics, music and language classes called tutorials, and by science labs.

Enrollment at St. John's is limited to 400 undergraduates and 100 graduate students. With a ratio of one faculty member for every eight students, teachers and students work together in discussion groups. There are no final examinations, and grades are recorded only for the benefit of those planning graduate work. In 1964 a second campus was opened in Santa Fe, New Mexico.

The Design

To paint the image of McDowell Hall for the postal card indicium stamp, art director Howard Paine chose an experienced designer of Historic Preservation series cards: Harry Devlin.

Devlin is one of the nation's leading architectural artists. He specializes in paintings of 19th-century homes of the eastern United States. His work captures the profuse details of the so-called Romantic era, when domestic architecture was exuberant, expressive and diverse, with such indulgences as fanlights and sidelights, wrought-iron filigree, cupolas, pillars and octagonal rooms.

His first painting for USPS was for the American Papermaking postal card of 1990 and depicted the old Rittenhouse paper mill in Germantown, Pennsylvania. Since then he has painted three other buildings for Historic Preservation cards: the Old Mill at the University of Vermont, Massachusetts Hall at Bowdoin College, and St. Louis Union Station.

Devlin's oil painting of McDowell Hall was based on color slides furnished by St. John's. It presents a straight-on view of the main entrance of the three-story square brick building with its green-hued cupola. Portions of two other campus buildings are seen in the background: Campbell Hall, a dormitory, on the left, and Randall Hall, a dining hall and dormitory, on the right. The time is twilight, with a yellow glow above the horizon that grades into a deep blue sky overhead.

The large tree in the left foreground, framing the picture, is actually much closer to the building than Devlin painted it. It's so close, in fact, a college spokesperson said, that it poses a problem for photographers, who can't command the artistic license to move it that was available to Devlin.

The Postal Service usually requires designers to provide art that is no more than five times stamp size, but Devlin is permitted to exceed those parameters for his postal card work. "We always know when another Harry Devlin painting comes through the door because it's so big," says Terrence McCaffrey, head of stamp design for USPS. Devlin does his buildings in painstaking detail, with windowpanes, brickwork and other small visual elements faithfully reproduced.

First-Day Facts

The McDowell Hall card was dedicated June 1 as part of a larger outdoor ceremony held to dedicate the college's new Greenfield Library.

Appropriately, the ceremony began with the singing of the National Anthem, written by Francis Scott Key, class of 1796, by Aaron Silverman, class of 1996.

Speakers included Christopher B. Nelson, president of St. John's College; Stewart Greenfield of the Board of Visitors and Governors; and Kathryn Kinzer, head librarian of St. John's.

The new Greenfield Library, home of the college's collection of some 90,000 books, was built with a gift from Stewart Greenfield, a 1953 graduate, and his wife, Constance Greenfield.

20¢ ALEXANDER HALL POSTAL CARD
HISTORIC PRESERVATION SERIES

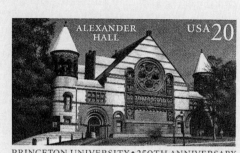

Date of Issue: September 20, 1996

Catalog Number: Scott UX263

Colors: black, cyan, magenta, yellow

First-Day Cancel: Princeton, New Jersey

First-Day Cancellations: 11,621

Format: Cards printed in 80-subject press sheets but available only as single-cut cards. Offset printing plates of 80 subjects (8 across, 10 down).

Size: 5½ by 3½ inches

Marking: "© 1996 USPS." "recycled" and recycled symbol.

Designer: Howard Koslow of Toms River, New Jersey

Typographer: John Boyd, Anagraphics Inc., New York, New York

Art Director: Derry Noyes

Project Manager: Vance Harris, USPS

Card Manufacturing: Cards printed by the Government Printing Office in Washington, D.C., on an offset 5-color MAN Roland sheetfed press. Cards processed and shipped by GPO.

Quantity Ordered and Distributed: 20,000,000

Tagging: vertical bar to right of stamp

The Postal Card

On September 20, USPS issued a postal card in its Historic Preservation series to commemorate the 250th anniversary of the founding of Princeton University in Princeton, New Jersey. The indicium stamp bore a picture of Alexander Hall, one of the university's landmark buildings.

400

The card had its origin in 1993 when Dorothy L. Bedford, Princeton '78, became executive director of the university's 250th anniversary steering committee. In consulting with other colleges and universities that had celebrated or were celebrating major anniversaries, Bedford learned that some of them had successfully petitioned the Postal Service for postal recognition. For example, Harvard University had gotten a 56¢ Great Americans stamp picturing its namesake, John Harvard, for its 350th anniversary in 1986, and the University of Chicago and the College of William and Mary had received Historic Preservation postal cards for their 1991 centennial and 1993 tercentenary, respectively.

Encouraged by these examples, Bedford wrote to USPS on behalf of the steering committee asking for a stamp for Princeton in 1996. The request was turned down. It wasn't until later that she learned of the Citizens' Stamp Advisory Committee's policy, adopted in 1987, specifying that postal recognition of a university's anniversary shall be limited to a Historic Preservation card picturing "an appropriate building on the campus."

Bedford and the committee then refined their request. They asked for a postal card that would depict the south facade of Nassau Hall, the historic centerpiece of the campus that was bombarded during the Battle of Princeton in the American Revolution and later, from June until November 1783, was home to the Continental Congress and thus in effect the capitol of the United States.

But this request also was rejected. The explanation given by the Postal Service was that Nassau Hall already had been postally honored. It was depicted on a 3¢ stamp in 1956 — printed, appropriately, in the university's colors, orange and black — that commemorated the building's 200th anniversary (Scott 1083).

"I was not daunted," Bedford said with a laugh.

She and the committee set out to rally support for their cause. In the spring of 1994 she placed notices in the student newspaper and the alumni weekly asking readers to write to CSAC on behalf of a postal card for Princeton. She also contacted alumni who held, or had held, high political office, seeking their endorsement.

One of these was Brendan T. Byrne, who had been governor of New Jersey from 1974 to 1982. Byrne wrote to President Clinton — a Yale

The 200th anniversary of Princeton University's Nassau Hall in 1956 was commemorated by this 3¢ stamp (Scott 1083), black on orange paper, designed by Victor S. McCloskey Jr.

Law School graduate — asking for help. Conceding in his letter that Nassau Hall had gotten a stamp in 1956, Byrne continued:

"This time it may be more difficult. The Post Office is independent, the stamp way more expensive, and everybody in Washington is from Yale.

"Still, I believe you have compassion and influence and so impose on you as an old friend and dynamic leader to intervene on behalf of a project to get a stamp (sic) for our 250th. I am sure Woodrow Wilson would have done the same for Yale." Wilson had been president of Princeton before becoming the nation's chief executive.

Clinton, in a return letter signed "Bill," made no commitment, but said he had forwarded the request to CSAC. "It is always a pleasure to hear from you," the president told Byrne.

Whatever the effect of the presidential attention to the matter may have been, the next decision by Bedford and her associates was the key one. It was to seek out and contact a member of CSAC who might be sympathetic to their cause.

Finding no Princeton alumnus or parent on the committee, the Princetonians next looked for "professional connections." Bedford identified the CSAC members who were active in the art world and showed the list to the director of the university art museum, who recommended that she contact C. Douglas Lewis, curator of sculpture at the National Gallery of Art and vice chairman of CSAC.

Lewis proved to be the ideal choice. Although he is another of the capital's Yale men, he had attended prep school in Lawrenceville, New Jersey, a few miles from Princeton, and was familiar with the university's campus and its architectural attractions. With his encouragement, Bedford and her committee reviewed the university's buildings, looking for those with the kind of architecture and history that would appeal to CSAC.

They ended up with three possibilities.

Nassau Hall had to be included because of its intimate association with the university from its earliest years. One problem, however, was that it resembled several other buildings shown on Historic Preservation cards in recent years, and Lewis warned that it might be difficult to sell CSAC on "another colonial brown shoebox," as he put it, for the series.

Another candidate was the university's graduate college, with its soaring Gothic tower that was named for President Grover Cleveland (who spent the last years of his life as a resident of the borough of Princeton) and built with funds donated by the public as a memorial to him.

Finally, there was Alexander Hall, which Lewis believed would be a strong contender because buildings of its style — Romanesque Revival — had been underrepresented on Historic Preservation postal cards.

With Lewis' strong support, CSAC approved the postal card. Surprisingly, the committee endorsed all three of the buildings nominated, and in effect left it up to the artist, Howard Koslow, and art director, Derry Noyes, in consultation with university officials, to decide which would make the best design. The consensus winner was Alexander Hall.

As the Postal Service had done with the Winter Scene and McDowell Hall postal cards issued earlier in the year, it sent the Alexander Hall card to the Government Printing Office in two sets of color separations, one with the 20¢ denomination, the other to cover the 21¢ rate that USPS hoped for but didn't get.

Princeton University was founded by education-minded Presbyterian ministers and chartered in October 1746 as the College of New Jersey. British North America's fourth college, it was first located in Elizabeth and later in Newark. It moved to Princeton in 1756, where it was housed in the newly built Nassau Hall, which contained the entire college for nearly half a century.

The school officially adopted the name "Princeton University" at the time of its sesquicentennial in 1896. Five years later, in 1901, the Graduate School was established.

Fully coeducational since 1969, Princeton in 1995-96 enrolled 6,419 students (4,609 undergraduates and 1,810 graduate students) who were taught by a faculty of 940.

Today, Princeton's main campus in Princeton Borough and Princeton Township covers 300 acres. The university's James Forrestal Campus in nearby Plainsboro adds another four complexes set on 340 acres.

Although much younger than Nassau Hall, Alexander Hall is also steeped in history. It was given to Princeton by Harriet Crocker Alexander to honor her husband's family, of which three generations had served Princeton as trustees. Construction began in 1891, and the building was formally dedicated in June 1894 at that year's commencement exercises.

In 1902 the building was the site of Woodrow Wilson's inauguration as president of the university. It later served as the site for the Stafford Little Lectures given by ex-President Cleveland. Dozens of men and women famous in politics, science, literature, the arts and other fields have spoken from its rostrum.

For 30 years, freshmen were welcomed and seniors graduated in Alexander Hall, but by 1922 commencement exercises had outgrown the building and threafter were held in front of Nassau Hall. A long-time practice of the university was to post all final course grades for all classes inside the building, where every student's grades became public knowledge. Thus, "Alexander Hall was the scene of much elation and heartache over the decades," Dorothy Bedford said.

Today, the building's Richardson Auditorium serves as the home of most of Princeton's performing-arts organizations.

Alexander Hall was designed by William A. Potter in Richardson Romanesque style, named for the great American architect Henry Hobson Richardson. Among its noteworthy features are the richly ornamented southeast facade, shown on the postal card; the four rounded towers capped by conical roofs, and the hall's massive, arcaded ambulatory, which describes a bulging curve on the north facade. Richardson Romanesque motifs are evident in Potter's use of light-brown granite trimmed in dark brownstone; the enormous, rounded arches; the geometric pattern under the eaves and across the gables; the high-pitched roof, originally red tiled; and the prominent dormers.

Several Princeton graduates have been depicted on U.S. stamps. These include two presidents, James Madison, class of 1771, and Woodrow Wilson, 1879. Other stamp subjects have been John Foster Dulles '08, Adlai Stevenson '22 and F. Scott Fitzgerald '17. Thornton Wilder (graduate school 1925-26) is scheduled for a stamp in 1997. John Witherspoon, an early president of Princeton College and a signer of the Declaration of Independence, was shown on a 9¢ postal card of 1975.

Nassau Hall, besides being featured on the 1956 stamp, can also be seen in the distance on a 13¢ stamp issued in 1977 to commemorate the bicentennial of the Battle of Princeton and depicting Charles Willson Peale's painting of George Washington in the midst of that engagement. The centennial of the first intercollegiate football game, between Princeton and Rutgers, was marked by a 6¢ stamp in 1969.

Princeton University also has a footnote in philatelic history because a block of four inverted Jenny airmail stamps (Scott C3a) is named for it. The "Princeton block," one of the few surviving multiples of the Jenny invert, was owned by the university from 1947 until 1976, when it was sold at auction for $170,000. In 1979 it was sold again for $500,000, which at that time was the highest price ever paid for a philatelic item.

The Design

Howard Koslow of Toms River, New Jersey, the designer of several previous U.S. stamps and Historic Preservation postal cards, was chosen to make the painting that would appear on the Princeton postal card.

In July 1995, Koslow drove to the Princeton campus and, with Dorothy Bedford, examined and photographed the three nominated buildings: Nassau Hall, Cleveland Memorial Tower and Alexander Hall. Bedford also turned over to him her own collection of photographs she had made of the buildings at various times of the year to help document Princeton's formal bid for a postal card.

Koslow prepared a color sketch of Alexander Hall and made pencil sketches of the other two buildings for art director Derry Noyes to show CSAC. The committee quickly ratified their choice of Alexander Hall.

"The problem with Nassau Hall was that you can't really see the building well because of the abundance of trees," Koslow said. "And, of course, it had been done before on a stamp. Cleveland Tower is a Gothic tower with a long, low building at right angles to it, so you get a giant L-shape, which isn't an ideal shape to work with for a horizontal stamp design. So we were left with Alexander Hall, and we were all very pleased with it."

Koslow delivered his finished painting in November 1995. Done in acrylic on illustration board, it shows the broad southeast facade of the building, with the sunlight illuminating its varying shades of brownstone. Among the distinctive features of this facade are a Tiffany rose window

404

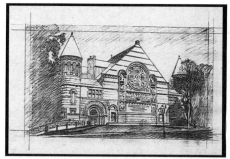

These are the three buildings that made the finals in the process of selecting a subject for Princeton University's postal card, as shown in pencil sketches by Howard Koslow: Alexander Hall, the building ultimately chosen for the card; Nassau Hall, the oldest and best-known structure on the campus; and the Graduate School's Gothic tower, named for President Grover Cleveland.

with four stained-glass roundels representing Study, Genius, Knowledge and Fame, and a gallery of brownstone figures by J. Massey Rhind. At the center is the seated figure of Learning, which is flanked by sculptures representing the arts, language, theology, law, history, mathematics and the sciences.

In Koslow's painting, three people are seen emerging from the arched entrance on the right side, and another person precedes them. "I felt they were necessary," Koslow said. "A picture of a building like that gets a little cold if you don't have some life in it."

A comparison of the painting with the actual postal card shows that the colors — the browns of the building, the green of the foliage and the blue of the sky — became darker and lost some of their brilliance in the translation of the artwork to the Government Printing Office's offset press.

The typography on the card consists of the words "PRINCETON UNIVERSITY • 250TH ANNIVERSARY" in black letters below the indicium stamp and "ALEXANDER HALL" within the image, dropped out of the blue sky.

First-Day Facts

The card was dedicated by William P. Bennett, Princeton '68, the Postal Service's chief counsel for purchasing, at the September 20 ceremony at Alexander Hall. Speakers were Harold T. Shapiro, president of Princeton University; Raymond T. Murphy, USPS district manager; and CSAC's C. Douglas Lewis.

Princeton alumnus Edward Tenner, writing in *The Guardian* of London, wrote that Lewis "stole the show" by delivering "without a prepared text a thumbnail history of 19th-century American academic architecture so urbane, effortlessly learned, and graceful that the audience did not mind his observation that Princeton chose Richardsonian Romanesque at the very end of its 15-year life, four years after Yale built its Osborne Hall." "After all," Tenner added, "Yale demolished Osborne 70 years ago, but Princeton has Alexander Hall and a postal card."

Dorothy Bedford introduced the guests, and Victor M. Zuczek, postmaster of Princeton, gave the welcome. Honored guests were Howard Koslow and Burton G. Malkiel, who chaired the 250th anniversary steering committee.

Two photographs of Alexander Hall, one of the southeast facade that Howard Koslow painted for the postal card, the other of the architecturally less-interesting north facade with northwest clerestory.
(Photos by Dorothy Bedford)

20¢ ENDANGERED SPECIES PICTURE POSTAL CARDS (15 DESIGNS)

Date of Issue: October 2, 1996

Price: $11.95 per set

Catalog Numbers: Scott UX264-UX278 (single cards); UX278a (booklet of 20)

Colors: black, cyan, magenta, yellow

First-Day Cancel: San Diego, California

First-Day Cancellations: 5,000 (cancellations applied by Philatelic Sales Division, Kansas City, Missouri, after which cards were returned to manufacturer for binding)

Format: Cards bound into booklets of 15 different varieties, 3 varieties to a page, arranged vertically, with rouletting for separating cards from each other and from illustrated vertical tab on left side. Offset printing plates made up of an introduction page and 5 pages of 3 cards each. Front cover printed separately with 4-color printing, embossing and two die-cut windows to show reproductions of 3 Endangered Species stamps on introduction page.

Size of Cards: 6 by 4 inches

Size of Booklet: 8 by 12 inches

Card Markings: "ENDANGERED SPECIES" and descriptive paragraph on message side of each card

Booklet Markings, Front Cover: "ENDANGERED SPECIES POSTAL CARDS."

Booklet Markings, Back Cover: "UNITED STATES/POSTAL SERVICE" and USPS logo. "© 1996 U.S. Postal Service. All Rights Reserved./To obtain additional information on Commemorative Stamps/and Stamp Products available from the U.S. Postal Service,/please write to:/Stamps, etc./U.S. Postal Service/P.O. Box 57,/Grand Rapids, MN 55744-0057/or/Visit our web site at http://www.stampsonline.com/All photographs except fern image: © James Balog;/Fern image provided by © 1996 PhotoDisc, Inc./James Balog uses the Mamiya 645 Pro with Mamiya Sekor lens."

Booklet Markings, Inside: On introduction page: "ENDANGERED/SPECIES/ Throughout the world, many species of plants and animals are endangered. This means that their ability to thrive or sustain viable natural populations is in jeopardy, and that extinction of the species is a real possibility. Species have become endangered from a variety of causes, including natural selection, diseases, and catastrophes. Today, the primary cause is man's encroachment into these animals' habitats." On second page: "As our own population grows, we expand into previously undisturbed areas and put increased pressure on natural resources. Fragile ecosystems, such as wetlands, deserts, and rain forests, become polluted or are cleared for man's use. This not only mars the pristine beauty of these environments, but it also adversely affects the species which call these areas home. Many animals have very specific needs and cannot survive elsewhere. Once their habitats are gone, the species are gone — forever. There are no easy answers. But, as the only species with the ability to protect and help the existence of all others, mankind is obligated to try. We must educate ourselves about our planet, its resources, and its inhabitants. As part of this effort, the United States Postal Service is proud to issue this set of postal cards honoring 15 of our country's most endangered species."

Designer (Photographer): James Balog of Boulder, Colorado

Stamp Typographer and Art Director: Richard Sheaff

Card and Booklet Designer: Supon Design Group, Washington, D.C.

Card Project Manager: Andrew Gunn Wilinski, USPS

Card Manufacturing: Cards printed by the Art Litho Company, Baltimore, Maryland, on 40-inch Planeta 5- and 6-color offset presses. Cards processed, bound and shipped by Art Litho.

Quantity Ordered and Distributed: 1,500,000 cards (100,000 booklets)

Tagging: vertical bar to right of stamp

The Cards

The second set of picture postal cards of 1996 was an unexpected addition to the year's postal stationery program.

Collectors had anticipated the previous set of cards, which was issued May 2 to accompany the 20 Centennial Olympic Games stamps that were issued on that date. The Olympic stamps were part of the Classic Collections series, and each of the sets in that series has come with a matching set of picture postal cards.

But the hobby was caught by surprise when matching cards also were issued for the 15 Endangered Species stamps of October 2, whose images were based on photographs taken by noted wildlife photographer James Balog. The Endangered Species set was not a part of the Classic Collections series.

Like the Olympic Games cards, the 15 Endangered Species cards were bound together in book form and could only be purchased in that form. The price of a book was $11.95, making the cost of each individual card $79^2/_3$¢, or nearly 60¢ over its 20¢ face value — a new record for a pre-

The Endangered Species postal cards are laid out on five pages, with three cards stacked on each page.

mium charged on a U.S. postage item. (The previous record, which was short-lived, had been the 45¢ surcharge that USPS had gotten for the 20¢ Olympics Games cards.)

The cards themselves are 6 inches long by 4 inches deep, considerably larger than the normal postal card size of 5½ by 3½ inches. They are laid out on five pages, with three cards stacked on each page. The cards can be separated from each other, and from the vertical tab that attaches them to the book, by tearing along rouletted lines. The size of the book and of the individual pages is 8 inches by 12 inches.

The cover of the book reproduces four of Balog's stamp photographs: the Schaus swallowtail butterfly, thick-billed parrot, San Francisco garter snake and Florida panther. The latter two images are embossed, to make the creatures "pop out at you," explained the project manager for the postal

Shown here are the picture sides of one page of cards.

410

cards, Andrew L. Gunn Wilinski. There are two die-cut windows in the cover, through which can be seen three stamp reproductions on the introduction page: the black-footed ferret, American crocodile and Gila trout.

Like the Classic Collections postal cards sets, this one was manufactured by Art Litho Company of Baltimore, Maryland. The printed and bound cards then were sent to Minnesota Diversified Industries in St. Paul, Minnesota, to be shrink-wrapped.

And like the Olympic Games cards, the Endangered Species cards were produced by the stamp and product marketing section of the Stamp Services office, rather than by the stamp development section, which normally is responsible for creating all stamps and postal stationery.

The Supon Design Group of Washington, D.C., designed the Endangered Species cards and booklet, as it had done with the Centennial Olympic Games set. The booklet text was written by a Supon Design Group staffer and edited by USPS project manager Wilinski. Wilinski wrote the brief descriptive paragraphs printed on the message sides of the postal cards from information furnished by the U.S. Fish and Wildlife Service.

"I thought that arranging the cards this way (in a booklet, three to a page) would appeal to people who were interested in stamp collecting and in the topic itself, endangered species," Wilinski said. "I thought the format would especially appeal to kids, who love animals."

One of the previous Classic Collections postal card sets, the 1995 Civil War set, had contained two typographical errors, including a highly visible one: the name of the Confederate General Stand Watie misspelled "Waite" in 18-point type on the picture side. A similar embarrassing error marred the Endangered Species postal cards.

On the picture side of the card depicting the Schaus Swallowtail butterfly, the last-mentioned word is misspelled "Butterly" in prominent capital letters. On the imprinted stamp design on the address side, "butterfly" is correctly spelled. The Postal Service was unaware of the mistake until *Linn's Stamp News*, alerted to it by three of its readers, published a story about it in its November 18 issue.

During the preprinting stage, "everybody and their mother" had looked at the misspelled word, Wilinski said. "And no one caught it." By the time USPS learned of the error, the booklets were in circulation.

"We thought about going back and reprinting it," Wilinski said. "But there was no error on the stamp portion, and reprinting it would have created a big rarity, which would have been unfair. So we decided against that."

Distribution of the Endangered Species postal cards was slow and spotty. They were unavailable at the Philatelic Fulfillment Service Center or at the philatelic window at USPS headquarters in Washington, D.C., for several weeks after the nominal issue date of October 2, and philatelic windows around the country had to specifically order them, as they do with other products of the stamp and product marketing office. However, postal retail stores received an automatic distribution, Wilinski said.

The Designs

Because of the larger size and glossy finish of the cards, the details in Balog's photography and the subtleties of his lighting are much more striking on the cards' picture sides than they are on the equivalent postage stamps. Such elements as the texture of the scaly skins of the American

413

crocodile and the Wyoming toad, and the swirl of bubbles surrounding the Gila trout, have a particular visual effectiveness on the postal cards.

Not all of the picture sides of these cards use the same photographs on which the corresponding postage stamps or indicium stamps were based. The picture sides of the Piping Plover and Florida Manatee cards display different Balog photographs. The change was made for "graphic design and layout" considerations, according to project manager Wilinski. In addition, several of the creatures on the picture sides are shown against white backgrounds instead of the tinted or natural backgrounds used on the stamps, and a few have been given artificial shadows that don't exist in Balog's photographs.

The indicium stamps on the postal cards are dull and poorly reproduced. They are smaller than the picture areas of the corresponding postage stamps, being only 1³/₁₆ inches wide by ⅞ inch deep compared to 1¹³/₃₂ inches wide by 1¹/₃₂ inches deep for the stamps. Much of the detail of the pictures has been lost in the printing process, and the typography lacks clarity. The indicium stamps are outlined in black, unlike the postage stamp designs, which have no outlines.

First-Day Facts

Details on the San Diego first-day ceremony can be found in the chapter on the Endangered Species stamps.

Because of the difficulty experienced by collectors in obtaining the postal cards, the Postal Service unofficially extended the grace period for submitting cards for first-day postmarks beyond the announced 30 days.

USPS sold booklets of the Endangered Species postal cards with first-day cancellations for $13.95.

ENDANGERED SPECIES

Wyoming toad – *Bufo hemiophrys baxteri*
The wetlands of southeastern Wyoming's Laramie River basin are the only natural habitat of the Wyoming toad. Believed extinct, about 100 individuals were found in 1987. Unlike other toads, the Wyoming toad spends most of its time in and around water. It preys on insects, larvae, and other small organisms.

WYOMING TOAD

ENDANGERED SPECIES

Woodland caribou – *Rangifer tarandus caribou*
The harsh, mountainous terrain of the Washington-Idaho border is the home of the U.S.'s "endangered" woodland caribou. Healthy populations exist in Alaska and British Columbia. Dense forests provide this hoofed animal with food and shelter. Tall, widely spread antlers and a shaggy mane beneath the neck characterize the male of the species.

WOODLAND CARIBOU

ENDANGERED SPECIES

California condor – *Gymnogyps californianus*
North America's largest bird, the California condor may weigh 20 pounds and have a wingspan of 10 feet. A triangular patch of white on the underside of each wing is visible only in flight. The condor is a scavenger, feeding on the carcasses of dead animals such as deer, elk, cattle, and pronghorn—which it can spot from high in the sky.

CALIFORNIA CONDOR

CAPEX 96 SOUVENIR CARD (BEP)

Date of Issue: June 8, 1996

Catalog Number: Scott 148

Colors: Offset: gold (overall background), yellow (stamp background), green (vignette enlargement and canceling lines), brown (titles, outlines), black (back text); foil stamp and embossing: gold metallic (title bar); intaglio: green (block of stamps).

First-Day Release: Capex 96, Toronto, Ontario, Canada, and Bureau of Engraving and Printing Visitors Center, Washington, D.C.

Size: 10 by 8 inches

Conceptual Design: Steve Manset (Bureau of Engraving and Printing)

Art Director: Leonard Buckley (BEP)

Typographer: Howard Brown (BEP)

Modeler: Brian Thompson (BEP)

Card Stock: white, Poseidon perfect

Card Manufacturing: 6-color sheetfed Miller offset press; Kluge letterpress for foil and embossing; intaglio die-stamping press

Quantity Printed: 8,500

The Card

The Bureau of Engraving and Printing issued its first philatelic souvenir card of the year June 8 to honor CAPEX 96, the World Philatelic Exhibition in Toronto, Ontario, Canada. CAPEX was held from June 8 to June 16 at the Metro Toronto Convention Center.

The card was one of seven philatelic and numismatic souvenir cards issued by BEP in 1996. The Bureau called this series of cards "The Era of Silver and Gold."

The CAPEX card featured a block of four intaglio die impressions of the 50¢ stamp in the Bureau's 1898 commemorative series honoring the Trans-Mississippi Exposition held that year in Omaha, Nebraska (Scott 291). The impressions were printed in sage green, the color of the original stamp. A green diagonal "cancellation" line was printed by the offset process across the lower-right corner of each stamp.

The background image on the souvenir card consisted of an enlargement of the stamp vignette, printed in green by offset. The vignette, enclosed in a shield-shaped frame and labeled "Western Mining Prospector," shows a bearded gold-seeker, pickax in hand, standing in a barren landscape. Two pack mules are beside him, and a dog lies wearily on the ground at the rear, tongue extended.

The inscription "THE ERA OF SILVER & GOLD" is contained in an embossed bar of gold foil across the top of the stamp. Beneath the bar, printed by offset in gold-colored ink, are the words "CAPEX '96/Toronto, Canada • June 1996."

On the back of the card is explanatory text: "A prospector diligently searching for gold is featured in this engraving of a 50¢ stamp issued in 1898 to commemorate the Trans-Mississippi and International Exposition in Omaha. The engraving (Post Office die #284) was taken from a Frederic Remington drawing, 'The Gold Bug.' G.F.C. Smillie engraved the picture, M.W. Baldwin did the ornamental framework and D.S. Ronaldson did the lettering and numerals."

The CAPEX card was the second BEP souvenir card to reproduce a block of four of the 50¢ Trans-Mississippi stamp from the original die. The first, produced in 1986, honored LOBEX 86, the annual exhibition of the Long Beach, California, Stamp Club. When the Bureau made the plate for the LOBEX card, it deleted from the die impressions the numerals and words that designated the stamp's denomination, as it did with all its souvenir cards prior to 1987.

Mint CAPEX cards were sold at the show for $5. They were also available at the Bureau's Visitors Center in Washington for $5 mint and $5.30 stamped and canceled. Prices for mail-ordered cards were $6.50 mint and $6.80 canceled.

1996-97 DUCK STAMP SOUVENIR CARD
U.S. FISH AND WILDLIFE SERVICE

Date of Issue: June 27, 1996

Catalog Number: none

Colors: Offset: magenta, yellow, cyan, black, green (duck stamp illustration), green (background), black (back text); foil stamp: gold (agency seals)

First-Day Release: June 27, 1996, Washington, D.C. Second-day release: June 29, 1996, Basking Ridge, New Jersey.

Size: 10 by 8 inches

Conceptual Design and Art Direction: Leonard Buckley (Bureau of Engraving and Printing)

Typographer: Howard Brown (BEP)

Modeler: Brian Thompson (BEP)

Card Stock: white, Poseidon perfect

Card Manufacturing: 6-color sheetfed Miller offset press; Kluge letterpress for foil stamping

Quantity Printed: 10,000 (750 numbered in gold)

The Card

In 1996, for the 10th consecutive year, the Bureau of Engraving and Printing produced a souvenir card bearing an offset-printed replica of that year's federal duck stamp. The sponsor was the U.S. Fish and Wildlife Service's Federal Duck Stamp Program, and all proceeds, after deduction of printing and marketing costs, went to buy wetlands for the National Wildlife Refuge System.

The card bore an enlarged full-color replica of the 1996 duck stamp, with simulated perforations around the stamp's edges, against a teal stone background. The stamp's design was based on Wilhelm J. Goebel's contest-winning oil painting of a pair of surf scoters in flight. On the front, the card reproduced the signatures and the agency seals or logos of Bruce Babbitt, secretary of the Interior, and Mollie Beattie, director of the Fish and Wildlife Service. It also carried a replica of artist Goebel's signature.

Printed on the back is a lengthy text, set in three columns. The first section gives the history of the Federal Duck Stamp Program, the second section explains the Federal Duck Stamp Licensing Program, and the third section describes the Federal Junior Duck Stamp Conservation and Design Program.

Ten thousand cards were printed. These cards, which came with a specimen of the $15 duck stamp, were sold for varying prices. A $5 shipping fee was charged for all orders.

The least expensive items were 8,250 cards without serial numbers or cancellations, which cost $20 each. With these, the duck stamp was included in a separate glassine envelope.

The remaining 1,750 cards each had a duck stamp and two 32¢ Smithsonian Institution Sesquicentennial postage stamps affixed; the stamps were tied with Goebel-designed pictorial first-day cancellations from Washington, D.C., where the cards went on sale June 27, and Basking Ridge, New Jersey, where they first were sold June 29. Of the canceled cards, 1,000 bore no numbers and sold for $25 each, and 750 were numbered in gold and sold for $150 each (numbers 1 through 10), $75 each (11 through 100) or $50 each (101 through 750). Unnumbered cards could be obtained with the autograph of the artist for an additional $2.

OLYMPHILEX 96 SOUVENIR CARD (BEP)

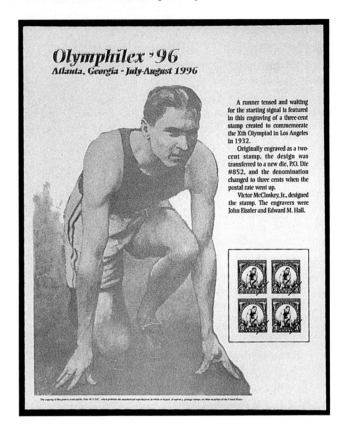

Date of Issue: July 19, 1996

Catalog Number: unassigned

Colors: Offset: gray (illustration), black (text, stamp frame and canceling lines); foil stamp and embossing: gold metallic (title); intaglio; purple (block of stamps)

First-Day Release: Olymphilex 96, Atlanta, Georgia, and Bureau of Engraving and Printing Visitors Center, Washington, D.C.

Size: 10 by 8 inches

Conceptual Design: Steve Manset (Bureau of Engraving and Printing)

Art Director: Leonard Buckley (BEP)

Typographer: Howard Brown (BEP)

Modeler: Peter Cocci (BEP)

Card Stock: ivory, artificial parchment

Card Manufacturing: 6-color sheetfed Miller offset press; Kluge letterpress for foil and embossing; intaglio die-stamping press

Quantity Printed: 8,500

The Card

The second philatelic souvenir card issued by the Bureau of Engraving and Printing in 1996 honored Olymphilex 96, the World Olympic and Sports Stamp Exhibition. Olymphilex 96 was held at the Merchandise Mart in Atlanta, Georgia, July 19 to August 3, during the staging of the Centennial Olympic Games in Atlanta.

The card featured a block of four intaglio die impressions of the U.S. 3¢ stamp of 1932 that commemorated the summer games of the Tenth Olympiad, held in Los Angeles, California (Scott 718). The stamp was part of a set of two; the other stamp bore a 5¢ denomination, which met the then-current international rate.

The impressions on the souvenir card were printed in reddish violet, approximating the color of the original stamp. A black diagonal "cancellation" line was printed by offset across the lower-right corner of each die impression.

The background image on the souvenir card consisted of an enlargement of the model, made by Victor S. McCloskey Jr. of the Bureau, from which the vignette of the stamp was engraved. This model consisted of a photograph of sprinter J. Alfred "Alf" Leconey of Lafayette College in Pennsylvania, on which McCloskey had made artistic revisions in the features to comply with the requirement that no living person should be shown on a U.S. stamp. The photograph reportedly was taken at the 1924 Olympic Games in Paris, where Leconey anchored the U.S. 4 x 100-meter relay team to a gold-medal victory in the then-world record time of 41 seconds flat. (In that race the runner-up team from Great Britain had as its leadoff man Harold Abrahams, whose story was told in the Academy Award-winning film *Chariots of Fire*.)

The text on the card reads as follows:

"A runner tensed and waiting for the starting signal is featured in this engraving of a three-cent stamp created to commemorate the Xth Olympiad in Los Angeles in 1932.

"Originally engraved as a two-cent stamp, the design was transferred to a new die, P.O. Die #852, and the denomination changed to three cents when the postal rate went up.

"Victor McCloskey, Jr., designed the stamp. The engravers were John Eissler and Edward M. Hall."

(The stamp was issued June 15, 1932, three weeks before the new 3¢ first-class rate took effect on July 6.)

The inscription "Olymphilex '96/Atlanta, Georgia • July-August 1996" is die-stamped in gold foil at the top of the card. Along the bottom, in small type, is this admonition: "The copying of this print is restricted by Title 18, U.S.C., which prohibits the unauthorized reproduction, in whole or in part, of currency, postage stamps, or other securities of the United States."

Mint Olymphilex cards were sold at the show for $5. They were also available at the Bureau's Visitors Center in Washington for $5 mint and $5.30 stamped and canceled. Prices for mail-ordered cards were $6.50 mint and $6.80 canceled.

Date of Issue: October 19, 1996

Catalog Number: unassigned

Colors: Offset: silver (overall background), yellow (stamp background), gray (vignette enlargement and cancelling lines), gray (titles, outlines), black (back text); foil stamp and embossing: silver metallic (title bar); intaglio: gray (block of stamps).

First Day Release: Billings Stamp Club Show, Billings, Montana, and Bureau of Engraving and Printing Visitors Center

Size: 10 by 8 inches

Conceptual Design: Steve Manset (Bureau of Engraving and Printing)

Art Director: Leonard Buckley (BEP)

Typographer: Howard Brown (BEP)

Modeler: Brian Thompson (BEP)

Card Stock: white, Poseidon perfect

Card Manufacturing: 6-color sheetfed Miller offset press; Kluge letterpress for foil and embossing; intaglio die-stamping press

Quantity Printed: 8,500

The Card

The Bureau of Engraving and Printing issued its third and final phila-telic souvenir card of 1996 in connection with the Billings Stamp Club Show at the West Park Plaza in Billings, Montana, October 19 and 20. Like the first card of the year, for CAPEX 96, it was part of a series that the Bureau called "The Era of Silver and Gold."

The Billings card features a block of four intaglio die impressions of a 4¢ stamp issued in 1959 to commemorate the centennial of the discovery of silver at the Comstock Lode in Nevada (Scott 1130). The impressions are printed in gray, the color of the original stamp. A gray diagonal "can-cellation" line printed by the offset process crosses the lower right corner of each stamp.

The background image on the souvenir card consists of an enlargement of the stamp vignette, printed in gray by offset. The inscription "THE ERA OF SILVER & GOLD" is contained in an embossed bar of silver foil across the top of the stamp. Beneath the bar, printed by offset in gray, are the words "Billings Stamp Club/Billings, Montana • October 1996."

The text on the back of the card describes the vignette: "The meeting of prospectors Henry Comstock, Peter O'Riley, and Patrick McLaughlin upon discovery of the rich Comstock Lode of gold and silver in Nevada in 1859 is depicted in this engraving of a 4-cent Silver Centennial commemora-tive stamp issued in 1959. Designers of the stamp were Robert L. Miller and William Schrage. Post Office die #1440 was engraved by Charles A. Brooks and Robert J. Jones."

Mint Billings cards were sold at the show for $5. They were also avail-able at the Bureau's Visitors Center in Washington for $5 mint and $5.30 stamped and cancelled. Prices for mail-ordered cards were $6.50 mint and $6.80 canceled.

Varieties

32¢ Comic Strip Classics pane (1995)

The Comic Strip Classics pane of 20 varieties, issued in 1995 as part of the Classic Collections series, has been found in two different part-perforate configurations.

In one configuration — listed in the Scott catalog as 3000u — the top eight stamps are imperforate and the four stamps spread horizontally in the center of the pane are only partly perforated.

The other is just the opposite. While the center four stamps have perforations along the top with part of one perforation extending down vertically between each, the bottom eight stamps on the pane are imperforate.

On the latter, the plate position diagram in the lower-left corner indicates that the pane came from the lower left of the six positions on the press sheet at the printer, Stamp Venturers.

Dealer Jacques C. Schiff Jr. sold the second pane in his February 6-7, 1997, auction for $2,200, plus the 10-percent buyer's commission. Schiff said the pane was brought to his attention by a dealer in New York state, but it isn't known exactly where or when it was discovered.

Two different part-perforate panes of the 1995 Comic Strip Classics stamps are known. In this configuration, the bottom eight stamps are imperforate.

This is the imperforate "Royal Favor Restored" souvenir sheet bearing reprints of the 6¢, 8¢ and $3 Columbians that surfaced in California.

Columbian souvenir sheet (1992)

An imperforate U.S. Columbian souvenir sheet from the set of six sheets issued in 1992 at World Columbian Stamp Expo in Chicago was discovered in California. The sheets, which were sold only in complete sets, contained reprinted stamps from the 1893 Columbian Exposition commemorative series, with the year dates changed from 1892 to 1992 and the colors approximating those of the originals. The error sheet was the "Royal Favor Restored" sheet bearing the 6¢, 8¢ and $3 stamp reprints and is listed in the Scott catalog as 2627d.

According to *Linn's Stamp News*, after the collector who — knowingly or unknowingly — had owned the error sheet died, his son went through his collection and discovered the error in a set containing five other normally perforated sheets. The son sold the sheet to a West Coast dealer, who in turn sold it to a dealer on the East Coast. That dealer consigned it to Weiss Philatelics in Bethlehem, Pennsylvania. Weiss offered it at auction September 21 with a $7,500 reserve price, but the lot didn't sell, and the sheet was returned to its owner.

American Bank Note Company, the producer of the souvenir sheets, perforated them off-line on a Bickel bull's-eye perforator. Because each of the six souvenir sheets was printed in large press sheets of 24, there could be up to 23 other imperforate specimens of the "Royal Favor Restored" sheet made, depending on the extent of the perforating malfunction.

15¢ Veterinary Medicine envelope (1979)

The American Philatelic Expertizing Service certified as genuine a previously unreported major color-omitted error on the 15¢ Veterinary Medicine stamped envelope issued July 24, 1979.

The normal version of the envelope is embossed, with printing in brown and gray inks. The envelope was released in four versions: regular size (number 6¾) and business size (number 10), each available plain or with window.

The error is a plain number 6¾ envelope that is completely missing the brown color of ink that printed the "15¢/USA" denomination and the group of five animals and a bird at the bottom left of the envelope. All that remains is the gray ink of the "V" and Caduceus crest in the top-right corner and in the inscription "Veterinary Medicine" along the bottom-left portion of the envelope.

In a previously reported major error of the Veterinary Medicine envelope, it was the gray color that was omitted. This brown-only variety, listed as Scott U595a, has a current Scott catalog value of $700. A completely unprinted version of the envelope, or so-called albino, also is known. It features only the embossed "V" and Caduceus crest in the top-right corner.

This shows the normal 15¢ Veterinary Medicine stamped envelope and the newly authenticated brown-omitted error.

32¢ Pink Rose self-adhesive (1995)

Panes of the 1995 Pink Rose self-adhesive stamps were found with horizontal pairs that lack the normal serpentine die cutting between them. The error panes bear the gravure cylinder number combination S444.

One such pane was shown to *Linn's Stamp News* by its owner, John Sampson of New Hampshire. It lacks vertical die cutting between the middle and right-hand vertical columns. The result is six pairs of stamps with no die cuts between them, plus a seventh such pair consisting of one stamp and the "Time to Reorder" label. They are the equivalent of imperforate-between errors on perforated stamps.

The pane has other unusual characteristics. It is formatted normally, but its right and bottom edges are die cut as well as sliced. For this pane and normal panes, it is slicing that separates them from the larger printing sheet or web.

The right-edge die cutting suggests that the die-cutting mechanism may have shifted one stamp row to the left (or the stamps may have shifted one stamp row to the right) when the stamps were die cut. The pane, however, seems to have been separated from adjoining panes with normal slices, and the "Time to Reorder" label's bull's-eye die cutting is positioned normally. The die-cutting at the bottom edge is a problem, *Linn's* wrote, be-

This is the bottom of the Pink Rose pane of 20 that was found with no vertical die cutting between the middle and right-hand vertical rows of the stamps. The pane is sliced normally, but it also has die cutting at the right and bottom edges, where die cutting isn't found on normal panes.

cause it apparently cannot be explained by an up or down shift of the die cutter or of the stamps; the horizontal die cuts for the pane's two selvage strips are in the right spots.

A possible explanation, *Linn's* wrote, is that the pane of 20 was made from stock that had been cut for the 32¢ Pink Rose panes of 15, 14 or 16 that are glued into cardboard, windowed covers and sold as folded booklets of 15 or 30. These panes are two stamp positions across by seven or eight down, and they do have die cutting at the bottom of the row with the label.

One other pane of Pink Rose stamps containing similar pairs with no die cutting between them was reported to *Linn's* by dealer Jacques C. Schiff Jr. Its error pairs, however, came about as a result of a properly die-cut pane being sliced vertically one and three-quarters stamp columns to the right. As a result, its "Time to Reorder" label was displaced to the middle column of the pane.

The Scott catalog has assigned number 2492c to a horizontal pair of Pink Rose stamps with no die cutting between.

32¢ Midnight Angel self-adhesive (1995)

A pane of the 1995 self-adhesive 32¢ Midnight Angel stamps printed on translucent green splicing paper was shown to *Linn's* by its owner, George B. Davis of Louisiana. The six stamps in the top two rows are printed entirely on top of the tape, while the three stamps in the third row are partly on the tape and partly on the face paper of the self-adhesive laminate. All stamps in the pane are die cut normally, including those with green tape. Green tape also is found on the back of the stamps' backing paper, with part of the enlarged stamp image and lettering on the backside printed on top of it.

The printed-on-tape variety isn't listed in the Scott catalog. Scott does, however, list a vertical pair of the Midnight Angel stamps with no die-cutting between (3012b).

32¢ Flag Over Porch self-adhesive (1995)

A pane of the 1995 Flag Over Porch self-adhesive stamps made by Avery Dennison was found with part of the face paper of the laminate torn away prior to printing. The result was that three of the stamps were printed entirely on the liner, or backing paper, and seven others were partly printed on the liner.

In the error pane, the affected positions are stamps 2 through 12 and 15, counting from left to right and top to bottom. The back of the pane is normal.

The unnamed dealer who owned the pane told *Linn's Stamp News* that it had been among 20 or so panes bought by a Virginia business for a mailing. The business used the good stamps on it but took what was left back to the post office to exchange.

However, the postal clerk told the owner to keep them because they

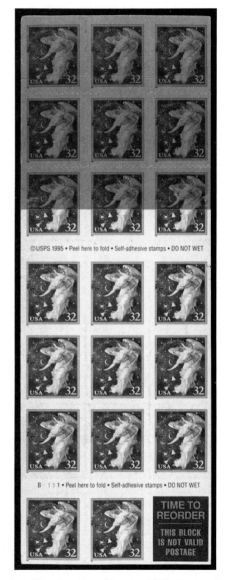

Green translucent splicing tape covers parts of the front and back of this pane of 32¢ Midnight Angel self-adhesive stamps. The six stamps in the top two rows are printed on top of the green tape. Three others are printed partly on the green tape.

might have collector value. The finder posted notice of what he had on the rec.collecting.stamps bulletin board on the Internet. Various potential buyers saw the notice before one of them bought the pane.

The pane's upper selvage strip, below positions 7-9, bears plate number combination V56665.

The face-paper tear begins in position 3 and heads southwest to position 7, where it turns southeast and exits the pane at position 15. The stamps in positions 6, 8 and 9 are printed entirely on the liner, while those in positions 2, 3, 4, 5, 7, 11 and 15 are partly on the backing and partly on the face paper.

The extreme upper-right corner of the face paper in position 10 was affected by the tear, but nothing is printed on the backing there, and the stamp there is gone.

The extreme lower-left corner of the face paper in position 12 is missing from the pane, but it probably was there at the time of printing, *Linn's* said. Most of the "1995" year date in the position 12 stamp's lower-left corner didn't print, probably because it is on the missing face paper.

A tear in the face paper of this 1995 Flag Over Porch pane of 20 self-adhesive stamps (only the top five rows are pictured) caused three stamps to be printed entirely on the backing.

Ten stamps, all normal examples except the one in position 4, have been removed from the pane and presumably were used on mail. Position 4 includes a tiny spot of blue ink from the lower-right corner of the stamp once there. The spot of blue is on the liner.

Scott catalog has assigned the partial pane the number 2920g.

8¢ Ernest Reuter (1959)

Four different kinds of color-missing error in varying quantities turned up in 1996 on a single pane of stamps that had been printed 37 years earlier. The stamp was the 8¢ Ernest Reuter commemorative of the Champions of Liberty series of 1959 (Scott 1137). No previous errors had been recorded for that particular stamp.

The stamp was printed in three intaglio colors — carmine, ultramarine and ocher — by the Bureau of Engraving and Printing and was distributed in panes of 72, 8 across by 9 down. In addition to the 14 color-missing errors, all remaining stamps on the pane are either misperforations or partially color-missing freaks. The pane is the lower-left position on a 288-subject printing sheet.

As described by Wayne Youngblood in *Stamp Collector*, the principal cause of the error was an extraneous piece of paper that was attached to the stamp paper prior to printing. As a result, that paper, extending diagonally from the upper left to lower right on the pane, received the three-color stamp impressions. The additional thickness on the sheet probably also caused it to misfeed into the perforator, creating the misperforation. Some time later, the extra paper detached itself from the pane, leaving a large void affecting 25 stamps.

Within this empty space, three stamps (positions 10, 20 and 30) are completely missing the ocher color. Three more (positions 17, 36 and 46) are completely missing the ultramarine. Two stamps from the pane (positions 27 and 37) are missing both ultramarine and ocher, and six stamps are missing all three colors, leaving blank, embossed stamps. Because of the wide distribution of the carmine ink in the design, none is missing carmine only.

The pane containing 14 errors received a March 13, 1996, certificate from the Philatelic Foundation stating that the errors are genuine.

The varieties were listed in the 1997 Scott catalog as 1137a (ocher omitted), 1137b (ultramarine omitted), 1137c (ocher and ultramarine omitted) and 1137d (all colors omitted).

Dealer Jacques C. Schiff Jr. sold the pane for $10,500 plus the 10-percent buyer's commission at his May 24-26 auction held in conjunction with Compex 96 in Rosemont, Illinois.

32¢ Christmas Children and Santa (1995)

The 1995 32¢ Christmas Children and Santa stamps, four varieties printed se-tenant in sheet form, were found imperforate. A block of four

Superior Stamp and Coin Company auctioned this imperforate pane of the Fall Garden Flowers booklet stamps, attached to its original folded booklet cover. The booklet had contained three other imperforate panes, but the stamps on them had been cut apart.

of the imperfs (Scott 3007d) was offered at auction by Richard E. Drews of Chicago November 22, 1996, but failed to reach its reserve price.

32¢ Garden Flowers booklet stamps (1995)

At least one booklet of the 1995 Fall Garden Flowers stamps with all four panes imperforate was purchased at a post office. Three of the panes reportedly were cut apart with scissors and the stamps used to pay bills. Superior Stamp and Coin of Beverly Hills, California, sold the remaining pane intact at its June 24-26 auction sale for $1,150, plus a 15-percent buyer's commission. The pane was in its original folded cover with plate number 2 printed on the binding stub. A horizontal ink marking crossed the top of the pane, partially over the 32¢ denomination on the stamps. The pane was folded between the second and third stamps, as is normal for a pane from this type of booklet.

THE YEAR IN REVIEW

Nixon inverts stolen; printing firm employee charged

In January 1996, the philatelic world was startled to learn that the 1995 Richard M. Nixon commemorative stamp had been found with the intaglio red name line inverted in relation to the offset portrait of the late president. The two kinds of printing were misaligned, so that the portraits on the error stamps were split in two, with the bottom of Nixon's face appearing at the top of the stamps, and the top of his face appearing at the bottom.

The first disclosure that such an error existed came when Christie's Inc. of New York City, without fanfare, illustrated a single specimen on the cover of the catalog for a February 1 stamp auction. *Linn's Stamp News* reported the story, and it then was picked up and carried in the general press and on radio and television.

A Christie's spokesman told reporters that the unidentified consignor of the stamp had said the invert was one of 160 such specimens. The stamps were bought at a post office in Virginia, near Washington, D.C., the spokesman said, but no other information was provided. When the auction was held, Christie's sold the stamp to an anonymous U.S. buyer for $14,500, plus a 15-percent buyer's premium that raised the total price paid to $16,675. Later, California stamp error dealer Dana Okey told *Linn's* that he had purchased 141 of the error stamps from their owner, using Christie's as the sales agent. The sale took place two days before the February 1 auction, and included the single that was sold by Christie's.

Okey, who made his purchase in partnership with Mark Morrow, said he had attempted to buy the entire holding of Nixon errors, but was told that the remaining 19 stamps weren't for sale. The dealer consigned a single copy of the invert to the March 27-28 auction of Ivy & Mader Philatelic Auctions Inc. The copy sold for $10,000, plus the 15-percent

An employee of Banknote Corporation of America was charged with stealing the Nixon inverts.

buyer's premium.

Okey then began advertising specimens for sale. In April he told *Linn's* he was selling single copies for $12,500 and that sales were "awesome."

On May 21, the Robert A. Siegel Auction Galleries Rarities of the World auction included a block of four Nixon inverts with two stamp-sized pieces attached, one of them bearing a set of plate numbers and both with the upper portion of Nixon's head printed on them. The item was unsold, however.

USPS spokespersons, in response to questions, said the Postal Service was aware of the error and "does not suspect improprieties." Nevertheless, the Scott catalog editors declined to give the invert a number or price pending further information, and some philatelic journalists were highly skeptical about the whole affair.

The most outspoken was Wayne Youngblood, then editor of *Scott Stamp Monthly*, who wrote a column citing "nagging unanswered questions — both about the stamps' origin and their subsequent handling and sale." Among the things he and others found troubling were the refusal of the printer, Banknote Corporation of America, to discuss the misprints; the absence of plate-position selvage on the error stamps that would shed light on their origin; and conflicts in dealers' accounts of how the errors were discovered and how many originally existed.

"If further investigation turns up evidence the stamps were illegally taken from Banknote Corporation of America, ... the stamps could be confiscated from collectors and dealers who bought them in good faith," Youngblood warned.

His concerns turned out to be well-founded. The stamps were printers' waste and never had been purchased by a postal customer. On December 12, 1996, the U.S. attorney for the Southern District of New York, Mary Jo White, announced that Clarence Robert Robie of Pearl River, New York, had been arrested and charged with theft and interstate transport of government property. Robie, who operated cutting machinery at BCA's plant in Suffern, New York, where the second stage (intaglio) of the Nixon stamp printing operation was performed, was accused of stealing the 160 Nixon inverts from the plant in March 1995.

According to the criminal complaint, Robie sold 120 of the stamps to an unnamed New Jersey stamp dealer for $60,000 the following June, and the remaining 40 stamps to an unnamed dealer in Brooklyn, New York, for $7,000 in cash and stamps worth $13,000 in August. The dealers' names weren't released, a postal inspector told *Linn's*, because there was no reason to believe that they knew the stamps were stolen.

The complaint stated that Christie's provided postal inspectors with information that 141 of the misprinted stamps were sold in January 1996 by the New Jersey dealer for a total price of approximately $800,000.

"These misprinted stamps, attractive as they may be to collectors, are the property of the United States Government," U.S. Attorney White said. "All buyers and sellers, philatelists everywhere, should understand they are dealing in stolen goods."

Shortly after Robie's arrest, postal inspectors obtained subpoenas for the recovery of the inverts from the dealers and collectors who possessed them. Inspector Pat Bossert told *Linn's* that Christie's and other dealers were cooperating fully and "we would expect cooperation from the collector community." She said "several" stamps had been recovered as of early January and would be used as evidence.

Robie was released after his arrest on a $50,000 personal recognizance bond. As of February 1997, no date had been set for a preliminary hearing. Conviction on the two charges would carry a maximum penalty of 10 years' imprisonment for each offense and a maximum fine of $250,000 or twice the gain realized from the sale of the stamps, whichever was greater.

Postal Service drops plans for 25th Anniversary stamps

On July 1, 1971, the old U.S. Post Office Department was officially succeeded by the United States Postal Service, an independent establishment of the executive branch of the U.S. government. The aim of Congress and the Nixon administration in reorganizing postal operations was to take politics and patronage out of the U.S. mails and make the service financially self-sufficient.

The April 25, 1996, issue of the *Postal Bulletin* reported that the Postal Service would commemorate its 25th anniversary by issuing a 32¢ stamp or stamps as a "book of 20 PSA," meaning a booklet of pressure-sensitive adhesives.

In response to a query by *Linn's Stamp News*, the Postal Service issued this statement on May 6: "Plans are in the works for a stamp which has the Postal Service as its theme. Unveiling and issue dates are still being worked out. Stay tuned for details."

But July 1 came and went with no stamp, although on that date the Postal Service held an anniversary celebration at its headquarters in L'Enfant Plaza in Washington and also held open houses at post offices around the country. USPS spokesman Barry Ziehl told *Linn's* at the time that a design would be unveiled later in the summer. The issue would refer to USPS as "America's first communications company," *Linn's* reported.

Questioned again in late September, Ziehl told the publication, "As far as I know, no official decision has been made, and it is still under consideration by the Citizens' Stamp Advisory Committee."

Finally, in December, Ziehl told *Linn's* there would be no 25th anniversary stamp after all. Designs were prepared for a stamp or stamps in 1996, but the issue was canceled by Postmaster General Marvin T. Runyon on the advice of CSAC, Ziehl said.

None of these public pronouncements hinted at the fervor of the behind-the-scenes struggle over the stamp proposal.

The Postal Service's Corporate Relations Department, under vice president Larry Speakes, had pushed for a stamp issue, against CSAC's strong objections. CSAC members pointed out that such a stamp would have violated the committee's fourth criterion for subject selection, that "events of historical significance shall be considered for commemoration only on anniversaries in multiples of 50 years."

The stamp also would have been openly self-serving, committee members argued. One member, a stamp collector, said his tally showed that the Postal Service had issued more than 40 commemorative stamps honoring itself since its inception, and insisted that this was more than enough.

Nevertheless, Corporate Relations was adamant, and the stamp design section went to work developing some concepts. At length, a set of designs was approved, consisting of multiple images reminiscent of the National Postal Museum block of four that was issued in 1993. "They were good designs, but it was just 'Son of National Postal Museum,'" one official said.

The designs were sent for approval to Postmaster General Runyon, whose immediate reaction, according to the official, was: "Why are we doing this? I thought we didn't honor 25th anniversaries." Runyon vetoed plans to unveil the designs.

Corporate Relations refused to give up completely, but as the year wore on the possibility that the design and acquisition sections could physically produce a stamp in 1996 dwindled to zero. The rationale for a stamp in 1997 would have been zero as well, of course.

The closest USPS came to philatelically commemorating its quarter-century of existence was to authorize a special postmark with a circular logo carrying the inscription "U.S. Postal Service 25th anniversary." Several post offices also used a pictorial handstamp with the USPS eagle logo and the word "Anniversary" in fancy script.

The Postal Service was asked by the *Yearbook* for permission to illustrate the proposed stamp designs for the 25th anniversary stamps, but decided against releasing them.

James Dean stamp is year's best-seller

The 32¢ James Dean stamp was "the most saved single commemorative stamp" of 1996, USPS announced.

According to the Postal Service's method of estimating stamp retention, which involves quarterly surveys of 50,000 households, individuals bought 31 million Dean stamps that they didn't use on letters during the fiscal year from mid-September 1995 to mid-September 1996. That gave the agency a $9.92 million profit from the stamp.

Only the Centennial Olympic Games commemoratives — panes of 20 designs — topped the Dean stamp in number of stamps saved, said USPS. By its estimate, 38.1 million Olympic stamps were retained.

The remaining issues in the top 10 in fiscal 1996 were: Comic Strip Classics, 20 designs (issued in 1995), 20 million stamps saved; Winter Garden Flowers, 5 designs, 17.8 million; American Indian Dances, 5 designs, 16.9 million; Big Band Leaders, 4 designs, 16.3 million; Folk Heroes, 4 designs, 15 million; Antique Autos, 5 designs (issued in 1995),

12.8 million; Riverboats, 5 designs, 12.8 million; Prehistoric Animals, 4 designs, 12.2 million.

The all-time top 10 most popular commemorative stamps, according to the Postal Service, are: Elvis Presley, 1 design (1993), 124 million; Wild-flowers, 50 designs (1992), 76.2 million; Rock & Roll Musicians, 7 designs (1993), 75.8 million; Moon Landing, 1 design (1994), 47.9 million; Civil War, 20 designs (1995), 46.6 million; Legends of the West, 20 designs (1994), 46.5 million; Marilyn Monroe, 1 design (1995), 46.3 million; Summer Olympics, 20 designs (1996), 38.1 million; Space Fantasy, 5 designs (1993), 36.5 million.

The Postal Service's survey method is viewed with skepticism by some stamp writers, who believe it overstates the number of stamps that won't be used for mailing purposes.

Civil War stamps top popularity polls for 1995

The 32¢ Civil War pane of 20 stamps was the favorite stamp issue of 1995 among collectors participating in the annual polls conducted by *Linn's Stamp News* and *Stamp Collector*.

The Civil War stamps, with 869 votes, received nearly twice the support (458 votes) given Great Lakes Lighthouses in *Linn's* "favorite stamp" category. American Comic Strips was third. Civil War also topped *Linn's* "best design, commemoratives" category, with Lighthouses and Carousel Horses as runners-up, and placed second to the World War II pane of 10 stamps in the "most important commemorative" group. The POW-MIA stamp was third.

At *Stamp Collector*, the Civil War stamps won the "best design" category. Great Lakes Lighthouses and American Comic Strips tied for second. *Stamp Collector*'s "most important commemorative" category had the same results as *Linn's* did: World War II, Civil War and POW-MIA, in that order.

Other results from the *Linn's* poll:

Commemoratives, worst design: Women's Suffrage, Florida Statehood, Recreational Sports. (Women's Suffrage received 2,710 votes in this category to Florida's 665.) Commemoratives, least necessary: Marilyn Monroe, Recreational Sports, American Comic Strips. Definitives, best design: Midnight Angel, Endeavour Space Shuttle, Challenger Space Shuttle. Definitives, most important: Challenger Shuttle, Eddie Rickenbacker, Madonna and Child. Definitives, worst design: Automobile Tail Fin, Automobile, Butte. Definitives, least necessary: Peaches and Pear, Nonprofit G, Love Cherub (nondenominated). Postal stationery, best design: American Clipper Ships card, Soaring Eagle card, Civil War cards. Postal stationery, most important: Civil War cards, Soaring Eagle card, Thaddeus Lowe aerogram. Postal stationery, worst design: Eagle envelope, Spiral Heart envelope, G postal card. Postal stationery, least necessary: American Comic Strips cards, Sheep envelope, Spiral Heart envelope.

Other results from the *Stamp Collector* poll:

Commemoratives, worst design: Women's Suffrage, Florida Statehood. (Women's Suffrage got 142 votes, 41 percent of the total in this category.) Commemoratives, least important: Recreational Sports, Marilyn Monroe, American Comic Strips. Definitives, best design: Endeavour Space Shuttle, Blue Jay, James K. Polk (which actually was a commemorative). Definitives, most important: Challenger Space Shuttle. Definitives, worst design: Auto Tail Fin, Automobile, Butte. Definitives, least important: Peaches and Pear, Juke Box and Nonprofit G (tie). Postal stationery, most important: Civil War cards, Space Station envelope, Soaring Eagle card and Liberty Bell envelope (tie). Postal stationery, best design: Red Barn card, Civil War cards, Soaring Eagle card. Postal stationery, worst design: Spiral Heart envelope, G postal card, Red Barn and G envelope (tie). Postal stationery, least important: Sheep envelope, Spiral Heart envelope.

Original wrong-Pickett pane sells for $525

The original pane of 1994 Legends of the West stamps with the "wrong" Bill Pickett pictured, canceled at Bend, Oregon, on December 13, 1993, and arguably the source of all the subsequent Pickett developments, sold in a Jacques Schiff auction at the Compex show in Chicago in May 1996 for $525. Adding in the 10-percent buyer's premium meant that the purchaser paid a total of $577.50 for one of the most interesting artifacts in the history of 20th-century commemorative stamps. If this pane, and several others that were sold by mistake before the scheduled first day of issue, hadn't reached the public, the Postal Service would have destroyed its entire printing of Legends panes containing one stamp with a portrait identified as Bill Pickett but actually that of his brother Ben Pickett. Instead, USPS tried to placate collectors and avoid creating a huge philatelic rarity by selling 150,000 of the error panes through a controversial lottery-style selection method.

Deaths in 1996

J. Edward Day, postmaster general under President John F. Kennedy, died October 29 at age 82. Day's most far-reaching act as postmaster general was to inaugurate the five-digit ZIP code July 1, 1963. But he is best remembered by stamp collectors as the man who ordered the deliberate reprinting of the 1962 Dag Hammarskjold inverted-color errors to destroy the value of a few of the error stamps that had been bought at post offices by stamp collectors.

Jacques Minkus, the Polish-born entrepreneur who started the stamp department at Gimbels department store in New York in 1931 and built it into the nation's largest stamp retailing operation, died September 17 at 94. He published albums and catalogs and represented Israel and other nations in distributing their stamps in the United States.

PLATE NUMBER COILS, SHEET, BOOKLET AND SELF-ADHESIVE STAMPS

Changes to the plate number listings that appeared in the 1995 *Linn's U.S. Stamp Yearbook*, as well as all new listings, are shown in bold typeface.

Transportation Coils (not precanceled)

Scott number	Stamp	Plate number	Tagging type
1897	1¢ Omnibus (1983)	1,2,3,4,5,6	overall
2225	1¢ Omnibus (1986)	1,2	block
2225a	1¢ Omnibus (1991)	2,3	untagged[2]
1897A	2¢ Locomotive (1982)	2,3,4,6,8,10	overall
2226	2¢ Locomotive (1987)	1	block
2226a	2¢ Locomotive (1993)	2	untagged
1898	3¢ Handcar (1983)	1,2,3,4	overall
2252	3¢ Conestoga Wagon (1988)	1	block
2252a	3¢ Conestoga Wagon (1992)	2, 3, **6**	untagged[15]
2123	3.4¢ School Bus (1985)	1,2	overall
1898A	4¢ Stagecoach (1982)	1,2,3,4,5,6	overall
2228	4¢ Stagecoach (1986)	1	block
2228a	4¢ Stagecoach (1990)	1	overall
2451	4¢ Steam Carriage (1991)	1	overall
2451b	4¢ Steam Carriage (1991)	1	untagged
2124	4.9¢ Buckboard (1985)	3,4	overall
1899	5¢ Motorcycle (1983)	1,2,3,4	overall
2253	5¢ Milk Wagon (1987)	1	block
2452	5¢ Circus Wagon (1990)	1	overall
2452a	5¢ Circus Wagon (1991)	1	untagged
2452B	5¢ Circus Wagon (gravure) (1992)	A1,A2,A3	untagged
2452D	5¢ Circus Wagon (gravure) (1995)	S1,**S2**	untagged[12]
1900	5.2¢ Sleigh (1983)	1,2,3,5	overall
2125	5.5¢ Star Route Truck (1986)	1	block
1901	5.9¢ Bicycle (1982)	3,4	overall
2126	6¢ Tricycle (1985)	1	block
2127	7.1¢ Tractor (1987)	1	block
1902	7.4¢ Baby Buggy (1984)	2	block
2128	8.3¢ Ambulance (1985)	1,2	overall
2129	8.5¢ Tow Truck (1987)	1	block
1903	9.3¢ Mail Wagon (1981)	1,2,3,4,5,6	overall
2257	10¢ Canal Boat (1987)	1	block
2257a	10¢ Canal Boat (1991)	1	overall
unassigned	10¢ Canal Boat (1992)	1,2,**3**	prephosphored[1]
2130	10.1¢ Oil Wagon (1985)	1	block
1904	10.9¢ Hansom Cab (1982)	1,2	overall
1905	11¢ Caboose (1984)	1	block
2131	11¢ Stutz Bearcat (1985)	1,2,3,4	overall
2132	12¢ Stanley Steamer (1985)	1,2	overall
2133	12.5¢ Pushcart (1985)	1,2	block

Scott number	Stamp	Plate number	Tagging type
2134	14¢ Iceboat (1985)	1,2,3,4	overall
2134b	14¢ Iceboat (1986)	2	block
2260	15¢ Tugboat (1988)	1, 2	block
2260a	15¢ Tugboat (1988)	2	overall
1906	17¢ Electric Auto (1981)	1,2,3,4,5,6,7	overall
2135	17¢ Dog Sled (1986)	2	block
2262	17.5¢ Racing Car (1987)	1	block
1907	18¢ Surrey (1981)	1,2,3,4,5,6,7,8,9,10,11, 12,13,14,15,16,17,18	overall
1908	20¢ Fire Pumper (1981)	1,2,3,4,5,6,7,8,9,10,11, 12,13,14,15,16	overall
2263	20¢ Cable Car (1988)	1,2	block
2263b	20¢ Cable Car (1990)	2	overall
2463	20¢ Cog Railway (1995)	1,2	prephosphored
2464	23¢ Lunch Wagon (1991)	2,3,**4**	prephosphored[17]
2136	25¢ Bread Wagon (1986)	1,2,3,4,5	block
2466	32¢ Ferryboat (1995)	2,3,4,5	prephosphored[13]
2468	$1 Seaplane (1990)	1	overall
unassigned	$1 Seaplane (1993)	3	prephosphored[1]

Transportation Coils (precanceled or service-inscribed)

Scott number	Stamp	Plate number	Tagging type
2123a	3.4¢ School Bus (1985)	1,2	untagged
1898Ab	4¢ Stagecoach (1982)	3,4,5,6	untagged
2124a	4.9¢ Buckboard (1985)	1,2,3,4,5,6	untagged
2453	5¢ Canoe (1991)	1,2,3	untagged
2454	5¢ Canoe (gravure) (1991)	S11	untagged
1900a	5.2¢ Sleigh (1983)	1,2,3,4,5,6	untagged
2254	5.3¢ Elevator (1988)	1	untagged
2125a	5.5¢ Star Route Truck (1986)	1,2	untagged
1901a	5.9¢ Bicycle (1982)	3,4,5,6	untagged
2126a	6¢ Tricycle (1985)	1,2	untagged
2127a	7.1¢ Tractor (1987)	1	untagged[3]
2127a	7.1¢ Tractor (1989)	1	untagged[4]
1902a	7.4¢ Buggy (1984)	2	untagged
2255	7.6¢ Carreta (1988)	1,2,3	untagged
2128a	8.3¢ Ambulance (1985)	1,2,3,4	untagged
2231	8.3¢ Ambulance (1986)	1,2	untagged
2256	8.4¢ Wheel Chair (1988)	1,2,3	untagged
2129a	8.5¢ Tow Truck (1987)	1,2	untagged
1903a	9.3¢ Mail Wagon (1981)	1,2,3,4,5,6,8	untagged
2457	10¢ Tractor Trailer (1991)	1	untagged
2458	10¢ Tractor Trailer (gravure) (1994)	11,22	untagged
2130a	10.1¢ Oil Wagon (1985)	1,2	untagged[5]
2130a	10.1¢ Oil Wagon (1988)	2,3	untagged[6]
1904a	10.9¢ Hansom Cab (1982)	1,2,3,4	untagged
1905a	11¢ Caboose (1984)	1	untagged[7]

Scott number	Stamp	Plate number	Tagging type
1905a	11¢ Caboose (1991)	2	untagged
2132a	12¢ Stanley Steamer (1985)	1,2	untagged
2132b	12¢ Stanley Steamer (1987)	1	untagged
2133a	12.5¢ Pushcart (1985)	1,2	untagged
2258	13¢ Patrol Wagon (1988)	1	untagged
2259	13.2¢ Coal Car (1988)	1,2	untagged
2261	16.7¢ Popcorn Wagon (1988)	1,2	untagged
1906a	17¢ Electric Auto (1981)	1,2,3,4,5,6,7	untagged
2262a	17.5¢ Racing Car (1987)	1	untagged
2264	20.5¢ Fire Engine (1988)	1	untagged
2265	21¢ Railroad Mail Car (1988)	1,2	untagged
2266	24.1¢ Tandem Bicycle (1988)	1	untagged

Flag coil series

Scott number	Stamp	Plate number	Tagging type
1891	18¢ Sea to Shining Sea (1981)	1,2,3,4,5,6,7	block
1895	20¢ Over Supreme Court (1981)	1,2,3,4,5,6, 8,9,10,12,13,14	block
1895e	20¢ Over Supreme Court precanceled (1984)	14	untagged
2115	22¢ Over Capitol Dome (1985)	1,2,3,4,5,6,7,8,10,11,12,13, 14,15,16,17,18,19,20,21,22	block
2115a	22¢ Over Capitol Dome (1987)	T1	prephosphored
2280	25¢ Over Yosemite (1988)	1,2,3,4,5,7,8,9	block
2280	25¢ Over Yosemite (1989)	1,2,3,5,6,7,8,9, 10,11,12,13,14,15	prephosphored
2523	29¢ Over Mount Rushmore (1991)	1,2,3,4,5,6,7,8,9	prephosphored
2523A	29¢ Over Mount Rushmore (gravure) (1991)	A111111, A222211	prephosphored
2609	29¢ Over White House (1992)	1,2,3,4,5,6,7,8,9, 10,11,12,13,14,15,16,18	prephosphored
2913	32¢ Over Porch (1995)	11111, 22221, 22222, **22322,** 33333, **34333,** 44444, 45444, 66646, **66666, 77767, 78767, 99969**	prephosphored[14]
2914	32¢ Over Porch (1995)	S11111	prephosphored[12]

Non-denominated rate-change coil stamps

Scott number	Stamp	Plate number	Tagging type
2112	D(22¢) Eagle (1985)	1,2	block
O139	D(22¢) Official (1985)	1	block
2279	E(25¢) Earth (1988)	1111, 1211, 1222, 2222	block
2518	F(29¢) Flower (1991)	1111, 1211, 1222, 2211, 2222	prephosphored
2893	G (5¢) Old Glory nonprofit (1995)	A11111, A21111	untagged
2888	G (25¢) Old Glory presort (1994)	S11111	prephosphored
2886	G (32¢) Old Glory self-adhesive (1994)	V11111	prephosphored
2889	G (32¢) Old Glory (1994)	1111,2222	prephosphored

Scott number	Stamp	Plate number	Tagging type
2890	G (32¢) Old Glory (1994)	A1111, A1112, A1113, A1211, A1212, A1222, A1311, A1313, A1314, A1324, A1417, A1433, A2211, A2212, A2213, A2214, A2223, A2313, A3113, A3114, A3314, A3315, A3323, A3324, A3423, A3426, A3433, A3435, A3436, A4426, A4427, A4435, A5327, A5417, A5427, A5437	prephosphored
2891	G (32¢) Old Glory (1994)	S1111	prephosphored[11]
2892	G (32¢) Old Glory (1994)	S1111, S2222	prephosphored

Miscellaneous coil stamps

Scott number	Stamp	Plate number	Tagging type
3044	**1¢ Kestrel (1996)**	**1111**	**untagged**
2149	18¢ Washington (1985)	1112, 3333	block
2529	19¢ Fishing Boat (1991)	A1111, A1112, A1212, A2424	prephosphored
2529a	19¢ Fishing Boat (1993)	A5555, A5556, A6667, A7667, A7679, A7766, A7779	prephosphored
2529c	19¢ Fishing Boat (1994)	S11	prephosphored
2005	20¢ Consumer Education (1982)	1,2,3,4	overall
O135	20¢ Official (1983)	1	block
2150	21.1¢ Letters (1985)	111111, 111121	block
2281	25¢ Honey Bee (1988)	1,2	block
2525	29¢ Flower (1991)	S1111, S2222	prephosphored
2526	29¢ Flower (1992)	S2222	prephosphored
31 and 31a	variable-rate coil (1992)	1	prephosphored[8]
31b and 31c	variable-rate coil (new font) (1994)	1	prephosphored[8]
32	variable-rate coil (1994)	A11	prephosphored
33	**variable-rate coil (1996)**	**11**	**prephosphored**

Miscellaneous precanceled (service-inscribed) coils

Scott number	Stamp	Plate number	Tagging type
2902	(5¢) Butte (1995)	S111, **S222, S333**	untagged[12]
2902B	**(5¢) Butte (1996)**	**S111**	**untagged[12]**
2903	**(5¢) Mountains (1996)**	**11111**	**untagged**
2904	**(5¢) Mountains (1996)**	**S111**	**untagged**
2904A	**(5¢) Mountains (1996)**	**V222222, V333323, V333333, V333342, V333343**	**untagged[12]**
2602	(10¢) Eagle & Shield (1991) "Bulk Rate USA"	A11111, A11112, A12213, A21112, A21113, A22112, A22113, A32333, A33333, A33334, A33335, A34424, A34426, A43324, A43325, A43326, A43334, A43335, A43426, A53335, A54444, A54445, A77777, A88888, A88889, A89999, A99998, A99999, A1010101010, A1011101010, A1011101011, A1011101012, A1110101010,	untagged

Continued on next page

Continued from previous page

Scott number	Stamp	Plate number	Tagging type
2602	(10¢) Eagle & Shield (1991) "Bulk Rate USA"	A1110101011, A1110111110, A1111101010, A1111111010, A1211101010, A1411101010, A1411101011, A1412111110, A1412111111	untagged
2603	(10¢) Eagle & Shield "USA Bulk Rate" (1993)	11111, 22221 22222, 33333	untagged[9]
2604	(10¢) Eagle & Shield (gold) "USA Bulk Rate" (1993)	S11111, S22222	untagged[16]
2905	(10¢) Auto (1995)	S111, S222, **S333**	untagged[12]
2906	**(10¢) Auto (1996)**	**S111**	**untagged[12]**
2907	**(10¢) Eagle & Shield (1996)**	**S11111**	**untagged[12]**
2908	(15¢) Tail Fin (1995)	11111	untagged
2909	(15¢) Tail Fin (1995)	S11111	untagged[12]
2910	**(15¢) Tail Fin (1996)**	**S11111**	**untagged[12]**
2149a	18¢ Washington (1985)	11121, 33333, 43444	untagged[10]
2150a	21.1¢ Letters (1985)	111111, 111121	untagged
2605	23¢ Flag Presort (1991)	A111, A112, A122, A212, A222, A333	untagged
2606	23¢ USA Presort (1992) (dark blue)	A1111, A2222, A2232, A2233, A3333, A4364, A4443, A4444, A4453	untagged
2607	23¢ USA Presort (1992) (light blue)	1111	untagged[2]
2608	23¢ USA Presort (1993) (violet blue)	S111	untagged
2911	(25¢) Jukebox (1995)	111111, 212222, 222222, **332222**	untagged
2912	(25¢) Jukebox (1995)	S11111, **S22222**	untagged[12]
2912	**(25¢) Jukebox (1996)**	**S11111**	**untagged[12]**

Self-adhesive miscellaneous coil stamps

Scott number	Stamp	Plate number	Tagging type
3053	**20¢ Blue Jay (1996)**	**S1111**	**prephosphored**
2480	29¢ Pine Cone (1993)	B1	prephosphored
2799-2802	29¢ Christmas Contemporary (1993)	V1111111	prephosphored
2598	29¢ Eagle (1994)	111	prephosphored
2599	29¢ Statue of Liberty (1994)	D1111	prephosphored
2813	29¢ Sunrise Love (1994)	B1	prephosphored
2873	29¢ Christmas Santa (1994)	V1111	prephosphored
2492	32¢ Pink Rose (1995)	S111	prephosphored
2495-95A	32¢ Peach/Pear (1995)	V11111	prephosphored
2915	32¢ Flag Over Porch (1995)	V11111	prephosphored
2915A	**32¢ Flag Over Porch (1996)**	**55555, 56666, 66666, 78777, 87888, 87898, 88888, 88898, 89878, 89888, 89898, 89899, 97898, 99899, 99999**	**prephosphored**
2915B	**32¢ Flag Over Porch (1996)**	**S11111**	**prephosphored[12]**
3014-17	32¢ Santa/Children with Toys (1995)	V1111	prephosphored
3018	32¢ Midnight Angel (1995)	B1111	prephosphored

444

Test stamps

To come	For Testing Purposes Only	Black (paper appears blue) (1996)	1111	untagged[12, 18]
To come	For Testing Purposes Only	Black on White (1996)	V1	untagged

Plate number coil notes

1 *Shiny gum*
2 *Plate number 3 shiny and dull gum*
3 *Service inscribed in black "Nonprofit Org."*
4 *Service inscribed in black "Nonprofit Org. 5-Digit ZIP +4"*
5 *Service inscribed in black "Bulk Rate" (between two lines)*
6 *Service inscribed in red "Bulk Rate Carrier Route Sort"*
7 *Has two black precancel lines*
8 *Shiny gum and dull gum*
9 *22222 shiny and dull gum, 33333 dull gum*
10 *11121 shiny gum, 33333 and 43444 dull gum*
11 *Rolls of 3,000 and 10,000 have back numbers*
12 *Has back numbers*
13 *2 shiny gum, 3, 4 and 5 low gloss and shiny gum*
14 *22221 shiny only and 11111, 22222 shiny and low gloss gum; all others low gloss gum only*
15 *2 dull gum, 3 dull and shiny gum, 6 shiny gum*
16 *S22222 has back numbers*
17 *Plate number 2 dull gum, 3 shiny and dull, 4 shiny*
18 *Tagged paper printed with three layers of opaque white*

Great Americans Sheet Stamps

Scott number	Stamp	Plate number	Perf type	Tagging type
1844	1¢ Dix	1 floating	bull's-eye	block
1844c	1¢ Dix	1,2 floating	L perf	block
2168	1¢ Mitchell	1	bull's-eye	block
1845	2¢ Stravinsky	1,2,3,4,5,6	electric-eye	overall
2169	2¢ Lyon	1,2	bull's-eye	block
unassigned	2¢ Lyon	3	bull's-eye	untagged
1846	3¢ Clay	1,2	electric-eye	overall
2170	3¢ White	1,2,3	bull's-eye	block
unassigned	3¢ White	4	bull's-eye	untagged[17]
1847	4¢ Schurz	1,2,3,4	electric-eye	overall
2171	4¢ Flanagan	1	bull's-eye	block
2171a	4¢ Flanagan	1,2	bull's-eye	untagged
1848	5¢ Buck	1,2,3,4	electric-eye	overall
2172	5¢ Black	1,2	bull's-eye	block
2173	5¢ Munoz	1	bull's-eye	overall
2173a	5¢ Munoz	2	bull's-eye	untagged
1849	6¢ Lippmann	1 floating	L perf	block
1850	7¢ Baldwin	1 floating	L perf	block
1851	8¢ Knox	3,4,5,6	L perf	overall
1852	9¢ Thayer	1 floating	L perf	block
1853	10¢ Russell	1 floating	L perf	block
2175	10¢ Red Cloud	1	bull's-eye	block
2175a	10¢ Red Cloud	1,2	bull's-eye	overall
2175c	10¢ Red Cloud	2	bull's-eye	prephosphored[17]
2175d	10¢ Red Cloud	2	bull's-eye	prephosphored[18]
1854	11¢ Partridge	2,3,4,5	L perf	overall
1855	13¢ Crazy Horse	1,2,3,4	electric-eye	overall
1856	14¢ Lewis	1 floating	L perf	block

Scott number	Stamp	Plate number	Perf type	Tagging type
2176	14¢ Howe	1,2	bull's-eye	block
2177	15¢ Cody	1,3	bull's-eye	block
2177a	15¢ Cody	2,3	bull's-eye	overall
2177b	15¢ Cody	1	bull's-eye	prephosphored
1857	17¢ Carson	1,2,3,4,13,14,15,16	electric-eye	overall
2178	17¢ Lockwood	1,2	bull's-eye	block
1858	18¢ Mason	1,2,3,4,5,6	electric-eye	overall
1859	19¢ Sequoyah	39529, 39530	electric-eye	overall
1860	20¢ Bunche	1,2,3,4,5,6,7,8,10,11,13	electric-eye	overall
1861	20¢ Gallaudet	1,2,5,6,8,9	electric-eye	overall
1862	20¢ Truman	1 floating	L perf	block
1862a	20¢ Truman	2	bull's-eye	block
1862b	20¢ Truman	3	bull's-eye	overall
1862d	20¢ Truman	4	bull's-eye	prephosphored[18]
2179	20¢ Apgar	B1,B2	bull's-eye	prephosphored
2180	21¢ Carlson	1	bull's-eye	block
1863	22¢ Audubon	1 floating	L perf	block
1863d	22¢ Audubon	3	bull's-eye	block
2181	23¢ Cassatt	1	bull's-eye	block
2181a	23¢ Cassatt	1,2	bull's-eye	overall
2181b	23¢ Cassatt	2,3	bull's-eye	prephosphored[19]
2182	25¢ London	1,2	bull's-eye	block
2183	28¢ Sitting Bull	1	bull's-eye	block
2184	29¢ Warren	S1,S2 (six positions)	bull's-eye	prephosphored
2185	29¢ Jefferson	S1,S2 (six positions)	bull's-eye	prephosphored
1864	30¢ Laubach	1 floating	L perf	block
1864a	30¢ Laubach	2	bull's-eye	block
1864b	30¢ Laubach	2	bull's-eye	overall
2933	32¢ Hershey	B1,B2	bull's-eye	prephosphored
2934	**32¢ Farley**	**B1**	**bull's-eye**	**prephosphored**
1865	35¢ Drew	1,2,3,4	electric-eye	overall
2186	35¢ Chavez	S1,S2 (six positions)	L perf	prephosphored
1866	37¢ Millikan	1,2,3,4	electric-eye	overall
1867	39¢ Clark	1 floating	L perf	block
1867c	39¢ Clark	2	bull's-eye	block
1868	40¢ Gilbreth	1 floating	L perf	block
1868a	40¢ Gilbreth	2	bull's-eye	block
2187	40¢ Chennault	1	bull's-eye	overall
2187a	40¢ Chennault	2	bull's-eye	prephosphored[17]
2188	45¢ Cushing	1	bull's-eye	block
2188a	45¢ Cushing	1	bull's-eye	overall
2938	46¢ Benedict	1	bull's-eye	prephosphored
1869	50¢ Nimitz	1,2,3,4	L perf	overall[18]
1869a	50¢ Nimitz	1,2	bull's-eye	block
1869d	50¢ Nimitz	2,3	bull's-eye	overall
unassigned	50¢ Nimitz	3	bull's-eye	prephosphored[17]
2189	52¢ Humphrey	1,2	bull's-eye	prephosphored[20]

Scott number	Stamp	Plate number	Perf type	Tagging type
2940	55¢ Hamilton	B1,B2	bull's-eye	prephosphored
2190	56¢ Harvard	1	bull's-eye	block
2191	65¢ Arnold	1	bull's-eye	block
2192	75¢ Willkie	1	bull's-eye	prephosphored[17]
2943	78¢ Paul	B1,B2	bull's-eye	prephosphored
2193	$1 Revel	1	bull's-eye	block
2194	$1 Hopkins	1	bull's-eye	block
2194b	$1 Hopkins	1	bull's-eye	overall
2194d	$1 Hopkins	2	bull's-eye	prephosphored[17]
2195	$2 Bryan	2	bull's-eye	block
2196	$5 Bret Harte	1	bull's-eye	block
2196b	$5 Bret Harte	2	bull's-eye	prephosphored

Great Americans sheet stamps notes

17 *Shiny gum and dull gum*
18 *Shiny gum*
19 *Plate number 3 shiny gum*
20 *Plate number 1 shiny and dull gum, plate number 2 shiny gum*

General Notes

Plate positions: Floating plate number positions are left or right, either blocks of six or strips of 20 (number must be centered in selvage in a block of six). All other plate number positions consist of upper left, upper right, lower left and lower right, with the following exceptions: 29¢ Warren, 29¢ Jefferson and 35¢ Chavez, which has positions of upper left, center upper right, upper right, lower left, center lower right and lower right. (Traditional corners have plate numbers to the side of the stamps; center positions have plate numbers above or below stamps.)

Tagging types

Block: tagging block centered over design of stamp; no tagging in selvage.

Overall: tagging applied to entire pane, often leaving an untagged strip at outer edge of large margin selvage.

Prephosphored: paper that has the phosphorescent taggant applied to the paper by the paper supplier prior to printing. On some stamps, under shortwave ultraviolet light, the appearance of the phosphorescent tagging is smooth and even (surface taggant), while on others, the taggant appears mottled (embedded taggant). Examples that exhibit both are the 10¢ Red Cloud, 23¢ Cassatt, 40¢ Chennault, 52¢ Humphrey, 75¢ Willkie and $1 Hopkins from the Great Americans and the 23¢ Lunch Wagon, 29¢ Flag Over Mount Rushmore and the variable-denomination coil (Scott 31, 31a, 31b and 31c) from the plate number coils.

Self-adhesive panes
Convertible (over-the-counter) booklets

Scott number	Stamp	Denomination	Total value	Number of subjects	Date of issue	Plate numbers	Notes
3048a	**Blue Jay**	**20¢**	**$2.00**	**10**	**8/2/96**	**S1111**	
2431a	Eagle & Shield	25¢	$4.50	18	11/10/89	A1111	1,2,3
2489a	Red Squirrel	29¢	$5.22	18	6/25/93	D11111, D22211 D22221, D22222 D23133	3
2490a	Rose	29¢	$5.22	18	8/19/93	S111	3,4
2491a	Pine Cone	29¢	$5.22	18	11/5/93	B1, B2, B3, B4, B5, B6, B7, B8, B9, B10, B11, B12, B13, B14, B15, B16	5
2595a	Eagle & Shield	29¢	$4.93	17	9/25/92	B1111-1, B1111-2, B2222-1, B2222-2, B3333-1, B3333-3, B3434-1, B3434-3, B4344-1, B4344-3, B4444-1, B4444-3	3,6,7
2596a	Eagle & Shield	29¢	$4.93	17	9/25/92	D11111, D21221, D22322, D32322, D32332, D32342, D42342, D43352, D43452, D43453, D54561, D54563, D54571, D54573 D54673, D61384, D65784	3,6,7
2597a	Eagle & Shield	29¢	$4.93	17	9/25/92	S1111	3,6,7
2598a	Eagle	29¢	$5.22	18	2/4/94	M111, M112	5
2599a	Statue of Liberty	29¢	$5.22	18	6/24/94	D1111, D1212	5
2802a	Christmas	29¢	$3.48	12	10/28/93	V111-1111, V222-1222, V222-2112, V222-2122, V222-2221, V222-2222, V333-3333	5
2813a	Sunrise Love	29¢	$5.22	18	1/27/94	B111-1, B111-2, B111-3, B111-4, B111-5, B121-5, B221-5, B222-4, B222-5, B222-6, B333-5, B333-7, B333-8, B333-9, B333-10, B333-11, B333-12, B333-14, B333-17, B334-11, B344-11, B344-12, B344-13, B434-10, B444-7, B444-8, B444-9, B444-10, B444-13, B444-14, B444-15, B444-16, B444-17, B444-18, B444-19, B555-20, B555-21	5

Scott number	Stamp	Denomination	Total value	Number of subjects	Date of issue	Plate numbers	Notes
2873a	Christmas	29¢	$3.48	12	10/20/94	V1111	5
2886a	G	32¢	$6.48	18	12/13/94	V11111, V22222	5
2492a	Pink Rose	32¢	$6.40	20	6/2/95	S111, S112, S333, S444, **S555**	5,9,**10**
2494a	Peach/Pear	32¢	$6.40	20	7/8/95	V11111, V11122, V11131, V11132, V11232, V12131, V12132, V12211, V12221, V12232, V22212, V22221, V22222, V33142, V33143, V33243, V33323, V33333, V33343, V33353, **V33363, V33453 V44424, V44434, V44454, V45434 V45464, V54365 V54565, V55365, V55565**	5,9,**10**
2920a	Flag Over Porch	32¢	$6.40	20	4/18/95	V12211, V12212, V12312, V12321, V12322, V12331, V13322, **V13831, V13834, V13836,** V22211, V23322, V23422, V23432, **V34743, V34745, V42556, V45554,** V56665, **V65976**	5,9,**10**
2920c	Flag Over Porch	32¢	$6.40	20	4/18/95	V11111	
2920e	**Flag Over Porch**	**32¢**	**$3.20**	**10**	**1/20/96**	**V11111, V12111, V23222, V31121, V32111, V32121, V44444, V55555**	
2949a	Love	(32¢)	$6.40	20	2/1/95	B1111-1, B2222-1, B2222-2, B3333-2	
3011a	Santa/Children with Toys	32¢	$6.40	20	9/30/95	V1111, V1211, V1212, V3233, V3333, V4444	5
3012a	Midnight Angel	32¢	$6.40	20	10/19/95	B1111, B2222 **B3333**	5, 10
3049a	**Yellow Rose**	**32¢**	**$6.40**	**20**	**10/24/96**	**S1111, S2222**	
3071a	**Tennessee Statehood**	**32¢**	**$6.40**	**20**	**5/31/96**	**S11111**	
3089a	**Iowa Statehood**	**32¢**	**$6.40**	**20**	**8/1/96**	**S1111**	
3112a	**Madonna w/Child**	**32¢**	**$6.40**	**20**	**11/1/96**	**1111-1, 1211-1, 2212-1, 2222-1, 2323-1, 3323-1, 3333-1, 3334-1, 4444-1, 5544-1, 5555-1, 5556-1, 5556-2, 5656-2, 6656-2, 6666-1, 6666-2, 6766-1, 7887-1, 7887-2, 7888-2, 7988-2**	
3116a	**Family Scenes**	**32¢**	**$6.40**	**20**	**10/8/96**	**B1111, B2222, B3333**	
3030a	**Love Cherub**	**32¢**	**$6.40**	**20**	**1/20/96**	**B1111-1, B1111-2, B2222-1, B2222-2**	
2960a	Love	55¢	$11.00	20	5/12/95	B1111-1, **B2222-1**	

Automatic teller machine (ATM) panes

Scott number	Stamp	Denomi-nation	Total value	Number of subjects	Date of issue	Plate numbers	Notes
2475a	Stylized Flag	25¢	$3.00	12	5/18/90	—	
2522a	F	29¢	$3.48	12	1/22/91	—	
2513Ab	Liberty Torch	29¢	$5.22	18	6/25/91	—	
	(revised back)	29¢	$5.22	18	10/??/92	—	8
2719a	Locomotive	29¢	$5.22	18	1/28/92	V11111	
2803a	Snowman	29¢	$5.22	18	10/28/93	V1111, V2222	
2874a	Cardinal	29¢	$5.22	18	10/20/94	V1111, V2222	
2887a	G	32¢	$6.48	18	12/13/94	—	
2919a	Flag Over Field	32¢	$5.76	18	3/17/95	V1111	
3013a	Children Sledding	32¢	$5.76	18	10/19/95	V1111	
3117a	**Skaters**	**32¢**	**$5.76**	**18**	**10/8/96**	**V11111**	

Notes for self-adhesive sheetlets

1 Selling price was $5, which included a 50¢ surcharge. On September 7, 1990, the USPS announced it was sending 400,000 Eagle & Shield stamps to the U.S. Forces in the Persian Gulf Area. The selling price would be $4.50, thus eliminating the surcharge.
2 Plate numbers are in two positions, upper left and lower right.
3 Also available in coil format
4 There are two different UPC bar codes on the back of the liner. The correct one is 16694. The other one, 16691, is the number for the African Violets booklet.
5 Also available in coil format with plate number.
6 When originally issued, the selling price was $5 (7¢ surcharge). The Postal Bulletin dated February 18, 1993, announced that beginning March 1, 1993, the new selling price would be $4.93, thus removing the surcharge.
7 The pane contains 17 stamps and one label the same size as the stamps.
8 Originally printed on prephosphored paper with and without a lacquer coating. When reissued with the revised back in October 1992, the panes were tagged on press (overall tagged). See Linn's Stamp News December 7, 1992, issue.
9 The Peach/Pear, Flag Over Porch, and the Pink Rose all have reorder labels in the lower right corner of the pane. To discourage the use of these labels as postage, later printings had a target and x die cut into the label. The Peach/Pear V12131, V33323 and V33333 exist both plain & die cut, while V33353,. V33363, V33453, V44424, V44434, V44454, V45434, V45464, V54365, V54565, V55365, V55565 exist die cut only. The Flag Over Porch V23422 exists both plain & die cut, while V12331, V13831, V13834, V13836, V23322, V34743, V34745, V42556, V45554, and V46665 exist die cut only. The Pink Rose S444 exists both plain and die cut while S555 exists die cut only.
10 In 1996 the USPS to lower costs instructed the printers that the printing on the inside of the liners would no longer be required. Several sheetlets that were originally issued with printed lines had imprinted liners on later releases. The following issue can be sound with both printed and unprinted liners. 32¢ Love Cherub (B2222-1 & B2222-2 both ways). 32¢ Pink Rose (S555 both ways), and Flag Over Porch (V23422, V42556, and V45554 both ways). The original Midnight Angel (B1111 & B2222) have printed liners while the reissue (B3333) has an imprinted liner.

Booklets with plate numbers

Scott booklet number	Booklet	Scott pane number	Denom-ination	Plate numbers	Notes
137	$3.60 Animals	2 panes 1889a	18¢	1-16	1, 2
138	$1.20 Flag	1 pane 1893a	two 6¢ & six 18¢	1	
139	$1.20 Flag	1 pane 1896a	20¢	1	3, 4
140	$2 Flag	1 pane 1896b	20¢	1, 4,	3, 4
140A	$4 Flag	2 panes 1896b	20¢	2, 3, 4	3, 4

Scott booklet number	Booklet	Scott pane number	Denom-ination	Plate numbers	Notes
140B	$28.05 Eagle	1 pane 1900a	$9.35	1111	2
142	$4 Sheep	2 panes 1949a	20¢	1-6, 9-12, 14-26, 28, 29	1, 2, 5
142a	$4 Sheep	2 panes 1949d	20¢	34	5
143	$4.40 D	2 panes 2113a	D (22¢)	1-4	5
144	$1.10 Flag	1 pane 2116a	22¢	1, 3	3
145	$2.20 Flag	2 panes 2116a	22¢	1, 3	
146	$4.40 Seashells	2 panes 2121a	22¢	1-3	
147	$4.40 Seashells	2 panes 2121a	22¢	1, 3, 5-8, 10	
148	$32.25 Eagle	1 pane 2122a	$10.75	11111	3
149	$32.25 Eagle	1 pane 2122a	$10.75	22222	
150	$5 London	2 panes 2182a	25¢	1, 2	6
151	$1.50 London	1 pane 2197a	25¢	1	
152	$3 London	1 pane 2197a	25¢	1	
153	$1.76 Stamp Collecting	1 pane 2201a	22¢	1	
154	$2.20 Fish	2 panes 2209a	22¢	11111, 22222	
155	$2.20 Special Occasions	1 pane 2274a	22¢	11111, 22222	
156	$4.40 Flag	1 pane 2276a	22¢	1111, 2122, 2222	6
157	$5 E	2 panes 2282a	E (25¢)	1111, 2122, 2222	
158	$5 Pheasant	2 panes 2283a	25¢	A1111	
159	$5 Pheasant	2 panes 2283c	25¢	A3111, A3222	
160	$5 Owl/Grosbeak	2 panes 2285b	25¢	1111, 1211, 2122, 2222, 1112, 1211, 1133, 1433, 1414, 1434, 1634, 1734, 2111, 2121, 2122, 2221, 2222, 2321, 3133, 3233, 3333, 3412, 3413, 3422, 3512, 3521, 2822, 4642, 4644, 4911, 4941, 5453, 5955	3
161	$3 Flag	2 panes 2285c	25¢	1111	
162	$4.40 Constitution	4 panes 2359a	22¢	1111, 1112	3
163	$4.40 Locomotive	4 panes 2366a	22¢	1, 2	6
164	$5 Classic Cars	4 panes 2385a	25¢	1	6
165	$3 Special Occasions	1 pane each 2396a/2398a	25¢	A1111	3, 6, 7
166	$5 Steamboat	4 panes 2409a	25¢	1,2	7
167	$5 Madonna	2 panes 2427a	25¢	1	6, 7
168	$5 Sleigh	2 panes 2429a	25¢	1111, 2111	6, 7
169	$5 Love	2 panes 2441a	25¢	1211, 2111, 2211, 2222	6, 7
170	$3 Beach Umbrella	2 panes 2443a	15¢	111111, 221111	6, 7
171	$5 Lighthouse	4 panes 2474a	25¢	1, 2, 3, 4, 5	6, 7
172	$2 Bluejay	1 pane 2483a	20¢	S1111	7
173	$2.90 Wood Duck	1 pane 2484a	29¢	4444	7
174	$5.80 Wood Duck	2 panes 2484a	29¢	1111, 1211, 2222, 3221, 3222, 3331, 3333, 4444	7, 8

Scott booklet number	Booklet	Scott pane number	Denom- ination	Plate numbers	Notes
175	$5.80 Wood Duck	2 panes 2485a	29¢	K11111	7, 9
176	$2.95 African Violet	1 pane 2486a	29¢	K1111	7
177	$5.80 African Violet	2 panes 2486a	29¢	K1111	7
178	$6.40 Peach/Pear	2 panes 2488a	32¢	11111	6, 7
179	$5 Indian Headdress	2 panes 2505a	25¢	1, 2	7
180	$5 Madonna	2 panes 2514a	25¢	1	6, 7
181	$5 Christmas Tree	2 panes 2516a	25¢	1211	6, 7
182	$2.90 F	1 pane 2519a	F (29¢)	2222	6
183	$5.80 F	2 panes 2519a	F (29¢)	1111, 1222, 2111, 2121, 2212, 2222	6
184	$2.90 F	1 pane 2520a	F (29¢)	K1111	9
185	$5.80 Tulip	2 panes 2527a	29¢	K1111, K2222, K3333	7, 9
186	$2.90 Flag	1 pane 2528a	29¢	K11111	7, 9
186A	$2.90 Flag	1 pane 2528a	29¢	K11111	3, 9
187	$3.80 Balloon	1 pane 2530a	19¢	1111, 2222	7
188	$5.80 Love	1 pane 2536a	29¢	1111, 1112, 1212, 1113, 1123, 2223	6, 7
189	$5.80 Fishing Flies	4 panes 2549a	29¢	A11111, A22122, A22132, A22133, A23123, A23124, A23133, A23213, A31224, A32224, A32225, A33233 A33235, A44446, A45546, A45547	6, 7, 10
190	$5.80 Desert Storm	4 panes 2552a	29¢	A11111111, A11121111	7
191	$5.80 Comedians	2 panes 2566a	29¢	1, 2	7
192	$5.80 Space Explorations	2 panes 2577a	29¢	111111, 111112	7
193	$5.80 Madonna	2 panes 2578a	(29¢)	1	6, 7
194	$5.80 Santa Claus	4 panes 2581b-2585a	(29¢)	A11111, A12111	7
195	$2.90 Pledge	1 pane 2593a	29¢	1111, 2222	7
196	$5.80 Pledge	2 panes 2593a	29¢	1111, 1211, 2122, 2222	
197	$5.80 Pledge	2 panes 2593c	29¢	1111, 1211, 2122, 2222 2232, 2333, 3333, 4444	6, 11
198	$2.90 Pledge	1 pane 2594a	29¢	K1111	7
199	$5.80 Pledge	2 panes 2594a	29¢	K1111	
201	$5.80 Humming- birds	4 panes 2646a	29¢	A1111111, A2212112, A2212122, A2212222, A2222222	3, 7
202	$5.80 Animals	4 panes 2709a	29¢	K1111	7,9
202A	$5.80 Madonna	2 panes 2710a	29¢	1	6,7
203	$5.80 Christmas Contemporary	5 panes 2718a	29¢	A111111, A112211, A222222	7
204	$5.50 Rock 'n' Roll	2 panes 2737a & 1 pane 2737b	29¢	A11111, A13113 A22222, A44444	7
207	$5.80 Space Fantasy	4 panes 2745a	29¢	1111, 1211, 2222	7
208	$5.80 Garden Flowers	4 panes 2746a	29¢	1, 2	6, 7
209	$5.80 Broadway Musicals	4 panes 2770a	29¢	A11111, A11121, A22222, A23232, A23233	7

452

Scott booklet number	Booklet	Scott pane number	Denom-ination	Plate numbers	Notes
210	$5.80 Country & Western	4 panes 2778a	29¢	A111111, A222222, A333323, A333333, A422222	7
211	$5.80 Madonna	5 panes 2790a	29¢	K1-11111, K1-33333, K1-44444, K2-22222, K2-55555, K2-66666	7, 10
212	$5.80 Christmas Contemporary	1 pane each 2798a, 2798b	29¢	111111, 222222	6, 7
213	$5.80 AIDS	4 panes 2806b	29¢	K111	7, 9
214	$5.80 Love	2 panes 2814a	29¢	A11111, A12111, A12112, A12211, A12212, A11311, A21222, A22122, A22222, A21311, A22322	7
215	$5.80 Garden Flowers	4 panes 2833a	29¢	1, 2	6, 7
216	$5.80 Locomotives	4 panes 2847a	29¢	S11111	7
217	$5.80 Madonna	2 panes 2871b	29¢	1, 2	6, 7
218	$5.80 Stocking	1 pane 2872a	29¢	P11111, P22222 P33333, P44444	7
219	$3.20 G	1 pane 2881a	G (32¢)	1111	6
220	$3.20 G	1 pane 2883a	G (32¢)	1111, 2222	
221	$6.40 G	2 panes 2883a	G (32¢)	1111, 2222	
222	$6.40 G	2 panes 2884a	G (32¢)	A1111, A1211, A2222, A3333, A4444	3, 10
223	$6.40 G	2 panes 2885a	G (32¢)	K1111	9
225	$3.20 Flag Over Porch	1 pane 2916a	32¢	11111, 22222, **23222**, 33332	6, 7
226	$6.40 Flag Over Porch	2 panes 2916a	32¢	11111, 22222, 23222, 33332, **44444**	6, 7
228	**$6.40 Flag Over Porch**	**2 panes 2921a**	**32¢**	**11111, 13111, 21221, 22221, 22222, 44434**	**3,6,7**
229	$6.40 Love	2 panes 2959a	32¢	1	6, 7
230	$6.40 Lighthouses	4 panes 2973a	32¢	S11111	7
231	$6.40 Garden Flowers	4 panes 2997a	32¢	2	6, 7
232	$6.40 Madonna	2 panes 3003b	32¢	1	6, 7
233	$6.40 Santa & Children	1 pane each 3007b & 3007c	32¢	P1111, P2222	7, 10
234	**$6.40 Garden Flowers**	**4 panes, 3029a**	**32¢**	**1**	**6,7**

Notes for booklets with plate numbers.

1 Joint lines on some panes.
2 Electric-eye (EE) marks on tabs.
3 Cover varieties.
4 Panes available scored or unscored.
5 Plate number either on top or bottom pane.
6 Various markings on either the selvage or the panes themselves allow these panes to be plated by position.
7 Available as never-folded or never-bound panes.
8 Panes issued either overall tagged or on prephosphored paper.
9 Panes can be found with cutting lines on either stamp number 5 or 6 (vertically oriented panes) or stamp number 3 or 8 (horizontally oriented panes).
10 Each of the panes in these booklets can have different plate numbers on them.
11 Shiny and dull gum.
For a complete understanding of position panes, Research Paper Number 2, Folded-Style Booklet Checklist, *is available from the Bureau Issues Association, 1710 University Avenue, Madison, WI 53705.*

No-hole panes

The following is a list of those panes that were officially issued by the U.S. Post Office Department and/or U.S. Postal Service as loose panes, i.e., not bound into a booklet and thus not having staple holes. Panes without staple holes can be found that aren't listed below. The aren't listed becuase they weren't officially issued without staple holes. The lack of staple holes can be caused by the following:

1. Staples passing through the perf holes.
2. Booklets assembled with one staple missing and the other passing through the perf holes or both staples missing.
3. Staple holes at the top of a wide tab that have been trimmed off.
4. Panes were bound by padding adhesive instead of staples.

Scott number	Pane	Notes
1035a	3¢ Statue of Liberty (6)	
1036a	4¢ Lincoln (6)	
1213a	5¢ Washington (5 + Slogan 1)	
1278a	1¢ Jefferson (8)	
1278b	1¢ Jefferson (4+2 Labels)	
1280a	2¢ Wright (5+1 Slogan 4 or 5)	
1280c	2¢ Wright (6)	1
1284b	6¢ Roosevelt (8)	
1393a	6¢ Eisenhower (8)	2
1393b	6¢ Eisenhower (5+1 Slogan 4 or 5)	
1395a	8¢ Eisenhower (8)	2
1395b	8¢ Eisenhower (6)	
1395c	8¢ Eisenhower (4 + 1 each Slogans 6 & 7)	2
1395d	8¢ Eisenhower (7 + 1 Slogan 4 or 5)	2
1510b	10¢ Jefferson Memorial (5 + 1 Slogan 8)	
1510c	10¢ Jefferson Memorial (8)	2
1510d	10¢ Jefferson Memorial (6)	
C39a	6¢ Plane (6)	
C51a	7¢ Jet, blue (6)	
C60a	7¢ Jet, carmine (6)	
C64b	8¢ Jet over Capitol (5 + 1 Slogan 1)	
C72b	10¢ Stars (8)	
C78a	11¢ Jet (4 + 1 each Slogans 5 & 4)	
C79a	13¢ Letters (5 + 1 Slogan 8)	

Never-bound panes

By definition a never-bound pane is one that was never assembled into a booklet. Loose panes such as Scott 1595a-d that were in booklets have small V-notches in the edge of the tab and traces of adhesive. The other panes in this category that were in booklets will have disturbed gum in the tabs showing that they were attached to either the booklet cover or each other.

Scott number	Pane	Plate number	Notes
1595a	13¢ Liberty Bell (6)		
1595b	13¢ Liberty Bell (7 + 1 Slogan 8)		2
1595c	13¢ Liberty Bell (8)		2
1595d	13¢ Liberty Bell (5 + 1 Slogan 9)		
2581b	(29¢) Santa Claus (4)	A11111	
2582a	(29¢) Santa Claus (4)	A11111	

Scott number	Pane	Plate number	Notes
2583a	(29¢) Santa Claus (4)	A11111	
2584a	(29¢) Santa Claus (4)	A11111	
2585a	(29¢) Santa Claus (4)	A11111	
2718a	29¢ Christmas Toys (4)	A111111, A112211, A222222	
2790a	29¢ Madonna (4)	K1-11111, K1-33333, K1-44444, K2-55555	

Never-folded panes

Scott number	Pane	Plate number	Notes
2398a	25¢ Special Occasions (6)	A1111	4
2409a	25¢ Steamboats (5)	1, 2	
2427a	25¢ Madonna (10)	1	4
2429a	25¢ Sleigh (10)	1	4
2441a	25¢ Love (10)	1211	4
2443a	15¢ Beach Umbrella (10)	111111	
2474a	25¢ Lighthouses (5)	1, 2, 3, 4, 5	3, 4
2483a	20¢ Bluejay	S1111	
2484a	29¢ Wood Duck (10)	1111	
2485a	29¢ Wood Duck (10)	K1111	5
2486a	29¢ African Violets (10)	K1111	
2488a	32¢ Fruits (10)	11111	4
2505a	25¢ Indian Headdress (10)	1, 2	
2514a	25¢ Madonna (10)	1	4
2516a	25¢ Christmas Tree (10)	1211	4
2527a	29¢ Tulip (10)	K1111	5
2528a	29¢ Flag w/Olympic Rings (10)	K11111	5
2530a	19¢ Balloons (10)	1111	
2536a	29¢ Love (10)	1111, 1112	4
2549a	29¢ Fishing Flies (5)	A11111, A22122, A23124, A23133, A23213, A32225, A33233	4
2552a	29¢ Desert Shield/Storm (5)	A11121111	
2566a	29¢ Comedians (10)	1	
2577a	29¢ Space Exploration (10)	111111	
2578a	(29¢) Madonna (10)	1	4
2593a	29¢ Pledge of Allegiance (10)	1111	
2594a	29¢ Pledge of Allegiance (10)	K1111	
2646a	29¢ Hummingbirds (5)	A1111111, A2212112, A2212122, A2212222, A2222222	
2709a	29¢ Animals (5)	K1111	5
2710a	29¢ Madonna (10)	1	4
2737a	29¢ Rock 'n' Roll (8)	A11111, A13113, A22222	6
2737b	29¢ Rock 'n' Roll (4)	A13113, A22222	
2745a	29¢ Space Fantasy (5)	1111, 1211, 2222	
2764a	29¢ Spring Garden Flowers (5)	1	4

Scott number	Pane	Plate number	Notes
2770a	29¢ Broadway Musicals (4)	A11111, A11121, A22222	
2778a	29¢ Country Music (4)	A222222	
2798a	29¢ Christmas Contemporary (10)	111111	4
2798b	29¢ Christmas Contemporary (10)	111111	4
2806b	29¢ AIDS (5)	K111	5
2814a	29¢ Love (10)	A11111	
2833a	29¢ Summer Garden Flowers (5)	2	4
2847a	29¢ Locomotives (5)	S11111	
2871b	29¢ Madonna (10)	1, 2	4
2872a	29¢ Stocking (20)	P11111, P22222, P33333, P44444	
2916a	32¢ Flag Over Porch (10)	11111	4
2921a	**32¢ Flag Over Porch (10)**	**21221, 22221, 22222**	**4**
2949a	32¢ Love (10)	1	4
2973a	32¢ Lighthouses (5)	S11111	
2997a	32¢ Fall Garden Flowers (5)	2	4
3003b	32¢ Madonna (10)	1	4
3007b	32¢ Santa and Children (10)	P1111	
3007c	32¢ Santa and Children (10)	P1111	
3029a	**32¢ Garden Flowers (5)**	**1**	**4**

Notes for no-hole, never-bound and never-folded panes

1 Shiny and dull gum.
2 Electric-eye (EE) marks on tabs.
3 Plate 1 panes available with and without scoring.
4 Various markings on either the selvage or the panes themselves allow these panes to be plated by position.
5 Panes can be found with cutting lines on either stamp 5 or 6 (vertically oriented panes) or stamp 3 or 8 (horizontally oriented panes).
6 Panes from A11111 have been found in 1993 Year sets only. They all had the bottom stamp removed and are thus (7).

For a complete understanding of position panes, Research Paper Number 2, Folded-Style Booklet Checklist, is available from the Bureau Issues Association, 1710 University Avenue, Madison, WI 53705.